Digestive Wellness

Completely Revised and Updated Third Edition

Elizabeth Lipski, Ph.D., CCN

McGraw·Hill

New York   Chicago   San Francisco   Lisbon   London   Madrid   Mexico City
Milan   New Delhi   San Juan   Seoul   Singapore   Sydney   Toronto

Library of Congress Cataloging-in-Publication Data

Lipski, Elizabeth.
    Digestive wellness / Elizabeth Lipski.— 3rd ed.
        p.   cm.
    Includes bibliographical references and index.
    ISBN 0-07-144196-4
    1. Indigestion—Popular works.   2. Digestion—Popular works.   I. Title.

    RC827.L57   2004
    616.3—dc22   2004020175

3 4 5 6 7 8 9 0   DOC/DOC   3 2 1 0 9 8 7 6 5

ISBN 0-07-144196-4

Interior design by Nick Panos

McGraw-Hill books are available at special quantity discounts to use as premiums and sales promotions, or for use in corporate training programs. For more information, please write to the Director of Special Sales, Professional Publishing, McGraw-Hill, Two Penn Plaza, New York, NY 10121-2298. Or contact your local bookstore.

This book is printed on acid-free paper.

Contents

Foreword

I've had the pleasure of having a professional exchange with Liz Lipski for nearly nineteen years and have been impressed with the way that she has kept abreast of the latest knowledge and information in nutritional sciences—and how it applies to nutritionally related chronic health problems. Her book, *Digestive Wellness*, opens the door to a new chapter in nutritional science. The result will be the alleviation of a number of health problems that many people have experienced for years, not knowing what to do about them. We now recognize that the intestinal tract plays an important role in determining our health other than just digesting our food and getting rid of waste products. We are not "what we eat" but rather "what we absorb from what we eat." It is this aspect of our digestive system that may, in fact, determine our immune function, glandular activity, and neurological function. I believe that Dr. Lipski's book identifies these relationships well and gets the reader to understand the complex interrelationships of our digestive process—and the bacteria living in our digestive tract that are in constant communication with us.

It may come as a great surprise to many readers of this book to learn that the bacteria that live in our digestive tract are the largest organ of the body, even though they're not tied directly to the body through the blood supply. Bacteria in our intestinal tract weigh nearly three and a half pounds and are metabolically active, releasing many substances into our blood that are absorbed across the intestinal barrier. A number of these substances, such as vitamins and amino acids, may be beneficial to our health, and others, which come from harmful bacteria, may, in fact, alter our immune, nervous, or glandular systems in such a way as to increase our susceptibility to chronic illness. Liz Lipski, in this book, defines these relationships and indicates how an individual might utilize nutritional intervention to reduce many of these problems.

This book will make a positive contribution to people's understanding of the important relationship between gastrointestinal physiology, diet, and health. For readers who are not familiar with this exciting and important topic, this book will provide an introduction and a guide to how they can gain better control over their digestive function and its relationship to their health. It seems hard to believe that our health is, to a great extent, controlled by that thin, three-millimeter lining of our intestinal tract that we call the gastrointestinal mucosa. The maintenance of its integrity so that it does not become "leaky" is of tremendous importance. Dr. Lipski's book helps the reader to understand how to approach this objective with precision.

Jeffrey Bland, Ph.D.

Preface

I originally wrote *Digestive Wellness* because I felt that new research and applications in the field of digestion ought to be in the hands of people who most need it. So I took the research and translated it into usable language. It's gratifying to be stopped in the grocery store and told, "My fibromyalgia is gone since I read your book and followed the advice" or "I sell *Digestive Wellness* in my office so that my patients can really understand what we are doing."

I even love hearing that it's the most stolen book from doctors' waiting rooms!

This book was originally published in 1995. Since then, the concepts presented have stood the test of time, gaining more recognition and a flood of new research each year. When I first wrote *Digestive Wellness*, only a small core of professionals used the tools I'd described. Now there are thousands. My clients used to come to me knowing little; now many of them are really knowledgeable about digestive flora, leaky gut syndrome, dysbiosis, and supplements.

The foundation of good health is lifestyle: eating foods that agree with us, becoming emotionally hearty, finding joy and pleasure in the life we lead and the people we interact with, taking the correct supplements to balance our unique biochemistry, and moving our bodies. When the body loses its ability to be adaptive, we become ill. Healthy people have acute medical problems that come and go. But when our health issues become chronic, it's time to figure out what we can do to stimulate our innate healing systems.

Digestive Wellness endeavors to give you the tools to help yourself and others. It's filled with practical information—steps you can take at home, questions to ask your doctor, and lab tests that can give you more insight into the underlying causes of your health issues. It's not meant to be read cover to cover. Pick a chapter and work with it. Then choose another or just look at a specific illness and work backward to fill in your understanding of how you might be adding gasoline to the flames of your illness.

In this edition, I've updated the information on health conditions and diseases, added new remedies and expanded on others, and highlighted some areas that deserve more attention, such as acid-alkaline balance. I've also added new sections on Barrett's esophagus, hepatitis, cirrhosis, and Behcet's disease.

I hope that you enjoy the journey through *Digestive Wellness*. Live each day fully and stay open to the glory of the surprises within it. Feel deeply. Appreciate the love and small and large kindnesses around you. Let the people you care about know how you feel. Laugh, live, love. Inhale the divine.

Acknowledgments

So many people to thank. I'll try to keep this short! Thanks to:

Stephen Long, who opened the space in my life so that I could initially write *Digestive Wellness*

My sons, Kyle and Arthur, who have generously shared me with my work and who keep me endlessly entertained

Christopher Dennen, my husband and devoted partner

Stephany Evans, my agent; Michele Pezzuti, my editor; Katherine Hinkebein, my project editor; and McGraw-Hill for believing in my work

Susan Davis for her editing of the first edition—which was considerable

Jeffrey Bland, Ph.D., for his foreword, again

Russell Jaffe, M.D., Ph.D., for his support and mentorship

And to the many people and companies who have shared their time, knowledge, and materials: Stephen Barrie, N.D.; Leo Galland, M.D.; Michael Murray, N.D.; Corey Resnick, N.D.; Bill Shaddle; the late William Crook, M.D.; Ann Louise Gittleman, M.S., CNS; Burt Berkson, M.D.; Patrick Hanaway, M.D.; Joanne Zeis; Dorena Rode; Great Smokies Diagnostic Laboratory; Elisa/Act Biotechnologies; Metagenics; and to my many clients who teach me every day.

Introduction

Who Can Benefit from This Book?

"If the patient has been to more than four physicians, nutrition is probably the medical answer."
—ABRAHAM HOFFER, M.D., PH.D.

Currently, our country is facing an epidemic of digestive illness directly related to the foods we eat and the way we live. One-third to one-half of all adults have digestive illness—more than sixty-two million people. According to the Digestive Disease Clearinghouse and Information Center, sixty to seventy million Americans have digestive diseases, and digestive diseases comprise 13 percent of all hospital admissions. Except for the common cold, digestive problems are the most common reason people seek medical advice. It is the third largest category of illness in the United States, with a cost of $87 billion in direct medical costs and an additional $20 billion from the resulting 229 million days of lost productivity.

Year after year, medications for digestive illness top the pharmaceutical bestseller list. As a category, antiulcer medications hold the top in worldwide sales of $17.4 billion. Zantac was introduced in 1981 and quickly became the world's bestselling drug and remained on top for a decade. It has been surpassed by Prilosec, which, initially a prescription drug, became available as an over-the-counter medication in the fall of 2001 and had national sales of more than $4 billion. Prevacid was introduced in 1995 for ulcers and had national sales of more than $1.2 billion by 1998.

Constipation plagues our nation. On average, each American pays more than $500 a year on laxatives and fiber supplements alone.

Unfortunately, most digestive problems are treated symptomatically. You have a symptom, you take some medicine, and voilà, you feel better again. This is a fairly good approach for an occasional concern, but if you have a chronic health concern, this remedy doesn't address the underlying cause of the problem. Symptoms of discomfort are our body's way of saying, "Pay attention to me!" *Digestive Wellness* offers a comprehensive guide to your total well-being. It gives you specific information so that you can begin to understand the messages your body is giving you.

The function of digestion is to break down foods into basic components for the cells to use for energy, as building materials and catalysts. The uninterrupted flow of these nutrients into our system is critical to our long-term health. When we eat poorly or our digestion becomes blocked and sluggish, we compromise our cells' ability to work efficiently and healthfully.

The food that we eat is our most intimate contact with our environment. We take food inside of our bodies and turn it into us. Each day, several pounds of this "foreign" matter must be processed. Seventy percent of the immune system is located in or around the digestive system. Often called the second brain, the digestive system can run independently of our brain, has more nerve endings than the spine, and manufactures more neurotransmitters than the brain. In fact, 90 percent of all serotonin is made in the gut.

Most of us don't think much about digestion unless it isn't working well. We don't have to because it works automatically. Michael Gershon, M.D., a great researcher in the field, says it well as he talks about the feedback that the bowels give to the brain—pain, bloating, and nausea. He says, "What these sensations from the gut have in common is unpleasantness. The information from the bowel that reaches consciousness, therefore, makes the gut an organ from which no one wishes to receive frequent progress reports."

This book is a resource for those with faulty digestion and the people who care about them. Some of you might have serious digestive illness, such as Crohn's disease, irritable bowel syndrome, or ulcerative colitis, while others might have simpler problems of heartburn, indigestion, or constipation. In addition to obvious digestive troubles, many other medical problems are caused by faulty digestion. Arthritis, many autoimmune diseases, eczema, food sensitivities, and psoriasis are digestive in origin. People with migraine headaches nearly always have food sensitivities that trigger the onset. Chronic fatigue syndrome, while initially triggered by a virus, has a major digestive component as well. When digestive competence is restored, many of these problems are resolved.

The causes of digestive problems are multifactorial. (See Figure I.1.) In fact, the only factor we can't control is our genetic makeup, and even that is more malleable than we previously believed. Virtually all human illness results from the interaction between our genetics and our environment and a balance between inflammation and anti-inflammation.

Digestive Wellness provides you with a step-by-step plan for making healthful changes in your lifestyle. The approach is from a biological rather than a medical viewpoint. The standard medical approach is to diagnose and provide "appropriate" treatment: either drugs or surgery. The biological approach involves cleansing, feeding, and nurturing your entire being—simple but effective tools to improve the way you feel. By understanding the function of the various parts of the gastrointestinal (GI) tract and looking for underlying causes of disease rather than mere treatment of symptoms, we can begin to understand how to correct our problems.

First, we explore the causes of digestive illness that are aggravated by the American lifestyle. Then we take a trip through the

Figure I.1 Causes of Digestive Problems

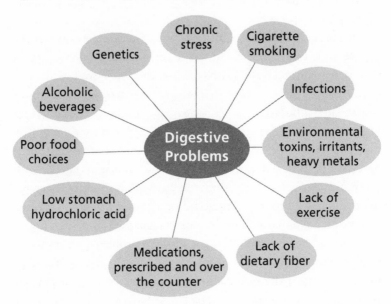

digestive tract where we find a beautifully orchestrated system of integrated harmony. Then we look at the microbes that populate our digestive universe. When they are out of balance, we feel the effects. We move on to discuss dysbiosis and leaky gut syndrome, which often underlie digestive illness and many seemingly unrelated health problems. These chapters provide the groundwork so you can really understand the causes and effects of poor lifestyle choices and medical therapies on your condition.

Functional medicine, which is concerned with early intervention in health problems, is presented next. Early intervention improves your chances of returning to full health. Information on functional lab tests is detailed. This information is new, and most physicians will be unfamiliar with many of these laboratory tests. Take this book to your doctor's office, and ask your doctor to work with you in this new way.

In the following chapters, we move on to self-improvement, with information and practical tips on how to develop a wellness lifestyle. You'll receive information about exercise, stress-reduction programs, detoxification food choices, and shopping lists. We'll focus on a personal exploration of what makes you feel better or worse and recommend approaches that support your body's ability to evoke its natural healing response. You will discover which habits make you feel vibrant and energetic and which drain you.

The biological approach treats you as a whole person with unique needs. It is based on the concept of biochemical individuality. Just as each of us has a unique face, body, and personality, so too do we each have a unique biochemistry. For example, one person's need for a specific nutrient can be thirty-fold higher or lower than another individual's. When it comes to food, one person's pleasure is another's poison. Although you may believe that it's important to eat certain foods—such as bread, eggs, meat, milk, oranges, and tomatoes—they may or may not be healthy for you. It depends on how well your body can use them. Detoxification programs are discussed as well: why you need to incorporate them into your life, recommended programs, and what to expect during detoxification.

Chapters 10 and 11 present self-care strategies for digestive and related health problems, including information about the latest research on nutritional and herbal therapies. Chapter 10 discusses common digestive illnesses and conditions, and Chapter 11 explores problems that are the consequence of faulty digestion, such as arthritic conditions, migraine headaches, and skin problems. Research has been gathered from clinicians and researchers who are striving to learn how your body works and why it fails. The goal is to help your body reach its own natural balance, which will allow it to heal. Day in and day out, cell by cell, your body continuously replaces itself. With the correct balance of work, rest, and nutrients, your body can become healthier each year. If you build your "house" with excellent materials, it will stand the test of time.

Finally, a resource guide is included. It lists professional organizations that can refer you to nutritionally oriented physicians, health professionals, and laboratories.

Throughout the book are exercises and questionnaires designed to increase your self-awareness of mind and body, help you shop more wisely, breathe more deeply, relax more fully, and live more freely. Even though we might not be aware of it, we all practice medical self-care. When we get a headache, we take an aspirin or go for a walk. If we have indigestion, we take an antacid or drink ginger tea. We know when we're too sick to go to work. Most of the time, we make our own assessment and treatment plan, expecting that the problem will pass with time. When these plans fail, we seek professional help. This book will expose you to more plans, new ideas, and the tools to be your own health expert. Just as one tool won't work for every job, not all of these tools will work for you. But some will, and even the failures might give you useful information.

The good news is that you can change the way you feel. The bad news is that it takes work and personal commitment. The journey can be an amazing voyage of self-discovery and self-mastery. This book provides you with some of the tools you need. In fact, the voyage is as interesting as the destination. So work, relax, laugh, and remember to look out the window and enjoy the scenery. This book is about taking control of your lifestyle to increase your chances of getting healthier and more vibrant each year.

DIGESTIVE HEALTH APPRAISAL QUESTIONNAIRE

Date: _____

This questionnaire will help you assess your digestive status. It is not meant as a replacement for a physician's care. The answers will help you focus your attention on specific areas of need.

Medications Currently Used

Circle any of the following medications you are taking. Write down the dosage and frequency.

Antacids
Laxatives
Cortisone
Antibiotic
Oral contraceptives
Prednisone
Antifungals
Ulcer medications
Tylenol (acetaminophen)
Anti-inflammatories
Aspirin
Stool softeners
Other _____

Food, Nutrition, and Lifestyle

Circle if you eat, drink, or use:

Alcohol
Luncheon meats
Candy
Margarine
Cigarettes
Soft drinks

Coffee
Sweets/pastries
Fast foods
Chewing tobacco
Fried foods

Circle if you:

Diet often
Do not exercise regularly
Are under excessive stress
Are exposed to chemicals at work
Are exposed to cigarette smoke

Total the number of items you circled in each list. When you have completed all sections of the questionnaire, refer to "Interpretation of Questionnaire" at the end for more information on what these answers mean for your digestive health.

This next part of the questionnaire will help you discover where your digestive system is imbalanced. It is a screening tool and does not constitute an exact diagnosis of your problem. However, it can point you in the right direction in determining where the highest priorities lie in your healing process.

Circle the number that best describes the intensity of your symptoms. If you do not know the answer to a question, leave it blank. For yes or no questions, score one point for yes, zero points for no. Total your score for each section to assess which areas need your attention.

0 = Symptom is not present/rarely present
1 = Mild/sometimes
2 = Moderate/often
3 = Severe/almost always

Section A: Hypoacidity of the Stomach

1. Burping	0	1	2	3
2. Fullness for extended time after meals	0	1	2	3
3. Bloating	0	1	2	3
4. Poor appetite	0	1	2	3
5. Stomach upsets easily	0	1	2	3
6. History of constipation	0	1	2	3
7. Known food allergies	0	1	2	3

Total

0–4: Low priority

5–8: Moderate priority

9+: High priority

Section B: Hypofunction of Small Intestines and/or Pancreas

1. Abdominal cramps	0	1	2	3
2. Indigestion one to three hours after eating	0	1	2	3
3. Fatigue after eating	0	1	2	3
4. Lower bowel gas	0	1	2	3
5. Alternating constipation and diarrhea	0	1	2	3
6. Diarrhea	0	1	2	3
7. Roughage and fiber causes constipation	0	1	2	3
8. Mucus in stools	0	1	2	3
9. Stool poorly formed	0	1	2	3
10. Shiny stool	0	1	2	3
11. Three or more large bowel movements daily	0	1	2	3

12. Dry, flaky skin and/or dry brittle hair	0	1	2	3
13. Pain in left side under rib cage or chronic stomach pain	0	1	2	3
14. Acne	0	1	2	3
15. Food allergies	0	1	2	3
16. Difficulty gaining weight	0	1	2	3
17. Foul-smelling stool	0	1	2	3
18. Gallstones/history of gallbladder disease	0	1	2	3
19. Undigested food in stool	0	1	2	3
20. Nausea	0	1	2	3
21. Acid reflux/heartburn	0	1	2	3
22. Connective tissue disease: lupus, rheumatoid arthritis, Sjögren's syndrome	0	1	2	3
23. Alcoholism, diabetes, osteoporosis	0	1	2	3

Total

Score 0–6: Low priority

Score 6–10: Moderate priority

Score 10+: High priority

Section C: Ulcers/Hyperacidity of the Stomach

1. Stomach pains	0	1	2	3
2. Stomach pains just before or after meals	0	1	2	3
3. Dependency on antacids for heartburn/acid reflux	0	1	2	3
4. Chronic abdominal pain	0	1	2	3
5. Butterfly sensations in stomach	0	1	2	3
6. Burping or bloating	0	1	2	3

7. Stomach pain when emotionally upset	0	1	2	3
8. Sudden, acute indigestion	0	1	2	3
9. Relief of symptoms by carbonated drinks	0	1	2	3
10. Relief of stomach pain by drinking cream/milk	0	1	2	3
11. History or family history of ulcer or gastritis	0	1	2	3
12. Current ulcer	0	1	2	3
13. Black stool when not taking iron supplements	0	1	2	3
14. Use or previous use of pain medications: aspirin, ibuprofen, and so forth	0	1	2	3

Total

Score 0–4: Low priority

Score 5–8: Moderate priority

Score 9+: High priority

Section D: Colon/Large Intestine

1. Seasonal or recurring diarrhea	0	1	2	3
2. Frequent and recurrent infections (colds)	0	1	2	3
3. Bladder and kidney infections	0	1	2	3
4. Vaginal yeast infection	0	1	2	3
5. Abdominal cramps	0	1	2	3
6. Toe and fingernail fungus	0	1	2	3
7. Alternating diarrhea and constipation	0	1	2	3
8. Constipation	0	1	2	3
9. History of antibiotic use	0	1	2	3

10.	Meat eater	0	1	2	3
11.	Rapidly failing vision	0	1	2	3
12.	Recurrent stomach pain	0	1	2	3
13.	Blood or pus in stool	0	1	2	3
14.	Family history of IBD	0	1	2	3

Total
Score 0–5: Low priority
Score 6–9: Moderate priority
Score 10+: High priority

Section E: Liver/Gallbladder

1.	Intolerance to greasy foods	0	1	2	3
2.	Headaches after eating	0	1	2	3
3.	Light-colored stool	0	1	2	3
4.	Foul-smelling stool	0	1	2	3
5.	Less than one bowel movement daily	0	1	2	3
6.	Constipation	0	1	2	3
7.	Hard stool	0	1	2	3
8.	Sour taste in mouth	0	1	2	3
9.	Gray-colored skin	0	1	2	3
10.	Yellow in whites of eyes	0	1	2	3
11.	Bad breath	0	1	2	3
12.	Body odor	0	1	2	3
13.	Fatigue and sleepiness after eating	0	1	2	3
14.	Pain in right side under rib cage	0	1	2	3
15.	Painful to pass stool	0	1	2	3
16.	Retain water	0	1	2	3
17.	Pain in big toe	0	1	2	3
18.	Pain radiates along outside of leg	0	1	2	3
19.	Dry skin/hair	0	1	2	3
20.	Red blood in stool	No	Yes		

21. Have had jaundice or hepatitis	No	Yes	
22. High blood cholesterol and low HDL cholesterol	No	Unknown	Yes
23. Cholesterol level is above 200	No	Unknown	Yes
24. Triglyceride level is above 115	No	Unknown	Yes

Total

Score 0–2: Low priority

Score 3–5: Moderate priority

Score 6+: High priority

Section F: Intestinal Permeability/Leaky Gut Syndrome/Dysbiosis

1. Constipation and/or diarrhea	0	1	2	3
2. Abdominal pain or bloating	0	1	2	3
3. Mucus or blood in stool	0	1	2	3
4. Joint pain or swelling, arthritis	0	1	2	3
5. Chronic or frequent fatigue or tiredness	0	1	2	3
6. Food allergy or food sensitivities or intolerance	0	1	2	3
7. Sinus or nasal congestion	0	1	2	3
8. Chronic or frequent inflammations	0	1	2	3
9. Eczema, skin rashes, or hives (urticaria)	0	1	2	3
10. Asthma, hay fever, or airborne allergies	0	1	2	3
11. Confusion, poor memory, or mood swings	0	1	2	3
12. Use of nonsteroidal anti-inflammatory drugs (aspirin, Tylenol, Motrin)	0	1	2	3
13. History of antibiotic use	0	1	2	3

14. Alcohol consumption, or alcohol makes you feel sick	0	1	2	3
15. Ulcerative colitis, Crohn's disease, or celiac disease	0	1	2	3
16. Headaches or migraine headaches	0	1	2	3
17. Chronic nasal congestion	0	1	2	3

Total

Score 1–5: Low priority

Score 6–10: Moderate priority

Score 7–19: High priority

Score 20+: Very high priority

Section G: Gastric Reflux

1. Sour taste in mouth	0	1	2	3
2. Regurgitate undigested food into mouth	0	1	2	3
3. Frequent nocturnal coughing	0	1	2	3
4. Burning sensation from citrus on way to stomach	0	1	2	3
5. Heartburn	0	1	2	3
6. Burping	0	1	2	3
7. Difficulty swallowing solids or liquids	0	1	2	3

Total

Score 0–3: Low priority

Score 4–6: Moderate priority

Score 7+: High priority

Interpretation of Questionnaire

This section will help you interpret your answers to the questionnaire. You can use this as a guide to be more specific about what your personal health and lifestyle needs are. The areas where we are weak give us the greatest opportunity for growth!

Medications

- Medications are good indicators that your body is in some sort of imbalance.
- Medications have drug-nutrient interactions. Some nutrient needs might be increased, some decreased; some nutrients might block absorption or usefulness of the drug.

Foods, Drinks, Tobacco

- Candy, alcohol, sweets, and soft drinks are "empty calorie foods" and contain few nutrients. But nutrients are needed to metabolize them, and they replace healthy foods in our diets. These foods have a detrimental effect on most digestive problems; for instance, simple sugars feed candida, bacteria, and parasites.
- If you use cigarettes and chewing tobacco, make sure to take a good antioxidant supplement and lots of vitamin C to compensate for the stress the tobacco causes. Tobacco has a negative effect on the digestive system.
- If you consume luncheon meats, pastries, fast foods, and margarine you are probably getting too much fat, especially saturated fat. Margarine and most pastries also contain hydrogenated oils, which are absorbed into our cells and are detrimental to our health. They make the cell membranes stiff and stifle the intake of nutrients and excretion of wastes, and they promote free radical activity and contribute to atherosclerosis and inflammatory diseases.

Lifestyle

- Weight problems can be caused by a hypoactive thyroid, food sensitivities, poor food choices, sedentary lifestyle, and emotional and social overeating. Chronic dieting leads to further metabolic slowdown. A wellness-centered approach works best for the overweight person.

- Exercise is the great stress reducer and enhances the health of our whole body, including our digestive system. Regular exercise at least three times a week for twenty to thirty minutes can significantly reduce the risk of cardiovascular disease and increase our total sense of well-being.

- A high stress level indicates the need for a good exercise program, skills to nurture oneself, and training to increase emotional heartiness. Food choices usually suffer during stressful periods, while nutrient needs are increased. Supplementation may be indicated.

- Prolonged exposure to chemicals can cause environmental illness, which can manifest as obvious illness or as nondiagnosable complaints of confusion, chronic fatigue, headaches, or just not feeling right. Chronic chemical exposure can also adversely affect the nervous system and trigger neurological diseases. Many women with breast cancer have had prolonged exposure to chemicals. Metabolic clearing as well as low-temperature saunas are important.

- Research indicates that secondhand smoke is detrimental to a healthy respiratory system. If you cannot get away from smokers, buy them "smokeless" ashtrays, open windows whenever possible, and take antioxidant supplements.

- Focus your attention on the sections where you scored in either the moderate- or high-priority range. These are the greatest arenas for health enhancement of your digestive system.

The American Way of Life Is Hazardous to Our Health

"Of the ten leading causes of death in the United States, four, including the top three, are associated with dietary excess: coronary heart disease, some types of cancer, stroke, and non-insulin-dependent diabetes mellitus. Together these conditions account for nearly two-thirds of the deaths occurring each year in the United States."

—BETTY FRZAZO, "THE HIGH COST OF POOR DIETS," *USDA FOOD REVIEW*

Our physical bodies are composed of the foods we eat. That's frightening because today we are part of a massive, uncontrolled food science experiment. What happens when, for more than three generations, people are fed highly processed foods that lack nutrients and fiber and are loaded with chemicals? What happens when you put these same people under high levels of stress in sedentary jobs with poor air and water quality? Is it a coincidence that men's sperm counts have declined by 50 percent since 1980 worldwide, that Americans are fatter than ever before, that we are more violent than ever before, and that more people are committing suicide? Is it a coincidence that 20 percent of our children have behavior or learning problems and that children and adults have rapidly increasing rates of allergies, asthma, and chronic ear infections? Is it a coincidence that our immune systems are breaking down or that diabetes and heart disease rates have risen dramatically over the past century? I don't think so.

Americans are the most overfed and undernourished people in the world. When you add up the calories that we consume each day from high-calorie, nutrient-poor foods, nearly half of our caloric intake comes from nutritionally depleted foods. We get 18.6 percent of our calories each day from sugar, 21.4 percent from fats and oils, and 5 percent from sweetened soft drinks. Compare this to only 4.5 percent of our calories from vegetables and 3 percent from fruits. No wonder the standard American diet is "SAD." Current studies report that we are consuming more nutrients than ever before, but this is because of the alarming increase in total number of calories consumed daily. (See Figure 1.1.) The result is that we are getting fat.

According to the United States Department of Agriculture (USDA), in 2001:

- Americans each ate on average 147 pounds of caloric sweeteners, which translates into nearly 6.5 ounces per day.
- Cane and beet sugar consumption was down to a mere 64.4 pounds, while hidden corn sweeteners rose substantially to 81.4 pounds per person. We each ate a little less than a pound each of syrups and honey.
- Americans drank 24.2 gallons or 258 cups of coffee.
- On average, Americans consumed 74.5 pounds of added fats and oils, which includes 23.1 pounds of hydrogenated vegetable shortening.
- Average Americans each ate 26.9 quarts of ice cream, sherbet, frozen yogurt, and ice milk.

Figure 1.1 The Changing American Diet, 1970–1998

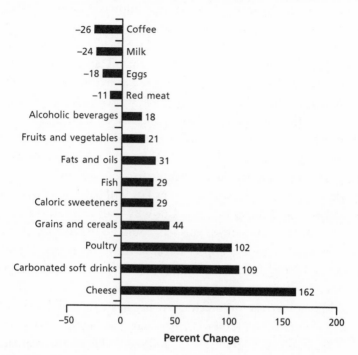

Source: Economic Research Service, USDA, Economics of Food, Farming, Natural Resources, and Rural America

- The average American drank 25 gallons of alcohol, or more specifically, 21.7 gallons of beer, 2 gallons of wine, and 1.3 gallons of distilled liquor.
- The average American drank 49 gallons of carbonated soft drinks, or more specifically, 11.8 gallons of diet soda and 37.2 gallons of caloric soft drinks.
- On average, Americans each ate 4.3 pounds of potato chips, 22.2 pounds of candy, and 38 donuts.

Aside from eating too much fat, Americans also eat the wrong kind. In 1910, a process called hydrogenation was invented, which turned liquid oils into solid fat that was inexpensive, suitable for frying and baking, and didn't go rancid. Since then, manufacturers replaced healthy oils with hydrogenated fats in thousands of products. On labels, you see them listed as hydrogenated or partially hydrogenated oils or as vegetable shortening. According to the FDA, these "trans" fats now comprise about 2.6 percent of daily calories for those of us age twenty and older. These restructured fats are detrimental to our health and have been implicated in cancer, heart disease, and inflammatory conditions.

Because of new regulations, trans fats will have to be listed on food labels by January of 2006. But why wait to eliminate them from your diet? Avoiding trans fats could be the dietary change that makes the largest impact because they are in nearly every processed food. This one change could help you vastly increase your consumption of more nutritious foods.

Although we eat too much fat, many of us are still deficient in essential fatty acids (good fats), especially the omega-3 fatty acids that are in seafood, grains, nuts, and seeds. These essential fatty acids are critical for growth, healing, reduction of pain and inflammation, healthy skin, reproduction, nervous system functioning, and overall well-being.

Dietary changes can substantially reduce the incidence of heart disease. Antioxidants, such as vitamins C and E, selenium, nitric oxide, glutathione, and carotenoids protect our blood vessels from inflammation—a process that is now believed to be associated with heart disease. But these nutrients are stripped from our highly processed foods. An elevated homocysteine level in our blood is another risk factor for cardiovascular disease. Increasing dietary and supplemental levels of vitamins B_6 and B_{12} and folic acid can normalize homocysteine levels. B vitamins are also lacking in the SAD diet. It's estimated that taking a multivitamin with B-complex vitamins could prevent 10 percent of deaths from heart disease.

The average person consumes 12 grams of fiber daily, according to studies done by the USDA and the National Institutes of Health. This falls far short of the recommendation of 20 to 30 grams and is half of what people ate 150 years ago. Dietary fiber, found in fruits, vegetables, legumes, and whole grains, is beneficial to our digestive tract and reduces risk of GI illness. Dennis Burkitt, father of the fiber revolution, found almost no appendicitis, colon disease, diabetes, or hiatal hernia in people eating traditional African diets, which are high in fiber. When these people move to cities or change to a Westernized diet—of high-sugar, highly processed, low-fiber, and low-nutrient-density foods—they begin to develop these illnesses at the usual rates. Fiber-rich foods help us manufacture short-chained fatty acids, which protect us against diseases of the colon.

We have changed not only our diets, but also the way we eat—for the worse. Often, we eat the same way we put gas in our cars: stop, fuel, go. We eat 45 percent of meals away from home, up from 39 percent in 1980 and 34 percent in 1970. Many of us skip breakfast, and others skip breakfast and lunch. Studies show that school-age children perform better when they've eaten breakfast. Adults are no different. In fact, small, frequent meals keep our energy levels even and our minds alert.

Americans often overeat socially and emotionally. This too contributes to digestive illness. We eat to give nourishment to our bodies, but meals are also a time for relaxation, rest, refreshment, and renewal. If we are relaxed while eating, we digest food better. People seem to know this intuitively. Saying grace or taking a couple of moments to center ourselves before eating is a global custom.

Food and the Environment

Thousands of years ago, people foraged and hunted for food. When populations increased, people learned how to farm and propagate plants and animals so that more people could be fed with regularity. Farmers used to grow many foods, rotate crops, and use natural fertilizers. Foods grown nearby were eaten fresh and primarily in season.

Today, we depend on the global economy to produce and supply our food. Are the foods that are shipped from far away just as nutritious as those grown locally? A ripe, juicy tomato from your backyard has about the same measurable nutritional value as those whitish-orange hothouse tomatoes on sale in winter. But, even though they have the same "scientific" measurements, our intuitive measurement tells us they are different.

The life in food gives us life. Once a plant is picked or an animal killed, a grain split or milk homogenized, it begins to lose its enzymatic activity. Transporting foods over long distances diminishes their life-giving capacity. Statistically, canned, frozen, and packaged foods often contain great nutrients, but we know instinctively that they're different from fresh or homemade foods. They don't have the essential enzymes that are critical aids to digestion and metabolism. Fresh fruits, vegetables, local fish and game, grains, beans, nuts, and seeds give us these necessary enzymes. If your body doesn't have to work overtime making enzymes, it has more energy for other processes. Whole foods are in balance with themselves and with nature. When we eat them, we benefit from their balance.

Not only are our foods processed, but they are also preserved. Preservation and packaging of food has killed much of the bacteria that cause food to spoil, helping to lengthen shelf life. But at the same time, we have also destroyed the beneficial bacteria and enzymes that help maintain our health.

Our soils are being depleted. Most food in America is grown on corporate agrifarms that grow monocrops. Chemical fertilizers add only the nutrients necessary for healthy plants, not nutrient-rich foods. Between 1993 and 1997, 19 to 24 percent of foods tested positive for pesticide residues. Pesticides have neurotoxic effects and can cause damage to our nervous systems. They are especially harmful to children whose small bodies are exposed to more pesticides per unit of weight than adults. The good news is that organic farming and integrated pest management are gaining momentum.

Most of our produce is hybridized. Its nutrient value is often sacrificed for pesticide resistance, ease of transportation, or appearance. Many of these hybridized foods look or taste better than their old counterparts, but corn, for instance, has 14 percent less protein now than it did forty years ago.

Throughout the world groups of people now collect seeds from nonhybrid food plants and grow them. Someday we may be very grateful for these pioneers who are helping to protect biodiversity.

Food Preparation and Technology

The average American diet is seriously depleted in many nutrients because of food processing that destroys or extracts nutrients. For example, whole wheat contains twenty-two vitamins and minerals that are removed to make white flour. After the bran and germ are removed from the whole wheat kernel, 98 percent of pyridoxine (vitamin B_6), 91 percent of manganese, 84 percent of magnesium, and 87 percent of fiber are extracted. One of the many lost nutrients is chromium, which is critical for maintenance of blood-sugar levels, normalizing high serum cholesterol levels, and fat burning. The incidence of diabetes has risen steadily in the past decade. It is estimated that 18 percent of all Americans over the age of sixty have diabetes. Most of this is largely preventable with improved diet, lifestyle, and micronutrients, such as chromium and magnesium.

Food Additives

From the earliest times, people salted meats and other foods to cure them. Later they canned foods with sugar, salt, and vinegar to keep them from perishing. Today, because food is produced and shipped from afar, manufactured chemical additives are put into foods to stabilize and preserve them. More than three thousand food additives are used in the United States alone—dyes, artificial flavors, dough conditioners, texturing agents, anticaking agents, and so on—to extend shelf life and enhance flavor, appearance, consistency, and texture. The average person eats an alarming fourteen pounds of additives each year.

While research shows that only a tiny percentage of the population is sensitive to food additives, I have seen many people in my practice with sensitivities. For instance, it is well documented that sulfites cause asthma and respiratory problems in sensitive individuals. The long-term effects of food additives on children are of special concern. Children consume more harmful substances per body weight than adults. Many researchers have found that additives caused significant behavior and learning problems in children who are sensitive to them. What are the long-term effects? No one really knows.

Additives have been tested singly but never in combination.

The chemistry experiment going on inside of us reminds me of my favorite experiment with a childhood chemistry set. I would mix two chemicals together and watch the test tube explode. Because the combining of food additives has not been tested, we have no idea what their synergistic effect really is. Healthy people can handle most food additives, but why burden your body with having to detoxify them?

Americans love the convenience of frozen foods. But if you read the labels, you'll find that most frozen foods contain additives that make the foods less perishable or less expensive. With careful shopping, you can find good-quality frozen foods.

The Microwave

Microwave cooking has spread like brush fire over the last two decades. Ninety percent of American homes have a microwave oven. Everyone seems to accept that cooking with microwave ovens is safe. Yet, a recent study from Swiss researcher Dr. Hans Ulrich Hertel reported that use of microwave cooking lowered hemoglobin levels and cholesterol levels while white blood counts rose. While this is only one study, I currently have a client who has used microwave cooking exclusively for the past fifteen years and he has found the same problems in his blood testing.

Studies show that when breast milk has been microwaved to 98.6° Fahrenheit, almost all the antibodies and lysozymes that protect us from infection are destroyed and vitamin C levels are diminished. One thing is for sure: microwaving foods is a recent innovation and we don't know what the long-term effects are. Until all the research has been done, I recommend conventional cooking methods—on the stove or in the oven.

Genetic Engineering

Genetically engineered foods are a new concern in our food supply. For the first time, we now have genetically engineered foods available to us. They appear—without labeling—in a large percentage of the foods you find in your local grocery store. Technologists are splicing genes into dozens of foods to make them last longer, be juicier, grow bigger, and be more pest resistant. Proponents of genetically modified foods (GMF) believe that these engineered crops will reduce pesticide and herbicide usage, make crops more resistant to frost damage, make them more drought hardy, and increase nutritional value. Opposition to these foods is based on the fact that little long-term testing was performed prior to the rapid release of these foods into our global food supply. While the outcry has been large in Europe, Americans have been relatively quiet about the new food technology even though most of us are eating it on a regular basis. Many people are completely unaware of the issues involved.

Generally, the biotechnology has engineered changes to seeds that are planted. Soy and corn have been engineered to be resistant to the herbicide Round-Up. Formerly, when herbicides were sprayed, the soy or corn would also be affected. Now just the "weeds" are killed. When you eat foods that contain soy or corn that has not been organically grown, you are probably consuming these food products. Despite consumer protest, use of these crops is increasing steadily. In 1997, 17 percent of soybean acreage was planted in genetically modified crops. By 2001, 68 percent of the soybean acreage was planted in these crops and rose to 80 percent in 2003. Many processed foods contain soy derivatives, corn syrup, or corn starch. Cotton crops went from 10 percent herbicide resistant in 1997 to 56 percent in 2001. Only 10 percent of corn crops are herbicide resistant; however, additional varieties have been engineered with the soil bacteria *Bacillus thuringiensis* (Bt), which makes the plant resistant to insects that go through a larval stage. Bt corn was introduced in 1996; by 1997 8 percent of corn was engineered with Bt, and that number was up to 30 percent in 2003. Because genetically modified foods were first developed in the mid-1990s, the long-term cost and environmental effectiveness is yet to be determined.

From an initial study done at Cornell University, there is concern that Bt corn will endanger monarch butterflies. Researchers dusted pollen from Bt corn onto the leaves of milkweed plants, which is the sole food of monarch butterflies. Nearly half of the caterpillars died and the remainder grew to only half their size. If monarch butterflies are so affected, what other animal species may also be impacted? Suffice it to say, more testing must be done before we can know the long-term environmental effects that these crops may produce.

The only sure way to avoid genetically modified foods is to buy and eat food products labeled "organic."

Food Irradiation

Food irradiation is now being used in food production. It's a "clever" way to use nuclear wastes to keep food fresh longer and to decrease the incidence of food poisoning. Irradiation kills all bacteria, such as salmonella, and leaves no radiation in the food itself. But, many researchers are opposed to irradiation. For instance, milk loses 70 percent of vitamin A, thiamine, and riboflavin. Moreover, irradiated foods have molecules that are found nowhere in nature. The Food and Drug Administration (FDA) dubs them "radiolytic by-products" and separates them into two categories: "known radiolytic products," such as formaldehyde and benzene, which are known carcinogens, and "unique radiolytic products," which are new molecules that haven't been characterized.

What's frightening is no one knows what the long-term effects of these molecules will be on health. Many people are opposed to such massive experimentation done at our risk. They are also worried about the risk of having small irradiating facilities throughout the country, which have all the problems associated with handling nuclear materials.

The Changing American Lifestyle

Though many people have a high standard of living today, the price is a hurried life that takes its toll on our bodies. Studies show we actually have less leisure time than we did just twenty years ago. Because our bodies and our minds work together, the stresses we feel in either one affects the other. This synergy can help calm us down or stress us out. The mind–body connection plays an important role in digestive wellness. Stress plays a large role in ulcerative colitis, skin conditions, and autoimmune problems. In fact, nearly all health problems are due to stress: physical, emotional, or environmental.

Over-the-Counter Pain Relievers

Commonly used drugs also play a role in the development of many digestive illnesses. Seventy million prescriptions for nonsteroidal anti-inflammatory drugs (NSAIDs) are written each year. The cost this contributes to the development of gastric ulcers is estimated to be more than $100 million a year.

Aspirin is especially hard on the stomach lining and overuse can contribute to the development of ulcers. NSAIDs—such as Tylenol, Motrin, Advil, and dozens of others—are somewhat gentler on the stomach lining but more irritating to the intestinal lining. They cause damage to the lining by blocking prostaglandins, small chemical messengers that stimulate repair. They are a direct cause of leaky gut syndrome, food sensitivities, and inflammatory problems, such as arthritis and eczema.

Antibiotics

Antibiotics kill not only disease-causing bacteria, but healthy ones as well. Healthful bacteria, such as *Lactobacillus acidophilus*, attach to the intestinal lining so that no parasites or disease-producing organisms can get a foothold. Antibiotics kill these friendly bacteria, allowing pathogenic microbes, viruses, and fungi to take hold. Antibiotics also disrupt the natural symbiosis of the gut and can cause gross imbalance of the natural flora, leading to chronic and systemic illness.

According to consumer drug advocate S. M. Wolfe, "After congressional hearings and numerous academic studies on this issue, it has become the general consensus that 40 to 60 percent of all antibiotics in this country are misprescribed."

Pollution and Environmental Toxins

We live in a toxic environment. Air quality is questionable, and water, our most precious resource, is becoming polluted. Although various localities are cleaning up their natural resources, the global balance is on average deteriorating. Our soils are becoming contaminated. Vast numbers of grazing livestock are destroying many habitats and causing erosion. World population has exploded, demanding material needs that are stripping the planet.

Many physicians believe that the underlying cause of digestive illness is a combination of poor nutrition and exposure to toxic substances. Daily, we are exposed to hundreds of chemicals: secondhand smoke, chlorine and fluoride from water, air pollution, cosmetics, toiletries, household cleaning supplies, medications, and workplace toxins. Healthy people can handle them fairly well, but when the liver gets overloaded, it fails to adequately protect us. Many holistic therapies integrate detoxification programs, which enhance the liver's ability to carry us through this chemical minefield. When our livers are not functioning optimally, our digestion doesn't work optimally, which leads to increased work for the already overtaxed liver, which leads to more digestive problems, and on and on.

The Will to Change

Most people are unaware of how closely their health problems are related to their lifestyle. We are overfed and undernourished. Poor food choices, use of alcohol and cigarettes, a sedentary lifestyle, and chronic stress shorten our lives and contribute to degenerative illness as well as how we feel daily. People are born with reserves of nutrients in their organs, but a lifetime of low-nutrient foods will deplete those reserves, weakening the body's ability to heal. We like to think of ourselves living robustly, rooting and tooting until we die, but the truth is most of us limp along, accepting poor health and declining quality of life for our last twenty years as though it were normal and customary. Many have come to accept digestive illness as an integral part of life. But we can change the way we feel by making changes in our way of life.

It's time to focus on health rather than convenience and develop better habits. Instead of asking, "Does it look and taste good?" we should ask, "Is this food healthful, will it contribute to my biochemical balance and help me feel better, and will it taste good?" We need to exercise regularly and think positive thoughts. We need to relax by ourselves and with friends. We need to create balance in our lives. Digestive problems offer an opportunity to change. You can see this as a curse or a blessing.

KEEP A FOOD DIARY

Write down everything you eat and drink in a diary and keep track of how your body feels. If you have diarrhea or pain after you eat or feel like a million bucks, write it down. See if you can correlate specific foods to the way your digestive system works. Keep track of where you were, who you were with, and your moods. Digestive problems are often related to how comfortable or uncomfortable we feel in a situation. A sample chart looks like this:

DAY 1			
Time of day	What did I eat?	Where was I? Who was I with? What was my mood?	How does my GI tract feel?

Examining Your Food Diary

1. Do you eat breakfast every day? Breakfast provides the fuel we need to get our bodies going for the day. It literally means "break the fast."

2. Is your indigestion better or worse at specific times of the day? This can be a clue to indigestion. Maybe it's something you ate, how fast or how much you ate, or where you ate.

3. Do you eat when you aren't really hungry? If so, examine the reasons, and try to find other outlets for your energies.

4. How often do you eat? Most people feel best when they eat three meals daily plus nutritious snacks. This meal plan keeps blood sugar levels even and facilitates digestion.

5. Do certain foods or beverages provoke symptoms?
   Eliminate suspicious foods for a week and note any
   differences in how you feel.
6. Are you relaxing at mealtimes? Eating more slowly aids
   digestion.
7. Do you get at least five servings of fruits and vegetables
   each day? A serving is a piece of fruit, a half cup of most
   vegetables, or a cup of lettuce.
8. What percentage of your foods and beverages are high-
   sugar, high-fat, low-fiber, or highly processed? Replace
   these with fresh, wholesome foods.
9. Do you consume enough high-fiber foods? We find fiber in
   whole grains, fruits, vegetables, and legumes.
10. Do you drink enough—six to eight cups—water, herb teas,
    and juices? Soft drinks and coffee don't count!

Take a few minutes to see what areas of your diet may be contributing to your health issues. Make a goal to work on one area
at a time and implement small, achievable improvements to your
lifestyle.

A Voyage Through the Digestive System

> *"The surface area of the digestive mucosae, measuring up and down and around all the folds, rugae, villi, and microvilli, is about the size of a tennis court."*
>
> —SIDNEY BAKER, M.D.

The digestive system is self-running and self-healing. Because this beautiful, intricate system works automatically, the average person knows very little about it. Let's take a trip through the digestive system to see what miraculous events occur inside us every moment of our lives.

Think of the digestive tract as a twenty-five- to thirty-five-foot hose that runs from the mouth to the anus. Its function is to turn the foods we eat into microscopic particles that the cells can use for energy, maintenance, growth, and repair. The old saying "You are what you eat" is primarily true. From birth to death, we continually create and re-create ourselves from the nourishment we put inside the body.

Whatever we eat is squeezed through the digestive system by a rhythmic muscular contraction called peristalsis. Sets of smooth muscles contract, alternately pushing food through the esophagus to the stomach and through the intestines. There it is acidified, liquefied, neutralized, and homogenized until it's broken down into usable particles. From the time you swallow, this process is involuntary and can occur even if you stand on your head. When my son, Arthur, was seven years old, he demonstrated this by eating upside-down. Yes, the food went down—or rather up—as usual.

The digestive system is like an irrigation system. A large source of water gets narrower and narrower, finally getting water to each tiny portion of a field. If the water becomes blocked upstream, the plants wither and die. In the body, the unblocked flow of nutrients is critical for optimal health and function. Along the way, the body breaks down food protein into amino acids, starches into glucose, and fats into fatty acids and glycerol. Enzymes, vitamins, and minerals are also absorbed. The cells use these raw materials for energy, growth, and repair. When digestion is compromised, our cells lose their capacity to function fully. Unlike a field, the body is innovative and will try to find ways to make things work. Eventually, however, its ability to seek new pathways fails, and we feel unwell. This is especially apparent in the lining of the digestive tract, which repairs and replaces itself every three to five days.

You Aren't Only What You Eat

On the path to digestive wellness, start with nutritious foods. But, remember that many people eat all the "right" foods and still have digestive problems. The best diet in the world won't help when you aren't digesting properly. You must be able to digest foods; break them down into tiny particles; absorb the food mash; take that through the intestinal lining and into the bloodstream; assimilate nutrients and calories into the cells where they can be used;

and eliminate waste products through the kidneys, bowels, lymph system, and skin. Health can and does break down at any of these phases. For example, people with lots of intestinal gas are fermenting their food. Difficulty with absorption (see Figure 2.1 for an absorption chart) can cause people to have food sensitivities, fatigue, skin rashes, and migraine headaches. Diabetics have a problem with assimilation of glucose into the cells. Constipation and diarrhea are problems of elimination.

The Digestive Process

Eating is voluntary when materials are put in the mouth. Food choices are related to lifestyle, personal values, and cultural customs.

Digestion occurs in the stomach and small intestine and requires cooperation from the liver and pancreas. Proper levels of hydrochloric acid (HCl) and intestinal bacteria are critical for full digestive capacity.

Absorption occurs when food is taken through the intestinal lining into the bloodstream and through the portal vein to the liver, where it is filtered. From the bloodstream it passes to the cells. Until food is absorbed, it is essentially outside the body—in a tube going through it.

Assimilation is the process by which fuel and nutrients enter the cells.

Elimination of waste products happens through the kidneys, bowels, lymph system, and skin. We absorb and excrete many substances through the skin, which is the largest organ in the body.

Water is essential to the digestive process. It softens foods and dissolves many components.

Figure 2.1 Digestive System Absorption

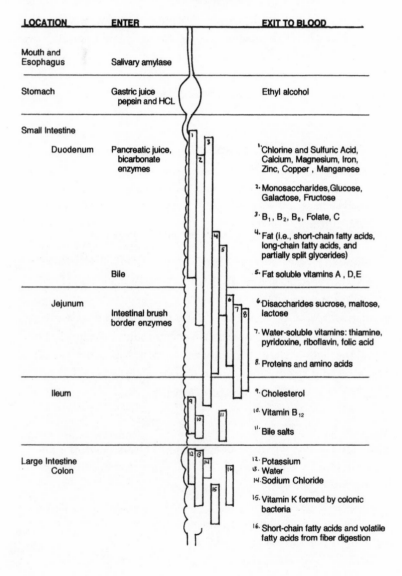

**DIGESTIVE SYSTEM
ABSORBTION**

A Guided Tour Through the Digestive System

To gain a thorough understanding of how the digestive system works, let's take a guided tour starting at the brain and ending at the colon.

The Brain

Digestion begins before we even put food into our mouths. Any sound, sight, odor, taste, or texture associated with food can trigger the body to prepare for what will arrive. Digestive juices, saliva, enzymes, and digestive hormones begin to flow in antici-

Digestive Process	Where in the Body	Function
Eating/food choices	Mouth/mind	Portal for all nutrients/materials to enter the body
Digestion	Stomach/small intestine; to a lesser degree, saliva in the mouth	Breaks down food into basic components for use by the cells
Absorption	Small intestine/large intestine, bloodstream, and liver	Food comes through the intestinal wall into the bloodstream.
Assimilation	Cellular	Nutrients enter cells and are used for energy, storage, and structure.
Elimination	Colon, kidneys, skin, lymph system, cells, and bloodstream	Wastes are excreted.

pation. In addition, the body "revs up" to prepare for the work of digestion, and the heart rate and blood flow can change.

Although this phase of digestion only lasts a short time, it emphasizes the importance of eating in a relaxed manner and of appreciating the food you are about to ingest. Some people find that taking time to say grace and to look at and smell the food, as well as making a special time and place for eating, can dramatically enhance their total digestive function.

The Mouth

The main function of the mouth is to chew and liquefy food. The salivary glands, located under the tongue, produce saliva, which softens food, begins dissolving soluble components, and helps keep the mouth and teeth clean. Saliva contains amylase, an enzyme for splitting carbohydrates. Only a small percentage of starches are digested by amylase, but if you keep a piece of bread in your mouth for a long time, you can begin to taste the increased sweetness that comes from splitting the starch into simple sugars. Chewing also stimulates the parotid glands, behind the ears in the jaw, to release hormones that stimulate the thymus to produce T-cells, which are the core of the protective immune system.

Healthy teeth and gums are critical for proper digestion. Many people eat too fast; they barely chew their food at all and then wash it down with liquids. So the stomach receives chunks of food instead of mush. This undermines the function of the teeth, which is to increase the surface area of the food. Fast eaters often complain of indigestion or gas. In *May All Be Fed*, John Robbins describes three men who survived in a concentration camp during World War II by chewing their food very well. Simply by chewing food thoroughly we can enhance digestion and eliminate some problems of indigestion.

The Esophagus

The esophagus is the tube that passes from the mouth to the stomach. Here, peristalsis begins to push the food along the digestive tract. Well-chewed food passes through the esophagus in about six seconds, but dry food can get stuck and take minutes to pass. The cardiac or esophageal sphincter—a little door at the bottom of the esophagus—separates the esophagus from the stomach, keeping stomach acid and food from coming back up. It remains closed most of the time, opening when a peristaltic wave, triggered by swallowing, relaxes the sphincter. The most common esophageal problems are heartburn (also called gastric reflux) and hiatal hernia.

The Stomach: The Body's Blender

The stomach chops, dices, and liquefies as it changes food into a soupy liquid called chyme, which is the beginning of the process of protein digestion. The stomach is located under the rib cage, just below the heart.

Protein molecules are composed of chains of amino acids—up to two hundred amino acids strung together. Hydrochloric acid (HCl), produced by millions of parietal cells in the stomach lining, begins to break apart these protein chains. HCl also kills microbes that come in with food, effectively sterilizing it. HCl is so strong that it would burn our skin and clothing if spilled. Yet, the stomach is protected by a thick coating of mucus (mucopolysaccharides), which keeps the acid from burning through the stomach lining. Prostaglandins, small chemical messengers, help keep the mucous layer active by sending messages to replace and repair the stomach lining and provide a protective coating. When this mucous layer breaks down, HCl burns a hole in the stomach lining, causing a gastric ulcer.

The stomach also makes pepsin, a protein-splitting enzyme that cuts the bonds between specific amino acids, breaking them down into short chains of just four to twelve. The stomach also produces small amounts of lipase, enzymes that digest fat. Most foods are digested and absorbed farther down the gastrointestinal tract, but alcohol, water, and certain salts are absorbed directly from the stomach into the bloodstream. That's why we feel the effects of alcohol so quickly.

Food stays in the stomach two to four hours—less with a low-fat meal, more with a high-fat or high-fiber meal. When the stomach has finished its job, chyme has the consistency of split pea soup. Over several hours, it passes in small amounts through the pyloric valve into the duodenum, the first twelve inches of the small intestine. Chronic stress lengthens the amount of time that food stays in the stomach, while short-term stress usually shortens the emptying time.

Vitamin B_{12} and Intrinsic Factor

Before vitamin B_{12} even had a name, scientists knew that there was something in food that joined with something in the stomach that helped its absorption. They named these two substances *intrinsic factor* (manufactured in our stomach) and *extrinsic factor* (from food), which is now called vitamin B_{12}. Vitamin B_{12} is essential for blood formation, energy, growth, and cell division and function. Intrinsic factor is made in the stomach in the parietal cells, and binds vitamin B_{12} so that it can be readily absorbed in the intestines. Hydrochloric acid is also produced by the parietal cells. As the parietal cells become less efficient, the production of both hydrochloric acid and intrinsic factor falls.

As we age, the ability to manufacture HCl decreases. Intrinsic factor is likewise decreased and vitamin B_{12} deficiencies occur. Many elderly people have vitamin B_{12} deficiencies that affect the body's ability to get oxygen into each cell. The main symptoms

The Man with a Window in His Stomach

We owe early information about how digestion works to a man who had a "window" in his stomach. In 1822, Alexis St. Martin, a young Canadian trapper, was shot at close range in his left side. U.S. Army doctor William Beaumont successfully treated St. Martin but was unable to close the wound completely. Over the next eight years, Dr. Beaumont observed the activity of St. Martin's stomach through the hole, watching what happened when various foods were eaten and how his emotions affected his digestive activity. Until this time, people had no idea what happened to food after it was swallowed. Science owes much to these two men.

are dementia, depression, nervous system problems, muscle weakness, and fatigue. Many people benefit from vitamin B_{12} injections, under a physician's care, even though many do not have low serum B_{12} levels or pernicious anemia (anemia caused by B_{12} deficiency). B_{12} shots or sublingual tablets can dramatically increase energy levels and decrease the symptoms listed.

The most common problems associated with the stomach are gastric ulcers and underproduction of hydrochloric acid.

Small Intestine

The small intestine is hardly small. If this coiled-up garden hose were stretched out, it would average fifteen to twenty feet long. If spread flat, it would cover a surface the size of a tennis court. In the small intestine, food is completely digested and nutrients are absorbed through hundreds of small fingerlike folds called villi, which are located in the intestinal wall and are covered, in turn, by millions of microvilli. (Think of them as small loops on a velvety towel that then have smaller threads projecting from them.) The villi and microvilli are only one cell layer thick but perform multiple functions of producing digestive enzymes, absorbing nutrients, and blocking absorption of substances that aren't useful to the body.

The intestinal lining repairs and replaces itself every three to five days. The sloughed material contains enzymes and fluids that are recycled to help digestion. The intestinal wall has a paradoxical function: it allows nutrients to pass into the bloodstream while blocking the absorption of foreign substances found in chemicals, bacterial products, and other large molecules found in food. Some foods we eat and medications we use cause the intestinal wall to lose the ability to discern between nutrients and foreign substances. When this occurs, there is a problem of increased intestinal permeability, commonly known as leaky gut syndrome. This syndrome contributes to skin problems, food sensitivities, osteoarthritis, migraine headaches, and chronic fatigue syndrome.

The small intestine has three parts: the duodenum, the jejunum, and the ileum. The duodenum is the first twelve inches of the small intestine, the jejunum is the next 40 percent, and the ileum is the last segment. Each nutrient is absorbed at specific parts of the small intestine. For instance, the duodenum has an acidic environment that facilitates absorption of some nutrients, including calcium, copper, iron, folic acid, thiamine, manganese, vitamins A and B_2, and zinc. People with low hydrochloric acid levels might become deficient in one or more of these nutrients because they need acid for absorption.

The Pancreas

The pancreas has two main roles. First, it produces digestive enzymes and insulin. When food passes from the stomach to the duodenum, the pancreas secretes bicarbonates, essentially baking soda, which neutralizes the acidity of the chyme so it won't burn the tissues of the intestines. Then, it manufactures and secretes specific enzymes that digest fats, carbohydrates, and protein. These enzymes are lumped into three categories: lipase, amylase, and protease. Lipase breaks fats into fatty acids and glycerol; amylase splits carbohydrates into simple sugars; and protease digests the links between amino acids from protein. Once digested, these nutrients can be absorbed into the bloodstream and used by the cells. Low secretion of pancreatic enzymes can also lead to nutritional deficiencies. For example, vitamin B_{12} requires protein-splitting enzymes to separate it from its carrier molecule, so poor pancreatic function can lead directly to vitamin B_{12} deficiency.

The second role of the pancreas is hormonal regulation of blood sugar levels. When the blood sugar is too high, the pancreas secretes insulin that signals the cells to store glucose. When this mechanism fails, people develop diabetes.

Gut-Associated Lymphatic Tissue (GALT)

Current research indicates that 70 percent of the immune system is located in or around the digestive system. The mucosal surface of the gut is only one cell thick. Underneath this is the gut-associated lymphatic tissue (GALT). It must continually distinguish between friend and foe in the foods we eat and in the gut bacteria. When the digestive system is presented with a foreign substance, an antigen, specialized cells called M-cells carry the antigen to the lining of the digestive tract. There they are "checked out," or sampled, by specialized cells called Peyer's patches in the intestinal lining. These cells in turn alert B- and T-cells to begin processing the antigens. The B- and T-cells carry the antigens back to the intestinal mucosa, where they are gobbled up by macrophages, part of the cell-mediated immune system.

Secretory IgA (sIgA) antibodies, which are like sentinels on constant alert for foreign substances, are also present in the gut mucosa. Their arousal signals cytokines, which begins the inflammatory process designed to rid our bodies of antigenic materials.

When microbes enter the digestive system, they are confronted with several nonspecific and antigen-specific defense mechanisms including: peristalsis, bile secretion, hydrochloric acid, mucus, antibacterial peptides, and IgA. This stops most microbes and parasites from infecting the body. Those that do get through this defense system are recognized by toll-like receptors (TLRs). When disease-causing microbes get through, the TLRs stimulate production of inflammatory cytokines by activation of NF-kappa B, triggering cytokine production and inflammation in the gut.

It is believed that the constant exposure to microbes in infancy and early childhood contributes to the health and responsiveness of the adult immune system. This theory is called the "Hygiene Hypothesis." In our culture, we don't challenge the immune system enough. We have improved sanitation, low bacterial availability in the foods we eat because of preservatives and food processing, decreases in consumption of fermented foods, fewer childhood infections, increased use of antibiotics, and routine use of vaccinations. Children who have little challenge to microbes are at risk for allergy, eczema, and asthma, which may continue throughout a lifetime.

Gut Serotonin

Serotonin is best known for its role in the brain, but 95 percent of our serotonin is manufactured in the gut. Without adequate amounts, we have insomnia and are depressed. Many selective serotonin reuptake inhibitor (SSRI) drugs are on the market to help keep serotonin in the synapses for a longer period of time. The most well-known of these is Prozac.

Serotonin in the gut plays a role in peristalsis, smooth muscle contraction, and mucosal secretions. A second gut hormone, called enterochromaffin cells (EC cells) also activate the gut nerves and can cause nausea that is associated with chemotherapy and possibly the bloating and pain associated with irritable bowel syndrome.

The Liver: The Body's Fuel Filter

The liver is the most overworked organ in the body because it plays many roles. It manufactures bile to emulsify fats for digestion; it makes and breaks down many hormones, including cholesterol, testosterone, and estrogens; it regulates blood sugar levels; and it processes all food, nutrients, alcohol, drugs, and other materials that enter the bloodstream and lets them pass, breaks them down, or stores them. The job of neutralizing environmental pollution inside the body is no small task—one that the liver never evolved to handle. Yet, the liver can lose as much as 70 percent of its capability and not show diagnosable liver disease.

The four-and-a-half-pound liver manufactures thirteen thousand chemicals and has two thousand enzyme systems, plus thousands of synergists that help with body functions. With these chemicals and enzymes, it "humanizes" nutrients so that the cells can use them. Practically all vitamins and minerals we take in need to be enzymatically processed by the liver before we can use them. If the liver is too congested to enzymatically process these nutrients, we do not get the benefit.

Bile, manufactured by the liver and stored by the gallbladder, buffers the intestinal contents because of its high concentration of bicarbonates. It also emulsifies fats. Bile is a soap-like substance made of bile salts, cholesterol, and lecithin. It makes fats more water soluble, increasing their surface area so that the enzymes can split them for the cells to use.

The liver has three lobes: main, left, and lower. The main lobe organizes and humanizes nutrients. It is the main chemical factory, producing enzymes and chemicals necessary for body functions. The left lobe regulates and maintains body functions. People with toxic left lobes are often environmentally sensitive or panallergic—allergic to nearly everything. Many times, allergic people crave what they are sensitive to. The body gets used to having nicotine, alcohol, wheat, dairy, or whatever, and when we remove it, the body's balance is disturbed. The left lobe works to maintain body homeostasis (staying the same) without the "missing" substance. The craving is, in some part, the liver's way of trying to get us what we "need." As Jack Tips writes in *The Liver Triad*, "As long as toxic residues from these substances are present in this lobe, the body will get a subtle signal to continue the addiction, to want to respond to allergens."

The lower lobe is where the essential fatty acids and fat-soluble vitamins A, D, E, and K are stored so the liver and other glands can produce cholesterol and hormones. Here, the liver also stores environmental toxins such as radioactive substances, pesticides, herbicides, food preservatives, and dyes. The liver will detoxify what it can, but if it can't break down a particular substance, it stores it in the lower lobe and in tissues throughout the body. It is important to detoxify the liver on a regular basis, perhaps twice a year, to help maintain its function. Many systems have been developed to help detoxify the liver, which we discuss at length in Chapter 8.

The Gallbladder: A Holding Tank for Bile

The gallbladder is a pear-shaped organ that lies just below the ction is to store and concentrate bile produced by the nulsifies fats, cholesterol, and fat-soluble vitamins by breaking them into tiny globules. These create a greater surface area for the fat-splitting enzymes (lipase) to act on during digestion. When we eat, the gallbladder and liver release bile into the common duct, which connects the liver, gallbladder, and pancreas to the duodenum. Between meals, the gallbladder concentrates bile. The most common problem of the gallbladder is gallstones. When bile becomes too concentrated, stones might form, which can cause pain, nausea, and discomfort. Gallbladder disease is directly related to diet.

The Large Intestine or Colon

When all nutrients have been absorbed, water, bacteria, and fiber pass through the ileocecal valve to the large intestine or colon. The ileocecal valve is located by your right hipbone and separates the contents of the small and large intestine. The appendix is a small, fingerlike sac that extends off the beginning of the colon. Until recently, the function of the appendix was a mystery. Now we know it contains a great deal of lymphatic tissue and is thought to be part of the immune system.

The colon is short—only three to five feet long. Its job is to absorb water and remaining nutrients from the chyme and form stool. Two-and-a-half gallons of water pass through the colon each day, two-thirds of which come from body fluids. The efficient colon pulls 80 percent of the water out of the chyme, which is absorbed into the bloodstream.

The large intestine has three main parts: the ascending colon (up the right side of the body), the transverse colon (straight across the belly under the ribs), and the descending colon (down the left side of the body) to the rectum, where feces exit the body. Stool begins to form in the transverse colon. If the chyme passes through the colon too quickly, water is not absorbed, causing diarrhea. Stool that sits too long in the colon becomes dry and hard to pass, leading to constipation. About two-thirds of stool is composed of water and undigested fiber and food products. The other third is composed of living and dead bacteria.

The large intestine contains trillions of bacteria. Helpful bacteria, called flora, lower the pH of the colon, killing disease-causing microbes. Intestinal flora also produce vitamins B and K, protect us from illness, enhance peristalsis, and make lactase for milk digestion. Probiotic bacteria ferment the dietary fiber, producing short-chained fatty acids—butyric, propionic, acetic, and valerate. Butyric acid is the main fuel of the colonic cells. Low butyric acid levels, or an inability of the colon bacteria to properly metabolize butyric acid, has been associated with ulcerative colitis, colon cancer, active colitis, and inflammatory bowel disease.

When the stool is finally well formed, it gets pushed down into the descending colon and then into the rectum. It is held there until there is sufficient volume to have a bowel movement. Two sphincters—rings of muscle—control bowel movements. When enough feces have collected, the internal sphincter relaxes and your mind gets the signal that it's time to relieve yourself. The external sphincter opens when you command it. Because this is voluntary, you can have the urge to defecate, but wait until it's convenient. If you ignore the urge, water keeps being absorbed back into the body and the stool gets dry and hard. Some people are chronically constipated because they don't want to take the time to have a bowel movement or don't like to have bowel movements at work. This book is about listening to your body signals. Take the time when your body calls you, not when it's convenient or ideal.

Many health problems arise in the colon: appendicitis, constipation, diarrhea, diverticular disease, Crohn's disease, ulcerative colitis, rectal polyps, colon cancer, irritable bowel syndrome, parasites, and hemorrhoids.

What Goes In Must Come Out

We can learn a lot about ourselves from stool. Dennis Burkitt, M.D., father of the fiber theory, found that on average people on Western diets excreted only five ounces of stool daily, whereas Africans eating traditional diets passed sixteen ounces. Well-formed stool tells us when it wants to come out; we don't need to coax it. It looks like a brown banana with a point at one end, is well-hydrated, and just slips out easily. Stool that looks like little balls all wadded together has been in the colon too long. The longer waste materials sit in the colon, the more concentrated the bile acids become; concentrated bile acids irritate the lining of the colon. Hormones that have been broken down by the body are also excreted via our feces. If the stools sit in the colon for too long, these hormones are reabsorbed into the bloodstream, increasing the risk for estrogen-dependent cancers. Betaglu-curonidase, an enzyme that may indicate formation of cancer-causing substances in the colon, can be measured as a marker of hormone reabsorption.

Frequency of bowel movements is a good health indicator. How often do you have a bowel movement? People on good diets generally have one to three each day. If you are not having a daily bowel movement, there can be many causes.

First, take a close look at your diet. You probably aren't eating enough fiber. If not, increase your intake of fruits, vegetables, whole grains, and legumes. These foods are generally high in magnesium, which helps normalize peristalsis. Make sure that you are drinking enough fluids. Coffee and soft drinks don't count. And get regular exercise.

Second, a good indicator of your colon's health is your bowel transit time—how long it takes food to move from the first swallow until it exits the body. When your system is working well, the average amount of time is twelve to twenty-four hours. On average, Americans have a transit time that is way too long—forty-eight to ninety-six hours—because we don't eat enough high-fiber foods or drink enough water. You can do a simple home test to determine your transit time, which gives you important information about the way your body works.

Testing Bowel Transit Time

Transit time is how long it takes from the time you eat a food until it comes out the other end. Buy charcoal tablets at a pharmacy or health-food store. Take 5–10 grams (5,000–10,000 milligrams) on an empty stomach. Note exactly when you took the charcoal. When you see darkened stool (charcoal will turn the stool black), calculate how many hours since you took the charcoal tablets. That is your transit time. You can also do the test with beets. Eating three or four whole beets will turn stool a deep garnet red.

The Results

Less than twelve hours: This usually indicates that you are not absorbing all the nutrients you should from your food. You may have malabsorption problems.

Twelve to twenty-four hours: This is the optimal transit time.

More than twenty-four hours: This indicates that wastes are sitting inside your colon too long. Poor transit time greatly increases the risk of colon disease. Substances that were supposed to be eliminated get absorbed back into the bloodstream, and they can interfere with and irritate your system. Take action now. Increase your fiber intake by eating more fruits, vegetables, whole grains, and legumes. Drink lots of water every day. Get thirty minutes of exercise at least three times a week.

CLEAN UP YOUR DIET

Let's take a look at which foods you are eating and begin the process of cleaning up your diet. Take last week's diary and get out some crayons or markers—you're going to color.

Circle the following foods red: sugar, caffeine, alcohol, junk foods, fried foods, high-fat foods, pastries, donuts, chips, microwave popcorn, highly processed foods, soft drinks, diet soft drinks, diet foods

Circle the following foods blue: dairy products—milk, cheese, yogurt, ice cream, frozen yogurt, ice milk

Circle the following foods green: fruits and vegetables

Circle the following foods yellow: protein foods—fish, poultry, beef, pork, lamb, veal, legumes, soy products

Circle the following foods purple: nuts and seeds, oils, butter, margarine

Circle the following foods black: grains—wheat, bread, corn, rice, millet, buckwheat, bulgur, quinoa, amaranth, barley, oats, rye

Look at those circles. Is there one food group that dominates your diary? If you eliminated one of these categories from your diet, which would be the easiest to give up and which would be the most difficult? Sometimes, the ones that are the hardest to give up are the ones that are causing us the most trouble. They temporarily make us feel better, even though they are really making us sicker. Why? Our bodies react negatively to cigarettes, dairy products, caffeine, sugar, wheat, pork, beef, citrus fruits, or any other foods, yet we crave them.

Tackle the Sweet Tooth

This week, focus on the foods you circled in red and eliminate all the sweets. Sugars ferment and can contribute to your digestive problems. Get rid of soft drinks, cookies, pastries, donuts, and sugar added to coffee or tea. We're not talking about perfection here. Let's just make some progress.

Next week, eliminate other items circled in red. Foods with hydrogenated oil or vegetable shortening, for example, may be a good pick. Keep reworking your diet until 90 percent or more of your food choices are optimal!

3

The Bugs in Your Body
Intestinal Flora

"There are more bacteria in our intestinal tract than cells in our body."
—Jeffrey Bland

A total of one hundred trillion bacteria live together in our digestive system, in either symbiotic or antagonistic relationships. That's ten times more intestinal bacteria than cells in our body. Their total weight is about four pounds—the size of the liver. They have many functions and act like a symbiotic organ to protect our health. Eighty percent of the dry weight of our stool is composed of gut bacteria, and half of that is still alive. Gut flora accounts for half of the volume of the contents of the large intestine.

We have four hundred to five hundred types of bacteria in our digestive systems, each of which has many types of strains. This variety may seem overwhelming, but twenty types make up three-quarters of the total. The most common are bacteroides, bifidobacteria, eubacterium, fusobacteria, lactobacillus, peptococcaceae, ruminococcus, and streptococcus. Most of these bacteria are anaerobic, meaning they do not need oxygen to thrive; some are aerobic and do need oxygen for survival. A third group produces lactic acid and can be either aerobic or anaerobic. Lactic acid–producing bacteria help acidify the intestinal tract and protect us from overgrowth of harmful bacteria.

Billions of bacteria inhabit our mouths. While the stomach has few because of its high acid content that prohibits their growth, the small intestine has many billions of bacteria. The overwhelming majority of intestinal flora reside in the colon—trillions and trillions. Each day, we produce several ounces of these microbes and eliminate several ounces in stool. These bacteria manufacture substances that raise or lower our risk of disease and cancer, the effect of drugs, immune competence, nutritional status, and rate of aging. Some of these bacteria cause acute or chronic illness. Other bacteria cause illness in people who are genetically susceptible but no problems in other people.

Another group of bacteria offers us protective and nutritive properties. These friendly bacteria are called intestinal flora, probiotics, or eubiotics. The last two terms mean "healthful to life." The term *probiotics* is commonly used to refer to supplemental use of these bacteria in powder or capsule form. It was coined in 1965 by researchers Lilly and Stillwell to mean organisms that promote life of microorganisms, in opposition to antibiotics, which kill microorganisms. The two most important groups of flora are the lactobacilli, found mainly in the small intestine, and bifidobacteria, found primarily in the colon. These bacteria live symbiotically within us in a mutually beneficial relationship that has evolved to enhance our health and theirs.

The bacteria within us live at about 98.6° Fahrenheit and thrive on the constant nourishment we provide in a warm, dark, moist environment. We allow them to inhabit us because they give us valuable preventive and therapeutic benefits.

Where did these trillions of bacteria come from? Up until birth, we receive predigested food from our mothers and are born with a sterile digestive tract. The trip down the birth canal initiates us into the world of microbes that thrive everywhere. Babies

Main Bacteria Types in Our Bodies

The following table gives us a breakdown of the most common types of bacteria in our digestive system.

Type	Aerobic/Anaerobic	Percent
Bacteroides, twenty species	Anaerobic	Almost 50
Bifidobacteria	Anaerobic	11
Peptostreptococci	Anaerobic	8.9
Fusobacteria, five species		7
Ruminococci, eleven species		4.5
Lactobacilli	Both	2–2.5
Clostridia		0.6
Enterobacteria, E. coli, klebsiella, aerobacter, etc.		Less than 0.5

are exposed to bacteria in breast milk and formula and when sucking on nipples, fingers, and toes. With every breath and touch, bacteria enter the body to colonize on the skin and mucous membranes. In no time, every conceivable space in the colon is occupied by microbes. Within the first few days of life, colonization of E. coli and streptococcus occurs. Within a week of birth, bifidobacteria, bacteroides, and clostridium are established in bottle-fed babies. Breast-fed infants have increased numbers of lactobacillus and bifidobacteria species.

The microbes set up homogeneous neighborhoods that push out competing microbes trying to break into their territories. This normally happens in a predictable way, and once established, the colonies flourish. When babies are unable to properly colonize friendly flora, they become irritable and colicky and have gas pains and eczema in their diaper area. Babies who don't develop the right balance of beneficial bacteria are more susceptible to allergy, asthma, and eczema. After weaning, the specific types and strains of dominant flora change from *Bifidobacteria infantis* in infants to other strains of bifidobacteria in children and adults. The colonization patterns we set up in infancy continue to prevail throughout our entire lifetime.

Successful colonization of the gut-associated lymphatic tissue (GALT) is necessary for the development and maintenance of the immune system. Lack of gut bacterial stimulation has resulted in a decreased amount of mucosal surface area, altered mucosal enzymes, defects in intestinal barrier function, reduction in inflammatory responses, defective secretory IgA (sIgA) protection of the mucosal membranes, and poor oral tolerance to protein antigens.

The Many Benefits of Intestinal Flora

Intestinal flora play an important role in our ability to fight infectious disease, providing a front line in our immune defense. As noted in a 1988 report by the U.S. surgeon general, "Normal microbial flora provide a passive mechanism to prevent infection." Friendly flora also manufacture many vitamins including the B-complex vitamins biotin, thiamine (B_1), riboflavin (B_2), niacin (B_3), pantothenic acid (B_5), pyridoxine (B_6), cobalamine (B_{12}), and folic acid, and vitamin K.

Lactobacillus acidophilus and bifidobacteria increase the absorption of minerals that require acid for absorption, such as calcium, copper, iron, magnesium, and manganese. Farm animals are routinely given supplemental flora, which enhance absorption of both vitamins and minerals.

Friendly flora help increase our resistance to food poisoning. In 1993, the Centers for Disease Control reported twenty to forty million cases of food poisoning, although the FDA estimates the true total to be eighty million. Many cases go unreported because

Benefits of *Lactobacillus acidophilus*

1. It prevents overgrowth of disease-causing microbes: candida species, E. coli, *Helicobacter pylori* (*H. pylori*), and salmonella.
2. It prevents and treats antibiotic-associated diarrhea.
3. It aids digestion of lactose and dairy products.
4. It improves nutrient absorption.
5. It maintains integrity of intestinal tract and protects against macromolecules entering bloodstream and causing antigenic response.
6. It lessens intestinal stress from food poisoning.
7. It acidifies intestinal tract. Low pH provides a hostile environment for pathogens and yeasts.
8. It helps prevent vaginal and urinary tract infections.

the symptoms closely resemble the flu. Some food-borne infections lead to chronic illness, causing heart and valve problems, immune system disorders, joint disease, and possibly even cancer. Use of supplemental acidophilus and bifidus can help prevent food poisoning by making the intestinal tract inhospitable to the invading microbes. It is a common misconception that friendly flora kill invading microbes. They actually change the environment by "competitive exclusion"—they secrete large amounts of acids (acetic, formic, and lactic acids) that make the area unsuitable for pathogens.

Probiotic Bacteria Help Us in Many Ways

Let's take a look at all the ways probiotic bacteria aid us.

Benefits of Bifidobacteria

1. They prevent colonization of the intestine by pathogenic bacteria and yeasts by protecting the integrity of the intestinal lining.
2. They produce acids that keep the pH balance in the intestine. This acid environment prevents disease-producing microbes from getting a foothold.
3. They decrease the side effects of antibiotic therapy.
4. They are the primary bacteria in infants, which helps them grow.
5. They inhibit growth of bacteria that produce nitrates in the bowel. Nitrates are bowel toxic and can cause cancer.
6. They help prevent production and absorption of toxins produced by disease-causing bacteria, which reduces the toxic load of the liver.
7. They manufacture B-complex vitamins.
8. They help regulate peristalsis and bowel movements.
9. They prevent and treat antibiotic-induced diarrhea.

Nutritional	Manufacture vitamins in our foods and bodies: B_1, B_2, B_3, B_5, B_6, B_{12}, K, and sometimes vitamin A.
Digestive	Digest lactose. Allow some people with lactose intolerance to eat yogurt and cultured dairy products. Help regulate peristalsis and regular bowel movements. Digest protein to free amino acids. Establish good digestion in infants, preventing colic, diaper rash, and gas.
Immune	Contribute to both humoral and cell–mediated immune function. Produce antibiotics and

	antifungals that prevent colonization of harmful bacteria and fungus. Protect against development of allergic conditions. Increase the number of immune system cells. Activate mucosal-associated lymphoid tissue (MALT). Manufacture essential fatty acids, 5 to 10 percent of all short-chained fatty acids. Increase the number of immune system cells. Create lactic acid that balances intestinal pH. Break down bacterial toxins and prevent production of bacterial toxins and colitis. Have antitumor and anticancer effects. Protect from xenobiotics like mercury, pesticides, radiation, and harmful pollutants. Break down bile acids. Manufacture hydrogen peroxide, which has antiseptic effects.
Heart	Play a role in normalization of serum cholesterol and triglycerides.
Metabolism	Break down and rebuild hormones. Promote healthy metabolism. Convert flavonoids—useful as antitumor factors and to reduce inflammation—to usable forms.

In addition to these nutritional and digestive benefits, probiotics enhance immune function. They manufacture antibiotics, such as acidophilin, produced by acidophilus, which are effective against many types of bacteria, including streptococcus and staph. *Lactobacillus acidophilus* and *Lactobacillus bulgaricus* have been shown to be effective in laboratory testing against the following pathogens: *Bacillus subtilis, Clostridium botulinum, Clostridium perfringens, Escherichia coli, Proteus mirabilis, Salmonella enteridis, Salmonella typhimurium, Shigella dysenteriae, Shigella paradysenteriae, Staphylococcus aureus,* and *Staphylococcus faecalis.*

Candida albicans, a fungus that causes infections in nails and eyes, thrush, and yeast infections, is controlled by acidophilus.

This works in at least two ways. First, acidophilus bacteria ferment glycogen into lactic acid, which changes the pH of the intestinal tract. Since candida and many other disease-causing microbes thrive in alkaline environments, this action discourages many disease-producing microbes. Second, specific strains of lactobacillus produce hydrogen peroxide, which kills candida directly. Studies show that supplementation with a hydrogen peroxide–producing strain of acidophilus, DDS-1, reduced the incidence of antibiotic-induced vaginal yeast infections threefold. Other probiotics have antitumor and anticancer effects. Probiotics also help us metabolize foreign substances, like mercury and pesticides, and protect us from damaging radiation and harmful pollutants.

Friendly bacteria also help us in other ways. Studies have repeatedly shown that lactobacillus bacteria can help normalize cholesterol levels. Probiotics also rebuild and break down hormones such as estrogen. Probiotics aid digestive function, improve peristalsis, and help normalize bowel transit time. Finally, bacterial balance is essential for healthy metabolism. Many superthin people have been able to gain weight when their bacteria were rebalanced, although the mechanism is not yet understood.

Lactobacillus bulgaricus and *Streptococcus thermophilus* are two other friendly inhabitants of our digestive tracts. Transient residents of the digestive tract, these flora are not native to it. They "vacation" in us for up to twelve days, which gives them time to have a beneficial effect on the intestinal ecology. Their most obvious function is to enhance the production of bifidobacteria. They have also been shown to have antitumor effects, and *Lactobacillus bulgaricus* has antibiotic and antiherpes effects as well. They are found in cultured dairy products or can be taken in supplement form.

Saccharomyces boulardii, another probiotic, is a friendly yeast that ᵇ⁻ᵛels of sIgA. In France, it's called "yeast against yeast." well studied and used clinically for more than fifty years. It is safe for people of all ages, including infants. It is resistant to antibiotics, except antifungal medications, so it can be used while taking antibiotics. It helps protect and restore normal flora. It stimulates the production of sIgA and IgG, antibodies that are the first line of defense against pathogens. It also stimulates enzymatic production, helping to repair and maintain normal gut mucosa, and stimulates the activity of short-chain fatty acids and disaccharide enzymes, such as lactase, maltase, and sucrase, which can help prevent diarrhea.

When used therapeutically, *S. boulardii* is useful for stopping diarrhea caused by traveling, antibiotics, AIDS, and severe burns. It has also been used effectively in people with Crohn's disease, significantly reducing the number of bowel movements and diarrhea, and it has been used to help people with diarrhea-type irritable bowel syndrome.

S. boulardii helps protect against bacteria and bacterial toxins by preventing them from attaching to the intestinal mucosa or specific receptor sites. Studies have shown its effectiveness against disease-causing strains of E. coli, *Clostridium difficile*, cholera, and *Entamoeba histolytica*. Studies indicate that it may also be effective against salmonella, the main cause of food poisoning.

E. coli Nissle strain has also been used effectively in digestive diseases. It's best studied for its role in protection from inflammatory bowel diseases and irritable bowel syndrome.

Probiotic supplements may be beneficial for the following health conditions:

- Vaginal infections
- Recurrent urinary infections
- Diarrhea in adults and children
- Complications from antibiotic therapy
- Traveler's diarrhea and/or colitis
- Lactose intolerance

- Hypertension
- Cancer
- Immune system stimulation
- Small bowel bacterial overgrowth
- Kidney stones
- Elevated blood cholesterol
- Allergy, including food allergies
- Inflammatory bowel diseases and pouchitis
- Flatulence
- Bacterial and fungal infections
- Rheumatoid arthritis
- Lupus erythematosus
- Alcohol-induced liver disease

Bacterial infections, antibiotics use, high stress levels, excessive alcohol intake, poor diet, and a number of other factors can disrupt the delicate balance of beneficial bacteria in our gut. Often, disease-producing bacteria and fungi will proliferate, causing symptoms such as diarrhea, bloating, and gas. If left unchecked, they can contribute to long-term conditions such as irritable bowel syndrome.

It would be impossible to write about each of the probiotic bacteria. Here are the highlights of a couple:

Lactobacillus reuteri (L. reuteri)
- Inhibits growth of disease-causing microbes including gram-negative and gram-positive bacteria, yeast, fungi, and protozoa
- Has a protective and therapeutic effect on vaginal infections
- Shortens duration of rotaviral infection, which causes diarrhea in children
- Has been found to colonize well in the human GI tract
- Appears to inhibit adherence of pathogens in gut

Bacteria and Yeasts Used as Probiotic Supplements

Bifidobacterium	Lactobacillus	Streptococcus	Other
B. bifidum	L. acidophilus	S. thermophilus	Enterococcus
B. breve	L. bulgaricus	S. faecium	faecium
B. infantis	L. rhamnosus	S. faecalis	S. boulardii
B. adolescentis	L. casei	S. lactis	Lactococcus
B. pseudocatenulatum	L. gasseri		cremoris
B. catenulatum	L. brevis		
B. angulatum	L. delbrueckii		
B. longum	L. lactis		
	L. kefir		
	L. plantarum		
	L. salivarius		
	L. reuteri		

Note: Some supplements contain soil-based probiotic organisms such as *Bacillus laterosporus*, *Bacillus subtilis*, and *L. sporogenes* (also known as *Bacillus coagulase*). Although there are many anecdotal stories of great success with these soil-based organisms for many digestive problems, there is no research yet to substantiate the claims.

Bifidobacteria infantis (*B. infantis*)

- Is the primary bacteria in the GI tract of infants
- Is useful in the treatment of colic, cradle-cap, and eczema in infants and babies
- May protect against bacteria that promote inflammatory bowel diseases
- Colonizes well in the GI tract after ingestion
- Contributes to reduction in illness and deaths associated with infants with necrotizing enterocolitis (NEC) when used with *L. acidophilus*

- Has antitumor properties in test research and possible therapeutic value in use with solid tumors, such as breast cancer

Not All Intestinal Bacteria Are Friendly

Friendly bacteria comprise only a small percentage of our total
bacteria. You could call the rest the OK, the bad, and the ugly.
Most intestinal residents are "commensal" bacteria: they have nei-
ther good nor bad effects on how we feel. Other intestinal bacteria are pathogens causing acute illness (salmonella causes food
poisoning) or chronic illness (*Helicobacter pylori* causes ulcers).
Disease-causing microbes produce bothersome gas and toxic
secretions that irritate the intestinal lining and get absorbed into
the bloodstream, making us sick.

Some bacteria are extremely virulent and cause sudden and violent illness. Our body reacts to a strong bacteria such as salmonella
with diarrhea, fever, loss of appetite, and vomiting. The body
screams, "Get this stuff out of me!" So, it attempts to rapidly flush
or starve it out. Most disease-causing microbes thrive at human
body temperature, while fever kills them by overheating them.

Bacteria that cause chronic illness are generally weak organisms
of low virulence. They are often found in small quantities in all of
us and have been assumed to be harmless. But when large colonies
are given the opportunity to thrive, they can and do cause illness.
This type of illness is called intestinal dysbiosis, which is discussed
in the next chapter.

Prebiotics

Prebiotics work with probiotics. They are saccharides, sugar molecules that are about half as sweet as sugar. Initial research focused
on their use as low-calorie sweeteners. As the research grew, how-

ever, it became apparent that these food molecules could play an important role in health maintenance. Studies found they stimulate the growth of good bacteria, such as bifidobacteria and lactobacilli, while promoting a reduction in disease-producing bacteria, such as clostridia, klebsiella, and enterobacter. They make the intestinal pH more acidic, creating an environment that enhances absorption of essential minerals, including calcium, magnesium, iron, and zinc.

We ingest prebiotics through our food. They pass through the digestive system whole and become fermented by the colonic microflora. There, they produce lactate and short-chain fatty acids, especially butyrate, the main energy source for the colonic cells. Butyrate helps cells maintain good function and repair. Because the great majority of gut bacteria are in the colon, butyrate is essential to protect the mucous lining and prevent leaky gut syndrome and translocation of bacteria to other organ systems.

Fructooligosaccharides (FOS) and inulin, two prebiotics that have been well-documented, are naturally found in our food. FOS has been shown to reduce serum triglyceride levels, protect against colon cancer, and help normalize insulin levels. Because of their health-building qualities, inulin and FOS are being researched as possible functional food additives by companies throughout the world. Dosages as low as 2.75 grams will dramatically increase bifidobacteria. They have also been shown to be antagonistic to at least eight disease-producing microbes including salmonella, listeria, campylobacter, shigella, and vibrio.

On average we consume about 2.5 grams per day of FOS alone. These fibers have been shown to increase levels of bifidobacteria in the colon. In addition, FOS has been shown to increase acidophilus. Foods containing FOS and inulin include Jerusalem artichokes, onions, chicory, garlic, leeks, fruit (especially bananas), soybeans, peas, legumes, eggplant, burdock root, aspa
maple, Chinese chive, and (in small amounts) whe
whole wheat.

High-Prebiotic-Containing Foods

Jerusalem artichokes	Onions	Chicory
Garlic	Leeks	Bananas
Fruit	Soybeans	Burdock root
Asparagus	Sugar maple	Chinese chives
Peas	Legumes	Eggplant

A recent study looked at the effect of honey on the growth of bifidobacteria in comparison to FOS, galactooligosaccharide (GOS), and inulin. Researchers reported that the honey worked as well to promote the production of lactic and acetic acid by the bifidobacteria. This study was a test-tube study, but it just may be helpful to add a spoonful of honey to your beverages. Yum!

Many people experience gas and bloating when they first begin to take FOS and prebiotics. This passes after a period of a couple of weeks. You can either persist or lower your dosage and increase gradually. Human studies show that the most growth of beneficial bacteria is seen in the people who need it most. Benefits increase up to 10 grams daily. After you stop taking prebiotics, your bacterial levels go back to where they were in about two to three weeks. They work synergistically with probiotics and can be taken together for best results—together they are being called synbiotics.

Foods and Herbs That Enhance Intestinal Flora

Cultured foods, such as yogurt, have significantly higher nutritional content than milk. The bacteria commonly used to produce yogurt—*L. bulgaricus* and *L. thermophilus*—produce biotin, a

Enhanced Nutrient Content of Selected Dairy Foods

Original Food	Fermented or Cultured Food	Increased Nutrition
Milk	Cheddar cheese	Vitamin B_1, 3 times
Milk	Cottage cheese	Vitamin B_{12}, 5 times
Milk	Yogurt	Vitamin B_{12}, 5 to 30 times
Milk	Yogurt	Vitamin B_3, 50 times
Skim milk	Low-fat yogurt	Vitamin A, 7 to 14 times

B-complex vitamin. The bacteria make this nutrient for their own good, but we benefit as well. By using cultured foods such as sauerkraut rather than cabbage; cottage cheese and yogurt rather than milk; tofu, miso, natto, tamari, or shoyu sauce; tempeh rather than soybeans; and wine rather than grapes, we get higher levels of vitamins A, B-complex, and K. In addition, fermented foods have increased probiotic content, aid digestion, and provide health-building enzymes and higher nutritional value.

People have long recognized the benefits of fermented foods. Although indigenous people didn't know the science behind their use, they easily noticed the healthful benefits. Sauerkraut, a traditional European food, has a long history of use to treat ulcers and digestive problems. Asian cultures traditionally use pickles and fermented foods as condiments—kimchi, pickled daikon radish, or a sweet rice drink called *amasake*. Because so many around the world are lactose intolerant, people have relied on cultured dairy products—cottage cheese, kefir, yogurt—for centuries. In India, *lassi*, a fermented dairy drink, is a household staple. In Israel, *leban*, which is similar to yogurt, is served daily.

Chinese green tea and ginseng also increase friendly flora. Polyphenols are believed to be the enhancing substance in green tea, which has beneficial effects on serum cholesterol, tumors, and ulcers. When polyphenols were tested to see their effect on intestinal flora, they increased the number of beneficial bacteria, such as lactobacilli and bifidus, while decreasing the number of disease-causing clostridium. A significant increase in beneficial flora was also found when ginseng extract was tested in vitro on 107 types of human bacteria.

The traditional Japanese diet takes advantage of several fermented foods—miso, tempeh, and tamari or soy sauce—that have antibiotic properties. Miso, a fermented soybean paste, was found to contain 161 strains of aerobic bacteria. Almost all of these were found to compete successfully with E. coli and *Staphylococcus aureus*, two main food-poisoning agents. Many lactic acid–producing bacteria were also found. Miso also helps reduce the negative effects of radioactivity and electromagnetic resonance. Several microbes, including yeast and *L. acidophilus*, are used in the fermentation process of soy sauce, also called shoyu or tamari, which produces a health-giving food. However, in the United States, rather than using living microbes, most soy sauce is manufactured from inorganic acids, such as hydrochloric acid, that break down the soybeans. This type of soy sauce doesn't have the same benefits as traditionally brewed soy sauce.

Probiotic Supplements

Because flora do not permanently stay in the gut, we need to get them either in our foods, such as yogurt or kefir, or to use a supplement. The composition of intestinal flora usually remains fairly constant in healthy people, but it can become unbalanced by aging, diet, disease, drugs, poor health, or stress. In fact, problems due to imbalanced flora have become widespread.

Eating yogurt and cultured dairy products can maintain healthful friendly flora colonies in people who are already healthy, but once disease-producing microbes have colonized, probiotic supplements are necessary. Taking daily probiotics increases our body's ability to protect itself from illness. Because of their acid-loving nature, they easily survive the high-acid environment of the stomach. Once in the intestinal tract, they colonize and replace less desirable residents. However, not all probiotic supplements provide the same benefits. According to Natasha Trenev, an expert on probiotics, various strains of acidophilus can differ genetically by as much as 20 percent. This is a huge difference, when you consider that the genetic difference between mice and man is about 2 percent.

What to Look for in a Probiotic Supplement

1. Look for *Lactobacillus acidophilus* and *Bifidobacteria bifidum*.
2. Choose an age-appropriate product. For a baby or toddler, *B. infantis* is appropriate; for children and adults, the most-studied strain of *L. acidophilus* is DDS-1.
3. Choose a product that is condition appropriate when it's available. There are now supplements that are specific for lactose intolerance, sugar malabsorption, irritable bowel syndrome, and diarrhea. There may soon be other specific products for psoriasis, vaginal infections, inflammatory bowel disease, and other health conditions.
4. Most of the best products come refrigerated. There are some viable products on the market that are stored at room temperature.
5. Bacteria multiply very quickly, but they need enough food once they reach the intestines. Some products contain inulin, FOS, or other prebiotics that help the flora grow. This can vastly improve the viability of the product. Just note that some people bloat from FOS.
6. Combination supplements with several types of flora are helpful. Bacteria compete for the same food supply, so look

for freeze-dried products. Freeze-drying puts the flora into suspended animation, keeping them dormant until placed in water or in your body.

Dosage

For preventive measures, take about a billion microbes of each protective species once a day. This is usually about ¼ to 1½ teaspoons or 1 to 3 capsules. For therapeutic purposes, take this amount three times a day or more. In one study, those with ulcerative colitis used 350 billion organisms. If you take probiotic supplements and have sudden bloating, diarrhea, gas, or worsening of symptoms, this is not necessarily a bad sign. As the disease-producing bacteria and fungus are killed, they release chemicals that aggravate symptoms. If this happens, begin again with tiny amounts and build up your dosage slowly to avoid the die-off reaction.

Probiotic supplements are also important for the prevention of traveler's diarrhea. If you plan to travel outside the United States, take a probiotic supplement daily. Studies show that it significantly increases your ability to withstand the new microbes you will be exposed to.

Dysbiosis
A Good Neighborhood Gone Bad

"Within these regions battles rage; populations rise and fall, affected just as we are by local environmental conditions, industry thrives and constant defense is exercised against interlopers and dangerous aliens who may enter unannounced; colonists roam and settle—some permanently, some only briefly, in general we have in miniature many of terrestrial life's vicissitudes, problems and solutions."
—NATASHA TRENEV AND LEO CHAITOW, *PROBIOTICS*

Early in the twentieth century, Dr. Eli Metchnikoff popularized the theory that disease begins in the digestive tract because of an imbalance of intestinal bacteria. He called this state *dysbiosis*, which comes from *symbiosis*, meaning "living together in mutual harmony," and *dys-*, which means "not." Dr. Metchnikoff was the first scientist to discover the useful properties of probiotics. He won the Nobel Prize in 1908 for his work on lactobacilli and their role in immunity and was a colleague of Louis Pasteur, succeeding him as the director of the Pasteur Institute in Paris.

Dr. Metchnikoff found that the bacteria in yogurt prevented and reversed bacterial infection. (He named it *Lactobacillus bul-*

garicus after the long-lived, yogurt-loving peasants of Bulgaria.)
His research proved that lactobacilli could displace many disease-
producing organisms and reduce the toxins they generated. He
believed these endotoxins (toxins produced from substances inside
the body) shortened lifespan. He advocated use of lactobacillus in
the 1940s for ptomaine poisoning, a widely used therapy in
Europe.

In more recent decades, Metchnikoff's work has taken a back-
seat to modern therapies, such as antibiotics and immunization
programs, which scientists hoped would conquer infectious diseases. For instance, because of an aggressive worldwide immunization program, the World Health Assembly formally declared
on May 8, 1980, that smallpox had been eradicated worldwide,
which was an enormous triumph for science and humankind. But,
subsequent efforts at eradicating other diseases have been unsuccessful. While parents in America routinely immunize their children against measles, mumps, and polio, parents in poor nations
are coping with the loss of half their children by age ten. Worldwide, we are finding an increase in new and deadly viruses for
which there are not yet effective vaccines.

Viruses and bacteria are extremely adaptable, and their success
ensures their survival. In our efforts to eradicate them we have
pushed them to evolve. Long before chemists created antibiotics,
yeasts, fungi, and rival bacteria were producing antibiotics to ward
each other off and establish neighborhoods. They became adept at
evading each other's strategies and adapting for survival. Because
people have used antibiotics prophylactically and indiscriminately
in humans and animals, the bacteria have had a chance to learn
from it, undergoing rapid mutations. As they shuffle their components, learning new evolutionary dance steps, superstrains of
bacteria have been created that no longer respond to any antibiotic treatment. For instance, our immune systems normally detect

bacteria by information coded on the cell walls. Now, in response to antibiotics, some bacteria have survived by removing their cell walls, so they're able to enter the bloodstream and tissues unopposed, causing damage in organs and tissues. Bacteria can also turn on specific genes when exposed to specific antibiotics.

Resistant strains of bacteria are communicating with each other and passing resistance information on to other types of bacteria. For example, we now have antibiotic-resistant gonorrhea, leprosy, staph, and strep. Similarly, many bacteria that cause disease primarily in the digestive tract—cholera, dysentery, E. coli, *Enterobacteriaceae*, *Enterococcus faecium*, klebsiella, proteus, pseudomonas, salmonella, *Serratia marcenscens*, and shigella—have mutated to become resistant to specific antibiotics. (For a lengthy but fascinating look at the world through the eyes of virologists, read Laurie Garrett's *The Coming Plague*.) In 1992, 13,300 hospital patients died of infections that resisted every drug doctors tried. Currently, forty thousand North Americans die each year from antibiotic-resistant infections.

The sexual revolution also helped the evolution of microbes. Multiple sex partners allowed bacteria, fungi, and virus more opportunity to replicate, increasing the possibility of mutation. Some of these mutant microbes became better at causing infection or deepening illness. Given people's rapid movement between countries, these new microbes are spread quickly throughout the world, increasing the risk of even more mutation and enhancement of the microbial defense system.

In *The Coming Plague*, Laurie Garrett spends nearly seven hundred pages discussing microbes, their increasing virulence, and the devastation of their epidemics. Her solutions offer little optimism. But she has neglected half the equation. If microbes are becoming more resistant and virulent, we must increase our own resistance and strength to outsmart them. We must boost immune function so that people will be less receptive to infection. We need to take a new look at Metchnikoff's work and at probiotic bacteria and the many immune-strengthening benefits they confer.

Optimum nutrition is a logical starting point. By definition, nutrients are essential for growth, immune function, repair, and maintenance of our bodies. But the diet of Americans will not protect our immune function. New research has shown that diets deficient in just one nutrient, in this case either selenium or vitamin E, could cause a benign virus to mutate to a disease-producing organism. Today, 80 percent of women and children do not meet the recommended daily intake (RDI) for vitamin E and zinc. Eighty percent of American women do not meet the RDI for magnesium. A study of high school runners found that 45 percent of girls and 17 percent of boys were deficient in iron, while 31 percent of female college athletes were also found to be iron deficient. A recent survey of nutritional status in elderly Americans showed that 25 percent were malnourished, and 50 percent of all hospitalized elderly suffer from malnutrition.

Dysbiosis weakens our ability to protect ourselves from disease-causing microbes, which are generally composed of low-virulence organisms. Unlike salmonella, which causes immediate food-poisoning reactions, low-virulence microbes are insidious. They cause chronic problems that go undiagnosed in the great majority of cases. If left unrecognized and untreated, they become deep-seated and may cause chronic health problems, including joint pain, diarrhea, chronic fatigue syndrome, or colon disease.

Because most doctors in our culture do not yet recognize dysbiosis, symptoms are treated with medication, but the underlying cause is never dealt with, and ultimately people do not get well. Published research has listed dysbiosis as the cause of arthritis, diarrhea, autoimmune illness, B_{12} deficiency, chronic fatigue syndrome, cystic acne, the early stages of colon and breast cancer,

Some Microbes and Their Relationship to Digestive and Autoimmune Problems

Bacteria	Gastrointestinal Effect
Candida	Candida is a fungus with more than two hundred species. The most common symptom is diarrhea but might also include constipation, abdominal discomfort, bloating, gas, rectal itching, menstrual complaints, vaginal infections, bladder infections, depression, irritability, inability to concentrate, memory lapses, headaches, hives, hay fever, asthma, ear fungus, and chemical sensitivities.
Citrobacter freundii, diversus, and *koseri*	Implicated in diarrheal diseases, they possess an antigen similar to some strains of salmonella, which may cause cross-reactive immune reactions. They might invade the intestinal mucosa, causing irritation and inflammation.
Clostridium difficile	In mild cases, symptoms are frequent, foul-smelling watery stools. In more severe cases, symptoms are diarrhea that contains blood and mucus and intestinal cramping. Approximately 20 percent of people in nursing homes are infected with *C. difficile.*
E. coli	Indicate intestinal flora imbalance when low levels are found in stool samples. Look for diet, drugs, environmental stress, excessive yeast, parasites, and pathogens as possible causes.
Enterobacter cloacae	This is associated with diarrhea in children when found in large numbers. Its presence indicates imbalanced flora.
Helicobacter pylori	This bacteria might cause stomach ulcers and gastritis with symptoms of abdominal pain, nausea, and vomiting. Its presence increases risk of developing stomach cancer. Fifty per-

	cent of the world's population is infected. Many people are completely without symptoms, which is probably due to their genetics.
Klebsiella	This bacteria can cause diarrhea, bacteremia, cystitis, pneumonia, or prostatitis. It is linked with such autoimmune diseases as ankylosing spondylitis and myasthenia gravis. It is usually asymptomatic in the intestine, although it can cause diarrhea. Klebsiella is generally very resistant to antibiotics. Infections often acquired in hospitals, mainly in patients with low resistance. Klebsiella thrives on a high starch diet.
Lactobacillus	Low levels of lactobacillus indicate flora imbalance. Look for diet, drugs, environmental stress, excessive yeast, parasites, and pathogens as possible causes.
Nonlactose E. coli	Ninety percent of normal strains of E. coli produce lactase, which ferments lactose. Half of the pathogenic strains fail to do so. May be causing symptoms if found in a stool culture in a patient with diarrheal symptoms.
Proteus	This is normally found in flora of feces, soil, and water. In large numbers, proteus may promote diarrhea and GI distress. *Proteus vulgaris* may be involved in the initiation of myasthenia gravis. It is also associated with ankylosing spondylitis and rheumatoid arthritis.
Pseudomonas	This may be acquired from contaminated water and leads to diarrhea and GI distress.
Salmonella	Gastroenteritis and diarrhea are casued by more than two thousand types of salmonella. It is the most often reported cause of food poisoning from eggs, milk products, and raw meat; salmonella infects 38 percent of commercial uncooked chickens. It may occur

	without symptoms in a carrier state and may also invade the mucosa and present as enteric fever, a focal disease with or without septicemia or gastroenteritis. Salmonella is an increasing health concern.
Staphylococcus aureus	This is a major cause of food poisoning, with abrupt onset of nausea and vomiting; symptoms may include diarrhea and abdominal cramps. *Staphylococcus aureus* is also implicated in pseudomembranous colitis and toxic shock syndrome.
Yersinia enterocolitica	This bacteria is implicated as a significant cause of gastroenteritis. Variable symptoms may resemble ulcerative colitis. Antigenic determinants, cross-reactive to the thyroid plasma membrane, may result in Grave's disease. *Yersinia enterocolitica* is also associated with such autoimmune diseases as arthritis, erythema nodosum, or Sjögren's syndrome.

These references were used with permission by Great Smokies Diagnostic Laboratory. Contact them for information on a huge number of additional dysbiotic organisms.

eczema, food allergy or sensitivity, inflammatory bowel disease, irritable bowel syndrome, psoriasis, and steatorrhea. These problems were previously unrecognized as being microbial in origin. Common dysbiotic bacteria are aeromonas, citrobacter, helicobacter, klebsiella, salmonella, shigella, *Staphylococcus aureus*, vibrio, and yersinia. Helicobacter, for example, is commonly found in people with ulcers. Citrobacter is implicated in diarrheal diseases. A common dysbiosis culprit, the candida fungus, causes a wide variety of symptoms that range from gas and bloating to depression, mood swings, and premenstrual syndrome (PMS).

What Causes Dysbiosis?

While there are many causes of dysbiosis, we generally bring it on ourselves. Constant high levels of stress, exposure to manufactured chemicals, poor food choices, oral contraceptives, surgery, and use of antibiotics and painkillers all change the healthy balance of the digestive tract.

The most common cause of dysbiosis is the use of antibiotics, which change the balance of intestinal microbes. Not terribly specific, antibiotics simultaneously kill both harmful and helpful bacteria throughout our digestive system, mouth, vagina, and skin, leaving the territory to bacteria, parasites, viruses, and yeasts that are resistant to the antibiotic that was used. In a healthy gut, parasites may be present in small numbers and not cause symptoms, but if allowed to flourish they can cause diarrhea, illness, and weight loss. Most people can recover fairly easily from a single round of antibiotics, but even those with strong constitutions have trouble regaining balance from repeated use of antibiotic drugs.

These microbes produce toxins that cause symptoms. The bacteria form chemicals that are poisonous to the cells around them and to the person they live in. A wide variety of substances are produced, including amines, ammonia, hydrogen sulfide, indoles, phenols, and secondary bile acids. These substances may hurt the intestinal lining directly by damaging the brush border and become absorbed into the bloodstream, causing system-wide effects. Initially, our body rushes white blood cells to the injured tissue to eat up the bacteria and carry away the debris via the lymphatic system. Inflammation, pain, and swelling are nature's message to stop and let your body heal. But we often ignore this basic instinct and reach for pain medication so we can continue our lives. If the pain and inflammation were initially caused by microbes and you never dealt with the cause, more endotoxins will be produced, causing chronic pain and inflammation, and setting up a continuing cycle.

Often, the pain medications we take become a factor in the continuation and severity of the problem. It becomes a vicious circle: The drug causes damage to the intestinal lining, causing more inflammation, irritation, and pain; so we take more pain medication, which causes further damage. The most common pain medications fall into three groups: steroidal drugs, such as cortisone and prednisone; nonsteroidal anti-inflammatory drugs (NSAIDs), such as aspirin, ibuprofen, and indomethacin; and cyclooxygenase 2 (COX2) inhibitors, such as Celebrex and Vioxx. Let's look at the long-term effects of these medications on the digestive system and their consequences on health.

Corticosteroids are naturally produced by the adrenal glands. Synthetic corticosteroids, such as cortisone and prednisone, are two of the most effective emergency drugs and used for a multitude of problems, including allergies, arthritis, asthma, Crohn's disease, eczema, lupus, poison ivy, psoriasis, and ulcerative colitis. They are generally prescription medications, but weaker over-the-counter remedies can be purchased everywhere.

Because cortisone and prednisone have such powerful anti-inflammatory effects, they are used long term by people with chronic illness. But long-term use of cortisone and prednisone depresses the immune system, causing side effects such as lowered resistance to infection and parasites, stomach and duodenal ulcers, thinning of bones, and dozens of other problems. Steroids are contraindicated for anyone who has a fungal infection because they provide excellent nourishment for fungi. Yet, many people with candida infections go undiagnosed. In turn, candida damages the intestinal lining, causing a wide variety of symptoms, including bloating, chronic fatigue, constipation, depression, diarrhea, fatigue, hypoglycemia, and premenstrual syndrome, to name but a few. Because corticosteroids are so strong, they suppress your body's ability to work through an illness on its own. They are best suited for an emergency, not daily use.

NSAIDs work by blocking prostaglandins, which are small protein messengers that circulate throughout the body. Some prostaglandins cause pain and inflammation; others cause healing and repair. NSAIDs block all prostaglandins. The pain is gone, but the healing process is blocked. Because the intestinal lining repairs and replaces itself every three to five days, prolonged use of NSAIDs blocks its repair. The GI side effects are well known: the lining becomes weak, inflamed, and "leaky," causing leaky gut syndrome or intestinal permeability. NSAID use also increases the risk of ulcers of the stomach and duodenum. These drugs also cause bleeding, damage to the mucous membranes of the intestines, and GI inflammation.

Because aspirin is hard on the stomach lining, doctors and advertisers have advised us to switch to anti-inflammatory drugs, such as ibuprofen. But we are not told that all NSAIDs cause irritation and inflammation of the intestinal tract, leading to colitis and relapse of ulcerative colitis. NSAIDs can cause bleeding and ulceration of the large intestine and may contribute to complications of diverticular disease. Even with moderate use, NSAIDs increase gut permeability. In fact, use of NSAIDs, steroids, antacids, and antibiotics are probably the greatest contributors to leaky gut syndrome.

These days, physicians are increasingly using a new class of drugs, COX2 inhibitors, for pain management. COX2 inhibitors block leukotrienes and do not appear to have the damaging effects to the stomach and mucous membranes of the digestive system.

Poor diet also contributes to dysbiosis. A diet high in fat, sugar, and processed foods may not have enough nutrients to optimally nourish the body or repair and maintain the digestive organs. The nutrients most likely to be lacking are the antioxidants—vitamins C and E, beta-carotene, coenzyme Q10, glutathione, selenium, the sulfur amino acids, and zinc—the B-complex vitamins, calcium, essential fatty acids, and magnesium.

Poor ileocecal valve function can contribute to dysbiosis. The valve's job is to keep waste matter in the colon from mixing with the useful material that is still being digested and absorbed in the small intestine. When this valve is stuck, either open or closed, dysbiotic problems can occur. Chiropractors can adjust the ileocecal valve to alleviate this problem.

Many other factors contribute to dysbiosis. Low levels of hydrochloric acid (HCl) in the stomach encourage bacterial overgrowth. Poor transit time in the intestinal tract also encourages proliferation of bacteria. For example, in twenty-four hours one E. coli bacterium produces nearly five thousand identical bacteria. The longer they sit inside us, the greater their potential to colonize.

Patterns of Dysbiosis

The four commonly recognized patterns of dysbiosis are putrefaction, fermentation, deficiency, and sensitization.

Putrefaction Dysbiosis

This is the most common type and occurs when food is not well digested, essentially rotting inside us. We may feel this as bloating, discomfort, and indigestion. The typical American high-fat, high-animal-protein, low-fiber diet predisposes people to putrefaction. It causes an increase of bacteroides bacteria, a decrease in beneficial bifidobacteria, and an increase in bile production.

...use vitamin B_{12} deficiency by uncoupling the B_{12}
...c factor necessary for its use. Other bacteria nor-
...make vitamin B_{12} directly for their own purposes, but it too
becomes unavailable to us. The most common signs of B_{12} deficiencies are depression, diarrhea, fatigue, memory loss, numbing
of hands and feet, sleep disturbances, and weakness. Vitamin B_{12}
deficiency is commonly seen in older people because of poor
hydrochloric acid (HCl) levels in the stomach.

Poor bifidobacteria levels decrease our body's ability to resist
infection, affect bowel health, and reflect a decreased production
of B-complex vitamins. Research has implicated putrefaction dysbiosis with breast and colon cancer. Bacterial enzymes change bile
acids into thirty-three substances formed in the colon that are
tumor promoters. Bacterial enzymes, such as betaglucuronidase,
re-create estrogens that were already broken down. These estrogens are reabsorbed into the bloodstream, increasing estrogen levels and estrogen-dependent breast cancers. Putrefaction dysbiosis
can be corrected by eating more high-fiber foods, fruits, vegetables, and grains and fewer meats and fats.

Fermentation Dysbiosis

This is characterized by bloating, constipation, diarrhea, fatigue,
and gas. People with fermentation dysbiosis have faulty digestion
of carbohydrates: sugars, fruit, beer, wine, grains, and fiber. Fermentation of carbohydrates provides food for multiplying bacteria
and produces hydrogen and carbon dioxide gases and short-
chained fatty acids, all of which can be tested.

Fermentation dysbiosis is often characterized by flora that
have been taken over by candida fungi or other disease-causing
microbes. These microbes damage the intestinal brush borders
(microvilli) and lead to increased intestinal permeability. People
with fermentation dysbiosis need to strictly avoid carbohydrate-
containing foods. It is recommended that they receive therapeu-

tic support to help regain bowel health. Up to 2,000 milligrams of citrus seed extract can be used daily. Use of probiotic supplements and repair of the intestinal mucosa are essential.

Deficiency Dysbiosis

This is characterized by a lack of beneficial flora, such as bifidobacteria and lactobacillus. Use of antibiotics and low-fiber diets are the primary cause of poor flora. Deficiency dysbiosis is often seen in people with irritable bowel syndrome and food sensitivities. Deficiency dysbiosis is often coupled with putrefaction dysbiosis, and the treatment is the same. To restore balance, supplementation with beneficial flora and fructooligosaccharides (FOS) is also recommended. Up to 2,000 milligrams of citrus seed extract may be used daily.

Sensitization Dysbiosis

This occurs when the immune system reacts with abnormal or aggravated responses to the digestive process. Microbes in the gut and foods produce exotoxins that irritate the gut lining. Our bodies recognize these toxins as foreign substances and produce antibodies that signal the immune system to get rid of them. Unfortunately, this local reaction might be the cause of some autoimmune diseases. Rheumatoid arthritis, ankylosing spondylitis, and perhaps skin diseases such as eczema and psoriasis are often the result.

In this process, our body initially reacts to a "bug" of some sort, but the antibodies formed to fight it are the perfect keys that fit into gene markers. These markers make us more susceptible to certain diseases. The mechanism by which these are turned on or off is unclear, but it appears that specific microbes cause disease only in people with specific gene markers who are exposed to specific microbes that are harmless in everyone else. Our body senses that as a systemic problem rather than just some imbalanced microbes in our intestines. It reacts with an all-out antibody reaction, attacking the body itself—an autoimmune reaction. What originated as a local infection becomes an autoimmune illness. For instance, rheumatoid arthritis has been linked to a prevalence of the bacteria proteus, which mimics gene marker HLA-DR4; 50 to 75 percent of people with rheumatoid arthritis have this gene marker.

People with sensitization dysbiosis often have food intolerances, leaky gut syndrome, and increasing sensitivity to foods and the environment. Symptoms may include acne, bowel or skin problems, connective tissue disease, and psoriasis. Sensitization dysbiosis may accompany fermentation dysbiosis, and similar treatments may be helpful. Replacing probiotic bacteria and repair of the intestinal mucosa are essential.

Candida: The Masquerader

The most prevalent and obvious form of dysbiosis is candidiasis, a fungal infection. Candida is found in nearly everyone, and in small amounts it is compatible with good health. Candida is usually controlled by friendly flora, our immune defense system, and intestinal pH. When the bacteria that normally balance candida are killed, it causes what's commonly known as a yeast infection because it produces a smell like yeasty bread. It's called a yeast infection in the vagina, a fungal infection in the nail beds and the eyes, and thrush in the throat. *Candida albicans* is the usual offender, but other species of candida fungus may cause health problems as well.

In the early 1980s, Orion Truss, M.D., noticed that many of his patients' other problems resolved when he treated them with nystatin for fungal problems. Indeed, one patient had a complete reversal of multiple sclerosis. After hearing Dr. Truss lecture on his findings, Abraham Hoffer, M.D., a doctor in the field of orthomolecular psychiatry, tried his first yeast protocol on a psychiatric patient who had suffered from depression for many years. One month after initiating Truss's program she was mentally and emotionally sound or stable.

Candida can also colonize in the digestive tract, causing havoc everywhere in the body. Candida colonies produce powerful toxins that are absorbed into the bloodstream and affect our immune system, hormone balance, and thought processes. The most common symptoms are abdominal bloating, anxiety, constipation or diarrhea (or both), depression, environmental sensitivities, fatigue, feeling worse on damp or muggy days or in moldy places, food sensitivities, fuzzy thinking, insomnia, low blood sugar, mood swings, premenstrual syndrome, recurring vaginal or bladder infections, ringing in the ears, and sensitivities to perfume, cigarettes, or fabric odors. Although these symptoms are the most prevalent, candida has many faces, and many types of symptoms can occur.

American physicians recognize candida in many forms, but in general they have been unwilling to recognize it in a systemic form. For those who do, it is a common diagnosis. In my own experience, I have found candida to be an underlying cause in many clients. Dr. Hoffer states that one-third of the world's population is affected by candidiasis.

Candida infections are usually triggered by use of antibiotics, birth control pills, steroid medications, and consumption of sugar. These drugs change the balance of the intestinal tract, kill the bacteria that keep candida in check, and the fungus quickly takes hold. Candida are like bullies that push their way into the intestinal lining, destroying cells and brush borders. Greater numbers of candida produce greater amounts of toxins, which further irritate and break down the intestinal lining. This damage allows macromolecules of partially digested food to pass through. The macromolecules are the perfect size for antibodies to respond to.

Your immune system then goes on alert for these specific foods so the next time you eat them, your antibodies will be waiting. The net result is increased sensitivity to foods and other food substances and the environment.

Many, many therapeutic programs are available for people to follow to rid themselves of candida. The standard therapeutic diet allows beef, chicken, fish, eggs, poultry, yogurt, vegetables, oils, nuts, and seeds. No alcoholic beverages, fruits or dried fruits, flours, grains, mushrooms, sugar, vinegar, or yeasted breads are allowed. When I had candida, I found that the worst foods for me were beer, sugar, and dried fruit. A sip of beer triggered symptoms within twenty minutes. However, at that time, I was a banana-holic, consuming three to five barely ripe bananas daily. I now know that bananas are loaded with fructooligosaccharides, which feed lactobacillus and bifidobacteria but not candida. Because of biochemical individuality, other people find other foods and substances to be the worst triggers for them. People are advised to go on a strict diet for three weeks and then reintroduce foods one at a time to test for reactions. If you know you're sensitive to a specific food, avoid it.

Candida often causes bowel problems—either diarrhea or constipation or both alternately—so it is essential that bowel transit time be normalized. Adding psyllium seed husks (found in fiber supplements) and probiotic supplements greatly helps to normalize this condition. Russell Jaffe, M.D., uses vitamin C flushes, which are described in Chapter 8.

Many substances are helpful in killing off candida. Garlic is my personal favorite—eat lots of it raw; women can use it as a vaginal suppository (make sure not to nick the garlic or it can sting!) or take in capsule form. Capryllic acid from coconuts, oleic acid from olive oil, oil of oregano, thyme oil, pau d'arco, olive leaf extract, and grapefruit seed extract are all valuable agents for killing candida. Mathake, a South American herb, has also been found to be extremely effective. While it isn't necessary to use all these health enhancers, you can buy many of them in combination products in health-food stores or from health professionals. Probiotics help keep candida in check.

When the candida are killed, the protein fragments and endotoxins released trigger an antibody response. This can initially produce a worsening of the person's symptoms and is commonly known as a die-off reaction, or a Herxheimer reaction. Therefore, it is important to begin therapeutics gently with small doses and gradually increase. If your symptoms are still initially aggravated, cut back and gradually increase supplements. Most people begin to feel dramatically better within two weeks. If you don't, you're probably not dealing with a candida problem. Ask your health professional to make therapeutic recommendations.

I recently advised a client to take probiotic supplements for peeling skin and a burning sensation on her feet. Although she scored rather low on the candida questionnaire, her symptoms fit those of candida. I advised her to take probiotics slowly, beginning with ¼ teaspoon daily and working up gradually to a full teaspoon once or twice a day. Six days later, she told me her feet were improving, but she had a horrible headache every time she took a teaspoon of probiotics. After she began again more slowly, she was soon relieved of both problems.

The following candida questionnaire can help you determine if it is a factor in your own health.

YEAST QUESTIONNAIRE—ADULT

Answering these questions and adding up the scores will help you decide if yeasts contribute to your health problems. Yet you will not obtain an automatic "yes" or "no" answer.

For each "yes" answer in Section A, circle the points score in that section. Total your score and record it at the end of the section. Then move on to sections B and C and score as indicated. Add the total of your scores to get your grand total.

Section A: History

Points Score

1. Have you taken tetracyclines (Sumycin, Panmycin, Vibramycin, Minocin, and so forth) or other antibiotics for acne for one month (or longer)?   35

2. Have you, at any time in your life, taken other "broad-spectrum" antibiotics* for respiratory, urinary, or other infections (for two months or longer, or in shorter courses four or more times in a one-year period)?   35

3. Have you taken a broad-spectrum antibiotic drug,* even a single course?   6

4. Have you, at any time in your life, been bothered by persistent prostatitis, vaginitis, or other problems affecting your reproductive organs?   25

5. Have you been pregnant two or more times?   5

   One time?   3

6. Have you taken birth control pills for more than two years?   15

   For six months to two years?   8

---

* Including Keflex, ampicillin, amoxicillin, Ceclor, Bactrim, and Septra. Such antibiotics kill off "good germs" while they're killing off those that cause infection.

7. Have you taken prednisone, Decadron, or other
   cortisone-type drugs for more than two weeks?   15

   For two weeks or less?   6

8. Does exposure to perfumes, insecticides, fabric shop
   odors, and other chemicals provoke:

   Moderate to severe symptoms?   20
   Mild symptoms?   5

9. Are your symptoms worse on damp, muggy days or
   in moldy places?   20

10. Have you had athlete's foot, ringworm, "jock itch,"
    or other chronic fungus infections of the skin or
    nails? Have such infections been:

    Severe or persistent?   20
    Mild to moderate?   10

11. Do you crave sugar?   10

12. Do you crave breads?   10

13. Do you crave alcoholic beverages?   10

14. Does tobacco smoke really bother you?   10

Total Score, Section A

Section B: Major Symptoms
For each of your symptoms, enter the appropriate figure in the
Points Score column:

If a symptom is occasional or mild score 3 points.

If a symptom is frequent and/or moderately severe score
6 points.

If a symptom is severe and/or disabling score 9 points.

Add total score and record it at the end of this section.

Points Score

1. Fatigue or lethargy

2. Feeling of being "drained"

3. Poor memory

4. Feeling "spacey" or "unreal"

5. Depression

6. Inability to make decisions

7. Numbness, burning, or tingling

8. Muscle aches or weakness

9. Pain and/or swelling in joints

10. Abdominal pain

11. Constipation

12. Diarrhea

13. Bloating, belching, or intestinal gas

14. Troublesome vaginal burning, itching, or discharge

15. Persistent vaginal burning or itching

16. Prostatitis

17. Impotence

18. Loss of sexual desire or feeling

19. Endometriosis or infertility

20. Cramps and/or other menstrual irregularities

21. Premenstrual tension

22. Attacks of anxiety or crying

23. Cold hands or feet and/or chilliness

24. Shaking or irritable when hungry

Total Score, Section B

Section C: Other Symptoms*

For each of your symptoms, enter the appropriate figure in the Points Score column:

If a symptom is occasional or mild score 1 point.

If a symptom is frequent and/or moderately severe score 2 points.

If a symptom is severe and/or disabling score 3 points.

Add total score and record it at the end of this section.

Points Score

1. Drowsiness

2. Irritability or jitteriness

3. Lack of coordination

4. Inability to concentrate

5. Frequent mood swings

6. Headaches

7. Dizziness/loss of balance

8. Pressure above ears, feeling of head swelling

---

* While the symptoms in this section commonly occur in people with yeast-connected illnesses, they are also found in other individuals.

9. Tendency to bruise easily

10. Chronic rashes or itching

11. Numbness, tingling

12. Indigestion or heartburn

13. Food sensitivity or intolerance

14. Mucus in stools

15. Rectal itching

16. Dry mouth or throat

17. Rash or blisters in mouth

18. Bad breath

19. Foot, body, or hair odor not relieved by washing

20. Nasal congestion or postnasal drip

21. Nasal itching

22. Sore throat

23. Laryngitis, loss of voice

24. Cough or recurrent bronchitis

25. Pain or tightness in chest

26. Wheezing or shortness of breath

27. Urgency or urinary frequency

28. Burning on urination

29. Spots in front of eyes or erratic vision

30. Burning or tearing of eyes

31. Recurrent infections or fluid in ears

32. Ear pain or deafness

Total Score, Section C

Total Score, Section A
Total Score, Section B
Total Score, Section C
Grand Total Score

The Grand Total Score will help you and your physician decide if your health problems are yeast connected. Scores in women will run higher as seven items in the questionnaire apply exclusively to women, while only two apply exclusively to men.

Yeast-connected health problems are almost certainly present in women with scores higher than 180 and 140 in men.

Yeast-connected health problems are probably present in women with scores higher than 120 and 90 in men.

Yeast-connected health problems are possibly present in women with scores higher than 60 and 40 in men.

With scores of lower than 60 in women and 40 in men, yeasts are less apt to cause health problems.

YEAST QUESTIONNAIRE—CHILD

Circle appropriate point score for questions you answer "yes." Total your score and record it at the end of the questionnaire.

Points Score

1. During the two years before your child was born, were you bothered by recurrent vaginitis, menstrual irregularities, premenstrual tension, fatigue, headache, depression, digestive disorders, or "feeling bad all over"?   30

2. Was your child bothered by thrush?

    Mild?   10
    Severe or persistent?   20

3. Was your child bothered by frequent diaper rashes
    in infancy?

    Mild?   10
    Severe or persistent?   20

4. During infancy, was your child bothered by colic and
    irritability lasting longer than three months?

    Mild?   10
    Severe or persistent?   20

5. Are his symptoms worse on damp days or in damp
    or moldy places?   20

6. Has your child been bothered by recurrent or
    persistent "athlete's foot" or chronic fungus
    infections of his skin or nails?   30

7. Has your child been bothered by recurrent hives,
    eczema, or other skin problems?   10

8. Has your child received:

    Four or more courses of antibiotic drugs during
    the past year? Or has he received continuous
    "prophylactic" courses of antibiotic drugs?   80
    Eight or more courses of "broad-spectrum"
    antibiotics (such as amoxicillin, Keflex, Septra,
    Bactrim, or Ceclor) during the past three years?   50

9. Has your child experienced recurrent ear problems?   10

10. Has your child had tubes inserted in his ears?   10

11. Has your child been labeled "hyperactive"?

    Mild?   10
    Severe?   20

12. Is your child bothered by learning problems
    (even though his early developmental history
    was normal)?   10

13. Does your child have a short attention span?   10

14. Is your child persistently irritable, unhappy, and
    hard to please?   10

15. Has your child been bothered by persistent or recurrent
    digestive problems, including constipation, diarrhea,
    bloating, or excessive gas?

    Mild?   10
    Moderate?   20
    Severe?   30

16. Has he been bothered by persistent nasal congestion,
    cough, and/or wheezing?   10

17. Is your child unusually tired or unhappy or depressed?

    Mild?   10
    Severe?   20

18. Has your child been bothered by recurrent headaches,
    abdominal pain, or muscle aches?

    Mild?   10
    Severe?   20

19. Does your child crave sweets?   10

20. Does exposure to perfume, insecticides, gas, or other
    chemicals provoke moderate to severe symptoms?   30

21. Does tobacco smoke really bother him?   20

22. Do you feel that your child isn't well, yet diagnostic
    tests and studies haven't revealed the cause?   10

Total Score

Yeasts possibly play a role in causing health problems in
children with scores of 60 or higher.

Yeasts probably play a role in causing health problems in
children with scores of 100 or higher.

Yeasts almost certainly play a role in causing health problems
in children with scores of 140 or higher.

Source: Used with permission from Crook, William. The Yeast Connection
and Women's Health. *Jackson, Tenn.: Woman's Health Connection Inc., 2003.*

Leaky Gut Syndrome

The Systemic Consequences of Faulty Digestion

"The gut is a major potential portal of entry into the body for foreign antigens. Only its intact mucosal barrier protects the body from foreign antigen entry and systemic exposure."

—RUSSELL JAFFE, M.D.

Leaky gut syndrome is really a nickname for the more formal term *increased intestinal permeability*, which underlies an enormous variety of illnesses and symptoms. It's not a disease or an illness itself. The list of health conditions associated with increased intestinal permeability grows each year as we increase our knowledge of the synergy between digestion and the immune system. If you do a Pubmed search on "intestinal permeability," you'll find it linked with nearly five thousand research articles.

A healthy intestinal lining allows only properly digested fats, proteins, and starches to pass through so they can be assimilated. At the same time, it also provides a barrier to keep out bacterial products, foreign substances, and large undigested molecules. This is called the barrier function of the gastrointestinal mucosal lining. This surface is often called the brush border because under a microscope its villi and microvilli look like bristles on a brush.

The intestinal lining lets substances move across this barrier in several ways. The process of diffusion is a simple one: it equalizes the concentrations inside and outside the cells. Diffusion is the way ions of chloride, magnesium, potassium, sodium, and free fatty acids pass into the cells. Most nutrients are moved through the brush borders via a process called active transport. Carrier molecules, all of low molecular weight, transport nutrients like molecular taxis. Amino acids, fatty acids, glucose, minerals, and vitamins cross cell membranes through active transport.

In between cells are junctions called desmosomes. Normally, desmosomes form tight junctions and do not permit large molecules to pass through. But when the area is irritated and inflamed, these junctions loosen up, allowing larger molecules to pass through. The substances that pass through the intracellular junctions are seen by our immune system as foreign, stimulating an antibody reaction. When the intestinal lining is damaged, larger substances of particle size are allowed to pass directly, again triggering an antibody reaction.

When the intestinal lining is damaged even more, substances larger than particle size—disease-causing bacteria, potentially toxic molecules, and undigested food particles—are allowed to pass directly through the weakened cell membranes. They go directly into the bloodstream, activating antibodies and alarm substances called cytokines. The cytokines alert our lymphocytes (white blood cells) to battle the particles. Oxidants are produced in the battle, causing irritation and inflammation far from the digestive system. That is the basis for a condition called increased intestinal permeability or leaky gut syndrome.

Intestinal mucus normally blocks bacteria from moving to other parts of the body. But when the cells are leaking, bacteria passes into the bloodstream and throughout the body. When intestinal bacteria colonize in other parts of the body, we call it bacterial translocation, and it is often found in people with leaky gut syndrome. For example, *Blastocystis hominis*, a bacteria that causes GI problems, has been found in the synovial fluid in the knee of an arthritis patient. Surgery or tube feeding in hospitals can also cause bacterial translocation.

Here's how leaky gut syndrome works. Imagine that your cells need a kernel of corn. They are screaming out, "Hey, send me a kernel of corn." The bloodstream replies, "I have a can of corn, but I don't have a can opener." So the can goes around and around while the cells starve for corn. Finally, our immune system reacts by making antibodies against the can of corn, treating the corn as if it were a foreign invader. Your immune system has mobilized to finish the job of incomplete digestion, but this puts unneeded stress on it. The next time you eat corn, your body already has antibodies to react against it, which triggers the immune system, and so on. As time goes on, people with leaky gut syndrome tend to become more and more sensitive to a wider variety of foods and environmental contaminants.

Depending on our own susceptibilities, we may develop a wide variety of signs, symptoms, and health problems. Leaky gut syndrome is associated with the following medical problems: allergies, celiac disease, Crohn's disease, HIV, and malabsorption syndromes. It is also linked to autoimmune diseases such as AIDS, ankylosing spondylitis, asthma, atopy, bronchitis, eczema, food and environmental sensitivities, other allergic disorders, psoriasis, Reiter's syndrome, rheumatoid arthritis, Sjögren's syndrome, and skin irritations.

The conditions presented in the box on page 84 can arise from a variety of causes, but leaky gut syndrome may underlie more classic diagnoses. If you have any of the common symptoms or disorders associated with leaky gut syndrome, ask your physician to order an intestinal permeability test to see if it is causing

Common Clinical Conditions Associated with Intestinal Permeability

Acne	Giardia
Aging	Hives
Alcoholism	HIV-positive status
Ankylosing spondylitis	Inflammatory joint
Autism	disease or arthritis
Behcet's syndrome	Intestinal infections
Burns (severe)	Irritable bowel syndrome
Celiac disease	Liver dysfunction
Chemotherapy	Malnutrition
Childhood hyperactivity	Multiple chemical
Chronic fatigue syndrome	sensitivities
Cirrhosis	NSAIDs enteropathy
Crohn's disease	Pancreatic insufficiency
Cystic fibrosis	Psoriasis
Eczema	Schizophrenia
Endotoxemia	Thermal injury
Environmental illness	Trauma
Food allergies and	Ulcerative colitis
food sensitivities	

your problem. In addition to clinical conditions, people with leaky gut syndrome display a wide variety of symptoms (see page 85).

Leaky gut syndrome puts an extra burden on the liver. All foods pass directly from the bloodstream through the liver for filtration. The liver "humanizes" the food and either lets it pass or changes it, breaking down or storing all toxic or foreign substances. Water-soluble toxins are easily excreted, but the break-

Symptoms Associated with Leaky Gut Syndrome

Abdominal pain
Diarrhea
Asthma
Bed wetting
Chronic joint pain
Recurrent bladder
    infections
Chronic muscle pain
Fevers of unknown origin
Confusion
Poor memory
Fuzzy thinking
Shortness of breath
Gas
Constipation

Indigestion
Bloating
Mood swings
Aggressive behavior
Nervousness
Anxiety
Poor exercise tolerance
Primary biliary cirrhosis
Poor immunity
Fatigue and malaise
Recurrent vaginal
    infections
Toxic feelings
Skin rashes

down of fat-soluble toxins is a two-stage process that requires more energy. When the liver is bombarded by inflammatory irritants from incomplete digestion, it has less energy to neutralize chemical substances. When overwhelmed, it stores these toxins in fat cells, much the same way that we put boxes in the garage or basement to deal with at a later date. If the liver has time later, it can deal with the stored toxins, but most commonly it is busy dealing with what is newly coming in and never catches up. These toxins provide a continued source of inflammation to the body. Increased intestinal permeability has been found to be a factor in liver diseases, such as cirrhosis.

What Causes Leaky Gut Syndrome?

Leaky gut syndrome has no single cause, but some of the most common are chronic stress, dysbiosis, environmental contaminants, gastrointestinal disease, immune overload, overuse of alcoholic beverages, poor food choices, presence of pathogenic bacteria, parasites and yeasts, and prolonged use of NSAIDs. Let's discuss some of these one at a time.

Chronic Stress

Prolonged stress changes the immune system's ability to respond quickly and affects our ability to heal. It's like the story of "The Little Boy Who Cried Wolf." If we keep hollering that there's a wolf every time we're late for an appointment or we need to finish a project by a deadline, our bodies can't tell the difference between this type of stress and real stress—like meeting a vicious dog in the woods or a death in the family. Our body reacts to these stressors by producing less secretory IgA (sIgA) (one of the first lines of immune defense) and less DHEA (an antiaging, antistress adrenal hormone) and by slowing down digestion and peristalsis, reducing blood flow to digestive organs, and producing toxic metabolites. Meditation, guided imagery, relaxation, and a good sense of humor can help us deal with daily stresses. We can learn to let small problems and traumas wash over us, not taking them too seriously.

Dysbiosis

The presence of dysbiosis contributes to leaky gut syndrome. Candida push their way into the lining of the intestinal wall and break down the brush borders. Candida must be evaluated when leaky gut syndrome is suspected. *Blastocystis hominis*, giardia, helicobacter, salmonella, shigella, *Yersinia enterocolitica*, amoebas, and other parasites also irritate the intestinal lining and cause gastrointestinal symptoms. People who have or have had digestive illness or liver problems have an increased tendency to leaky gut syndrome. Which came first: the chicken or the egg?

Environmental Contaminants

Daily exposure to hundreds of household and environmental chemicals puts stress on our immune defenses and the body's ability to repair itself. This leads to chronic delay of necessary routine repairs. Our immune systems can only pay attention to so many places at one time. Parts of the body far away from the digestive system are affected. Connective tissue begins to break down, and we lose trace minerals like calcium, potassium, and magnesium. Environmental chemicals deplete our reserves of buffering minerals, causing acidosis in the cells and tissue and cell swelling. This is known as leaky cells—like having major internal plumbing problems!

Overconsumption of Alcoholic Beverages

Alcoholic drinks contain few nutrients but take many nutrients to metabolize. The most noteworthy of these are the B-complex vitamins. In fact, alcoholic beverages contain substances that are toxic to our cells. When alcohol is metabolized in the liver, the toxins are either broken down or stored by the body. Alcohol abuse puts a strain on the liver, which affects digestive competency, and also damages the intestinal tract.

Poor Food Choices

Poor food choices contribute to an imbalance of probiotics and pH. An intestinal tract that is too alkaline promotes dysbiosis. Low-fiber diets cause an increase in transit time, allowing toxic by-products of digestion to concentrate and irritate the gut mucosa. Diets of highly processed foods injure our intestinal lining. Processed foods invariably are low in nutrients and fiber, with high levels of food additives, restructured fats, and sugar. These foods promote inflammation of the GI tract. In fact, even foods we normally think of as healthful can be irritating to the gut lining. Milk, an American staple, can be highly irritating to people with lactose intolerance.

Use of Medication

As was discussed more fully in Chapter 4, NSAIDs damage brush borders, allowing microbes, partially digested food particles, and toxins to enter the bloodstream. Birth control pills and steroid drugs also create conditions that help feed fungi, which damage the lining. Chemotherapy drugs and radiation therapy can also significantly disrupt GI balance.

Restoring Gut Integrity

If you believe you suffer from leaky gut, it's best to work with a health professional who can help you determine the underlying factors. Fortunately, you can find many ways to heal your gut. Some involve changing your habits, like chewing your food more completely; others involve taking specific supplements that will help your body repair itself. If you have food allergies or sensitivities, deal with them. Find out if you have dysbiosis or candida and get appropriate treatment. Replenish your bacterial flora with probiotics and prebiotics such as fructooligosaccharides (FOS). You may need to support your digestive function with enzymes, bitters, or hydrochloric acid tablets.

Once the intestinal tract has been damaged, free radicals are often produced in quantities too large for the body to process. This causes inflammation and irritation, which exacerbate a leaky gut. Increasing use of antioxidant nutrients such as vitamin E, selenium, N-acetyl cysteine, superoxide dismutase (SOD), zinc, manganese, copper, coenzyme Q10, lipoic acid, and vitamin C can help quench the free radical fire.

Supportive nutrients can help repair the mucosal lining directly. Glutamine is the preferred food of the cells of the small intestine. Dosages can range from 1 to 30 grams daily, depending on your needs. Zinc may be an essential nutrient for gut repair. Other nutrients and supplements that are helpful include gamma oryzanol, Seacure, vitamin A, vitamin C, pantothenic acid (vitamin B_5), deglycyrrhized (DGL) licorice, folic acid, concentrated whey immunoglobulin concentrates, schizandra, and aloe vera.

Food and Environmental Sensitivities

Food and environmental sensitivities are usually the result of leaky gut syndrome. The prevalence of these sensitivities is more widely recognized today than in the past; 24 percent of American adults claim they have food and environmental sensitivities. These sensitivities, also called delayed hypersensitivity reactions, differ from true food allergies, also called Type I or immediate hypersensitivity reactions.

True food allergies are rare occurrences. They affect 0.3 to 7.5 percent of children and 1 to 2 percent of adults. The foods that most often trigger these reactions are eggs, cow's milk, nuts, shellfish, soy, wheat, and white fish. Food allergies trigger reaction of type IgE antibodies that bind to the offending food antigens. The IgE antibodies attach to mast cells that stimulate the release of cytokines and histamines. This results in closing of the throat, fatigue, tearing, hives, itching, respiratory distress, watery or runny nose, skin rashes, itchy eyes or ears, and sometimes severe reactions of asthma and anaphylactic shock. These symptoms occur within minutes after the food is eaten and people usually know what they are (hives or difficulty breathing). Physicians diagnose food allergies through the use of patch skin tests and RAST (radioallergosorbent test) blood testing, which are great for testing for food allergies but do not accurately determine food sensitivities.

Sensitivity reactions, also called delayed or hidden hypersensitivities, occur when IgA, IgG, and IgM antibodies are triggered in response to foods, chemicals, and bacterial toxins. The most common antibody reactions are IgG to mold and foods; exposure to molds and foods is quite high compared to pollens. For example, in an entire hay-fever season, we might inhale a teaspoon of pollen, but we take pounds of food inside us each day. It is estimated that 95 percent of all food allergy is of this delayed type. In the past, these delayed allergies were called serum sickness. The sensitivities cause symptoms that are delayed, taking several hours to several days to appear, which makes tracking them down very difficult.

Food and environmental sensitivities cause a wide number of symptoms typical of a leaky gut reaction. Food particles enter the bloodstream through damaged mucosal membranes; the body recognizes them as foreign substances (antigens) and triggers an immune reaction. Prolonged antibody response can overwhelm the liver's ability to eliminate these food antigens. Subsequently, the antigens enter the bloodstream and trigger delayed hypersensitivity response, inflammation, cell damage, and disease. Almost any food can cause a reaction, although the most common are beef, citrus, dairy products, egg, pork, and wheat. These foods provoke 80 percent of food sensitivity reactions.

Symptoms of Food and Environmental Sensitivity

The following symptoms occur because of many health conditions. Professional evaluation is necessary to uncover the source of these symptoms and to establish if food sensitivities are involved.

Head: Chronic headaches, migraines, difficulty sleeping, dizziness

Mouth and throat: Coughing; sore throat; hoarseness; swelling or pain; gagging; frequently clearing throat; sores on gums, lips, and tongue

Eyes, ears, and nose: Runny or stuffy nose; postnasal drip; ringing in the ears; blurred vision; sinus problems; watery and itchy eyes; ear infections; hearing loss; sneezing attacks; hay fever; excessive mucus formation; dark circles under eyes; swollen, red, or sticky eyelids

Heart and lungs: Irregular heartbeat (palpitations, arrhythmia), asthma, rapid heartbeat, chest pain and congestion, bronchitis, shortness of breath, difficulty breathing

Gastrointestinal: Nausea and vomiting, constipation, diarrhea, irritable bowel syndrome, indigestion, bloating, passing gas, stomach pain, cramping, heartburn

Skin: Hives, skin rashes, psoriasis, eczema, dry skin, excessive sweating, acne, hair loss, irritation around eyes

Muscles and joints: General weakness, muscle or joint aches and pains, arthritis, swelling, stiffness

Energy and activity: Fatigue, depression, mental dullness and memory lapses, difficulty getting your work done, apathy, hyperactivity, restlessness

Emotions and mind: Mood swings, anxiety and tension, fear, nervousness, anger, irritability, aggressive behavior, binge eating or drinking, food cravings, depression, confusion, poor comprehension, poor concentration, difficulty learning

Overall: Overweight, underweight, fluid retention, dizziness, insomnia, genital itch, frequent urination

Additional Signs of Food Sensitivities in Children

In addition to the symptoms listed in the previous section, children with food sensitivities may have:

Attention deficit disorder
Behavior problems
Learning problems
Recurring ear infections

These problems are often not recognized as being related to food sensitivities. Children with these problems will benefit from a food evaluation and environmental sensitivity testing.

Antibodies and antigens form what is known as *immune complexes*. If you have many antibodies and few antigens, you have a small immune complex. Conversely, if you have many antigens and only a few antibodies, you also have a small immune complex. The worst symptoms and cravings appear when you have moderate amounts of both antibodies and antigens—when you have a large immune complex. When you try to eliminate foods while in this state, you are left with enormous cravings for them, and symptoms often worsen before they improve. It can take seven to ten days to get through this stage. These large immune complexes can cause rashes in the skin and cheeks, as those seen in lupus.

Blood testing for IgG or IgG4, IgM, and/or IgA antibody reactions can help determine sensitivities to a variety of foods and environmental substances. You may want to screen for food allergies with IgE testing at the same time. Some labs test for another indicator of delayed hypersensitivity: white blood cell blastogenesis, where lymphocytes are stimulated and produce protein, DNA, and RNA at a rapid rate. Environmental screening panels measure antibody reaction to chemicals commonly found in our homes, yards, workplaces, and public places. People often test positive to household cleaning supplies and petroleum-based chemicals. Several laboratories perform antibody testing for foods, dusts, environmental chemicals, heavy metals, molds, and pollens. These labs are listed in the Resources section.

Lectins

Lectins that are incompatible with our genetics can also cause negative reactions to foods. We each have a genetically determined blood type—A, B, AB, or O. Our blood types contain specific antibodies that helped our ancestors live successfully in their environment. We no longer stick to our ancestor's specific environment and are continually exposed to new substances. When we eat a food that contains lectins that are incompatible to our blood type, they target an organ or tissue and begin to collect blood cells in clumps, a process called agglutination.

Peter D'Adamo, N.D., author of *Eat Right 4 Your Type*, hypothesized that when we eat foods containing lectins incompatible with our blood type, we experience negative health reactions. For example, if I have type A blood and drink milk, my body will begin to agglutinate and reject that milk. When I drink milk, the next morning I wake up with a clump of mucus in my throat. I know this and usually avoid uncultured dairy products. The lectins don't get digested and then cause reactions. According to D'Adamo, the lectin proteins settle somewhere in our bodies and have a magnetic effect on the cells there. The cells clump together and are targeted for destruction as though they were foreign invaders. This can appear to us as irritable bowel syndrome, arthritis, or nearly any inflammatory condition.

Lectin reactions mimic food allergies. The digestive system and nervous system are especially sensitive to lectin reactions. The people whose arthritis responds to elimination of the nightshade family of foods (potatoes, eggplant, tomatoes, peppers) probably have lectin sensitivities. If you want to know much more about blood type diets and lectins, read *Eat Right 4 Your Type*.

Elimination-Provocation Diet

If you wish to determine food and chemical sensitivities on your own, you can use the elimination-provocation challenge. Only eat foods that you are unlikely to be sensitive to for a week and then add back the foods you normally eat to "challenge" your system. Removal of offending foods calms down symptoms, while careful addition of only one food every two days makes it easier to determine which cause reaction.

Although the elimination-provocation challenge sounds simple, it can be tricky. People usually have no problem with the elimination part—a restricted food plan for a week is easy. Slowly adding foods back into your diet may be more difficult, because recipes and restaurant foods have many ingredients. Sometimes it's hard to determine which ingredient caused the distress. Reactions that are delayed for a day or two also complicate the situation. It then becomes necessary to remove all suspected foods for four days and try them again one at a time. If you have the same reaction each time you add the food, you've found the culprit.

Unfortunately, if you have sensitivities to one food, you are often sensitive to all foods in the same family. For example, some people who are sensitive to wheat are sensitive to all grains in the grass family. It is common to be sensitive to more than one food or food family. (See Chapter 6 for more on elimination-provocation testing.)

To cure food and environmental sensitivities, you'll do best with a holistic approach. Begin by avoiding substances you are sensitive to for a period of six months, and your body will gradually stop reacting to most of them. That will help detoxify the body, especially the liver. (Detoxification programs are discussed in Chapter 8.) A comprehensive program of nutritional supplements will help in the healing process. The Elisa/Act Patient Handbook, provided by Elisa/Act Biotechnologies, reads, "Persons suffering from immune system dysfunction and overload due to delayed hypersensitivity reactions often have a need for even greater supplementation because of poor functioning of the body's normal biochemical pathways." Organically grown and nutrient-rich natural foods also help repair the body. Exercise programs and use of stress-management tools also play a part in recovery. With a holistic program you will find that over time you will become less and less sensitive to foods and the environment.

6

Functional Medicine and Functional Testing

"The best measure of quality is not how well or how frequently a medical service is given, but how closely the result approaches the fundamental objective of prolonging life, relieving distress, restoring function, and preventing disability."
—LEMBEKE, QUOTED BY JEFFREY BLAND IN AN ARTICLE IN
FUNCTIONAL MEDICINE JOURNAL

Modern medicine equates the absence of disease with health. Often, people walk into a doctor's office feeling tired and run down, have an exam and a battery of tests, and come back a week later to hear, "Nothing's wrong with you. You're perfectly healthy." While relieved, they still don't feel well. This is where functional, complementary, and alternative medicines play a critical role, helping people focus on wellness and improved function.

The primary concern of functional medicine, a new paradigm in nutritional healing, is finding health problems before they become illnesses. Questionnaires and lab testing are used to determine how well organs and systems are functioning. Functional medicine recognizes that each of us has specific biochemical needs that are determined by our lifestyle, genetic structure, and environment. It focuses on restoration of health and health status, rather than progression of disease. It looks for improvement in the quality of life and an increase in a person's health span. The ultimate goal is for people to live a healthful existence throughout life.

Many years before most illnesses occur, people have a steady, cumulative, measurable decline in body function. To quantify this, holistic health practitioners require different tools than those most commonly used over the past fifty years. By the time you need a cardiogram, you already have heart symptoms. By the time you have a lower or upper GI test, you are experiencing some digestive problems. Even so-called preventive medical testing such as mammograms and cholesterol screenings are really tests for early detection of disease rather than true prevention. Innovative individuals in medical laboratories worldwide have been designing tests to determine function rather than disease. A few of the leading laboratories in functional testing are listed in the Resources. Others can be found at www.digestivewellness.us.

Tests for functional medicine are numerous. The following are the ones I've found to be most useful for digestive problems. Most of these are laboratory tests, but a few are home tests you can perform on your own.

Acid-Alkaline Balance and pH Testing

Most of us are not in good acid-alkaline balance. This contributes to disease, fatigue, and most health conditions. *This may be the most important overall health test that you can do.* It's inexpensive and you can do it at home.

Our body pH is maintained just above 7.0 for optimal health. When we keep this pH, our metabolism, enzymes, immune system, and repair mechanisms work most effectively. And, when our pH is kept at this level it indicates that we have enough buffering minerals to balance the acids in our body.

Our metabolism is kept in balance by a variety of mechanisms that produce acid by-products. So, it's essential that our foods contain buffering minerals to offset this natural acid metabolism. Our standard American diet (SAD) contributes to the overall acid load, rather than helping balance it. High protein, fat, sugar, and refined foods increase acid load. Generally, grains are acid producing. Stress, alcohol, and cigarettes compound the problem. Fruits, vegetables, seaweeds, and some other foods help alkalize our systems.

Most of us unknowingly have a slightly acidic body environment. Imagine that our air was filled with sulfuric acid (like in acid rain). It would be harder for us to function. And, with more sulfuric acid in the air, the environment would become more caustic and detrimental to our health. Our cells react the same way to an acid environment. When we are acidic, our cells become sluggish and cannot function properly. Wastes build up, toxins are not excreted, and nutrients are not properly used. We begin to feel less well than we'd like.

To maintain homeostasis in our blood, which is very sensitive to changes in pH, we pull potassium from our extracellular fluid. When stores have been used up, we begin to pull calcium, magnesium, and other alkalizing minerals from our bones. This is one of the underlying causes in osteoporosis and arthritic conditions.

Foods we eat can dramatically change our pH. For example, one twelve-ounce can of cola contains enough phosphoric acid to significantly change our pH. The kidneys cannot excrete urine that is more acidic than about 5.0 without damaging them or the bladder. The pH of the cola is between 2.8 to 3.2, about a hundred times more acidic than a pH of 5.0. To dilute this to an appropriate level, you'd need thirty-three liters of urine. So, the body has another mechanism—use buffering minerals from elsewhere in the body. If there are enough reserves, the body will pull sodium and potassium to do this. If not, it will pull calcium, magnesium, and other minerals from bone. The amount of minerals necessary would be equivalent to the buffering capability of four Tums. One can imagine the long-term effects of drinking several cans of cola—or one Big Gulp—daily. On the other hand, if you drink sparkling water with juice, the pH remains stable.

The standard American diet is not sufficient in its buffering capacity. When diets are higher in protein, as many are today, the need for buffering minerals is also higher. When diets are low in fruits and vegetables, the need for buffering minerals is higher still. When we are under stress, we need more buffering minerals. And when we drink soft drinks, we need more buffering minerals. In total, most of us are continually taking minerals from bone to keep our cells and blood balanced. If we don't replenish these minerals, the long-term effect is bone loss, joint degeneration, and overall lack of health.

Home pH Testing

PH testing is a simple home urine test with a dipstick. Purchase a packet of pH test paper. Make sure that it has the ability to test between a pH of 5.5 and 8.0. You simply place a two- to three-inch piece of pH paper into your first morning urine and read it to see what your pH is. To do this, match the color of the test strip with the color chart on the back of the test tape packet. Optimally, the level will be between 6.5 and 7.5, or fairly neutral. If needed, you can bring this into an optimal range by manipulating your foods, which will give support to your body's own innate healing and balancing capacities. Any number lower than 7 indicates that your urine is on the acid side. The lower the number, the more acidic you are. This works logarithmically, so a reading of 6.0 is ten times more acidic than a reading of 7.0, and a reading of 5.0 is

Figure 6.1 First Morning Urine pH After Rest

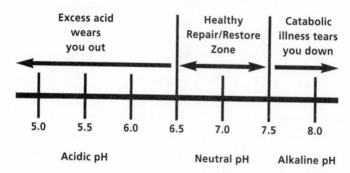

one hundred times more acidic than a 7.0 reading. Figure 6.1 shows the ranges of pH levels and their effects on the body.

If your readings fall below 6.5, begin to make dietary changes to bring your pH back into an optimal range. Use Figure 6.2A to learn which foods are most alkalizing. The further to the right of the chart, the more alkalizing the foods are. Be sure to eat lots of fresh fruits and vegetables, at least two cups twice daily. Eating daikon radish and steamed greens daily is strongly recommended. Lentils, miso soup, and yams are also extremely alkalizing. Fresh vegetable juices offer a way to flood your body with alkalizing minerals. Drink the juice of half of a lemon or lime or 1 to 2 tablespoons of apple cider vinegar in water each day. Favor alkalizing grains like oats, quinoa, and wild rice.

If you are healthy, eat 60 percent of your foods from the alkaline chart and 40 percent from the acidic chart (see Figure 6.2B). If you are trying to rebuild health, eat 80 percent alkaline and 20 percent acid-producing foods. Eating fruits and vegetables in abundance helps maintain the normal balance of acid and alkaline.

Figures 6.2A and 6.2B will help you easily figure out the net effect of food on your pH. Fat, protein, carbohydrate, mineral, and other factors were used to calculate the relative degree of

Figure 6.2A Alkaline Levels in Select Foods

Food Category	Lowest Alkaline	Low Alkaline	More Alkaline	Most Alkaline
Spices/Herbs		Herbs (most)	Spices/cinnamon	Baking soda*
Preservatives	Sulfite		Sea salt	Table salt (NaCl)
Beverages	Ginger tea	Green or mu tea*	Kambucha*	Mineral water
Sweeteners	Sucanat*	Rice syrup	Molasses	
Vinegar	Umeboshi vinegar*	Apple cider vinegar	Soy sauce	
Therapeutics	Algae, blue-green*	Sake*		Umeboshi plums*
Processed dairy	Ghee (clarified butter)*			
Cow				
Soy				
Goat/sheep				
Eggs	Duck eggs*	Quail eggs*		
Meat				
Game				
Fish/shellfish				
Fowl				

Category				
Grains/cereal/grass	Oats/quinoa*/wild rice			
Nuts			Chestnuts/almonds	
Seeds/sprouts	Seeds (most)	Sesame seed	Poppy seed/sprouts	Pumpkin seed
Oil	Avocado oil/coconut oil/olive oil/linseed oil	Primrose oil/cod liver oil		*Hydrogenated oil*
Vegetables	Brussels sprouts/squashes/okra/jicama	Bell pepper/mushroom/cauliflower/eggplant/pumpkin	Broccoli	
Beans				
Legumes			Lentil	
Roots	Beets	Potato/rutabaga/salsify	Kohlrabi/parsnip/garlic/ginger root	Onion/daikon/taro root/burdock/lotus root/sweet potato/yam
Greens	Chive/cilantro/lettuces/turnip greens	Collard greens	Endive/mustard greens/kale/parsley	
Citrus fruits	Orange	Lemon	Grapefruit	Lime/tangerine/pineapple
Fruits	Apricot/banana/blueberry/raisin/currant/grape/strawberry	Pear/apple/avocado/blackberry/cherry/peach/papaya	Cantaloupe/honeydew/dewberry*/loganberry/mango	Nectarine/persimmon/raspberry/watermelon

*Indicates foods that are therapeutic, exotic, or gourmet.

Italics indicate a food or substance that is not recommended.

Source: Used with permission from Russell Jaffe, M.D., Health Studies Collegium, Elisa/Act Biotechnologies.

Figure 6.2B Acid Levels in Select Foods

Food Category	Lowest Acid	Low Acid	More Acid	Most Acid
Spices/Herbs	Curry	Vanilla	Nutmeg	Pudding/jam/jelly
Preservatives	MSG	Benzoate	Aspartame	
Beverages	Kona coffee	Alcohol	Coffee	Beer (yeast, hops, malt)
Sweeteners	Honey/maple syrup		Saccharin	Sugar/cocoa
Vinegar	Rice vinegar	Balsamic vinegar		White/acetic vinegar
Therapeutics		Antihistamines	Psychotropics	Antibiotics
Processed dairy	Cream	Cow's milk	Casein, milk protein*	Processed cheese
Cow	Yogurt	Aged cheese	New cheeses	Ice cream
Soy		Soy cheese	Soy milk	
Goat/sheep	Goat/sheep cheese	Goat's milk		
Eggs	Chicken eggs			
Meat	Gelatin/organs	Lamb/mutton	Pork/veal	Beef
Game	Venison	Boar/elk	Bear	
Fish/shellfish	Fish	Shellfish	Mussels/squid*	Lobster
Fowl	Wild duck	Goose/turkey	Chicken	Pheasant*

Grains/cereal/ grass	Triticale/millet/kasha/ amaranth/brown rice	Buckwheat/wheat/spelt/ teff/farina/semolina/ white rice	Maize/barley groats/ corn/rye/oat bran	Barley
Nuts	Pine nuts		Pecans	Hazelnuts/walnuts/ Brazil nuts
Seeds/sprouts			Pistachio seed	
Oil	Pumpkin seed oil/grape seed oil/sunflower oil/canola oil	Almond oil/sesame oil/safflower oil	Chestnut oil/*lard*/ palm kernel oil	Cottonseed oil
Vegetables	Rhubarb		Green pea/peanut/ snow pea	
Beans	Fava bean/kidney bean/string or wax bean	Pinto bean/white bean/ navy bean/red bean/ adzuki bean/lima bean		Soybean/carob
Legumes			Chickpea/legumes (other)	
Roots			Carrot	
Greens	Spinach	Chard		
Citrus fruits				
Fruits	Guava/pickled fruit/dried fruit/figs/persimmon/dates	Plum/prune/ tomato	Cranberry/ pomegranate	

*Indicates foods that are therapeutic, exotic, or gourmet.
Italics indicate a food or substance that is not recommended.
Source: Used with permission from Russell Jaffe, M.D., Health Studies Collegium, Elisa/Act Biotechnologies.

acid- or alkaline-forming effects of the specific food on body chemistry.

Meditation, outdoor walks, and baking soda and Epsom salt baths can also help bring pH back to normal. Use ½ cup each of baking soda and Epsom salts, and soak in a warm to hot tub regularly. Your supplements can also help you alkalize. Take a mineral supplement daily, and use a fully buffered vitamin C mineral ascorbate. Avoid soft drinks.

If your readings are always between 7.5 and 8.0, this represents a "false alkalinity" and indicates that you are in a state of tissue breakdown, also called catabolism. If so, see your health-care practitioner. If you see an occasional reading of 7.5 to 8.0, this is acceptable.

Comprehensive Digestive Stool Analysis (CDSA)

The CDSA checks for bacterial balance and health, digestive function, and dysbiosis and is used to determine which types of bacteria are present and measures beneficial, possibly harmful, and disease-producing microbes. It also checks to see levels of candida. If present, they are cultured to see if they grow and which agents will be most effective in eliminating them.

In addition, the CDSA measures digestive function by determining how well a person can digest proteins, fats, and carbohydrates; the level of pancreatic enzymes produced; and the amount of short-chain fatty acids and butyric acid in the colon. Some labs also include a dysbiosis index, which uses the combined testing to give a measure of normalcy or abnormalcy. The CDSA provides a quick reference for your health-care provider and can determine your therapeutic needs. Many labs also culture any abnormal fungi, bacteria, and parasites to determine which medications and herbal preparations may be most effective at bringing you back into balance.

CDSA is useful for everyone who has digestive problems. If you only choose one test, do this one in conjunction with the comprehensive parasitology screening.

Parasitology Testing

We tend to think of parasites as something we get from traveling in other countries. However, according to the June 27, 1978, *Miami Herald,* the Centers for Disease Control (CDC) in Atlanta found that one out of six randomly selected people had one or more parasites. Great Smokies Diagnostics Laboratory in North Carolina has similar results. They find parasites in 20 percent of samples tested. More than 130 types of parasites have been found in Americans. Parasites have become more prevalent for many reasons, including contaminated water supplies, day-care centers, ease of international travel, foods, increased immigration, pets, and the sexual revolution. Most people will meet a parasite at some point in their lives. Contrary to popular myths, having parasites isn't a reflection of your cleanliness. My family contracted giardia in Chicago. We hadn't traveled and have absolutely no idea how we contracted it.

If you have prolonged digestive symptoms, you should really consider having a comprehensive parasitology screening. Some symptoms of parasites can appear to be like other digestive problems: abdominal pain, allergy, anemia, bloating, bloody stools, chronic fatigue, constipation, coughing, diarrhea, gas, granulomas, irritable bowel syndrome, itching, joint and muscle aches, nervousness, pain, poor immune response, rashes, sleep disturbances, teeth grinding, unexplained fever, and unexplained weight loss. Sometimes parasites are found without accompanying digestive symptoms. Other health problems, such as arthritis, that seem to be unrelated are resolved after the parasites are treated.

Many physicians request parasitology testing on random stool samples. This can be highly inaccurate, so repeated testing is often necessary to get definitive results. For example, eight random stool samples would be needed to definitively rule out giardia. Because numerous parasites live farther up the digestive tract, many labs now give an oral laxative to induce diarrhea to detect these parasites. The most accurate stool testing is usually done by labs that specialize in parasitology testing.

PARASITE QUESTIONNAIRE

Check If Yes

1. Have you ever been to Africa, Asia, Central or South America, China, Europe, Israel, Mexico, or Russia?

2. Have you traveled to the Bahamas, the Caribbean, Hawaii, or other tropical islands?

3. Do you frequently swim in freshwater lakes, ponds, or streams while abroad?

4. Did you serve overseas while in the military?

5. Were you a prisoner of war in World War II, Korea, or Vietnam?

6. Have you had an elevated white blood count, intestinal problems, night sweats, or unexplained fever during or since traveling abroad?

7. Is your water supply from a mountainous area?

8. Do you drink untested water?

9. Have you ever drunk water from lakes, rivers, or streams on hiking or camping trips without first boiling or filtering it?

10. Do you use plain tap water to clean your contact lenses?

11. Do you use regular tap water that is unfiltered for colonics or enemas?

12. Can you trace the onset of symptoms (intermittent constipation and diarrhea, muscle aches and pains, night sweats, unexplained eye ulcers) to any of the above?

13. Do you regularly eat unpeeled raw fruits and raw vegetables in salads?

14. Do you frequently eat in Armenian, Chinese, Ethiopian, Filipino, fish, Greek, Indian, Japanese, Korean, Mexican, Pakistani, Thai, or vegetarian restaurants; in delicatessens, fast-food restaurants, steak houses, or sushi or salad bars?

15. Do you use a microwave oven for cooking (as opposed to reheating) beef, fish, or pork?

16. Do you prefer fish or meat that is undercooked, i.e., rare or medium rare?

17. Do you frequently eat hot dogs made from pork?

18. Do you enjoy raw fish dishes like Dutch green herring, Latin American ceviche, or sushi and sashimi?

19. Do you enjoy raw meat dishes like Italian carpaccio, Middle Eastern kibbe, or steak tartare?

20. At home, do you use the same cutting board for chicken, fish, and meat as you do for vegetables?

21. Do you prepare gefilte fish at home?

22. Can you trace the onset of symptoms (anemia, bloating, distended belly, weight loss) to any of the above?

23. Have you gotten a puppy recently?

24. Have you lived with, or do you currently live with, or frequently handle pets?

25. Do you forget to wash your hands after petting or cleaning up after your animals and before eating?

26. Does your pet sleep with you in bed?

27. Does your pet eat off your plates?

28. Do you clean your cat's litter box?

29. Do you keep your pets in the yard where children play?

30. Can you trace the onset of your symptoms (abdominal pain, distended belly in children, high white blood count, unexplained fever) to any of the above?

31. Do you work in a hospital?

32. Do you work in an experimental laboratory, pet shop, veterinary clinic, or zoo?

33. Do you work with or around animals?

34. Do you work in a day-care center?

35. Do you garden or work in a yard to which cats and dogs have access?

36. Do you work in sanitation?

37. Can you trace the onset of symptoms (gastrointestinal disorders) to any of the above?

38. Do you engage in oral sex?

39. Do you practice anal intercourse without the use of a condom?

40. Have you had sexual relations with a foreign-born individual?

41. Can you trace the onset of symptoms (persistent reproductive organ problems) to any of the above?

Major Symptoms

Please note that although some or all of these major symptoms can occur in any adult, child, or infant with parasite-based illness, these symptoms might instead be the result of one of many other illnesses.

Adults

1. Do you have a bluish cast around your lips?

2. Is your abdomen distended no matter what you eat?

3. Are there dark circles around or under your eyes?

4. Do you have a history of allergy?

5. Do you suffer from intermittent diarrhea and constipation, intermittent loose and hard stools, or chronic constipation?

6. Do you have persistent acne, anal itching, anemia, anorexia, bad breath, bloody stools, chronic fatigue, difficulty in breathing, edema, food sensitivities, itching, open ileocecal valve, pale skin, palpitations, PMS, puffy eyes, ringing of the ears, sinus congestion, skin eruptions, vague abdominal discomfort, or vertigo?

7. Do you grind your teeth?

8. Are you experiencing craving for sugar, depression, disorientation, insomnia, lethargy, loss of appetite, moodiness, or weight loss or gain?

Children

1. Does your child have dark circles under her eyes?

2. Is your child hyperactive?

3. Does your child grind or clench his teeth at night?

4. Does your child constantly pick her nose or scratch her behind?

5. Does your child have a habit of eating dirt?

6. Does your child wet his bed?

7. Is your child often restless at night?

8. Does your child cry often or for no reason?

9. Does your child tear her hair out?

10. Does your child have a limp that orthopedic treatment has not helped?

11. Does your child have a brassy, staccato-type cough?

12. Does your child have convulsions or an abnormal electroencephalogram (EEG)?

13. Does your child have recurring headaches?

14. Is your child unusually sensitive to light and prone to blinking frequently, eyelid twitching, or squinting?

15. Does your child have unusual tendencies to bleed in the gums, the nose, or the rectum?

Infants

1. Does your baby have severe intermittent colic?

2. Does your baby persistently bang his or her head against the crib?

3. Is your baby a chronic crier?

4. Does your baby show a blotchy rash around the perianal area?

Interpretation of Questionnaire

1. If you answered "yes" to more than forty items, you are at high risk for parasites.

2. If you answered "yes" to more than thirty items, you are at moderate risk for parasites.

3. If you answered "yes" to more than twenty items, you are at risk.

4. If you are not exhibiting any overt symptoms now, remember that many parasitic infections can be dormant and then spring to life when you least expect them. Be

aware that symptoms that come and go may still point to an underlying parasitic infection because of their reproductive cycles. The various developmental stages of parasites often produce a variety of metabolic toxins and mechanical irritations in several areas of the body. For example, pinworms can stimulate asthmatic attacks because of their movement into the upper respiratory tract.

Source: Used with permission from Ann Louise Gittleman, Guess What Came to Dinner? *Garden City Park, N.Y.: Avery Publishing Group, 1993.*

Elimination-Provocation Food Sensitivity Testing

Elimination–provocation testing for food and environmental irritants is a two-stage process: an elimination diet and then a provocation challenge test. Elimination–provocation testing requires your determination and commitment because you must radically change your diet to find out which foods you are reacting to. Often, the foods we are sensitive to are the ones we depend on most, so you may have to do without some of your favorite foods for a while.

Over the past few years, I have been using an elimination diet that works well for nearly all of my clients (except those with candida). This program allows all fruit (except citrus), all vegetables (except tomatoes, eggplant, potatoes, and peppers), and white rice. You can eat as much of these foods as you like, plus olive oil and safflower oil for stir-frying and on salads. In addition, I often use a rice-protein, nutrient-enriched drink that helps detoxify your system and ensures your protein needs are met. The foods allowed during the elimination diet are unlikely to cause food sensitivities.

If food sensitivities are provoking symptoms, you'll find you feel terrific eating this way. In fact, some people feel better than they have in years. Elimination of the offending foods gives your digestive system a chance to heal over several months' time because you are no longer irritating it.

After seven to fourteen days on the elimination diet, you begin the provocation challenge. By slowly reintroducing foods into your diet, you can test yourself for your reactions. Do you become sleepy thirty minutes after eating wheat? Does cheese give you diarrhea? Do you itch all over after eating oranges? Do your joints ache after eating tomatoes? Through careful observation, you can detect many foods you have become sensitive to. Once you become familiar with your body's reaction, you can identify sensitivities, though it may be necessary to test a food several times to be certain of your reaction.

Food Allergy/Sensitivity Testing

To enhance the elimination-provocation food testing process, many people also find it useful to have a blood test for IgG and IgE antibody reactions to determine food and environmental sensitivities. Some labs also include testing for IgA and IgM antibodies. While many foods may be unmasked during the elimination-provocation challenge, others may remain hidden. If you suspect that chemicals, molds, or pollens are causing problems, you should also be screened for them. (Labs offer these tests either separately or as part of a complete screening package.) Sensitivities are rated from normal to severe reactions. In addition to a detailed readout documenting your personal reactions, most laboratories also include a list of foods that contain hidden sources of the offending foods, a rotation menu, and other educational material to help you in the healing process.

Leaky Gut Syndrome or Intestinal Permeability Testing

The method that has rapidly become the recognized standard for intestinal permeablility testing is the mannitol and lactulose test. Mannitol and lactulose are water-soluble sugar molecules that our bodies cannot metabolize or use. They come in differing sizes and weights and are absorbed into the bloodstream at different rates. Mannitol is easily absorbed into cells by people with healthy digestion; lactulose has such a large molecular size that it is only slightly absorbed. A healthy test shows high levels of mannitol and low levels of lactulose. A leaky gut condition is indicated when large amounts of mannitol and lactulose are present. A general malabsorption of all nutrients is indicated when low levels of both sugars are found. Low mannitol levels with high lactulose levels have been found in people with celiac disease, Crohn's disease, and ulcerative colitis.

Your doctor can give you a test kit to collect urine samples. After collecting a random urine sample, you drink a mannitol-lactulose mixture and collect urine for six hours. The samples are then sent to the laboratory. This test is often done in conjunction with a CDSA or a parasitology test.

Heidelberg Capsule Test

The Heidelberg capsule test has proven to be accurate and sensitive in determining stomach pH levels. A radiotelemetry test for functional hydrochloric acid (HCl) levels, it is a simple, effective technique to determine how much HCl your stomach is producing. After you swallow a radio transmitter that's about the size of a B-complex vitamin, the transmitter measures the resting pH of your stomach, alternating with challenges of baking soda, which is very alkaline. By observing how well the stomach returns to an acid condition after administration of the baking soda, the physician can determine whether or not you produce adequate amounts of HCl.

Normally produced by the parietal cells of the stomach, HCl is necessary for the initial stage of protein digestion and the absorption of vitamin B_{12} and many minerals. Common symptoms of low-stomach acidity include belching or a burning sensation immediately after meals, bloating, a feeling that the food just sits in the stomach without digesting, and an inability to eat more than small amounts at any one sitting.

Poor HCl levels have been associated with childhood asthma, chronic hepatitis, chronic hives, diabetes, eczema, gallbladder disease, lupus erythematosus, osteoporosis, rheumatoid arthritis, rosacea, under- and overactive thyroid conditions, vitiligo, and weak adrenals. As we age, we produce less HCl. As many as half of all people over the age of sixty may be deficient in this important substance. The test, unfortunately, is not widely available.

Functional Liver Profile Testing

Liver profile testing is useful for determining how well you are able to handle toxic substances. The liver is responsible for transforming toxic substances into harmless by-products that the body can excrete. It does this in a variety of ways, including acetylation, conjugation, sulfation, sulfur transferase, and via the cytochrome P450 system. The functional liver profile looks at the total toxic load in your body and sees how well your body handles it by measuring the abilities of your liver detoxification systems.

When we are exposed to substances that the body sees as toxic, cytochrome P450 levels go up. The cytochrome P450 system, called phase 1 liver detoxification, transforms endotoxins (toxins produced within the body) and exotoxins (those taken into the body from outside) into water-soluble forms that can be excreted in urine. By measuring the cytochrome P450 levels and seeing how quickly the toxic materials are transformed, tests can provide useful information about how well the body is able to detoxify a wide variety of substances. Many substances can stimulate cytochrome P450 production, including alcohol, barbiturates, carbon tetrachloride, charcoal broiled meats, dioxin, exhaust fumes, high protein diets, niacin, oranges, organophosphorus pesticides, paint fumes, riboflavin, sassafras, saturated fats, steroid hormones, sulfonamides, and tangerines.

When cytochrome P450 is released, a second phase of detoxification is also activated, which causes an elevation of D-glucaric acid. D-glucaric acid is released by the liver and is a by-product of turning toxic substances into glucuronidase, which is excreted in urine. A sulfur/creatinine ratio is used to test this function. This ratio helps determine leaky gut syndrome, low glutathione levels, and the level of free radical activity.

For the test, take small amounts of caffeine, aspirin, and acetaminophen at home and send urine samples off to the laboratory for analysis. By measuring your urine and saliva, your liver's ability to process toxins can be determined. Normal levels of cytochrome P450 are found in 50 percent of people tested. A low-caffeine clearance is found in about one-third of all people tested and indicates that your body is having difficulty detoxifying. High-caffeine clearance levels are found in people who have been exposed to high levels of toxins or smoke.

Another way to measure liver detoxification pathways is to measure D-glucaric acid and mercapturic acid in the urine. D-glucaric acid is a general marker for cytochrome P450 liver detoxification pathways. High levels of D-glucaric acid indicate the presence of environmental toxins such as pesticides, herbicides, fungicides, petrochemicals, and excessive alcohol intake. Mercapturic acid provides a measurement of glutathione conjugation. This test is easier on those who do not tolerate caffeine, aspirin, or acetaminophen.

Indican Test

The indican test gives a general indication of how well you are digesting foods by measuring the amount of putrefaction in your digestive system. High indican levels are found in people with dysbiotic conditions and malabsorption. Indican testing offers a quick way to screen for faulty digestion but does not give enough detailed information to know exactly why or where the problem originates. Some doctors find it a useful office screening test because it is inexpensive and noninvasive.

Lactose Intolerance Testing

Lactase is an enzyme that digests lactose, a sugar naturally found in milk products. The inability to digest lactose affects about 75 percent of the world's population and is highly prevalent in African Americans, Asian Americans, Caucasian Americans of Mediterranean and Jewish descent, Hispanics, and Native Americans: 25 percent of Americans are lactose intolerant, including 15 percent Caucasians, 70 percent of African Americans, 74 percent of Native Americans, 53 percent of Mexican Americans, and 90 percent of Asian Americans. Lactose intolerance is caused by an enzymatic deficiency and is not a milk allergy, which is the inability to digest milk proteins. Lactose intolerance causes a wide variety of symptoms including abdominal cramping, acne, bloating, diarrhea, gas, headaches, and nausea. Most people with lactose intolerance fail to recognize that the food they eat has any relationship to how they feel.

There are two ways to test for lactose intolerance—a self-test and a laboratory test. To self-test, you must restrict intake of all dairy products for at least ten days. Obvious sources include milk, yogurt, cheese, ice cream, creamed soups, frozen yogurt, powdered milk, and whipped cream. Less obvious sources are bakery items, cookies, hot dogs, lunchmeats, milk chocolate, most non-dairy creamers, pancakes, protein powder drinks, ranch dressings, and anything that contains casein, caseinate, lactose, sodium caseinate, and whey. If you're not sure what's in a food, avoid it during the testing period. It's probably best to eat all your meals at home or prepare all food yourself.

If lactose intolerance is causing your problems, you will probably notice your symptoms have disappeared significantly. Reintroduction of dairy products will trigger a return of symptoms. However, the results may be inconclusive because you may be sensitive to other foods in addition to dairy—in which case your symptoms might not change much. A laboratory test would then be indicated.

Your doctor can order a simple, noninvasive hydrogen breath test to pinpoint if lactose intolerance is causing your problems. This challenge test is ideal for people who find it difficult to complete a self-test or are confused about their findings. After you breathe into a bag to collect a baseline sample, you drink a small amount of a lactose solution and breathe into a different bag. Lab technicians measure the levels of hydrogen and methane gas you exhaled in both samples. Normal methane levels are 0 to 7 parts per million (ppm). If levels increase at least 12 ppm between the two samples, it indicates lactose intolerance, even if your hydrogen production is normal. Normal hydrogen levels are 10 ppm.

Levels of 20 ppm or more are commonly found in people with lactose intolerance. When both methane and hydrogen are measured, false results are narrowed considerably. Use of antibiotics, enemas, and laxatives are common reasons for false negative results, which occur 5 percent of the time. This test has a few false positive results that are generally caused by eating high-fiber foods before the test, exposure to cigarette smoke, or sleeping during testing.

Hair Analysis

Hair analysis is a useful tool to see how well you absorb essential minerals and screen for heavy metal accumulation. Hair is cut as close to your head as possible—only the one to two inches that grow closest to your head will be tested because it reflects your mineral status during the past few months. The lab burns your hair in an electrochromatography scan to measure the levels of minerals present. Low levels of six or more essential minerals indicate a problem with absorption of nutrients, which could be due to drug therapy, dysbiosis, low HCl levels, or poor flora. Hair analysis is also an accurate screening test to determine whether you have high levels of toxic minerals such as aluminum, arsenic, cadmium, lead, and mercury.

Small Bowel Bacterial Overgrowth Test

The small bowel bacterial overgrowth test measures breath levels of hydrogen and methane to determine if a bacterial infection is present in the small intestine. This test differs from the comprehensive digestive and stool analysis in that it tests for dysbiosis of the small rather than the large intestine. Small bowel overgrowth occurs when bacteria in the large intestine travel to the small intestine, often the result of poor HCl production in the stomach or an insufficient amount of pancreatic enzyme function. It is often found in conjunction with parasitic infections. Chronic pancreatitis, Crohn's disease, and lupus erythematosus can also cause small bowel overgrowth.

People with small bowel bacterial overgrowth experience diarrhea, poor nutrient absorption, and weight loss. Other people who may be affected are those with poor ileocecal valve function, poor intestinal motility, scleroderma, or recent gastric surgery. People infected with small bowel overgrowth often have difficulty with digestion of fats, which come through undigested in the stool, called steatorrhea. They may also experience B_{12} deficiency, chronic diarrhea, and poor absorption of the fat-soluble vitamins A, D, E, and K.

Breath testing provides a simple, noninvasive alternative to the more widely used method of obtaining a small bowel aspirate and is more accurate. To perform the test, you drink either a lactulose or a glucose drink and collect breath samples. Hydrogen is produced when lactulose or glucose come in contact with the gut flora. A significant rise in hydrogen levels indicates small bowel overgrowth.

Electrical Acupuncture Voltage (EAV) Testing

After much promising research, the EAV test is widely used in Europe. Although it has met with FDA resistance in the United States, many skillful professionals use this test to successfully diagnose and determine appropriate therapies.

The test measures the electrical activity of your skin at designated acupuncture points. You hold a negative rod in one hand, the practitioner places a positively charged pointer on a variety of points on your skin, and a meter measures the voltage reading between the points. The test can determine which organs are strong or weak, which foods help or hurt you, which nutrients you need or have excessive levels of, and how old patterns are contributing to your health today. It is a fast, noninvasive screening test.

Organic Acid Testing

Organic acids are produced throughout the body and by intestinal microbes as metabolic products. High levels of organic acids in the urine can indicate metabolic problems, hormone irregularities, and dysbiosis. They can also give good indication about detoxification pathways, inherited enzyme deficiencies, and drug effects. Organic acid testing is a simple way to screen for a large variety of nutritional and immunological factors in one simple urine test, including fatty acid metabolism, neurotransmitter metabolism, carbohydrate metabolism, oxidative damage, energy production, detoxification status, B-complex sufficiency, dysbiosis, methylation abilities, and inflammatory reactions.

Moving Toward a Wellness Lifestyle

"Health approaches seek to identify the causes (or potential causes) of disease and employ therapies designed to eliminate host susceptibility and hospitality to ill health. Health approaches give priority to therapies of minimum risk and high therapeutic gain, tailored to the individual's attitudes and circumstances."

—RUSSELL JAFFE, M.D.

In a wellness scenario, the time to tackle the problem is when you have the first small signs. The first principle of wellness is paying attention to what your body is trying to tell you. Indigestion is not caused by a Rolaids deficiency. Listening to your body can help you make healthful changes in your lifestyle that will affect not only your tummy, but your entire well-being. For example, if your indigestion happens when your stress level is high, then you can focus on building stress-management tools. If your indigestion happens after you eat milk products, then the solution may be the elimination of dairy products. If your indigestion is worse when you are out of shape, then an exercise program may be in order.

The following exercise is a great way to discover and prioritize which areas of your life need attention. You may feel that your relationships have little or nothing to do with the fact that you have chronic diarrhea, but until you balance your relationships, you can't know for sure. The mind is not separate from the body. It is well documented that the thoughts we have influence our physical condition. All domains of wellness affect our sense of well-being.

WELLNESS WHEEL

How satisfied are you today in each of the areas of your life illustrated in Figure 7.1? Rate them on a scale from 1 to 10, with 1 being the most dissatisfied and 10 being the most satisfied. A 1 is placed nearest the center, a 10 farthest from the center.

Now look at your wellness wheel. Would it roll? Which spokes are the shortest? The short spokes are the areas you've paid less attention to recently, so they offer the greatest areas of discovery and opportunity. They help you prioritize which areas you need to pay attention to the most today.

Next, study the overall look of your wheel. Are you generally satisfied or dissatisfied with your life? People with 8s, 9s, and 10s generally feel pretty good about themselves; their lives are moving in the right direction. People with 1s, 2s, and 3s may be feeling a lack of confidence and have low self-esteem. If you have lots of short spokes on your wheel, you may want to boost your support systems. Find a friend to talk to or get a professional counselor to help you sort out your priorities. My wellness wheel changes each time I do this exercise, depending on what's going on in my life at that particular time. It is a dynamic, ever-changing wheel.

Now that you have looked at the spokes, choose one or two areas where you see an opportunity for growth and change. Set a small, achievable goal, such as "I will only eat dessert one time this week" or "I will spend time in nature twice this week." Be reasonable and easy on yourself. Small, attainable goals lead to success, which leads to more goal setting and more success. If you've never exercised, begin by walking or biking twenty minutes once or twice a week. If you'd like to cut out coffee, you can quit or cut back. Some people find they only "need" the first cup of the day; other people switch to decaf, while others mix it half regular coffee and half decaf. Remember that the journey toward wellness is as important as the destination. Don't worry about "getting there"; just enjoy the scenery.

Figure 7.1 The Wellness Wheel

Wellness is more than the absence of illness. Wellness is having the energy to do the things you dream of. It is the belief that your body wants to heal itself and that you can improve your health over time, rather than stand by and watch it deteriorate. Does that mean you won't age? No, all people age. But we can build a strong house so that we age gracefully. Having a healthy body prevents chronic, degenerative illnesses that are primarily products of our lifestyle. Wellness demands that we take responsibility for our own health and make changes in the way we live to help our body function more optimally. We are required to ask questions, rather than just accept the cultural norm.

Complementary medicine is rapidly becoming integrated into American culture and into conventional care. The therapies most used include herbal medicine, massage, acupuncture and Chinese traditional medicine, Ayurvedic medicine, megavitamins, self-help groups, folk remedies, energy healing, and homeopathy. People seek out alternative medicine mainly for chronic health problems such as back pain and headaches.

Although it will probably take at least another decade for complementary practices to be fully integrated into current standard medical practice, the changes are happening rapidly. Complementary medicine is cost-effective; honors the feelings, wisdom, and knowledge of the patient; and empowers each person to be active in her own care. It puts the soul and spirit back into medicine, and this is what we are all embracing. (But obviously, you know this— you have this book in your hands.)

In the following chapters, you will be given a wellness prescription, which includes general guidelines, followed by specific guidelines. Because you are unique, you need to tailor these plans to suit your current needs and lifestyle. You would benefit from a consultation with a certified clinical nutritionist (CCN), a certified nutrition specialist (CNS), or a physician who specializes in nutritional or functional medicine. These professionals can help you determine the essentials of your program, its duration, and how to work with it over time.

When you find a health professional whom you like, trust, respect, and are attuned to, listen to his or her advice. When you agree on a plan of action, follow through. Many people "shop around" for therapeutics and practitioners and never really complete any given program. You aren't doing yourself a favor if you don't make a commitment. If you want to add another therapy or modality to your program, talk it over with the health professional you are working with. Team efforts often give the best results, but only with commitment and communication.

You can only really tell what the results will be if you follow the plan over a set period of time. If you feel that a given therapy isn't helping after a certain amount of time, it may not be the correct one for you. If you have a bad feeling about a therapy or about the person you are working with, do something about it. Be bold, ask questions, educate yourself, and direct your own care. Or find someone else to work with.

Here are some people you may want to put on your wellness team: medical doctor, chiropractor, naturopathic physician, homeopath, energetic healer, clinical nutritionist, physical therapist, acupuncture practitioner, herbalist, psychologist, counselor, colon therapist, massage therapist, or body worker. Each of these professionals can guide you toward health from their own perspective.

8

First Things First

Detoxification

"It can be strongly said that the health of an individual is largely determined by the ability of the body to detoxify."
—JOSEPH PIZZORNO, N. D., AND MICHAEL MURRAY, N.D.,
ENCYCLOPEDIA OF NATURAL HEALTH

Cleansing and fasting are integral to holistic healing. The basic tenets of functional medicine are clean the body; remove any irritants, whether they be food, medicine, or microbes; provide the proper nutrients for the body to use as building materials; replace missing intestinal flora, enzymes, and hydrochloric acid; and give the body time to heal itself.

We are exposed to toxins everywhere—from the air we breathe to the foods we eat, even as a result of metabolism. These toxins cause irritation and inflammation throughout our bodies. People have always been exposed to toxic substances, but today's exposure to contaminants far exceeds that of previous times. Each week, approximately 6,000 new chemicals are listed in the Chemical Society's Chemical Abstracts, which adds up to more than 300,000 new chemicals each year. Each year, we consume, on average, fourteen pounds of food additives, including colorings, preservatives, flavorings, emulsifiers, humectants, and antimicrobials. In 1990, the EPA estimated that 70,000 chemicals were commonly used in pesticides, foods, and drugs.

Our body normally produces toxins as a by-product of metabolism. We call them *endotoxins*, which means they come from within us. If not eliminated, these endotoxins can irritate and inflame our tissues, blocking normal functions. Endotoxins formed by bacteria and yeasts can be absorbed into the bloodstream. Antibodies formed to protect us against the harmful effects of these endotoxins often trigger a systemic effect, causing an autoimmune reaction, so our body begins fighting itself. By assisting your body in removal of stored toxins through detoxification programs, your body can more easily heal itself.

One of the many functions of the liver is to act as a filter, to let nutrients pass, to "humanize" other substances if possible, and to transform toxins into safe substances that can be eliminated in urine and stool. When the liver enzymes fail to break down these toxins, they are stored in the liver and fatty tissue throughout our bodies. Common medications can inhibit the liver's ability to adequately process toxins. Acetaminophen (Tylenol) causes liver damage when used in combination with alcoholic beverages. Cimetidine, an ulcer medication, limits the liver's ability to detoxify foreign substances. A thorough cleansing program works systemically, cleansing all the cells in your body of harmful toxins.

Throughout time and in various cultures, people have seen the need for periodic internal cleansing. Native Americans and Mexicans use sweat lodges. Ancient Roman bathhouses had rooms for bathing in steam, warm water, and cold water. Jewish women have used ritual *mikva* baths to cleanse both body and spirit. Most Swedish people have home saunas, and our own health clubs have saunas, steambaths, and jacuzzis. People "take the waters" in Europe and parts of the United States. Hawaiians use steam and a form of massage, called *lomilomi*, where they scrub people clean with the red Hawaiian dirt and sea salt. In fact, mud and clay have been used worldwide to draw toxins from the body while simultaneously providing essential nutrients.

Fasting is an important part of many religious holidays and customs. Both Jesus and John the Baptist fasted to gain mental and spiritual clarity. During Ramadan, an important Muslim holiday, people fast during daylight hours for a month. Jewish people fast on Yom Kippur. Indigenous people of many cultures use fasting as a way to clarify thought and provoke visions.

Removal of waste material—detoxification—is essential to the healthy functioning of our bodies. This is shown in the many different ways the body cleanses itself. Skin is our body's largest organ. In addition to being a protective organ, it is also an organ of elimination through perspiration. Sneezes clear our sinuses. Lungs breathe out carbon dioxide, and even the breath allows for removal of some wastes. Kidneys filter wastes from the bloodstream. Stool is the residue from the digestive process. The liver filters the substances that are absorbed through the digestive barrier into the bloodstream. White blood cells gobble up bacteria and foreign substances, and the lymphatic system clears the debris from circulation. During a cleansing program, your body more rapidly recycles materials to build new cells, take apart aged cells, and repair damaged cells.

Most detoxification programs focus on the liver or colon. The liver is, in my opinion, the most overworked organ of the body. It has responsibility for manufacturing thirteen thousand different enzymes, producing cholesterol, breaking down estrogen, regulating blood sugar, filtering blood, manufacturing bile, breaking down old red blood cells, and detoxifying harmful substances. When the liver loses its ability to easily perform these functions, we begin to feel ill, with many systems out of balance.

It is best if you follow a detoxification program under the supervision of a medical or health professional who can guide you through the process. Toxins released too quickly can make you feel worse than when you began and can aggravate your symptoms.

Detoxification Programs

Detoxification programs such as fasting, modified fasting, metabolic cleansing, colonic irrigation, steaming, mud packs, saunas, herbal detoxification programs, and hot tubs all have therapeutic benefits. When choosing a detoxification program, it must meet specific criteria: it needs to (1) work with your life and your values, (2) be thorough, and (3) be gentle and nurturing to your body.

During the past several years, I have personally and professionally relied on three main detoxification programs that are effective and gentle: fruit and vegetable cleansing, metabolic cleansing, and low-temperature steams and saunas. I also recommend vitamin C flushes between cleansings. Other professionals may prefer fasting programs or colonic irrigation, which in the right hands can be powerful tools for healing. Because there are many fine books on fasting and colonic irrigation, I have not included information about them here.

Fruit and Vegetable Cleansing

This gentle cleansing method is outlined in Chapter 6 as the elimination portion of the elimination-provocation challenge.

In this challenge, you may eat all you want of fruits, vegetables, and rice and use olive and safflower oils as condiments for seven to ten days. Fresh fruit and vegetable juices are an excellent source of easily assimilated nutrients and alkalizing minerals and can enhance the detoxification pathways. It's important to eat every two to three hours to keep your blood sugar levels normal. The major benefit of this detox method is that you can do this on your own without professional supervision. Of course, if you are under a doctor's care or taking medication of any kind, you'll need to let your physician know of your plans. The first few days may require mental and physical adjustments to your new regimen, but most people feel a sense of general well-being. You may notice that many of your outstanding symptoms have disappeared or become less aggravated.

You may also experience some discomfort during the first three or four days. Headaches, bad breath, skin breakouts, and changes in bowel habits are fairly common and may be the result of withdrawal from caffeine, sugar, alcohol, or other substances. They are an indicator that toxins are being flushed out or that your body is going through withdrawal. To facilitate this, drink a lot of water, diluted juices, and all herbal teas except those containing caffeine. Dandelion tea is especially useful.

Some people develop rashes or pimples as the skin works hard to eliminate toxins. Taking saunas, steambathing, and massaging your skin with a soft, dry brush or loofa can help your skin. If you are constipated, make sure you eat enough fiber-rich fruits and vegetables (apples, broccoli, pears, sweet potatoes, peas, brussels sprouts, corn, potatoes, carrots, greens, blackberries, bananas, strawberries, raspberries, and spinach). Constipation opens up a chance for toxins to be reabsorbed into your bloodstream, causing symptoms such as headaches and nausea. So add a fiber supplement; psyllium seeds or psyllium seed husks work well. Begin with 1 teaspoon in water, and drink up quickly before it turns into a gel. Aloe vera juice may also help regulate your bowels.

After the cleansing, slowly reintroduce healthful foods such as beans, tofu, chicken, and fish. Then add healthful grains, nuts, seeds, and cultured dairy products.

Metabolic Cleansing

Metabolic cleansing is a gentle yet deep method of detoxification, and it is the best, most thorough program I have used. The foundation of this program is a hypoallergenic-sensitive, rice-based protein and nutrient drink that is designed specifically for liver detoxification. The first week, you consume only the drink and all you want of rice, all fruits except citrus, all vegetables except nightshade-family foods, and small amounts of oils. Citrus fruits are excluded because many people are sensitive to them. Nightshade vegetables—potatoes, tomatoes, eggplant, green peppers, and chili peppers—are excluded because 10 to 15 percent of people with joint pain become pain-free when these vegetables are removed from the diet. If you know that you are sensitive to bananas, melons, or other foods that are allowed on the plan, then avoid them as well. It is possible for people to continue their normal daily routine while on this program.

This program is administered only through health professionals who can monitor your progress, determine when you should quit, and help you adjust if you have any difficulties. Most people find a dramatic alleviation of symptoms and a distinct improvement in energy levels. The high levels of nutrients found in the rice protein drink and in the fruits and vegetables help the liver activate its detoxification pathways and move unwanted materials out of the body. The intention here is to allow your digestive system to rest, relax, and heal itself.

Once you have completed the cleansing, it is important to slowly reintroduce foods back into your diet. Being a food sleuth takes a lot of patience; it's not always apparent which foods cause adverse symptoms. But with persistent detective work you can discover many of them. Keep a running record of everything you eat and of your symptoms. Food sensitivities often display delayed reactions, so it may take up to forty-eight hours to feel the effect of a newly introduced food.

You may want to have testing done for food allergies and sensitivities at this time. If you have uncovered a problem, these tests can further pinpoint which foods and substances are making you ill.

Vitamin C Flush

Vitamin C has been well researched for its ability to help detoxify bacterial toxins, drugs, environmental toxins, and heavy metals from our bodies. Its gentle and potent detoxification counteracts and neutralizes the harmful effects of manufactured poisons.

High levels of vitamin C help detoxify the body, rebalance intestinal flora, and strengthen the immune system. The vitamin C flush can be used between metabolic cleansing therapies or at the first sign of a cold or infection. If your immune system is weak or you've been exposed to a lot of toxins, you may want to do a vitamin C flush once a week for a month or two. On days when you are not doing a vitamin C flush, take a minimum of 2,000 to 3,000 milligrams. Humans are one of the only animals that do not produce their own vitamin C, so we need to replenish our supply daily.

To do a vitamin C flush, you take vitamin C to the level of tissue saturation. You'll know you've reached it because you will have watery diarrhea. You'll need to purchase powdered mineral ascorbate C, which is more easily tolerated by most people because it doesn't change your pH balance. The amount you take varies depending on your personal needs that day. Many of us require about 5,000 milligrams; others need fifteen or twenty times as much. For instance, if you're coming down with a cold, have chronic fatigue syndrome, or are under excessive stress, you'll probably need a lot more.

To do a vitamin C flush, take ½ teaspoon, about 2,500 milligrams, of vitamin C powder, mix with water or fruit juice, and drink. Repeat in fifteen minutes. Keep taking ½ teaspoon of ascorbate every fifteen minutes until you have watery diarrhea. Do not stop with just gas. Adding vitamin C rapidly helps prevent bloating and cramping. Stop once you get diarrhea. Keep track of how much vitamin C you take. This will help you determine your optimal dosage. Take daily one-half to three-quarters of the amount it takes to produce a vitamin C flush in divided amounts. Over time your needs may increase but then substantially decrease as repair occurs.

Low-Temperature Saunas and Steams

Low-temperature saunas or steambaths are useful to eliminate fat-soluble chemicals from our systems. They are commonly used to help detoxify those who have had high exposure to pesticides, solvents, pharmaceutical drugs, and petrochemicals. Slow, steady sweat encourages the release of fat-soluble toxins through the skin from their storage sites in our tissues. Most saunas and steambaths are set at temperatures too high to accomplish this, so be sure the dry sauna is set between 110 and 120° Fahrenheit and the steambath is at 110° Fahrenheit so you can stay in for at least forty-five minutes without getting too hot or chilled. It is best to spend thirty to sixty minutes in a sauna or steam at least three to five times a week. Releasing toxins cannot be accomplished with higher heat or shorter amounts of time. The object is to sweat slowly and steadily.

After you are done sweating, you must shower immediately afterward using a glycerin-based soap such as Neutrogena. It will wash away the toxins and keep you from reabsorbing them.

If you have extreme toxicity from environmental chemicals, you'll need to detox under the supervision of a physician. The temporary release of toxins into your circulation can be quite severe and debilitating. Some clinics specialize in using saunas for medical detoxification. In her excellent book, *Poisoning Our Children*, Nancy Sokol Green describes her experience in a detox clinic in depth: "On the fourteenth day of detox, I started experiencing allergic symptoms, such as eyelid swelling, while I was in the sauna! . . . I was actually beginning to reek of the pesticides that had been sprayed in my home. . . . Several of the patients at the clinic who were sensitive to pesticides had to stay away from me as I triggered adverse reactions in them."

METABOLIC SCREENING QUESTIONNAIRE

Use this questionnaire to monitor your health and progress. Rate each of the following symptoms based on your health profile for the past thirty days.

Point Scale
    0 = Never or almost never have the symptom.
    1 = Occasionally have it; effect is not severe.
    2 = Occasionally have it; effect is severe.
    3 = Frequently have it; effect is not severe.
    4 = Frequently have it; effect is severe.

Digestive Tract
    _____ Nausea or vomiting
    _____ Diarrhea
    _____ Constipation
    _____ Bloated feeling

_____ Belching or passing gas
_____ Heartburn

_____ *Total*

Ears

_____ Itchy ears
_____ Earaches, ear infections
_____ Drainage from ear
_____ Ringing in ears, hearing loss

_____ *Total*

Emotions

_____ Mood swings
_____ Anxiety, fear, or nervousness
_____ Anger, irritability, or aggressiveness

_____ *Total*

Energy/Activity

_____ Fatigue, sluggishness
_____ Apathy, lethargy
_____ Hyperactivity
_____ Restlessness

_____ *Total*

Eyes

_____ Watery or itchy eyes
_____ Swollen, reddened, or sticky eyelids
_____ Bags or dark circles under eyes
_____ Blurred or tunnel vision (Does not include near- or farsightedness)

_____ *Total*

Head

_____ Headaches
_____ Faintness
_____ Dizziness
_____ Insomnia

_____ *Total*

Heart

_____ Irregular or skipped heartbeat
_____ Rapid or pounding heartbeat
_____ Chest pain

_____ *Total*

Joints/Muscles

_____ Pain or aches in joints
_____ Arthritis
_____ Stiffness or limitation of movement
_____ Pain or aches in muscles
_____ Feeling of weakness or tiredness

_____ *Total*

Lungs

_____ Chest congestion
_____ Asthma, bronchitis
_____ Shortness of breath

_____ *Total*

Mind

_____ Poor memory
_____ Confusion, poor comprehension
_____ Poor concentration
_____ Difficulty in making decisions

_____ Stuttering or stammering
_____ Slurred speech
_____ Learning disabilities

_____ *Total*

Mouth/Throat
_____ Chronic coughing
_____ Gagging, frequent need to clear throat
_____ Sore throat, hoarseness, loss of voice
_____ Swollen or discolored tongue, gums, lips
_____ Canker sores

_____ *Total*

Nose
_____ Stuffy nose
_____ Sinus problems
_____ Hay fever
_____ Sneezing attacks
_____ Excessive mucus formation

_____ *Total*

Skin
_____ Acne
_____ Hives, rashes, or dry skin
_____ Hair loss
_____ Flushing or hot flashes
_____ Excessive sweating

_____ *Total*

Weight

_____ Binge eating/drinking
_____ Craving certain foods
_____ Excessive weight
_____ Compulsive eating
_____ Water retention
_____ Underweight

_____ *Total*

Other

_____ Frequent illness
_____ Frequent or urgent urination
_____ Genital itch or discharge

_____ *Total*

Scoring

0–50: Significant if 10 points or more in any one organ system
51–75: Early indication of need for metabolic clearing
76–100: Chronic symptoms associated with the need for
  metabolic clearing
101+: Acute symptoms associated with need for metabolic
  clearing

The Metabolic Screening Questionnaire is used with permission from Jeffrey
Bland, Ph.D., and Metagenics.

9

Diet Means "A Way of Living"

"We are what we repeatedly do. Excellence, then, is not an act, but a habit."

—ARISTOTLE

Eating is our most intimate contact with our environment. Each day, we put pounds of food inside of our bodies and turn it into us, a truly amazing process. But how much attention do we really pay to what goes into our mouths? And how much do we really understand about nutrition? I often find that my clients have many misunderstandings and confusion about nutrition and food.

The word *diet* comes from Greek and means "a manner of living" or "way of life." The Latin root means "a day's journey." The key is to make real changes—ones you can live with successfully on a long-term basis—in the way you approach food, fitness, and the challenges and opportunities of living.

In this chapter, I will outline a plan that can help you take charge of your health and feel good on every level. Because I don't know you and your specific needs, you will have to modify these general recommendations. If you have a specific digestive condition—candidiasis, chronic fatigue, migraines, or ulcers—look at the reference material for that condition and incorporate those ideas into this plan. For instance, if you have Crohn's disease or ulcerative colitis, you'll probably want to avoid grain and dairy products totally. If you have arthritis, you may find that tomatoes, peppers, eggplant, and potatoes aggravate your condition. Integration of your specific needs with a general life plan will give you the best results.

There are many healthful ways to eat. You need to find one that works for you and your lifestyle. Healthful eating relies on natural, home-cooked, genuine-food meals; they are devoid of artificial colors and flavors, trans fatty acids, and sugar; and they are loaded with phytonutrients (plant nutrients), fiber, and good-quality fats. Today the marketplace is buzzing with low-carbohydrate foods. A few years ago, it was low-fat foods. Many of these so-called foods are fancy packages of food technology and profits for the companies. The temptation to use them is high because they are abundant and heavily marketed. Stick to real foods and ultimately you'll do much better.

The world of nutrition is certainly confusing, but it is important to find what works best for you.

Clean Out the Pantry

Go into your cabinets, refrigerator, and freezer and toss out any foods that contain hydrogenated vegetable oil, vegetable shortening, or partially hydrogenated vegetable oils. If you read labels, you'll find them in margarine, cookies, crackers, cereals, frozen foods, packaged foods, breads, snack foods, salad dressings, mayonnaise, and so on.

Why am I asking you to throw out food? Hydrogenated oils are used in foods because they are cheap, have a long shelf life, and give a buttery texture to foods. While this enables manufacturers to use inexpensive materials to reap high profits, these oils are extremely unhealthy for your body.

Liquid oils are turned into solid vegetable shortenings by the hydrogenation process. Hydrogenation converts the naturally occurring *cis* form of fat molecules into a *trans* form. When our body tries to use trans fats, they block normal biochemistry, inhibiting the function of enzymes that are involved in the synthesis of cholesterol and fatty acids. In an analogy, trans fats are like using the wrong key to open a lock and then having the key break in the lock. The trans fats jam the position so the cis fats don't fit. Trans fatty acids are found nowhere in nature and have been associated with hardening of the arteries (atherosclerosis), some types of cancer, and all inflammatory illnesses—like arthritis, eczema, irritable bowel syndrome, and more. Recent research indicates that these fats play at least as large a role in heart disease as do saturated fats.

Trans fatty acids also affect our body's electrical circuitry. European research has shown that essential fatty acids found in the cis formation are necessary for electrical and energy exchanges that involve sulfur-containing proteins, oxygen, and light. Trans fatty acids are not suitable in these processes and jam the "plug" for the cis fats. These electrical currents are responsible for all body functions, from the way our minds work to heartbeat, cell division, muscle coordination, and energy levels.

Says Udo Erasmus, Ph.D., expert on fatty acids and author of *Fats That Heal, Fats That Kill*, trans fats are stickier than cis fats, "increasing the likelihood of a clot in a small blood vessel causing strokes, heart attacks, or circulatory occlusions in other organs, such as lungs, extremities, and sense organs." Our hearts use fatty acids as their main fuel. Trans fats are less easily broken down by enzymes and have slower use as an energy source, which could have serious consequences in a high-stress situation. Trans fatty acids also interfere with our liver detoxification pathways.

Each cell in our bodies has a fatty membrane around it. Cell membranes that incorporate hydrogenated fats lose their flexibility and become more rigid because trans fats are fairly solid at body temperature. This interferes with normal cellular function. Trans fats also change the permeability of the cell membranes, which allows substances to enter where they don't belong. If we eat hydrogenated oils, and the average American consumes 6 to 8 percent of his or her total daily calories in them, then our body fat is comprised of these fatty acids.

While you're cleaning out your kitchen, toss out the following foods: high-sugar foods, highly processed foods including white flour products and enriched foods, foods that contain a lot of food additives and colorings, and foods that have an expiration date of more than a few years from now. If you feel guilty about tossing out these foods, donate them to a soup kitchen.

Now you're ready to go shopping. It's important to read food labels carefully. It will take you longer the first few times you go shopping, but soon you'll be zipping through the store with your new food recognition. The foods that you bring into your home need to provide excellent nourishment. If you're careful about what you eat at home, the treats you eat at parties and restaurants will be indulgences you can feel good about. The idea isn't to be perfect, but to make progress and build good health habits slowly.

Great treasures that add flavor, fun, and variety are waiting to be uncovered in your local market and health-food store.

Rules for Eating, Cooking, and Shopping

Following these rules will go a long way toward improving your digestive health:

1. Eat local foods in season, when possible.
2. The life in foods gives us life.

3. Plan ahead. Carry food with you.
4. Eat small, frequent meals to sustain even energy levels.
5. Eat when you are hungry; stop when you are satisfied.
6. Relax while eating.
7. Choose organically grown produce, dairy, poultry, and meats whenever possible.
8. Eat as many fruits and vegetables as possible.
9. Eat lean protein. Include EPA and DHA fish one to two times a week.
10. Drink clean water.
11. Respect your own biochemical uniqueness.
12. Increase high-fiber foods.

Eat Local Foods in Season

Local foods are fresh and have the highest levels of nutrients. They also have the largest energy fields and the greatest enzyme activity. Ask the produce manager at your supermarket to purchase locally grown products whenever possible. Make it part of your routine to shop at local farm stands and farmer's markets. Eating local foods in season is the concept behind macrobiotics.

Eating foods in season also helps cut down on the amount of pesticides and herbicides we consume. Foods that are flown in from outside the country—grapes from Chile, coffee from South America, bananas from Mexico—are not regulated by the same pesticide standards as foods grown in the United States. Often we get back on imported produce the very pesticides that we banned. Eating local foods also helps the local economy and the environment by cutting down transportation costs and reducing consumption of fossil fuels. Act locally, think globally.

In winter, focus on cabbage-family foods, winter squash, and root vegetables. You'll find that cooked vegetables in soups and stews will keep you warmer. Winter fruit includes citrus, apples, and pears. If you are lucky enough to live in a climate that is moderate year round, you'll find an abundance of fresh produce all year.

The Life in Foods Gives Us Life

Food is fuel. Food gives us energy. Because we really are what we eat, when we eat foods that have little enzyme activity, they don't "spark" our body to work correctly. Enzymes are to our body what spark plugs are to the engine of our car. Without those sparks, the car doesn't run right. So if a food isn't biologically useful, who needs it? If it won't spoil or rot, don't buy it! It's a "dead" food and won't provide you the energy you need.

Plan Ahead: Carry Food with You

I've found that planning ahead and carrying food with me are two of the greatest tools for healthful eating. If you carry a bag lunch, you know it'll be healthful because you made it at home where you have only healthful foods. If you don't bring your lunch, you are at the mercy of what's available within five minutes of your workplace, which in many cases limits the healthful options.

Eat Small, Frequent Meals to Sustain Even Energy Levels

Snacking is the best trick I know for boosting energy levels. If you find that from 3:00 to 6:00 P.M. you have difficulty concentrating, try this simple trick. Have something to eat in the middle of the afternoon and again just before you leave work. Here are a few quick snack ideas. Eat half a sandwich you saved from lunch plus a piece of fruit, a bagel and cream cheese with tomatoes, a rice cake with peanut butter and apples, a cup of soup and several pretzels, or a handful of nuts and raisins. You'll find your energy level will stay more constant throughout the day.

Eat When You Are Hungry; Stop When You Are Satisfied

This sounds like a simple statement, but often we eat when we aren't hungry because we're lonely, angry, depressed, bored, or because we're at a social event and everyone else is eating. Before you eat anything, ask yourself the simple question: Am I hungry? If you are, then eat. If you aren't, divert your attention to other activities. Eating when you're not hungry contributes to poor digestion. Let your body use what it has before you put more into it.

Relax While Eating

Many times, we don't even stop long enough to sit down when we eat. Yet eating is a time of rejuvenation of body and spirit. Take a few extra minutes to enjoy and relish the food that you eat. Take a few moments to reflect on your day and your life. Doing this can help keep your whole day in balance.

One way I've found to encourage peace of mind during meals is to say grace. In our home we close our eyes and hold hands in silence for a moment. It puts me in touch with the bounty of the earth we live on, makes me pay attention to the people I am with and be grateful for their presence in my life, helps me thank the people who produced the food, and reminds me that we all depend on each other and on community.

Choose Organically Grown Foods Whenever Possible

Organic foods generally have higher levels of nutrients because organic farmers pay more attention to their animals' health and to their soils. Animals raised on organic farms are given foods that nature intended. For example, cows that graze on grasses, rather than being fed corn, produce meat and dairy products with cis-linoleic acid, a fat that is lacking in our food supply. We also benefit because we don't get extra doses of hormones added to our foods. Organic farmers add more nutrients to the soil because they know that healthy plants can better fend off pests and that those nutrients end up in the foods. Bob Smith, while at Doctor's Data, produced a study that analyzed organic versus commercially grown apples, pears, potatoes, wheat, and wheat berries. He found that mineral levels in organically grown foods were twice as high on average as commercially grown foods.

Antibiotics are used as growth promoters in healthy animals. It's estimated that up to 70 percent of antibiotics, twenty-five million pounds, are used in animal production. The small amounts used in their food create the perfect environment for the bacteria to develop resistance to these antibiotics. It's the bacteria's job to survive and adapt. We develop stronger and newer antibiotics, and they develop ways to become resistant to them. These antibiotic-resistant strains are passed to humans directly in the food we eat and in our contact with farm animals.

For example, quinolones are a class of antibiotics that include ciprofloxacin, commonly known as cipro. A growth promoter called sarafloxacin is from the same group of antibiotic. Even though sarafloxacin is only used in animal farming, it is creating bacteria that are becoming resistant to cipro. We now have bacteria that are resistant to five or more antibiotics, including vancomycin. Many of these infections were originally confined to hospitals and nursing homes, but now there are many more resistant infections out in the public. When we eat meat, poultry, eggs, and dairy products that are not organically farmed, we ingest small amounts of these antibiotics. Those most at risk are the elderly, infants and small children, and people with chronic illnesses. Each time we eat food that contains antibiotic growth enhancers, we risk decreasing the overall effectiveness of these drugs we so rely on.

While nearly all countries in Europe have banned the use of these antibiotic growth enhancers, we still use them freely. In July 2002, McDonald's joined with the Environmental Defense Fund and its suppliers, Tyson Foods and Cargill, to announce that it will no longer accept growth enhancers in its products. They will be phased out by the end of 2004. Several poultry producers have voluntarily stopped using antibiotics except to treat sick birds. They include Perdue Farms, Tyson Foods, and Foster Farms. These three companies produce one-third of our chicken. Smith Food, Inc., one of the world's largest hog producers, has also stopped using antibiotic growth promoters. There is still concern, however, because there are no clear lines between use of antibiotics for growth promotion and treatment of sick animals. It's left up to the individual farmer to decide when to use antibiotics. For information on organic and antibiotic-free products in your area, log on to: keepantibioticsworking.org/pages/consumers.

By refusing to purchase foods that have antibiotics, we are doing our small part to help save lives. If enough of us are aware of this issue and make enough noise about it, our regulatory administrators may be courageous enough to stand up to the farming industry. If we don't, our precious antibiotic drugs will soon become useless as we create superstrains of microbes. If you want to read more about this, I recommend *The Killers Within: The Deadly Rise of Drug-Resistant Bacteria*, by Michael Shnayerson and Mark Plotkin. Buying organic foods also ensures that you are not getting genetically modified foods. These are rampant in our food supply but have not been adequately tested.

Eat as Many Fruits and Vegetables as Possible

They are chock-full of vitamins, minerals, fiber, and phytonutrients that protect us from heart disease, cancer, and probably everything else. Research on phytonutrients is in its infancy, yet very promising. Citrus fruits, berries of all types, garlic, onions, chives, tomatoes, grapes, soybeans and other legumes, green tea, and cabbage family foods, which include broccoli, kale, kohlrabi, cauliflower, collards, mustard greens, rutabaga, turnips, brussel sprouts, and bok choy, all contain phytochemicals that protect us from developing degenerative diseases. The high fiber in fruits and vegetables protects our colons and reduces the incidence of polyps and bowel diseases and the risk of developing colon cancer. Eat at least five half-cup servings a day, but more is better—up to nine or eleven.

Eat Lean Protein Including High EPA and DHA Fish One to Two Times a Week

On average, Americans eat too much protein, and this excess can tax the kidneys. The saturated fats found in beef, pork, and poultry skin are artery clogging and ought to be limited or avoided altogether. Focus instead on lean protein sources such as legumes, skinless poultry, and fish. Other protein sources may be higher in good fats and are also recommended; these include cold-water fish, tofu, nuts, and seeds.

Cold-water fish are an excellent source of EPA and DHA fatty acids. These essential fats are critical to the eyes (more than 60 percent of the retina is composed of DHA), brain, thought processes, nervous system, and heart. Studies show that people who eat cold-water fish at least twice a week have a reduced incidence of heart disease. Although many of us can make DHA from other fats, others lack the enzymes and nutrients essential for this conversion to occur. The most beneficial sources of DHA are salmon, mackerel, sardines, halibut, tuna, and herring. It's best to eat these fish at least twice each week. Finally, algae and sea vegetables also contain some DHA and EPA.

Drink Clean Water

Our bodies are 70 percent water. If we don't adequately hydrate the cells with this essential substance, they cannot function properly. Moreover, the water we drink and consume in food is a carrier, bringing nutrients to cells and taking away wastes. Making sure that you get plenty of high-quality water every day is one of the most promising routes to digestive wellness.

The issue for many, then, becomes the quality of water. When a chemical is used in our culture, it will show up in the water supply. These chemicals are now detectable in parts per trillion. Unfortunately, many cities fail to provide excellent water. The sources are often groundwater that is easily contaminated by runoff. The EPA estimates that 1.5 trillion gallons of pollutants leak into the ground each year, with the highest incidence of contaminants from lead, radon, and nitrates (from fertilizers). More than seven hundred chemicals have been found in tap water.

There isn't one correct answer about where to get the best drinking water. If you have a well, have the water tested for bacterial content and pollutants. Find out about your local drinking water: where it originally comes from, how it's processed, and if it has fluoride added to it. Ask your water department for an analysis, and if the results please you, drink tap water. The use of chlorine in tap water has created much controversy today. The levels of chlorine needed to kill bacteria are rising because of increasing bacterial resistance, but chlorine has been strongly associated with elevated cancer risks. A simple water filter can efficiently remove chlorine from tap water. Activated charcoal filters are inexpensive and can remove many pollutants. I don't recommend the regular use of distilled water. The distillation process removes all minerals from water, and because minerals are generally transported through the body through diffusion, the regular consumption of distilled water leads to leaching of minerals from the body.

If you want to use a more sophisticated system than activated charcoal, look for a home water purifying system that alkalizes water. It is believed that drinking this alkalized water helps change the biological terrain of the individual, which ultimately makes it less possible to become or stay ill. People with digestive disorders and other health conditions often see changes in how they feel in days. This may actually be the simplest and most direct route to true digestive wellness because it can help normalize pH, dysbiosis, and candida, as well as keep your body easily alkalized.

Bottled water isn't necessarily any better than tap water. Often it's local, city tap water that has just been carefully filtered. And if you are buying spring water, you'll want to know about the water source and its purity. If you are buying water in plastic bottles, you may also be ingesting small amounts of plastic, which have known hormone-disrupting effects. If you do regularly buy bottled water, ask the manufacturer for information on water source, type of plastics used, mineral content per glass, and a report on levels of toxic substances in the water. In European countries, bottled water is preferred because of its high mineral content.

Respect Your Own Biochemical Uniqueness

Remember the foods that are best for you are foods that agree with your body and your unique biochemistry. In practice, about half the people I work with do best on a high-complex-carbohydrate, high-fiber, natural-foods diet. The other half seem to do best on a low-carbohydrate, relatively high-protein diet abundant in fruits and vegetables. Many people with digestive problems do best avoiding all grains and dairy. It's important to experiment with your own diet to find out what works best for you specifically.

Many eating plans are publicized by books and other media. Whether you try the Zone diet, the blood-type diet, macrobiotics, a vegan diet, Ayurvedic eating plans, natural hygiene/food combining, or some other program, how it makes you feel and whether you can live with it over the long term is important. The eating programs listed in this book are all based on real, natural food. None contain sugars, processed foods, alcohol, high levels of saturated fats, or other harmful food components. The body was designed to run on real foods; a natural-foods diet is the ultimate direction in eating for all of us, no matter exactly how we shape it. A proper diet ought to make you feel energetic and keep your immune system strong. It's always fun to experiment with eating plans, but please make sure that whatever you try is well balanced.

The rest of your family may have little or no problem eating wheat products, dairy, or any other food, but if you do, it's best to avoid them. If you really want to get well and stay well, you and your needs must come first. Your family will understand when you eat something different. If you are invited to someone's home, call several days ahead of time and let the host know you are on a restricted eating program. With advance notice, you may be able to eat nearly everything. If not, have a snack before you go and eat what you can. Perhaps you can bring a dish that suits your needs. Remember that restaurants are there to cater to you. Tell the food server if you need a menu item prepared a special way.

Increase High-Fiber Foods

The connection of diet to constipation is well substantiated. Dr. Dennis Burkitt was the first researcher to connect a high-fiber diet with better health. He noticed that people eating a traditional African diet in rural areas had almost no diabetes, irritable bowel syndrome, constipation, diverticular disease, colon cancer, or heart disease. In comparison, Africans consuming a Western diet had the expected incidence of these problems. In India, he found a hospital where the incidence of appendicitis was only 2 percent of that in a similar American hospital. At the same hospital, virtually no hiatal hernia, which affects nearly 30 percent of Americans over the age of fifty, was found. After looking at many factors, Dr. Burkitt concluded that the high amount of fiber in traditional diets was necessary for maintaining good health.

Known as the father of the fiber hypothesis, Dr. Burkitt made his discoveries in the 1970s. Since then, we have learned much more about fiber and how it contributes to health. For instance, we now know low-fiber diets lead to digestive disorders found in one out of four Americans. Improvement in bowel function can help prevent diverticulosis, appendicitis, colon polyps, colon cancer, hemorrhoids, and varicose veins. Diets high in soluble fiber are helpful to people with irritable bowel syndrome, Crohn's disease, hiatal hernia, and peptic ulcer. Dietary fiber also helps prevent obesity by slowing down digestion and the release of glucose and insulin. Fiber has been shown to normalize serum cholesterol levels. High-fiber diets reduce the risk of heart disease, high blood pressure, and certain types of cancer.

Americans eat twelve grams of fiber on average a day. The National Cancer Institute recommends that we consume twenty to thirty grams of fiber daily, the same amount that Americans ate in 1850. So we are really trying to replace the fiber that was eliminated from our diet over the past 150 years. The foods that are the richest sources of fiber are whole grains (brown rice, whole wheat, bulgur, millet, buckwheat, rye, barley, spelt, oats), legumes (all beans except green beans), vegetables, and fruits. These foods comprise the bulk of a healthy food plan, with nuts, seeds, protein foods, and oils used as condiments. Although soluble and insoluble fibers work differently inside the body, it's important to remember that these fibers are mixed in foods. If you eat a wide variety of high-fiber foods, you will get both types of fiber without counting and measuring grams of soluble and insoluble fiber.

Amount of Fiber in Select Foods

Fruits

Apple, raw, with skin	1 medium = 4 grams
Peach, raw	1 medium = 2 grams
Pear, raw	1 medium = 4 grams
Tangerine, raw	1 medium = 2 grams

Vegetables

Asparagus, fresh, cooked	4 spears = 1 gram
Broccoli, fresh, cooked	½ cup = 2.5 grams
Brussels sprouts, fresh, cooked	½ cup = 2 grams
Cabbage, fresh, cooked	½ cup = 1.5 grams
Carrot, fresh, cooked	½ cup = 2.5 grams
Cauliflower, fresh, cooked	½ cup = 1.5 grams
Romaine lettuce	1 cup = 1 gram
Spinach, fresh, cooked	½ cup = 2 grams
Summer squash, cooked	1 cup = 3 grams
Tomato, raw	1 = 1 gram
Winter squash, cooked	1 cup = 6 grams

Starchy Vegetables

Baked beans, canned, plain	½ cup = 6.5 grams
Kidney beans, fresh, cooked	½ cup = 8 grams
Lima beans, fresh, cooked	½ cup = 6.5 grams
Potato, fresh, cooked	1 = 3 grams

Grains

Bread, whole-wheat	1 slice = 2 grams
Brown rice, cooked	1 cup = 2.5 grams
Cereal, bran flake	¾ cup = 5 grams
Oatmeal, plain, cooked	¾ cup = 3 grams
White rice, cooked	1 cup = 1 gram

A Guide to Buying Food

By learning more about the foods you eat, you can begin to make a healthful food plan that will allow you to enjoy eating and feel better. Once you make a decision to rely on natural foods, your body and mind will adjust so that natural foods taste more delicious than manufactured derivatives. Once your sugar and salt taste buds calm down, fruit will taste sweet and you won't need that salt shaker as much. Ninety percent of your food should be excellent for your body, and 10 percent excellent for your soul!

Cereals and Grains

Cereals are an excellent way to increase your fiber and mineral intake. Unfortunately, the bulk of breakfast cereals contain too much sugar, hydrogenated oils, and other unhealthful ingredients, though some low-sugar, low-sodium cereals are sold in health-food stores. Read package labels carefully. Check for the amount of sugar (4 grams = 1 teaspoon) and for the amount of fiber. If you have gluten or other grain sensitivities, you will be able to find many, nongluten breakfast cereals in natural-food stores. Healthy cereals are made with the whole grain. You can also choose cereals with organically grown ingredients such as oatmeal and bulgur. Purchasing organic products ensures that you have not purchased genetically modified foods.

Eggs

Eggs have been given a bad rap because they've been linked to cholesterol. In fact, eggs have high amounts of phospholipids that are integral to our cell membranes. They are a precursor to acetylcholine, an important neurotransmitter.

Many researchers now believe that eating eggs has little or no effect on the serum cholesterol levels of people who have normal serum cholesterol. Recent studies found no significant change after six weeks in the cholesterol levels of healthy people after eating two hard-boiled eggs daily. Other studies have concurred that eating eggs can actually raise the good HDL cholesterol. Current thinking is that if your cholesterol levels are normal, it's fine to eat egg yolks that have not been oxidized (exposed to oxygen)—eggs that are hard-boiled, soft-boiled, or poached—since oxidized cholesterol can damage arteries and raise blood pressure.

It's best to buy organic or free-range eggs. Commercially raised chickens live in unnatural settings, never seeing the light of day, never touching the earth beneath their cages, pumped with hormones to stimulate growth and antibiotics to prevent disease. If you believe that the quality of a seed determines the health and vibrancy of the plant it produces, then by the same token if a chicken is artificially manipulated to produce eggs, how good can the quality of those eggs possibly be? For more information on this subject, the best resource is *Diet for a New America* by John Robbins.

Fish and Seafood

When selecting fish, it's important to know where the fish came from. Do not eat fish found in polluted or questionable waters. Fish and shellfish found close to shore, in rivers, or in lakes may be environmentally contaminated. Mollusks that filter water, such as oysters, clams, mussels, and scallops, can concentrate pesticides up to seventy thousand times the concentration of seawater. The EPA and FDA have recommended that we avoid eating shark, swordfish, king mackerel, and tile fish because of high mercury content. Blue fish also may be highly contaminated. Many farm-raised fish have fats that resemble chicken fat because they were fed grains instead of algae. If you purchase farm-raised fish, ask questions about what they were fed. Eat high EPA/DHA-containing fish, such as salmon, twice a week.

Seaweeds

Seaweeds, also called sea vegetables, are nutritious foods that are often neglected in American cuisine, though we have been exposed to them through macrobiotics and Japanese culture. Because we evolved from the sea, sea vegetables and seaweeds contain nutrients that are nearly identical in ratio and quality to those we use best. Many people find that eating sea vegetables gives them a tremendous energy boost, probably because the seaweed is filling some minute nutrient need.

Meat and Poultry

When eating meats, make sure to choose lean cuts and remove the skin from poultry, which contains most of the fat and half of the calories. So by removing it, you can eat twice as much and stay within the same calorie count. Pork is marketed as "the other white meat," but the only truly low-fat cut of pork is the tenderloin.

Environmentally, food animals are a disaster. Most water pollution comes from runoff from animal farming. The antibiotics they are given go into our rivers and streams, fields, crops, and bodies. The hormones they are fed affect us after we eat their meat. This doesn't even touch on the inhumane conditions in which these animals are raised and slaughtered.

It takes sixteen pounds of grain to produce one pound of beef, which is an extremely wasteful use of our global natural resources. If we, as a nation, would consume just 10 percent less meat, we would have additional stores of grain to feed sixty million people each year. Undeveloped countries that switch from a grain-based to a meat-based economy become poorer, have more hunger and starvation, and strip their land of natural resources.

By changing the foods you eat, you have an opportunity to help the world become a better, gentler place. For more information on this subject, read *Diet for a Small Planet* and *Food First* by Frances Moore Lappe and *May All Be Fed* and *Diet for a New America* by John Robbins.

Oils, Nuts, and Seeds

When purchasing oils, it is essential to find ones that have been expeller pressed, cold pressed, or are extra virgin (for olive and coconut oil). These oils have undergone a simple process of warming and pressing, unlike most grocery store oils which have been chemically treated with solvents, heated to temperatures that destroy all natural antioxidants, deodorized, bleached, refined, degummed, defoamed, and preserved. One should also avoid all products that contain cottonseed oil, hydrogenated oil, partially hydrogenated oil, margarine, or vegetable shortening.

Keep all oils, except olive oil, in the refrigerator so they don't go rancid. Good-quality oils vary in flavor and color—walnut oil tastes different from corn oil. You'll find it's best to use less of the stronger flavored oils.

The fat in nuts and seeds provides minerals and essential fats. However, a cup of nuts contains between eight hundred and twelve hundred calories, most of which come from fat, so beware of quantity if you are watching your weight. Chestnuts, which are delicious steamed or roasted, are an exception to this rule. Buy raw or roasted nuts that have not been seasoned, dry roasted, or coated with sugar and/or salt. Store nuts and seeds in the refrigerator or freezer to keep them fresh.

Peanuts are in the bean family and grow underground rather than on trees. Some peanuts have a mold, called aflatoxin, which is toxic and can cause cancer. Aflatoxin is tasteless, so it's impossible to tell if it's on your peanuts or peanut butter. A healthy person should be able to handle any aflatoxin they're exposed to, but a sick person may have a difficult time. As for peanut butter, be sure to buy only the old-fashioned kind—ground up peanuts and salt. Almond butter, cashew butter, and sesame tahini are good alternatives.

Shopping List

Here is a shopping list of healthful foods. It includes some brand names I know, but hundreds more are equally fine. Because "natural" and organic foods are often less available and sometimes more expensive than other foods, many people have banded together to form informal food co-ops. Together, they can order from wholesale distributors of natural foods, and buy foods in bulk or by the case. Buying foods in bulk saves time and money, and most grocery and health-food stores are happy to give a discount when you buy cases.

Fruits and Vegetables

Eat at least five to nine servings a day of all fruits and vegetables. They are rich in nutrients and fiber, contain no cholesterol, and are low in fat.

Legumes (Beans and Peas)

Use all types freely and often.

Black beans
Fava beans
White beans
Great northern beans
Kidney beans
Garbanzo beans (chickpeas)
Pinto beans

Split peas, green and yellow
Lentils: green, yellow, orange
Soybeans: tofu, tempeh, miso, flour, grits
Lima beans

Whole Grains

Many people with digestive illness have difficulty handling grains of any type. If so, you may need to limit or eliminate this food group from your diet for a period of time or permanently. Note that an asterisk denotes a grain that contains gluten.

Brown rice
Wild rice
Millet
Whole wheat★: whole wheat flour, wheat berries, cracked
    wheat, bulgur, wheat bran, couscous
Buckwheat
Spelt★
Barley★
Quinoa
Rye★
Kamut
Oats: oatmeal, whole oats, oat bran
Corn: flour, meal, bran, polenta, popcorn
Amaranth

Whole Grain Breads

These can be found in some grocery stores, bakeries, and natural-food stores. Look for "whole wheat" or "stone ground wheat" on the label. If it says "wheat flour" or "enriched" flour, it's white flour. Dense, heavy breads usually contain the most nutrients and fiber.

Breads and Pastas

Many stores are now carrying breads and pastas made with gluten-free flours such as quinoa, rice, millet, and soy. These products are terrific for people with celiac disease and wheat or gluten sensitivities.

Breads: whole grain
Crackers: Akmak, Health Valley, Hain, Finn crisp, Ry-Krisp, Barbara's pretzels and breadsticks, Wasa (rye only), whole wheat matzoh
Tortillas, corn or wheat
English muffins
Pita bread
Rice cakes
Whole grain muffins, pancakes, waffles
Pasta: whole wheat, corn, quinoa, semolina
Jerusalem artichoke
Rice, soba, udon, cellophane noodles

Cereals

Here are some healthier cereal brand choices. They use organic whole grains, have less or no refined sugar, and are generally high-fiber.

Health Valley
Nature's Path
Barbara's Bakery
Kashi
Perky's
Shredded wheat with bran
All Bran

Erewhon
New Morning
Oatmeal
Uncle Sam's cereal
Seven-grain cereal
McCann's Oatmeal

Dairy Products and Eggs

Many people with digestive problems need to eliminate dairy products from their diet, so use only if you are able to digest them easily.

Low- or nonfat yogurt
Skim milk
Skim milk ricotta
Buttermilk
Low-fat cottage cheese
Parmesan
Kefir
Butter and ghee in small quantities
Yogurt cheese
Goat's milk and cheese
Eggs: chicken, duck

Fish and Seafood

All seafood can be healthful, but these are highest in omega-3 fatty acids.

Salmon (all types)
Mackerel
Atlantic sturgeon

Tuna
Anchovy
Sablefish
Eel
Sardines
Seaweed and sea vegetables
Herring
Lake trout
Shellfish

Meats and Poultry

Choose low-fat cuts of meat and take the skin off poultry.

Lean hamburger and beef
Ground turkey
Leg of lamb
Venison
Buffalo
Pork tenderloin
Turkey, light meat, no skin
Chicken, without skin

Beverages

Water is the most healthful beverage. Make certain your drinking water is uncontaminated. Fresh juices made from organic produce offer a delicious and healthful option. Check labels carefully for sugars added to juice drinks; only 100 percent pure juices can be labeled "juice."

Pure water
Grain coffee

Fruit juices
Vegetable juices
Pure carbonated waters
Black tea/green tea/Rooibos tea
Herbal teas

Oils, Nuts, and Seeds

Use only extra-virgin or expeller-pressed oils, organic oils whenever possible, and olive oil, except for stir-frying or baking.

Olive oil
Sesame oil
Canola oil
Sunflower oil
Safflower oil
Corn oil
Walnut oil
Almond oil
Soybean oil
Peanut oil
Rice bran oil
Macadamia nut oil
Pistachio nuts
Macadamia nuts
Cashews
Almonds
Chestnuts
Pecans
Walnuts
Peanuts
Sunflower seeds

Pumpkin seeds
Sesame seeds
Coconut, unsweetened
Pine nuts

Condiments

Condiments add great flavor to foods, with few calories or grams of fat. Read labels carefully; many sauces are salty, fatty, sugar laden, or filled with food chemicals. Homemade salad dressings are best.

Mustard
Horseradish
Salsa
Worcestershire sauce
Tamari or shoyu sauce
Vinegars: balsamic, rice, fruit
Herbs and spices
Pepper: white or black
Olives: black and green
Anchovy paste
Pickles
Sun-dried tomatoes
Gomasio
Seaweed flakes
Capers
Sauerkraut
Herbal blends in shakers

And you thought I wasn't going to leave you anything to eat!

10

Natural Therapies for Common Digestive Problems

"Disease bias means that we take health for granted, waiting to act when health is gone and disease emerges. Once we make this assumption, we can soon become so preoccupied that our horizon is filled with diseases to combat. Because disease looms so large, our sight is obscured to the possibilities of health."

—Russell Jaffe, M.D.

This chapter provides a comprehensive list of self-care ideas for the most common digestive problems. The remedies are mostly nutritional and herbal because those are the fields I know best; I have included other modalities whenever possible. The most important ones are listed first. Read each section that applies to you, find the remedies for your symptoms, and try those recommended more than once first. Also try the remedies that make the most sense intuitively.

Each herb or nutrient is listed separately, but often they can be found in combination supplements. You'll notice that specific recommendations are repeated for many problems. Although each health condition has its own unique properties, many have similar characteristics that respond to similar treatment programs. You may want to work with a health professional to tailor a program that will best suit your needs.

Health care is both a science and an art. You may need the science in the form of lab testing, diagnosis, and evaluation of your needs. Your doctor will order the customary lab work. I have included information about functional lab tests that are most likely to reveal new information; these tests will probably be unfamiliar to your physician. The Resources directory will help you connect with the appropriate labs.

The art of healing comes into play when determining which paths to follow, which ideas have the most merit, and which dosages are appropriate. Healing often happens in layers. Sometimes you try the right thing at the wrong time. Later, you try it again with great results because the initial obstacle has been removed. If the first program you try doesn't work or only works partially, try another. You can feel better when you are persistent and patient. Remember, our symptoms are our body's way of telling us to pay attention, that something is out of balance. By listening, we often have the inner wisdom to know exactly what we need.

This chapter contains classic digestive problems. We start our journey at the mouth and move south. Some of the following ideas alleviate symptoms, while others work to help your body heal the underlying cause. You can begin your program by taking a multivitamin and mineral supplement. Be sure to purchase one that is hypoallergenic.

Think of a multivitamin with minerals as inexpensive health insurance, and arm yourself with an excellent supplement. Your diet is likely to be deficient in several nutrients that it can provide. Because minerals are bulky, you'll find yourself taking anywhere from two to nine pills daily. Read the ingredients on the label carefully. If it contains artificial colors, preservatives, shellac, or carnauba wax, put it back on the shelf and keep looking. Also, look for an expiration date and batch number. Look for a multi-vitamin and mineral supplement that contains at least the following:

- 1,000 milligrams of calcium
- 400–600 milligrams of magnesium
- 400 IU of vitamin D
- At least 100 IU of vitamin E
- At least 250 milligrams of vitamin C
- 200 micrograms of chromium
- 200 micrograms of selenium
- 5–10 milligrams of manganese
- At least 15 milligrams of zinc
- At least 400 micrograms of folic acid
- At least 10 milligrams of each B vitamin

If you do this, the rest of the nutrients will be in line.

Mouth

The mouth is the first digestive organ, after the brain. (See Chapter 2.) The health of our teeth, tongue, and gums is integral to the health of the rest of the digestive tract. Digestive enzymes in saliva begin the process of carbohydrate digestion, and chewing sends signals to the brain, which in turn sends signals to the stomach that food is on the way. Thorough chewing of food can help with indigestion.

Irritation and inflammation in the mouth can be signs of food or chemical sensitivities or allergies. The mouth is our first contact with ingested allergens. Careful investigation of the mouth area can give information about a person's nutritional status. Cracks down the center of the tongue are an indication of the need for increased B-complex vitamins. Bleeding gums indicate the need for vitamin C and bioflavonoids. Receding gums indicate bone loss, so bone nutrients are needed. Deep pockets in gums indicate the need for vitamin C, bioflavonoids, and coenzyme Q10 (CoQ10).

Bad Breath or Halitosis

Yes, bad breath can be digestive in origin. It can be caused by low HCl levels in the stomach, poor flora, and/or constipation. But, first, consult a dentist to see if it is caused by poor dental hygiene, periodontal disease, or tooth infections. If so, follow your dentist's advice, and also look in the section on gum and tooth health that follows. If your gums and teeth are healthy, look to your digestive capacities. Using mouthwash is like putting a Band-Aid on a broken leg.

Healing Options

Eliminate constipation. See the section on stool transit time in Chapter 2 and do the self-test. Make sure you are getting plenty of fiber and liquids and are having one to two bowel movements each day. Magnesium is essential for normal peristalsis. Take 400–800 milligrams of magnesium daily.

Try a probiotic supplement. Take 1 or 2 capsules of acidophilus and bifidus between meals.

Consider possible lactose intolerance. Lactose intolerance can cause bad breath, other digestive symptoms, and headaches. The simplest way to discover if you have lactose intolerance is to avoid all dairy products and dairy-containing food for two weeks, then see if your symptoms have improved.

Look for other causes if the problem persists. If you continue to have problems, you might be fermenting rather than digesting your foods. (1) Check out your HCl levels. Try one teaspoon vinegar in a glass of water with meals or betaine HCl tablets. If the HCl causes burning, you probably don't need it. You can neutralize the acid with milk or baking soda. (2) Ask your doctor to run a comprehensive digestive stool analysis (CDSA) with parasitology evaluation. You may have dysbiosis, parasites, or a helicobacter infection (the bacteria implicated in ulcers). A CDSA can help you find out what's amiss.

Cheilosis or Cracks in the Corners of the Mouth and Lips

Our skin is continuously replacing itself, and the places where our skin folds need to be replaced even more often. B-complex vitamins, particularly vitamins B_2 (riboflavin) and B_6 (pyridoxine), assist in formation of new skin. Cracks at the corners of our lips, called cheilosis, are most often associated with these nutrient deficiencies. They can easily become infected by yeast (*Candida albicans*). If they do not respond to nutritional therapy, have a physician look for other causes.

Healing Options
Take B-complex vitamins. Try 50–100 milligrams one to three times daily in trial for four weeks.

Gingivitis and Periodontal Disease

Gingivitis is an inflammation of the gums that, if left alone, often progresses to periodontal disease, an inflammation of the bone around the teeth. Periodontal disease increases with plaque buildup, age, long-term use of steroid medications, and in diabetics, people with systemic disease, and smokers. The presence of silver fillings, which contain 50 percent mercury, has also been found to predispose people to periodontal disease. One study showed that when silver fillings were removed, 86 percent of the 125 oral cavity symptoms were eliminated or improved.

Gingivitis and periodontal disease are complex problems that have complex solutions. Periodontal disease will affect nine out of ten Americans during their lifetimes, and four out of ten will lose all their teeth. Regular dental care is essential. Follow your dentist's advice and practice consistent oral hygiene: brush and floss daily.

Nutrition plays a critical role in dental health. One recent study looked at gingivitis, plaque adhesion, and calculus deposit with regard to the eating habits of teenagers. They concluded that teenagers with diets adequate in nutrients had better oral health than teenagers with diets that contained fewer nutrients.

Teeth are made of bone material and need the same nutrients for rebuilding as other bones. It has long been considered that receding and inflamed gums were a sign that people brushed too hard, causing damage to the gums, but new theories propose that gums recede because bone throughout the body, including the teeth, is demineralizing. If other bones need seventeen nutrients to remineralize, the same goes for teeth. Calcium alone cannot reverse the problem. Stress and fast-paced living can cause bone loss by making the body more acidic. To compensate, the body takes alkaline materials from bones and teeth. Read and follow the section on acid-alkaline balance in Chapter 6.

Vitamin C deficiency causes bleeding gums and loose teeth and contributes to gingivitis. Bleeding gums is one symptom of scurvy, a vitamin-C-deficiency disease. We rarely see outright scurvy in our population, but we often see people with bleeding gums. Vitamin C is also important for bone formation and collagen synthesis and is essential for gum repair. Vitamin A is also necessary for collagen synthesis and formation of gum tissue.

Other researchers look to zinc deficiency or a low zinc-to-copper ratio as the culprit in gum disease. Zinc is integral to maintenance and repair of gum tissue, inhibits plaque formation, and reduces inflammation by inhibiting mast cell release of histamine. It also plays a role in immune function.

Vitamin E has been used clinically for periodontal disease. Bacterial plaque, long known to be a culprit in tooth decay and gingivitis, produces compounds that weaken and irritate the gum tissue. They include endotoxins and exotoxins, free radicals, connective tissue–destroying enzymes, white blood cell poisons, antigens, and waste products.

Antioxidant nutrients and CoQ10 have been associated with improved gum health, reduced periodontal pocket depth, and decreased tooth movement. Bioflavonoids make the tissues stronger and reduce inflammation and cross-link with collagen fibers, making them stronger. Because bioflavonoids work synergistically with vitamin C, bleeding gums often respond to vitamin C and bioflavonoid supplementation. My favorite bioflavonoid is quercetin.

Folic acid, a B-complex vitamin, is important for maintenance and repair of mucous membranes. The need for extra folic acid was first noted for pregnant women, while subsequent studies have shown that it plays an important role for gingival health in all people.

Healing Options

Make dietary changes. Focus on fresh fruits, vegetables, whole grains, and beans. Foods rich in flavonoids are beneficial: blueberries, blackberries, and purple grapes.

Take a multivitamin with minerals. Because you are depleted in many nutrients, arm yourself with an excellent multivitamin with minerals. Because minerals are bulky, you'll probably take anywhere from four to nine pills daily. Look for a supplement that contains the following: 1,000 milligrams of calcium, 500 milligrams of magnesium, at least 400 IU of vitamin D, at least 250 milligrams of vitamin C, at least 100 IU of vitamin E, 100–200 micrograms of chromium, 100–200 micrograms of selenium,

5–10 milligrams of manganese, at least 15 milligrams of zinc, and at least 25 milligrams of each B vitamin.

Try coenzyme Q10. Take 75 to 200 milligrams daily for a trial period of three months.

Take antioxidants. Vitamins C and E, selenium, glutathione, N-acetyl cysteine (NAC), superoxide dismutase (SOD), beta-carotene, and other antioxidant nutrients are depleted in diseased gum tissues. Supplementation can facilitate repair. For ease of use, purchase an antioxidant supplement. Use as directed for three months.

Take vitamin C. Try 500–1,000 milligrams one to three times daily. For maximum benefits, use until your tissues are saturated. See section on vitamin C flush in Chapter 8.

Try bioflavonoids. Use quercetin, bilberry (blueberry), grape seed extract, or pycnogenol for their anti-inflammatory and antioxidant effects.

Try myrrh. Myrrh has been used since biblical times. It has soothing and antiseptic properties for mucous membranes.

Use a folic acid mouthwash. Use of a 0.1 percent folic acid mouthwash can be quite effective. Be sure to have your blood tested for pernicious anemia first, because folate supplementation can cause nerve damage in people with vitamin B_{12} deficiencies.

Try fish oil capsules. In a controlled placebo trial, it was found that MaxEPA fish oil capsules significantly reduced gingival bleeding and reduced inflammatory factors. Take 2–4 grams EPA/DHA daily.

Mouth Ulcers or Canker Sores

Mouth sores are common. Most of us have experienced mouth ulcers, canker sores, or cold sores, but some have chronic problems. Usually found inside the mouth, canker sores, called aphthous stomatitis, or aphthous ulcers, are the result of poor intestinal flora, food sensitivities or allergies, stress, hormonal changes, and nutritional deficiencies. High-sugar and high-acid foods, such as pineapples, citrus, and tomatoes, sometimes trigger canker sores.

If you have recurring canker sores, thoroughly investigate the possibility of food sensitivities. Also, make sure your toothpaste, mouthwash, and floss aren't causing the problem. A study showed that use of Piroxicam, an NSAID, caused mouth ulcers that resolved when the patient was taken off the medication. If you have canker sores that don't resolve after several weeks, let your doctor or dentist examine you.

Healing Options

Investigate allergies and sensitivities. Cigarettes, toothpaste, mouthwash, and flavored dental floss can cause irritation. Make sure they are not the source of your problem. Food sensitivities often are. Rule them out carefully with the elimination-provocation diet and/or food allergy or sensitivity blood testing.

Try a probiotic supplement. Lactobacillus acidophilus is often beneficial in prevention and treatment of canker sores. Take one to two capsules or ¼ to 1½ teaspoons of the powder three times daily; take between meals.

Take B-complex vitamins. Deficiencies in vitamin B_1, B_2, B_6, B_{12}, and folic acid have been associated with recurrent canker sores. People with B-complex deficiencies showed significant improvement of mouth ulcers during three months of supplementation with B-complex vitamins.

Consider gluten sensitivity. Gluten is a protein fraction found in wheat, rye, spelt, barley, and oats. A considerable amount of research has been done on the connection between gluten intolerance and mouth ulcers because people with celiac disease (sprue) often have recurring mouth sores. About 25 percent of people with chronic canker sores have elevated antibodies to gluten, which indicates a specific sensitivity. When they avoid gluten-containing grains, their mouth sores go away.

Address iron deficiency anemia. Iron deficiency is associated with canker sores. If you get recurrent canker sores and are anemic, you may respond to iron supplementation. People who are not anemic will not benefit. Ask your physician to test you for anemia. Take 30–75 milligrams of elemental iron daily. Because iron tends to be constipating, a slow-release iron, like Feosol or generic equivalents, may be helpful. Floradix, an herbal iron supplement, is gentle and works well. Cooking in cast-iron pots and pans is another way to gain iron from your diet.

Practice stress-management skills. Ask yourself if stress plays a significant role in your canker sores. If so, work on your stress-management skills.

Take zinc. Zinc deficiencies have been linked to mouth ulcers. Zinc plays an important role in healing wounds and immune system function. In one study, zinc supplementation helped heal canker sores 81 percent of the time in people with low zinc levels or a low zinc-to-copper ratio.

Topical Remedies

Use ice. Ice compresses dry up canker sores quickly. Apply ice directly to the sore for either forty-five minutes once a day, or several times a day for five minutes. You'll still have a scab that needs to heal, but the sores won't be painful.

Try licorice root. Licorice root is soothing to the mucous membranes of the digestive tract, and chewable licorice can help reduce inflammation and pain from mouth ulcers. Licorice promotes healing of mucous membranes by stimulating production of healing prostaglandins. Just be sure to buy deglycyrrhized (DGL) licorice that has had the glycyrrhizins removed. Glycyrrhizins can raise blood pressure and lower serum potassium levels. Chew two licorice tablets between meals as needed up to four times daily, or eat real licorice, such as Panda brand. Most licorice is made with anise, not licorice.

Try myrrh. Myrrh is an herb that has been used since biblical times to soothe mucous membranes. It has antiseptic properties and can be used in a variety of ways. Chewing gum with myrrh can be temporarily soothing, and a glycerin tincture can be used topically to soothe the sores. It can be combined with the herb goldenseal in tea, paste, or tincture.

Try goldenseal. Goldenseal is soothing to mucous membranes and also has antiseptic properties. It can be taken internally, dabbed directly on the sores, or drunk as a tea.

Try castor oil. An old Edgar Cayce remedy is to soak a cotton swab in castor oil and apply to the canker sore.

Thrush

Thrush is a yeast infection in the mouth and throat. It has a white, cottage cheesy look and is common after use of antibiotics. Thrush can be treated with either prescription or natural medicines. If it persists, you must treat yourself systemically. It is of primary importance to use probiotic supplements of acidophilus and bifidus to reestablish normal mouth-throat flora. Natural remedies such as garlic, grapefruit seed extract, pau d'arco, and mathake tea, along with dietary changes, can make your body inhospitable to candida. Follow the protocols for candida infections. In one study, one-third of people with thrush were found to have folic acid, vitamin B_6, or vitamin B_{12} anemias, so it's worth having your doctor check you for anemias and B-vitamin status.

Tongue Problems

Glossitis is an inflammation of the tongue, which can be extremely red and smooth, like a bald tire. Other people may also develop what's called a geographic tongue, where the center of your tongue looks like a miniature Grand Canyon. Look in a mirror, look at your friend's and family's tongues, and you'll probably find one. People may also have scalloping on the edges of their tongues.

Tongue problems can arise from systemic illness, so celiac, diabetes, Behcet's disease, anemia, and syphilis should be ruled out by your physician. More often, tongue problems are indicators of nutritional needs or mouth irritants, such as smoking or other chemicals. Studies have found that glossitis is a sign of protein calorie malnourishment, nutritional deficiencies, or marginal nutritional deficiencies of several vitamins and minerals. It affects 5 percent of our elderly. It most often signals the need for increased B-complex vitamins and iron. You will often find a reddened tongue with pellagra, which is caused by a deficiency of niacin (vitamin B_3). Therapeutics for glossitis are almost identical to those for canker sores.

Healing Options
Take B-complex vitamins. The most important B vitamins for tongue health are riboflavin (B_2), niacin (B_3), vitamin B_{12}, and folic acid. Choline is found in B-complex vitamins and also plays a vital role in tongue health. Take 50–100 milligrams of B complex one to three times daily for a trial period of four to six weeks to see if it helps.
Address iron deficiency anemia. Iron deficiency anemia can also cause a sore and inflamed tongue. Have your physician check to make sure your iron status is normal. Thorough testing would include hematocrit, hemoglobin, ferritin, TIBC, and transferrin.
Take zinc. Zinc is important for healing. Take 25–50 milligrams daily.
Investigate food sensitivities. Check for food sensitivities.
Take vitamin E. One study of elderly people with glossitis found that they had lower serum levels of vitamin E. It is not known if

vitamin E is just a marker or if it will help therapeutically, but vitamin E has low toxicity and is worth trying. You should take 400 IU every day.

Esophagus

The most common problems in the esophageal area are belching, medically called eructation; heartburn, also called gastric reflux; and Barrett's esophagus.

Belching or Eructation

Belching is a symptom of gas in the upper part of the digestive tract. It is a release of trapped air from the stomach and usually comes from swallowed air. Just as a baby needs to be burped if she swallows air, we also burp if we swallow air—it's normal. Other than being culturally embarrassing, it's usually without problem. In fact, in China it's considered polite to belch after a meal—it means you really enjoyed it!

Foods and drink that contain air contribute to belching. Without fail, when I have a carbonated drink, I burp. Whipped cream and egg whites can have the same effect on many people. Gulping drinks and food causes us to take in more air, while eating slowly prevents us from swallowing air. People also swallow air during exercise and while chewing gum, and sucking on pipes, straws, or cigarettes. If you are overweight, you are more likely to belch from exercise.

Be thankful that you belch; air trapped in the stomach can be painful and belching is a safety valve that relieves the pressure. If you have a problem with the amount of belching you do, here are some suggestions.

Functional Laboratory Testing

Sometimes *H. pylori* infection can cause belching, with or without other digestive symptoms. Ask your doctor to test for *H. pylori*.

The Heidelberg capsule test measures your ability to produce hydrochloric acid when challenged with alkaline substances. See Chapter 6 for complete details.

Healing Options

Make lifestyle changes. Eat slowly and chew your food well. Avoid carbonated beverages. Stop smoking. If you smoke, stop. Be glad you have such a benign reason to stop. Reach and maintain ideal body weight. If you are significantly overweight, lose some weight. Stop chewing gum or sucking on candy. As an alternative, you can suck on or eat umeboshi plum, or you can make it into a tea. These salty, fermented plums are highly alkalizing and aid in indigestion.

Try charcoal tablets. These can absorb toxins, make breath smell better, and calm an overexcited digestive system.

Check your supplements. Some can cause belching, such as fish oils. Try any of the remedies for heartburn, gastric reflux, and hiatal hernia.

Heartburn or Gastric Reflux and Hiatal Hernia

Heartburn is caused by stomach acid backing up into your esophagus. The esophageal sphincter is supposed to keep the stomach contents in place, but if the sphincter relaxes, acid can push up into the esophagus. The most common symptoms are a burning sensation above the stomach, excessive salivation, belching, regurgitation, and a sour taste in the mouth. One-third of Americans experience frequent heartburn, also known as GERD. Another 3 to 7 percent suffer from Barrett's esophagus, an esophageal illness caused from acid reflux that results in scarring, constriction of the esophagus, and swallowing disorders. Some drugs can cause heartburn, including birth control pills, diazepam, nicotine, nitroglycerine, progesterone, provera, and theophylline.

Four to five million Americans seek medical advice each year for heartburn and hiatal hernia. Heartburn is common among pregnant women whose organs are squashed in a most peculiar way. For most people, heartburn is a mild, self-limiting problem, yet for 20 percent of those affected, it becomes a serious health problem. Stress plays some part in it. Other triggers include wearing tight-fitting clothes, lying down, bending over, and eating large meals or specific foods. If you experience heartburn in the middle of the night, be sure to eat at least four hours before going to bed.

Hiatal hernia occurs when a portion of the stomach gets pushed through the diaphragm and into the thoracic cavity where it doesn't belong. Hiatal hernias may or may not cause symptoms, the most common of which is heartburn. It's found in about 20 percent of all middle-aged Americans. Dr. Dennis Burkitt, father of fiber, hypothesized that hiatal hernia was a contemporary problem and the result of a modernized diet.

Gastric reflux and hiatal hernia have been on the rise over the past twenty years and occur most often in people of Caucasian descent. These problems are rarely seen in people eating high-fiber diets. Straining with bowel movements can push the stomach out of place, what's called a hiatal hernia. Chiropractic adjustment can gently put the stomach back in place, and in many cases only a single adjustment is necessary.

Heartburn sufferers commonly take antacids for temporary relief. Initially, use of antacids causes the body to produce more HCl, which helps digest food. Parietal cells respond by making more acid. Eventually the parietal cells get exhausted, so over the long term, antacids cause the parietal cells to make less HCl.

There are other repercussions of taking antacids. A recent study looked at 155 healthy people who had been using antacids for heartburn over long periods of time. The study found that 47 percent had erosion of the esophagus and 6 percent had Barrett's esophagus, a more serious condition. Most bacteria can't live in a high-acid environment and are killed in the stomach. Low stomach acid predisposes people to dysbiosis. Antacids also decrease your stomach's ability to digest protein by reducing the effectiveness of protease enzymes. H2 blockers, such a Tagamet and Zantac, and protein-pump inhibitors, such as Prilosec, are the most common prescription medications used for acid reflux. These medications are effective while you take them, but once you discontinue their use, your problem often recurs.

Functional Laboratory Testing
H. pylori
Heidelberg capsule test

Healing Options
Try osteopathic care and chiropractic adjustment. Seek chiropractic care for hiatal hernia. Cranial-sacral adjustments can often correct gastric reflux, especially in children. Chiropractic or osteopathic adjustment is often all the therapy you need for these problems.
Make dietary changes. Eat healthy foods. Increase fruits, vegetables, grains, beans, and high-fiber foods. Foods that are more acidic, like tomatoes and citrus, are more likely to cause heartburn. Dairy products have been shown to trigger symptoms, but more symptoms were provoked with milk with higher fat contents, suggesting that fat was the culprit, rather than the milk. Alcoholic beverages, coffee, and to a lesser extent, tea provoke heartburn, as well as high-fat, fried, and spicy foods; onions; and chocolate. Trigger foods are individual—you need to discover what yours are. If you are overweight, lose weight.

Drink plenty of water. Some people find that increasing water consumption up to a gallon of water a day resolves acid reflux.

Place a six-inch beam under the head of your bed. If you suffer from nighttime heartburn, raising the head of your bed can alleviate symptoms. Although you might think that raising your bed would feel strange, the difference is barely noticeable, and the heartburn improves.

Consider possible Helicobacter pylori *infection.* Helicobacter pylori is a bacteria that has been implicated in gastric and duodenal ulcers. In some cases, it is also involved in gastric reflux. Treatment with antibiotics and bismuth-containing supplements or drugs can eradicate *H. pylori*.

Try hydrochloric acid supplements. Heartburn has traditionally been treated with antacid therapy, but often it responds well to supplementation with hydrochloric acid pills. Often, the symptoms of excess stomach acid and decreased stomach acid are the same. To test yourself, dilute a tablespoon of apple cider vinegar with water and drink with meals. If the vinegar is not strong enough to show results, take one to two HCl tablets with meals. If you do not need the HCl, you will feel a burning sensation, which can be neutralized with milk or baking soda. If you need it, you'll feel relief of symptoms. (See section on hypochlorhydria.)

Drink cabbage juice. Cabbage juice has been a long-standing folk remedy for heartburn. Its high glutamine content is probably the key to its success. Cabbage juice has a strong flavor, so dilute with other vegetable juices.

Try slippery elm bark. Slippery elm bark has demulcent properties, and it's gentle and soothing to mucous membranes. It has been a folk remedy for both heartburn and ulcers in European and Native American cultures and was used as a food by Native Americans. It can be used in large amounts without harm. Drink as a tea or chew on the bark. To make a tea, take 1 teaspoon of slippery elm bark in 2 cups of water. Simmer for twenty minutes and strain.

Sweeten if you want, and drink freely. You can also purchase slippery elm lozenges at health-food stores and some drugstores.

Use lobelia. Massage tincture of lobelia externally onto the painful area and take 2 to 3 drops internally. This is a remedy recommended by Dr. Christopher, one of the greatest American herbalists of our times.

Use ginger. This root can provide temporary relief in a tea. Steep 1½ teaspoons of powdered ginger or a few slices of fresh ginger per cup of boiled water for ten minutes and drink. If you like, sweeten it with honey. Use freely.

Try meadowsweet herb. Also a demulcent, meadowsweet soothes inflamed mucous membranes. To make a tea, steep 1 to 2 teaspoons of the dried herb in 1 cup of boiled water for ten minutes. Sweeten with honey if you like. Drink 3 cups daily.

Barrett's Esophagus

Barrett's esophagus is a condition in which some of the lining of the esophagus is replaced by a type of tissue that is normally found in the intestine. It is estimated to affect about 700,000 adults in the United States. It is more common in men than in women, and especially in Caucasians.

Barrett's itself may or may not cause any symptoms. Barrett's does not cause cancer, but often precedes it. The risk of developing esophageal cancer is 30 to 125 times higher in people who have Barrett's esophagus than those who don't. The risk of developing cancer is low, about 0.5 percent of people with Barrett's esophagus will develop esophageal cancer each year. People with known Barrett's esophagus should be frequently monitored for early detection of possible cancer. Barrett's esophagus can occur in people without gastric reflux, but is three to five times more common in people who do have it. Treatment with acid-blocking drugs sometimes improves the extent of the Barrett's, but it doesn't correlate with a reduction in cancer rates. Production of peroxynitrite, a damaging free radical, contributes to Barrett's esophagus. Vitamin C, glutathione, and folic acid are known to help reduce the formation of damaging peroxynitrites. Barrett's is diagnosed by doing an upper GI endoscopy and biopsy.

The healing options may help with the symptoms of Barrett's esophagus. They may also help prevent cancer of the esophagus, which is the long-term problem to be concerned about. Very little literature about this is available, but I am working with what is known in other areas of the digestive tract and personal experience with clients. It is necessary to continue to have medical testing and to be vigilant about this illness. You may also benefit from the many suggestions in the section on heartburn or gastric reflux.

Healing Options

Take folic acid. Folic acid is well documented to help prevent colon cancer. In a Chinese study, folic acid and beta-carotene were studied to see what long-term effect they would have on the prevention of esophageal, stomach, and colon cancers. They gave 20 milligrams (20,000 micrograms) of folic acid daily plus 1 milligram vitamin B_{12} as an injected shot once a month for one year. (Vitamin B_{12} was given as a precautionary measure, because if someone who has a folic acid deficiency is treated with folic acid, it can hide neurological damage that may be caused by the B_{12} deficiency.) After the first year, the folate was continued twice a week plus 1 milligram of vitamin B_{12} every three months. There were no incidences of digestive cancers in the folate test group. It has long been used in patients with ulcerative colitis to help prevent colon cancer. Folic acid works as an antioxidant to control peroxynitrite scavenger. In the 1970s, Butterworth, a medical researcher, did several studies on the use of folic acid, 10 milligrams daily, to successfully treat women with cervical dysplasia. This condition is not dissimilar to Barrett's. It may not be necessary to use such high dosages, but the research has not yet been done and folate appears to be nontoxic at extremely high dosages.

Because folic acid can mask vitamin B_{12} deficiency, most products contain only 0.8 milligrams per dose (800 micrograms). At this time, there is only one company I know of that sells folic acid in a 10 milligram dosage, available through Emerson Ecologics. Take 20 milligrams daily for one year, plus 1 milligram vitamin B_{12} by injection each month, or take sublingual B_{12} hydroxycobalamine 1,000 milligrams weekly. Second year, reduce dosage as noted above.

Try antioxidant nutrients. Several studies indicate that free radical damage helps initiate Barrett's esophagus. Antioxidant nutrients are useful in nearly every condition. Selenium levels in people with Barrett's esophagus are lower than in controls. Glutathione levels are reduced, malondialdehyde, and NF-kappa B levels are increased. It is prudent to increase levels of antioxidant nutrients such as vitamin C, carotenoids, vitamin E, selenium, N-acetyl cysteine (NAC), lipoic acid, folic acid, and others. You can begin with a combination antioxidant supplement with at least 200–400 micrograms selenium. Add an additional 1,000 IU of vitamin E, 1,000–2,000 milligrams NAC, and at least 1,000–2,000 milligrams vitamin C. You may want to use the vitamin C flush. (See Chapter 8.)

Try probiotics and digestive enzymes. No published research on the use of probiotic bacteria or on the use of digestive enzymes in Barrett's is available, but it would make sense to give each a trial.

Stomach

Gastric Hypofunction or Hypochlorhydria

Hypochlorhydria (low stomach acid) has been associated with many common health problems. Stomach acid is used to begin the process of protein digestion. A normal stomach acid level is a pH of 1.5 to 2.5. As we age, the parietal cells in the stomach lining produce less hydrochloric acid. In fact, half of people over the age of sixty have hypochlorhydria, and by age eighty-five, 80 percent of the healthy people tested had low stomach acid.

Use of acid-blocking medications increases stomach pH to 3.5 or higher. This inhibits pepsin, which can irritate the stomach, but it's also essential for digestion of protein. Stomach acid is also necessary for absorption of many minerals, so mineral depletion may occur with use of these medicines. Minerals that can become depleted include iron, calcium, magnesium, zinc, and copper. Stomach acid also provides our first defense against food poisoning, *H. pylori*, parasites, and other infections. Without adequate acid, we leave ourselves open to decreased immune resistance.

Overgrowth of bacteria in the intestinal tract occurs in 20 percent of people age sixty to eighty and in 40 percent of people over age eighty. Adequate HCl is necessary for the absorption of vitamin B_{12} from food. B_{12} deficiency causes weakness, fatigue, and nervous system problems. Most B-complex vitamins require normal levels of stomach acid. Vitamin C levels are also low in people with poor stomach acid. Acid is critical for the breakdown of protein bonds in the stomach. Poor acid content in the stomach causes indigestion. The symptoms of hypoacidity often mimic those of hyperacidity.

Hypochlorhydria may be caused by the following: pernicious anemia, chronic *H. pylori* infection, long-term treatment with proton pump inhibitors (like Prilosec), autoimmune gastritis, and mucolipidosis type IV; it is also common in autoimmune diseases.

Functional Laboratory Testing

Heidelberg capsule test

Healing Options

Try betaine HCl. Begin with 1 10-milligram capsule of betaine HCl with meals. If you do not respond, build slowly to a maxi-

Low Gastric Acidity

The following are common symptoms of low gastric acidity:

- Bloating, belching, burning, and flatulence immediately after meals
- A sense of fullness after eating
- Indigestion, diarrhea, or constipation
- Multiple food allergies
- Nausea after taking supplements
- Itching around the rectum
- Weak, peeling, and cracked fingernails
- Dilated blood vessels in the cheeks and nose (in nonalcoholics)
- Acne
- Iron deficiency
- Chronic intestinal parasites or abnormal flora
- Undigested food in stool
- Chronic candida infections
- Upper digestive tract gassiness

The following are diseases associated with low gastric acidity:

- Addison's disease
- Asthma
- Celiac disease
- Chronic autoimmune disorders
- Chronic hives
- Dermatitis herpetiformis (herpes)
- Diabetes
- Eczema
- Gallbladder disease

- Graves disease
- Hepatitis
- Hyper- and hypothyroidism
- Lupus erythematosis
- Myasthenia gravis
- Osteoporosis
- Pernicious anemia
- Psoriasis
- Rheumatoid arthritis
- Rosacea
- Sjögren's syndrome
- Thyrotoxicosis
- Vitiligo

Used with permission from Michael Murray, N.D. "Indigestion, Antacids, Achlorhydria and H. pylori." American Journal of Natural Medicine (January–February 1997): 11–16.

mum of 5 capsules with each meal. If you experience burning, immediately neutralize the acid with one teaspoon baking soda in water or milk. That indicates that you now have too much HCl and are irritating your stomach lining. Cut back your dosage to a comfortable level.

Try umeboshi plum. You can suck on, eat, or make into a tea. These salty, fermented plums are highly alkalizing and aid in indigestion.

Increase acidity with vinegar. Dilute 1 teaspoon of vinegar in water and drink with each meal. Gradually increase the amount of vinegar, up to 10 teaspoons. If you experience burning, immediately neutralize the acid by drinking a glass of milk or taking a teaspoon of baking soda in water.

Test for vitamin B_{12} insufficiency. Have your physician test your B_{12} by testing homocysteine or methylmalonic acid. Serum B_{12} levels

decrease only when tissue levels are very depleted. A more expe-
dient and less expensive route is to ask your physician to give you
1,000 micrograms of vitamin B_{12} by injection weekly for four
weeks. Then you and your doctor can evaluate the benefits. Or
you can use sublingual (under the tongue) hydroxocobalamin at
2,000 micrograms daily for four weeks. People who are deficient
in vitamin B_{12} feel much more energetic and can accomplish more
when levels are normalized.

Take a multivitamin with minerals. Adequate HCl is necessary for
absorption of vitamins and minerals. Because you are depleted in
many nutrients, arm yourself with an excellent multivitamin with
minerals. Because minerals are bulky, you'll probably find yourself taking anywhere from four to nine pills daily. Look for a supplement that contains the following: 1,000 milligrams of calcium,
500 milligrams of magnesium, at least 400 IU vitamin D, 100–200
micrograms of chromium, 100–200 micrograms of selenium,
5–10 milligrams of manganese, at least 15 milligrams of zinc, and
at least 25 milligrams of each B vitamin.

Try digestive enzymes. I recommend plant-derived enzymes because
they work in both the low pH of the stomach and in the neutral
environment of the intestines. They provide protease and lipase for
the stomach and serve your enzyme needs throughout the digestive tract. Take 1 to 2 with meals for a trial period of four weeks.

Use Swedish bitters. Bitters are a long-standing remedy for poor
digestion in Europe. They stimulate production of HCl. Take bitters either in tablet or liquid form as needed.

Change your eating habits. Chew food thoroughly and eat small
meals frequently. Small meals are easier to digest. Avoid drinking
liquids with meals. Fluids dilute stomach acid.

Gastric Ulcers and Gastritis

A 1994 National Institutes of Health statement reports that "peptic ulcer disease is a chronic inflammatory condition of the stom-

ach and duodenum that affects as many as 10 percent of people in the United States at some time in their lives. The disease has relatively low mortality, but it results in substantial human suffering and high economic costs."

Gastric ulcers: Gastric ulcers occur in the stomach and the duodenum (the first section of the small intestine) where gastric juice has burned a hole in the lining. It hurts! Gastric juice is so acid it would burn your hand if you spilled some on it. A mucus layer protects the stomach tissue from being eaten away by pepsin (a protein-splitting enzyme) and the gastric juices. Secretions of bicarbonate (baking soda) from the stomach lining are mixed into the mucus, buffering the acid. This makes an effective barrier to keep the stomach lining from harm. Pepsin, the real villain in this story, slowly digests this mucus layer, and if the mucus isn't replaced, gastric juices come into contact with the stomach lining and ulcers occur.

Eighty percent of ulcers are caused by a bacterial infection called *Helicobacter pylori* (*H. pylori*), 10 percent are caused by the use of NSAID medications, and another 10 percent are of unknown origin.

In 1982, Australian physician Barry Marshall discovered the presence of *H. pylori* between the stomach lining and the mucous membrane. *H. pylori* infections deplete vitamin C levels in the gut. This bacteria is found in 80 percent of people with duodenal and stomach ulcers and with gastritis. *H. pylori* is found in about 30 percent of all people, but only 10 percent will experience ulcers. This poses a curious question. Why do some people have helicobacter infection yet no GI upset? It's probably due to a difference in genetics. If you have "lucky" genes in this case, you remain unaffected by the bacteria.

About 10 percent of stomach and duodenal ulcers are caused by the use of NSAIDs, such as aspirin, Tylenol, Motrin, and prescription pain relievers. Continued use of these therapies has been widely shown to cause ulcers and hospitalizations. It has been estimated that 107,000 people are hospitalized each year because of NSAID complications, and at least 16,500 NSAID-related deaths occur each year among arthritis patients alone.

The stomach has three defense mechanisms against the highly acid stomach environment: (1) mucus that coats the stomach lining, (2) bicarbonate that neutralizes the acids, and (3) blood circulation in the stomach lining that aids in cell growth and repair. NSAIDs hinder all three of these mechanisms, and ulcers result. The ulcers usually heal once you've stopped taking the NSAIDs, but you may want to use medications or herbs to help with the discomfort in the meantime.

Ten percent of people with ulcers and gastritis do not have *Helicobacter pylori* infection, nor have they used NSAID medications. For these people, the cause of ulcers and gastritis is still a mystery. Looking at stress, diet, and lifestyle may yield important clues. Stress plays a significant role in ulcers and gastritis. While low-grade stress probably won't cause an ulcer, severe stress has been shown to cause ulcers in both animal and human studies. Psychological stress increases stomach acid and causes the mucus to become more fragile, making it easier for ulcers to form.

In the 1970s, receptor sites on the stomach lining were found that regulate secretion of HCl, and drugs were developed to block these receptor sites. These drugs, called H2 blockers, have been effective in healing ulcers but not in preventing recurrence.

More recently, a new class of drugs called protein-pump inhibitors has been used, the most common of which is Prilosec. These drugs absolutely block stomach acid production. They appear to be safe, although approximately 2.5 percent may experience severe side effects. Long-term use can lead to gastric atrophy, poor HCl production, and poor vitamin B_{12} and mineral absorption. Protein-pump inhibitors are metabolized in the liver via the CP450 pathways. It may be a good idea to do a liver cleanse/detox before going onto these drugs to increase their effectiveness.

It is known that when *H. pylori* is eradicated, ulcers heal and don't recur. It's important to treat diagnosed helicobacter infections; long-term infection increases the risk of duodenal or gastric ulcers, asymptomatic chronic gastritis, chronic indigestion, and stomach cancer. The most common therapies used by physicians are called triple therapies and consist of the use of an antibiotic or antiparasitic drug, an H2 blocker or a protein-pump inhibitor, and bismuth. Bismuth is an elemental mineral that protects the stomach lining by protecting the mucous membrane from being dissolved by pepsin.

Your doctor will choose the specific medications that will be most effective and most cost-effective. These short-term therapies are quite effective at eradicating *Helicobacter pylori* infections. Despite treatment, 20 percent have a relapse of their ulcer within six months without aggravation from NSAID medications. Although this treatment has minor side effects, the overall outcome shows improved quality of living and less psychological stress after therapy.

Because ulcers have been experienced throughout history, people have found effective natural therapies. Most physicians are not aware of these therapies, but nutritionally oriented physicians have been using them with promising results. Some have been using a combination of antibiotic therapy and bismuth, with DGL licorice, citrus seed extract, goldenseal, activated charcoal, and aloe vera. Glutamine, gamma oryzanol, SanoGastril, cabbage juice, comfrey, and calendula have also been shown to heal ulcers. Dietary recommendations for people with ulcers may be useful. Low-fiber diets may contribute significantly to ulcers. A South African physician, G. Borok, studied more than a thousand patients with ulcers and concluded that elimination of refined sugars, white-flour products, milled maize, chocolate, fries, soft drinks, and desserts will reduce gastric irritation. He also suggests avoiding tea and coffee. Another plug for a whole-foods diet!

A recent study on the diet of people with duodenal ulcers found that people who had good vitamin-A intake, followed a high-fiber diet, or ate seven or more servings of fruits and vegetables per day, rather than three servings or fewer, reduced risks of developing ulcers by 54 percent, 45 percent, and 33 percent, respectively. Again, this shows that a great diet can reduce your risk of all sorts of health problems.

Gastritis: Gastritis is a stomach inflammation without an ulcer or sore. It's usually caused by medications, including corticosteroids, NSAIDs, cancer drugs, and antibiotics; drinking alcoholic beverages; excessive coffee consumption; organ failure; and severe stress or trauma. Common symptoms of gastritis include hiccups, loss of appetite, indigestion, nausea, vomiting, vomiting of blood, and dark stools. It is common in the elderly, affecting 20 percent of people between the ages of sixty and sixty-nine, and 40 percent of people over age eighty. The lack of hydrochloric acid secretion in the elderly allows for bacterial growth, such as *H. pylori*; however, when treated with antibiotics, symptoms improve.

Long-term effects of gastritis include poor vitamin B_{12} status in all people. Signs of B_{12} deficiency often mimic those of senility. Many people have B_{12} deficiencies with normal serum levels. Tests for B_{12} status include homocysteine and methylmalonic acid.

Atrophic gastritis is usually treated with H2 blockers or protein-pump inhibitors. Looking at triggers, such as stress, medications, and poor HCl production is also an important step toward prevention.

One new therapy uses lactoferrin, or cow's colostrum, to eradicate *H. pylori*. Research has shown that use of triple therapy with added lactoferrin improves the success rate. Alone, it probably won't do the job. People with high levels of gastritis and heli-cobacter also have concurrent high levels of lactoferrin in their stomach. Is the lactoferrin helping the *H. pylori* gain a foothold and helping it gain necessary iron for its metabolism? Or is the lactoferrin called in by the body's immune system to help rid us of the bacteria? At this point, no one really knows.

Functional Laboratory Testing
H. pylori test

Healing Options
Drink water. One very simple remedy for ulcers and gastritis is to drink huge amounts of water. Drink four to six glasses of water during the pain, and then it may magically disappear. A fascinating book on this subject is *Your Body's Many Cries for Water*, by Fereydoon Batmanghelidj, M.D. Drink at least eight to ten glasses of water each day.

Try licorice. DGL licorice helps heal the stomach's mucous lining by increasing healing prostaglandins that promote mucus secretion and cell proliferation. Licorice enhances the blood flow and health of intestinal tract cells. It's important to use DGL licorice to avoid side effects caused by whole licorice. Take capsules or chew 2 to 4 tablets three times daily.

Use aloe vera. Aloe vera is a folk remedy for ulcers and has been approved by the FDA for use in oral ulcers. It is soothing and healing to mucous membranes.

Try gamma oryzanol. Gamma oryzanol, a compound found in rice bran oil, is a useful therapeutic tool in gastritis, ulcers, and irritable bowel syndrome. It acts on the autonomic nervous system to normalize production of gastric juice and has also been shown to be effective in normalizing serum triglycerides and cholesterol, symptoms of menopause, and depressive disorders. Studies involving 375 hospitals in Japan indicate that gamma oryzanol was effective in reducing symptoms from 80 to 90 percent, with more than half of the participants experiencing total or marked improvement. Typical dosage was 100 milligrams three times daily for three weeks. Occasionally, the dosage was doubled, and often the therapy was used longer. Minimal side effects were experienced by 0.4 percent of the people.

Take 100 milligrams of gamma oryzanol three times daily for a trial period of three to six weeks to determine if it relieves the problem.

Drink cabbage juice. Cabbage juice is a long-standing folk remedy for heartburn. Drink 1 quart of cabbage juice daily for a trial period of two weeks.

Try glutamine. Glutamine is the most popular antiulcer drug in Asia today. The digestive tract uses glutamine as a fuel source and for healing. It is effective for healing stomach ulcers, irritable bowel syndrome, and ulcerative bowel diseases. Begin with 8 grams daily for a trial period of four weeks.

Try grapefruit or citrus seed extract. Citrus seed extract has widely effective antiparasitic, antiviral, and antibiotic properties. Take 75 to 250 milligrams three times daily.

Use goldenseal. Goldenseal is soothing to mucous membranes, enhances immune function, and has antibiotic and antifungal properties.

Try SanoGastril. SanoGastril is a chewable tablet that buffers the acidity of the stomach. (SanoGastril is marketed in this country by Nutri-Cology/Allergy Research Group; this is not an endorsement, but the only product of its type.) SanoGastril is composed of an extract called glycine-max and a specific strain of *Lactobacillus acidophilus* plus vitamin C and other nutrients. A study using 2 tablets three times daily was done on ninety-three people with ulcers and gastritis. After one month, each participant was x-rayed to see progress. At that time, twelve out of twenty-two people with gastric ulcer, twenty-five out of fifty-eight people with duodenal ulcer, and four out of twelve people with gastritis were completely healed. Two tablets of SanoGastril three times daily before meals relieved heartburn completely within five to ten minutes in 76 percent of 158 people.

Try slippery elm bark. Slippery elm bark has demulcent properties and has been a folk remedy for both heartburn and ulcers. It can be used in large amounts without harm. Drink as a tea, chew on the bark, or take in capsules. To make a tea, simmer 1 teaspoon of slippery elm bark in 2 cups of water for twenty minutes and strain. Sweeten if you want, and drink freely. Or, take 2 to 4 capsules three times daily for a trial period of three weeks.

Use evening primrose, borage, or flaxseed oils. These oils increase the levels of prostaglandin E2 series, which promotes healing and repair. Take 1,000 to 2,000 milligrams of one of these oils or a combination oil three times a day for a trial period of four weeks. Low dietary intake of linoleic acid, an essential fatty acid, has been associated with duodenal ulcers. Flaxseeds are excellent sources of linoleic acid. A benefit to using ground flaxseeds rather than the oil is that the mucous portion of the flaxseed buffers excess acid, which makes it ideal for inflammation in the stomach and throughout the gastrointestinal tract. Grind them fresh daily or buy products with enhanced shelf life, and store in the refrigerator.

Linoleic acid is also found in pumpkin seeds, tofu, walnuts, safflower oil, sunflower seeds and oil, and sesame seeds and oil. Use 2 to 3 teaspoons in smoothies or protein drinks, or on salads and vegetables.

Take zinc. Zinc increases the rate of healing and can prevent damage to the stomach lining. Take 50 milligrams daily.

Take vitamin A. Vitamin A is protective and promotes healing of gastric ulcers. Take 10,000 to 25,000 IU daily. Daily short-term treatment dosage may be 50,000 to 75,000 IU for up to three weeks. Pregnant women should not exceed 10,000 IU vitamin A.

Take other important nutrients. You should also take 2 milligrams of copper daily, 400 IU of vitamin E daily, B complex, and N-acetyl cysteine.

Try Turkish herbs. Six Turkish plant medicines were studied for their effectiveness against *H. pylori* in a laboratory setting. Five were found to be highly effective, with *Cistus laurifolius* (laurel rockrose) being the most effective. The effective herbs were the flowers of *Cistus laurifolius*, cones of *Cedrus libani* (cedar of Lebanon), herbs and flowers of *Centaurea solstitialis* (yellow starthistle), fruits of *Momordica charantia* (bitter melon), herbaceous parts of *Sambucus ebulus* (danewort or dwarf elder), and flowering herbs of *Hypericum perforatum* (St.-John's-wort). We may begin to see research on some or all of these plant medicines. We may also begin to see them in supplements. There have been no human studies.

Try comfrey and calendula. A Bulgarian study used comfrey and calendula either with antacid medications or alone in patients with peptic ulcers. Eighty-five percent of both groups felt better, but people who also used antacids felt better a few days earlier. Gastric scoping showed equal healing of ulcers in both groups. Comfrey, one of my favorite herbs, has come under fire lately. It contains small amounts of pyrrolizidine alkaloids, which have liver damaging and possible carcinogenic effects. Although there have been no known cases of toxicity in humans from comfrey, rat testing has caused it to be removed from many products and banned in several countries. Studies were done using the specific pyrrolizidine alkaloids, but in studies with whole comfrey, no adverse reactions were found.

While the controversy continues, be cautious about using comfrey internally. Restrict its internal use to two weeks. Comfrey has been used medicinally for hundreds of years to promote wound and bone healing. The combination of comfrey and calendula makes sense in terms of today's triple therapy. Comfrey promotes healing and protects the gastric mucosa. Calendula has antibacterial effects. Dosage in the Bulgarian study was unclear, but comfrey leaf and calendula flower tea at 3 to 4 cups daily would be appropriate.

Liver

The liver is the most complex organ in the body. Unlike the heart, which has one major function—to beat, the liver has a multitude of functions that include regulation of blood sugar levels, making thirteen thousand different enzymes, humanizing food by acting as a filter, breaking down toxins, manufacturing cholesterol and bile, breaking down hormones, and more. Because of its complexity and the ten thousand pounds of toxins it must filter over a lifetime, the liver can easily become overwhelmed.

Hepatitis

The eight types of hepatitis are A, B, C, D, E, autoimmune, alcoholic, and nonalcoholic steatohepatitis (NASH). Types A through E are caused by a blood-borne viral infection that causes inflammation in the liver. Autoimmune hepatitis, alcoholic hepatitis, and NASH are not caused by infection.

Hepatitis A: Hepatitis A can occur in isolated cases or spread among large groups of people. You can catch it from close personal contact with a person who has it or from food or water that has been contaminated. It is usually a self-limiting illness with flu-like symptoms. Once you've had hepatitis A, you cannot get it again. It may take several months to recover fully. A vaccine for people over the age of two is available for lifelong protection against hepatitis A.

Hepatitis B: Hepatitis B is the most common serious liver infection in the world and is more serious than hepatitis A. It can lead to cirrhosis, liver cancer, or liver failure. In most people, it is a self-limiting illness. But, 90 percent of infected babies, 30 to 50 percent of infected children, and 5 to 10 percent of infected adults will also develop a chronic infection. A vaccine is available to help prevent hepatitis B infection. It is currently recommended that all babies be vaccinated.

Each year 100,000 Americans contract hepatitis B and 5,000 to 6,000 Americans will die from it. It is estimated that 1.25 million Americans have chronic hepatitis B. Worldwide, it affects 400 million people and there are 1 million deaths per year. It is passed directly through blood. Since 1992, blood collected for transfusions is carefully screened for hepatitis B (and C). Prior to that time, infection through blood transfusion was common.

You can get hepatitis B from having unprotected sex with someone who has it, by sharing needles for drug use or tattooing, or by an accidental needle poke with an infected needle. During childbirth, a mother could pass it on to her child.

Hepatitis C: Hepatitis C accounts for about 15 percent of acute viral hepatitis, 60 to 70 percent of chronic hepatitis, and up to 50 percent of cirrhosis, end-stage liver disease, and liver cancer. In America, four million people, or 18 percent of our population, have been diagnosed with antibodies to the disease. This indicates that they currently have an infection or previously were exposed to the virus. There are 10,000 to 12,000 deaths each year because of hepatitis C. Seventy-five percent of people with acute hepatitis C will ultimately develop chronic hepatitis. Millions more of us may be infected but have not been diagnosed.

Many people with hepatitis C are asymptomatic and may not know they have the disease. In those who do have symptoms, they are generally mild and include fatigue, liver discomfort or tenderness, nausea, muscle and joint pains, and a poor appetite.

The course of this disease varies radically. No symptoms might occur for up to twenty years and liver enzymes might not be elevated. If a liver biopsy is performed and the injury is mild, the outcome is usually good. On the other hand, if severe symptoms occur and liver enzymes are elevated, many people will ultimately develop cirrhosis and end-stage liver disease. Or the illness may be characterized by elevated liver enzymes with few symptoms, with an uncertain outcome. It is estimated that 20 percent of those with chronic hepatitis C will develop cirrhosis within ten to twenty years. After that time, a small group will develop liver cancer. Hepatitis C is the most common reason for liver transplants.

Hepatitis C is passed via blood. The hepatitis C virus was only isolated in 1988, so many people were infected by blood transfusion prior to that time. Since 1992, blood has been routinely screened for hepatitis. You can get hepatitis C from having unprotected sex with someone who has it, by sharing needles for drug use or tattooing, or by an accidental needle poke with an infected needle. During childbirth, a mother could pass it to her child. In 10 percent of cases, the source of the infection is unknown.

Standard treatment for hepatitis C is interferon and antiviral medications. Their success rate is only 30 percent and the side effects can be severe. This is why so many people with chronic hepatitis are looking at alternative therapies. Patients on interferon therapy have found St.-John's-wort and ginger to help with side effects of treatment.

Hepatitis D: You can only get hepatitis D if you already have hepatitis B. It exists as a co-infection. You contract it the same way you contract hepatitis B and C.

Hepatitis E: Hepatitis E spreads by consuming contaminated drinking water and food. At this point in time, the only Americans who contract this form of hepatitis get it outside of the country, probably in a developing nation. For best prevention, drink bottled water when traveling, and only use ice made with bottled water. Don't eat raw shellfish, and avoid uncooked fruits and vegetables that are not peeled by you personally.

Autoimmune hepatitis: Autoimmune hepatitis occurs when your body's immune system attacks your own liver cells and is probably due to a genetic defect. About 70 percent of people with this illness are women, and it's usually diagnosed between the ages of fifteen and forty. It is a long-term illness and if left untreated can lead to cirrhosis and eventual liver failure. With treatment, about 70 percent of people with autoimmune hepatitis go into remission or experience a decrease in symptoms. It is usually treated with prednisone and azathioprine, both of which have unwanted side effects. About half also have another autoimmune illness, such as Hashimoto's thyroiditis, Grave's disease, Sjögren's syndrome, ulcerative colitis, or autoimmune anemia. The most common symptoms are fatigue, enlarged liver, jaundice, itching, skin rashes, joint pain, lack of menstrual periods in women, and abdominal discomfort.

Alcoholic hepatitis: Alcoholic hepatitis is a self-inflicted, progressive liver disease caused by the toxicity of alcohol. Unlike hepatitis A, B, C, and D, it is not an infectious disease. It is also known as alcoholic steatohepatitis, acute hepatic insufficiency of patients with chronic alcoholism, florid alcoholic cirrhosis, subacute alcoholic cirrhosis, and fatty liver with hepatic failure.

Alcoholic liver disease affects more than two million people (1 percent of our population) but affects many more who remain completely asymptomatic. It is the fourth leading cause of death in urban adult men age twenty-four to sixty-five. It is estimated that up to 35 percent of heavy drinkers have alcoholic hepatitis. This is often undetected until the disease has progressed. Women and nonwhite males are more susceptible to alcoholic liver damage with smaller amounts of alcoholic consumption. On average, it is estimated that men develop cirrhosis taking in about two ounces daily of ethanol, and women with less than one ounce daily. This is an illness that can kill you. Overall, the one-year survival rate after hospitalization for alcoholic hepatitis is about 40 percent.

Symptoms, when present, can include abdominal pain, fever, jaundice, and liver failure. It can progress to cirrhosis or liver cancer.

The long-term outcome depends on whether the person stops drinking alcohol and whether they have progressed to cirrhosis. If you have this and keep drinking alcohol, you will develop cirrhosis. If you stop drinking, it gradually resolves over a period of weeks to months. People may experience a worsening of liver function during the first weeks of abstinence. Because of alcohol excess, many people with alcoholic hepatitis are malnourished and deficient in antioxidant nutrients. They drink instead of eating. Use of Tylenol while drinking alcoholic beverages is well documented to accelerate liver disease. No one should drink booze and take Tylenol.

N-acetyl cysteine (NAC), catechin (from green tea), and milk thistle (silymarin) have been shown to be helpful in recovery.

Nonalcoholic steatohepatitis (NASH): NASH is another non-infectious type of hepatitis. It also is called pseudoalcoholic hepatitis, diabetic hepatitis, fatty-liver hepatitis, and alcohol-like hepatitis. It causes few problems in most people who have it but can lead to cirrhosis. Children especially may experience vague discomfort located at the liver. It often goes unrecognized but is common in those with elevated liver enzymes who have no other diagnosis. In a recent study of children with NASH, nearly all were very obese.

NASH was first discovered in 1980. Until recently, it was believed to be primarily a disease that affected obese, diabetic women. However, recent studies have shown that healthy, lean men, women, and children can all be affected. Inflammation of the liver, mitochondrial damage, and free radical pathology are apparent in this disease. Liver enzymes are elevated, and there is an increased need for antioxidant nutrients. Iron, on the other hand, is a pro-oxidant. It has been shown that high iron levels accelerate progression of NASH.

Ultimately, NASH is diagnosed with a liver biopsy. It is believed that a rich diet and lack of exercise can cause this illness. It can also be caused by drugs such as amiodarone, perhexiline maleate, glucocorticoids, synthetic estrogens, and tamoxifen. Surgeries, such as jejunal bypass, gastroplasty (stomach stapling), biliopancreatic diversion, or extensive small bowel resectioning can also trigger NASH.

If you are overweight and trying to lose weight, be sure to do so gradually. Quick weight loss can aggravate the disease.

Many people with hepatitis have no obvious symptoms. But when they do, the most common ones are fatigue, mild fever, headache, muscle aches, tiredness, loss of appetite, nausea, vomiting, and diarrhea. As the illness progresses, sufferers become jaundiced, which is evident by the yellow color of the skin and whites of the eyes. They may experience stomach pain and have dark-colored urine with pale-colored bowel movements.

Diagnosis of hepatitis is done with a routine blood test for liver enzymes. Further testing needs to be done to determine which type of hepatitis is present. A liver biopsy may be performed.

It is well documented that people with hepatitis have an increased need for antioxidants. While much more research could be done in this area, taking antioxidants offers a simple and effective way to help protect liver function. It is advisable to take several antioxidant nutrients either in combination or separately. Antioxidants include: vitamin C, E, selenium, N-acetyl cysteine, lipoic acid, S-adenosylmethionine (SAMe), flavonoids, and many herbs have antioxidant properties as well. In foods, they are found in fruits and vegetables, preferably fresh and organically grown.

Bert Berkson, M.D., is one of the leading experts on lipoic acid. He reports that a combination of lipoic acid, selenium, and milk thistle rapidly dropped viral levels and brought three of his patients with hepatitis C back to normal health. Dosages were 300 milligrams of lipoic acid twice daily, 300 milligrams of milk thistle three times daily, and 200 micrograms of selenomethionine once daily. He is currently doing a larger study using these three antioxidants. In a German study from 1976, forty-two patients with hepatitis were given intravenous lipoic acid. The treatment showed promise for many of the patients and, because of the low toxicity and lack of side effects, was recommended for long-term treatment.

Rest, sleep, and healthful eating help with an easy recovery. It's also critically important not to drink any alcohol because alcohol is a direct liver toxin.

If you are planning on traveling outside of North America, check to see if you are going to a country with known hepatitis problems. You may want to get vaccinated against hepatitis A and B before you go.

There are a huge number of nutrients, antioxidants, herbs, flavonoids, and phytonutrients that may be beneficial in helping reduce symptoms and the long-term effects of hepatitis and cirrhosis. I found information on hepatitis and B-complex vitamins, phyllanthus, shiitake mushrooms, astragalus, fenugreek, schizandra, andrographis, phosphatidylcholine, thymus extract, chlorophyll, and many more natural compounds. If you don't find something here that really helps, keep looking. I could have spent weeks researching this one topic.

Functional Laboratory Testing
Routine medical testing is adequate for diagnosis of hepatitis. People who are infected may also want additional information.

Vitamin and mineral status
Antioxidant status
Glutathione levels
Small bowel bacterial overgrowth

Healing Options
Hepatitis is a serious illness. For best results, these healing options are meant to be used in combination. You don't need to use them all, but pick several at least.

Avoid alcoholic beverages. Alcohol is damaging to the liver. Don't drink if you have any type of hepatitis.

Eat lots of fruits and vegetables. They contain antioxidant nutrients, vitamins, and minerals that help support your immune system. Eat at least five servings daily, preferably a lot more. Fresh juicing of organic vegetables is a great way to quickly multiply your nutrients and antioxidants.

Take a multivitamin with minerals. Cover your bases. A good multivitamin will have base amounts of antioxidants, vitamins, and minerals. Look for one with at least 400 IU of vitamin E, 200 micrograms of selenium, and 250 milligrams or more of vitamin C.

Take vitamin C. Studies have shown vitamin C levels to be very low in people with hepatitis. Vitamin C is well known for its antiviral and antioxidant effects. Much research was also done in the 1970s and early 1980s on vitamin C's ability to naturally stimulate interferon production. Interferon is the drug treatment of choice for people with chronic hepatitis (hepatitis C). Interferon is isolated at great expense, is only 30 percent effective, and the side effects make many people decide not to even try it. Linus Pauling theorized that vitamin C could be used to increase natural production of interferon. Other researchers also reported that this was so.

Robert Cathcart, M.D., a long-standing advocate of complementary medicine, uses high doses of intravenous vitamin C for hepatitis. He found that with doses of 40 to 100 grams, he was able to greatly improve symptoms in two to four days and clear jaundice within six days. Other people have found similar effects. As little as 2 grams was able to prevent hepatitis B in hospitalized patients. However, there is little published research specifically on vitamin C and hepatitis.

At a minimum, I recommend taking 2,000 milligrams of vitamin C daily. Preferably, use dosages up to bowel tolerance and recalibrate your dosage every week. Determine your personalized dosage with a vitamin C flush. (See Chapter 8.)

Take zinc. People with hepatitis are commonly zinc deficient. Zinc helps with healing of tissues and is important for prevention of scarring. Take 50 to 75 milligrams daily.

Try whey protein or transfer factor. There are numerous studies on the use of transfer factor in people with hepatitis. They have been very positive. Transfer factor is isolated from cow colostrum, and is loaded with protective antibodies that help us fight infection. A current study also demonstrates that a whey protein product called Immunocal was shown to be effective in patients with hepatitis B, but not hepatitis C. Take 12 to 30 grams of whey protein, daily and 300 milligrams transfer factor, 1 to 2 times daily.

Try N-acetyl cysteine (NAC). Several research studies have found that glutathione levels are inversely related to the viral loads for hepatitis B and C. German researchers found that when NAC was added to hepatitis cultures, viral load decreased fifty fold. Take 1,000 to 2,000 micrograms twice daily.

Try lipoic acid. Lipoic acid, also called thiotic acid, is a strong antioxidant and has been shown to be liver protective in mushroom and chemical poisoning. In studies with chemically induced hepatitis, lipoic acid has been shown to be effective in treatment. Take 200 to 300 milligrams twice daily.

Try S-adenosylmethionine (SAMe). SAMe was given to 220 patients with liver disease. Twenty-six percent of them had hepatitis. There was a reduction of symptoms of itching and fatigue and an improved sense of well-being. Laboratory testing of conjugated bilirubin and alkaline phosphatase showed significant improvement. Patients were given 1,600 milligrams daily.

Take vitamin E. People with hepatitis have lower levels of vitamin E. A 2001 pilot study published in *Antiviral Research* studied people with hepatitis B. Thirty-two patients were given either 300

IU of vitamin E twice daily for three months or no treatment. They were followed for one year. In the vitamin E group, 47 percent (seven patients) had normalized alanine aminotransferase (ALT), a liver enzyme. Only one of the controls normalized ALT. Hepatitis B DNA was normalized in 53 percent of the vitamin E group and in only 18 percent in the control group. A normalization of both ALT and DNA was seen in 47 percent of the vitamin E group and none of the control group. In another study, people with hepatitis B were given 600 IU of vitamin E daily for nine months. All symptoms of hepatitis disappeared in five of the twelve people tested.

In yet another study, looking this time at people with hepatitis C, there was some additional improvement when people were given 544 IU of vitamin E with interferon therapy. And in a different study, people with hepatitis C were given 400 IU of vitamin E twice daily for twelve weeks. There was improvement in eleven out of twenty-three patients, 48 percent. ALT levels were decreased by 45 percent and AST, a liver enzyme, decreased 37 percent after a six-month follow-up. Vitamin E is nontoxic and worth trying in all types of hepatitis. Take 600 to 1,000 IU of vitamin E daily. Look for d-alphatocopherol and mixed tocopherols, rather than dl-alphatocopherol.

Try milk thistle or **Silybum marianum** *(silymarin).* Milk thistle has been used for liver protection for centuries and has few side effects. There is currently an ongoing human study sponsored by the National Center for Complementary and Alternative Medicine (NCCAM) at the NIH. They hope the research will show if silymarin reduces symptoms in people with hepatitis C and/or cirrhosis, whether it prevents the progression of liver disease in people with hepatitis C but who have normal liver enzyme levels, whether it helps clear up the infections, and finally whether it improves people's quality of life. Another study at the NIH is looking at optimal dosages of silymarin. Silymarin has already been shown to be useful in people with cirrhosis caused by alco-

hol abuse. Look for a product that has been standardized for silymarin content. A company that has done that will clearly label it
on the bottle. Take 420 milligrams daily

Try Picrorhiza kurroa. Picrorhiza, an herb commonly used in
Ayurvedic medicine, has been less well studied than milk thistle,
but studies indicate that it is equally effective with nearly identical effects. It has anti-inflammatory and liver protective properties. Indian researchers also used Picrorhiza in acute hepatitis A
and showed it to be helpful in a speedy recovery. Take 400 to 1,500
milligrams in capsules.

Try licorice. Licorice has been shown to reduce elevated liver
enzymes in people with hepatitis. It appears to be the glycyrrhizin
that tempers NF-kappa B and inflammatory cytokines. It also naturally raises the body's interferon levels. In Japan, it is often used
intravenously for hepatitis B and C. Glycyrrhizin can elevate
blood pressure levels, so use with caution.

Try sho-saiko-to. Sho-saiko-to is a Chinese remedy that contains
bupleurum and other traditional Chinese herbs. Several trials were
done in people with hepatitis B infection and one small trial in
people with hepatitis C. Sho-saiko-to helps reduce symptoms and
normalize blood liver enzymes in people with active viral hepatitis. It has also been found to help reduce the incidence of liver
cancer in people with hepatitis. Take 2.5 grams three times daily.
It should not be used in combination with interferon therapy.

Take catechins. Catechins are a type of flavonoids found in green
tea. Study results have been mixed, but favorable results have been
seen in dosages of 500 to 750 milligrams three times daily. A
recent Chinese study on ducklings showed significant reduction
in liver damage and protected liver function. In two recent studies, catechin was found to reduce liver damage and hepatitis that
was chemically induced by halothane, an anesthetic drug used in
surgery. Halothane is known to induce hepatitis in people.
Regarding dosage, I recommend that you drink green tea as often
as you like.

Drink Rooibos tea **(Aspalathus linearis)**. Rooibos tea is also called red tea. It is a relatively new food product and offers a delicious caffeine-free alternative to people who drink tea. Research was done in rats, but I was delighted to see that, at least in this initial report, it showed a regression of liver damage and cirrhosis and a lowering of liver enzymes (ALT and AST). The researchers consider it to be a useful plant for patients with liver disease. Other studies show it to have antioxidant effects. It appears to have the same properties as green tea. I recommend that you drink it as often as you like.

Try quercetin. Another flavonoid with antioxidant effects is quercetin. Although studies need to be done in people, animal research shows that treatment with quercetin dehydrate reduced oxidative damage from hepatitis twofold. Another mouse study found liver protective effects of quercetin when combined with amla. *Bougainvillea spectabilis* has been used in Chinese folk medicine for treatment of hepatitis. The active component of *Bougainvillea* is quercetin. Take 1,000 to 3,000 milligrams of quercetin daily, plus 900 to 2,700 milligrams of amla daily.

Cirrhosis

Cirrhosis is a disease of the liver. Scar tissue replaces normal tissue and blocks the flow of blood and nutrients. It kills about 26,000 Americans each year and is the twelfth leading cause of death. The most common causes of cirrhosis are alcoholism and hepatitis. Some people have diseases that may lead to cirrhosis, which include alpha-1 antitrypsin deficiency, hemochromatosis, Wilson's disease, galactosemia, and glycogen storage diseases. Nonalcoholic steatohepatitis (NASH) is a condition where fat accumulates in the liver and eventually causes scarring. NASH is usually associated with diabetes, protein malnutrition, obesity, heart disease, and treatment with steroid medications. Blocked bile ducts can also cause cirrhosis, called biliary cirrhosis. Because the liver is our body's main filtering system for drugs and toxins, bad reactions to them may also lead to cirrhosis. Overdosing with vitamin A supplements can also cause cirrhosis. Vitamin A toxicity in the liver is accentuated in an alcoholic.

About one-third of people with cirrhosis have no symptoms during the initial stages of the disease. Loss of liver function may be picked up on routine blood testing. As the scarring progresses, liver function begins to fail. People with cirrhosis may experience some of the following symptoms: exhaustion and fatigue, loss of appetite, nausea, light-colored stools, weakness, weight loss, abdominal pain, or spiderlike blood vessels that break out on the skin. Cirrhosis may also lead to water retention, bruising and bleeding, jaundice, itching, gallstones, increased sensitivity to medication and environmental contaminants, increased insulin resistance, diabetes, liver cancer, osteoporosis, impotence, and infection in other organs.

The scarring caused by cirrhosis cannot be reversed. But treatment can help stop or slow the disease progression. The liver is remarkably able to recuperate when we eliminate the factors that hurt it. Many find that with a nutritious diet, rest, and supplements, they can begin to feel healthy again. It is critical that you stop drinking all alcoholic beverages if you are diagnosed with cirrhosis. Alcohol is a direct liver poison. It is known to cause cirrhosis, liver cancer, and liver failure and generates a large need for antioxidant nutrients, such as vitamin E, selenium, vitamin C, and N-acetyl cysteine. Alcoholics are notoriously deficient in B-complex vitamins.

If possible, stop using hazardous chemicals. If you do need to use them, protect your skin, be in a well-ventilated area, and wear a breathing apparatus. If your work involves use of paint, solvents, cleaning products, or other chemicals, it's probably time to look for a different job.

Research indicates that many people with cirrhosis have increased intestinal permeability, which can lead to infection and problems elsewhere in the body. Nutrients such as glutamine, quercetin, and probiotics can help heal a leaky gut.

Methionine, an amino acid, from our food is metabolized in the liver into S-adenosylmethionine (SAMe). People with cirrhosis have problems metabolizing methionine. SAMe increases glutathione levels, an important antioxidant for detoxification. SAMe is an important methyl donor and is used as a supplement for people with elevated homocysteine levels, heart disease, joint diseases, and depression.

Functional Laboratory Testing
Functional liver testing
Intestinal permeability testing
Vitamin and mineral analysis

Healing Options
Avoid alcoholic beverages. Alcohol is damaging to the liver. Don't drink at all if you have hepatitis or cirrhosis. If you are an alcoholic, you might find Alcoholics Anonymous or a residential program to be of benefit. Support helps ease the way.

Eat lots of fruits and vegetables. They contain antioxidant nutrients, vitamins, and minerals that help support your immune system. Eat at least five servings daily, preferably a lot more. Fresh juicing of organic vegetables is a great way to quickly multiply your nutrients and antioxidants.

Take a multivitamin with minerals. Cover your bases. A good multivitamin will have base amounts of antioxidants, vitamins, and minerals. Look for one with at least 400 IU of vitamin E, 200 micrograms of selenium, at least 250 milligrams of vitamin C, and at least 15 milligrams of zinc.

Take an antioxidant supplement. In addition to a good multivitamin with minerals, it would be wise to take additional antioxidants.

These can be found in a combination supplement and may include mixed carotenoids, selenium, vitamin E, vitamin C, N-acetyl cysteine, lipoic acid, and more.

Try lipoic acid. Lipoic acid, also called thiotic acid, is a strong antioxidant and has been shown to be liver protective in mushroom and chemical poisoning. In studies with chemically induced hepatitis, lipoic acid has been shown to be effective in treatment. Take 200 to 300 milligrams twice daily.

Try S-adenosylmethionine (SAMe). SAMe was given to 220 patients with liver disease. Sixty-eight percent had cirrhosis, 6 percent had biliary cirrhosis, and 26 percent had hepatitis. A reduction of symptoms of itching and fatigue were noted along with an improved sense of well-being. Laboratory testing of conjugated bilirubin and alkaline phosphatase showed significant improvement. Patients were given 1,600 milligrams daily.

Try sho-saiko-to. Sho-saiko-to, also called TJ-9, is a Chinese remedy that contains bupleurum and six other herbs. It is being extensively used in Japan for people with hepatitis and cirrhosis and to prevent the development of liver cancer. Take 2.5 grams three times daily. It should not be used in combination with interferon therapy.

Try milk thistle or **Silybum marianum** *(silymarin).* Milk thistle has long been used for all liver disease. It appears to retard progression of cirrhosis primarily through its antioxidant effects. Animal research has been consistent in its results; human research has been less so. Still, there is little or no risk and the possibility of great benefit. Take 420 milligrams daily. Look for a product that has been standardized for silymarin content. A company that has done that will clearly label it on the bottle.

Take zinc. People with cirrhosis often have a zinc deficiency. Take 50 to 75 milligrams daily.

Drink Rooibos tea **(Aspalathus linearis).** Rooibos tea is also called red tea and is a relatively new food product. It offers a delicious caffeine-free alternative for tea drinkers. Research was done in rats, but I was delighted to see that, at least in this initial report, it showed a regression of liver damage and cirrhosis and a lowering of liver enzymes (ALT and AST). The researchers consider it to be a useful plant for patients with liver disease. It contains small amounts of vitamin C, iron, magnesium, phosphorus, sodium, chloride, and potassium. Other studies show it to have antioxidant effects. For dosage, I recommend that you drink as much as you like.

Pancreas

The pancreas has three main functions in the body: to (1) neutralize stomach acid, (2) produce digestive enzymes, and (3) produce insulin to regulate blood sugar levels. When food passes from the stomach to the duodenum, the pancreas secretes bicarbonates. This is essentially baking soda that neutralizes the acidity of chyme so that it won't burn the internal tissues of the intestines. The pancreas also secretes enzymes that digest carbohydrates, protein, and fats. Proteins are broken down by these molecules into single amino acids. When protease enzymes are doing their job, they also protect us from allergic reactions caused by protein particles being absorbed into the bloodstream that trigger an antigenic response. Poor production of pancreatic juice is called pancreatic insufficiency.

The signs of pancreatic insufficiency include gas, indigestion, bloating, discomfort, undigested food in our stools, undigested fat in our stools, and food sensitivities. It is common in people with candidiasis or parasite infections and is an underlying cause of hypoglycemia. Pancreatic insufficiency also increases as we age. People with pancreatitis and cystic fibrosis have pancreatic insufficiency.

Stool testing with the comprehensive digestive stool analysis provides an indirect measure of pancreatic function by measuring chymotrypsin, or pancreatic elastase, and by measuring how well you are able to digest meats and vegetables. The Chymex test is a standard used to measure pancreatic activity. In this test, people swallow a tablet that contains p-aminobenzoic acid (PABA—a B vitamin) and benzyl-L-tyrosine. If you have adequate chymotrypsin function, the PABA will show up in the urine. If not, you have chymotrypsin pancreatic insufficiency.

Causes of pancreatic insufficiency are stress (mental and physical), nutritional deficiencies, poor diet, eating only cooked foods, exposure to radiation or toxins, hereditary weaknesses, drugs, and infections.

Functional Laboratory Testing

Comprehensive digestive stool analysis (CDSA)

Chymex testing for pancreatic function

Food allergies—IgE; food sensitivities—IgG or IgG4

Healing Options

Improve your eating habits. Eat in a relaxed manner. Chew your food thoroughly. Limit beverage intake with meals. Drinking liquids at meals dilutes the gastric juices in the stomach and pancreatic juice in the small intestines.

Take pancreatic enzyme supplements. Clinical experience shows that pancreatic enzymes work well as a digestive aid. Glandular-based supplements, like pancreatic enzyme preparations, are directed to specific tissues, helping to initiate repair. Pancreatic enzymes also help restore the balance of GI flora. In studies done on monkeys, it was shown that pancreatic enzymes were able to kill clostridium, bacteroides, pseudomonaceae, enterobacter, E. coli, and klebsiella. Continued use of pancreatic enzymes can help with repair and maintenance of pancreatic tissue.

Pancreatic tissue from pigs has been widely used over the past fifty years to supply missing pancreatic enzymes. You can purchase products from health-food stores or ask your physician to pre-scribe them. The United States Pharmacopoeia (USP) regulates the strength of pancreatic enzymes. Take 1 to 2 tablets or capsules at the beginning of meals.

Try vegetable enzymes. For people who would rather have a vege-tarian alternative to pancreatic enzymes, vegetable enzymes are a suitable option. These enzymes are derived from a fungus called *Aspergillus oryzae*, which is used to ferment soy sauce, tamari, and miso.

These enzymes work in a much wider range of pH than pan-creatic enzymes, enhancing digestion in the stomach as well as in the intestines. Because they are not broken down by stomach acid, the required dosage is much smaller than that for pancreatic enzymes. Vegetable enzymes are also less likely to cause food allergy reactions. Some companies include probiotic bacteria along with the enzymes for an added effect. Take 1 to 2 capsules at the beginning of meals.

Gallbladder

The gallbladder, a pear-shaped organ that lies just below the liver, holds bile for the liver. The gallbladder's function is to store and concentrate bile that emulsifies fats, cholesterol, and fat-soluble vitamins by breaking them into tiny globules. These create a greater surface area for the fat-splitting enzymes (lipase) to act on for digestion. Between meals, the gallbladder concentrates bile. Gallbladder problems usually indicate poor liver function.

When we eat a meal that contains fat, the liver and gallbladder are stimulated to release bile. Each day, the liver secretes about a quart of bile, which is absorbed into the body from the ileum and colon and returned to the liver to be used again. Drugs and other toxins are eliminated from the liver through bile. The brown color of stool comes from the yellow color of bilirubin in bile. When you eat food containing fat, bile is released from the liver, and concentrated bile is released from the gallbladder. However, people who have had their gallbladders removed don't get this burst of bile. To reproduce this infusion, it is recommended that they take bile salts with fatty meals.

Gallstones

The most common digestive problem associated with the gallbladder is gallstones. One in five Americans over the age of sixty-five has gallstones, and half a million surgeries are performed each year for removal of the gallbladder. Women are two to four times more likely to be affected by gallstones than men. However, most people who have gallstones are never bothered by them, and doctors only treat them if they are causing problems. An inflammation of the gallbladder can lead to pain and discomfort. Symptoms can take the form of abdominal discomfort, bloating, belching, or food intolerances. When you have more than one stone, you may experience a sharp pain or a spasm under the ribs on the right side. Occasionally, the pain will be felt under your right shoulder blade. These pains are often strongest after eating a high-fat meal.

Diet plays an important role in prevention of gallbladder disease. Low-fat, low-meat, and vegetarian diets are recommended, as is a low-sugar, high-fiber intake. In fact, a recent study of over 1,100 people found that none of the 48 vegetarians in the group had any gallstones at all. There was an increase in gallstones in people who were heavy coffee drinkers. Dennis Burkitt, a British physician who lived and worked in Africa for twenty years, found that he performed only two surgeries for gallbladder removal among Africans eating an indigenous diet.

If you are overweight, losing weight will reduce your risk of developing gallstones. Be careful, because several studies have shown that fasting and extremely low-fat, low-calorie diets increase your risk of developing gallstones. Fasting for more than fourteen hours raises the risk of problems due to gallstones. So easy does it while dieting. And always eat breakfast.

Exercise is also important for the prevention of gallstones. It has been postulated that thirty minutes of exercise, five times each week, could reduce the risk of gallstones by 34 percent. In a 1998 study, men who watched fewer than six hours of television per week had a gallstone rate lower than that of men who watched more than forty hours. The researchers concluded that 34 percent of the cases of symptomatic gallstone disease in men could be prevented by increasing exercise to thirty minutes of an endurance-type training, five times per week.

Medical treatment for gallstones consists of an injection of a drug that dissolves the gallstones, oral medication to dissolve stones, lithotripsy that breaks stones with sound waves, or surgical removal of the gallbladder.

Physicians familiar with natural therapies have favorable results treating gallstones without use of drugs or surgery by having their patients detoxify the liver and strengthen liver function. Metabolic cleansing or other detoxification programs are a critical first step in treatment. Food sensitivities also play an important role in the development of gallstones—most patients with gallbladder disease have them and they must be identified.

Functional Laboratory Testing
   Liver function profile
   Home test for bowel transit time
   IgG or IgG4 testing for food sensitivities and IgE testing for
      food allergies
   Heidelberg capsule test for levels of hydrochloric acid
      production
   Acid-alkaline home testing

Healing Options

Make dietary changes. Low-fat diets help prevent gallstones and also reduce pain and inflammation associated with gallstones. Saturated fats found in dairy products, meats, coconut oil, palm oil, hydrogenated oils, and vegetable shortening stimulate concentration of bile. While a low-fat diet is optimal, essential fatty acids are vital to gallbladder function and overall health. Make sure you get 1 to 2 tablespoons of uncooked expeller-pressed oils or extra-virgin olive oil each day—the easiest way is in homemade salad dressing. Also, vegetarian diets have been found to be helpful in reducing the incidence of gallbladder disease.

Several studies have indicated that people who consume a lot of sweets are more likely to develop gallstones. And remember to eat breakfast. Fasting for more than fourteen hours raises your risk of problems due to gallstones.

Decrease coffee intake and increase water consumption. Coffee may trigger gallbladder attacks in susceptible people. Use of either regular or decaffeinated coffee raises levels of cholecystokinin, a hormone that stimulates the release of bile from the gallbladder and digestive enzymes from the pancreas, and causes gallbladder contractions. Stop drinking coffee and see what effect this produces. Some people get horrible headaches or flulike symptoms when they withdraw from caffeine. If you do, wean yourself gradually. And don't forget to drink six to eight glasses of water every day.

Reduce bowel transit time. People with gallstones have significantly slower transit times than healthy people. Eat more high-fiber foods and drink more fluids.

Investigate food sensitivities. In 1968, James Breneman, a pioneer in the area of food allergies, found that food sensitivities play a role in gallbladder disease. He put sixty-nine patients on an elimination diet consisting of beef, rye, soy, rice, cherry, peach, apricot, beet, and spinach. After three to five days, all people were free of symptoms. With a slow reintroduction of foods they were sensitive to, symptoms returned. The most common food offenders were eggs (3 percent), pork (64 percent), and onions (52 percent). Interestingly, beef and soy are often trigger foods for food sensitivity reactions.

Rule out deficient levels of hydrochloric acid (HCl). A study published in *The Lancet* found that about half of the people with gallstones had insufficient levels of hydrochloric acid (HCl). A Heidelberg capsule test can determine if you have sufficient levels of hydrochloric acid. You can also take HCl supplements with meals. Begin with 1 500-milligram capsule of HCl with 150 milligrams of pepsin. If you don't need the HCl, you'll experience a burning or warm sensation. If this is uncomfortable, you can drink some milk or a teaspoon of baking soda in water to neutralize the acid. Many people with low-acid secretion need several HCl tablets per meal; increase the dosage slowly to find the correct one for you. Too much will cause a warmth or burning sensation.

Try milk thistle or **Silybum marianum** *(silymarin).* Extracts of the herb milk thistle have been used historically since the fifteenth century for ailments of the liver and gallbladder. It helps normalize liver function, detoxify the liver, which it does gently and thoroughly, and improves the solubility of bile. Silymarin promotes the flow of bile and helps tone the spleen, gallbladder, and liver. Take 3 to 6 175-milligram capsules daily of standardized 80 percent milk thistle extract with water before meals.

Try lipotrophic supplements. Lipotrophic supplements contain substances that help normalize liver and gallbladder functions. They may contain dandelion root, milk thistle, lecithin or phosphatidylcholine, methionine, choline, inositol, vitamin C, black radish, beet greens, artichoke leaves (*Cynara scolymus*), turmeric, boldo (*Peumus boldo*), fringe tree (*Chionanthus virginicus*), greater celandine, and ox bile. Lipotrophics may also contain magnesium and B-complex vitamins (B_6, B_{12}, and folate) to enhance their function. Use as directed on the label. Use 1,000 milligrams each of methionine and choline daily.

Try lecithin. Phosphatidylcholine, the most biologically active form of lecithin, and lecithin have been shown to make cholesterol more soluble, which reduces formation of gallstones. Studies have shown that as little as 100 milligrams of lecithin three times daily will increase lecithin concentration in bile. I recommend 500 milligrams daily.

Take vitamin C. Vitamin C has been shown to prevent formation of gallstones. Vitamin C is required for the enzymatic conversion of cholesterol to bile salts. People with high risk for developing gallstones have low ascorbic acid levels. Take 1 to 3 grams daily.

Do a liver or gallbladder flush. Anecdotal stories about people showing up at their doctor's office with a jar full of stones after a gallbladder flush are abundant, but there is little documentation to validate whether what they passed are really gallstones or just congealed olive oil. Nonetheless, many people testify to the benefits of the gallbladder flush. Do this procedure at home only under the supervision of a physician.

From Monday through Saturday, drink as much natural apple juice as possible. Continue to eat normally and take your usual medications or supplements. On Saturday, eat a normal lunch at noon. Three hours later (3:00 P.M.) dissolve 1 tablespoon of Epsom salts (magnesium sulphate) in ¼ cup of warm water and drink it. This is a laxative and helps peristalsis move the stones through your digestive system. It doesn't taste great, so you may want to follow it with some orange or grapefruit juice. Two hours later (5:00 P.M.) repeat the Epsom salts and orange or grapefruit juice. For dinner, eat citrus fruits or drink citrus juices. At bedtime, drink 1½ cups of warm extra virgin olive oil blended with 1½ cups of lemon juice. Go to bed immediately and lie on your right side with your knees pulled up close to your chest for half an hour. On Sunday morning, take 1 tablespoon of Epsom salts in ¼ cup of warm water an hour before breakfast. If you have gallstones, you will find dark green to light green stones in your bowel movement on Sunday morning. They are irregular in shape and size, varying from small, like kiwi seeds, to large, like cherry pits. If you have chronic gallbladder problems, you may want to repeat this again in two weeks. The flush can be repeated every three to six months if you continue to form stones.

Try black radish. Black radish, *Raphanus sativus niger*, has long been used as a folk remedy to stimulate bile production and aid in the digestion of fats. Radishes of all types seem to be of benefit. A recent rat study showed that the inflammation and other abnormal parameters that were observed in rats fed a fat-rich diet were reversed with treatment with black radish. Radishes are also high in bioflavonoids and other immune protective substances. You can eat radishes for the same benefit. Daikon radish, an Asian variety, is a mild tasting radish for those of us who aren't radish lovers. Or, you can take black radish in capsule or tablet form.

Try bile salts. These are useful for people who have already had their gallbladders removed. Take 1 to 2 with fatty meals.

Small Intestine

Gas and bloating are the most common symptoms of small intestinal problems. Other problems that occur in the small intestines are parasites, celiac disease, food sensitivities, and increased intestinal permeability (leaky gut). When you are having digestive discomfort, it is important to rule out candidiasis, food sensitivities, pancreatic insufficiency, parasites, and small bowel bacterial overgrowth, which may be underlying causes. Use of digestive supplements and beneficial flora can also be helpful.

Flatulence or Intestinal Gas

Everyone has gas. It's normal. In fact, we "pass gas" an average of ten to fifteen times a day. Most of our gas comes from swallowed air. Chewing gum, drinking carbonated drinks, and eating whipped foods such as egg whites and whipped cream all contribute to swallowed air. The gas we pass is mainly nitrogen (up to 90 percent), carbon dioxide, and oxygen, which are odorless. Gas and bloating are also a product of the fermentation of small pieces of undigested foods by the bacteria in our intestines. Fermentation produces stinky gases like methane and hydrogen sulfide, which has the odor of rotten eggs. Other substances, like butyric acid, cadaverine, and putrescine are present in tiny amounts, but they are noted for the mighty fragrance they give to gas.

Some of us experience excessive amounts of gas, which can be not only embarrassing but also an uncomfortable sign that something is out of balance. Millions of people have bloating and discomfort associated with gas. If you've ever made wine, you'll recall putting a balloon on the top during the fermentation process that allowed for expansion of the gasses produced. Our bellies act like a balloon, expanding to contain the gas produced by fermentation.

Foods from the cabbage family, dried and sulfured fruits, and beans all contain sulfur that gives gas a rotten-egg odor, but sulfur also has critical use throughout our bodies. Cucumbers, celery, apples, carrots, onions, and garlic are all commonly known to cause gas. People with lactose intolerance often experience gas when they eat dairy products. Eating a high-fiber diet is healthful, but can cause gas until your intestinal flora adjust. You may have insufficient levels of hydrochloric acid, intestinal flora, pancreatic enzymes, or a dysbiosis that is causing your problems. Food sensitivities, especially to wheat and grains, can also cause excessive gas.

Functional Laboratory Testing

Small bowel bacterial overgrowth test

Comprehensive digestive stool analysis with parasitology

IgE and IgG allergy testing

Lactose breath test

Self-test for lactose intolerance by eliminating all dairy from
your diet

Healing Options

Chew your food well and eat slowly. These simple activities can
have far-reaching effects on healthy digestive processes and gas
reduction.

Increase fiber gradually. Most of us need to dramatically increase the
amount of dietary fiber we eat, but raising these levels too quickly
can cause a lot of gas and discomfort. Our flora go wild with sudden increases in dietary fiber, and the fermentation causes gas.
Increasing your fiber intake more slowly will solve this problem.
High-fiber foods include whole grains, beans, and many fruits and
vegetables.

Consider possible lactose intolerance. The inability to digest lactose,
the sugar in milk, is a frequent cause of gas. Eliminate all dairy
products for at least two weeks and see if there is improvement.
Make sure to eliminate all hidden dairy products found in foods.
These are listed in the section on lactose intolerance in Chapter 6.
Products such as Lactaid and Digestive Advantage LI really help
for the times you do eat dairy products.

Supplement with acidophilus and bifidobacteria. Use of a supplement
probiotic bacteria can make a tremendous difference in your ability to digest foods. Beneficial flora can help reestablish the normal
microbial balance in your intestinal tract. Take 1 to 2 capsules or
¼ to 1½ teaspoons powder two to three times daily on an empty
stomach. Mix powdered supplement with a cool or cold beverage;
hot drinks kill the flora.

Try digestive enzyme supplementation. Many people find that supplementation with digestive enzymes at meals, either vegetable,

bromelain, papaya, or pancreatic enzymes, really help prevent gas. Take 1 to 2 digestive enzymes with meals.

De-gas your beans. Beans are an excellent source of vegetarian protein, containing both soluble and insoluble fibers, and sitosterols that help normalize cholesterol levels. However, beans are notorious for their gas-producing effects. They contain substances that are difficult for us to digest. For instance, beans, grains, and seeds hold their nutrients with phytic acid. Soaking or sprouting releases the nutrients so that we can absorb more of them. First, soak the beans for four to twelve hours, then drain off the water, replace with new water, and simmer for several hours until they are soft. Some people find that putting a pinch or two of baking soda in the water helps reduce gas. Others add kombu, a Japanese sea vegetable, or ginger. Beano is an enzyme product that contains the enzymes necessary for digestion of beans. Place a drop or two on your food; it helps reduce flatulence for most people. Beano is sold widely in drugstores and health-food stores.

We produce digestive enzymes for foods we commonly eat. If you eat beans rarely, start by eating a tablespoon or two of beans each day. Your body may begin to produce the enzymes necessary for their digestion.

Explore food sensitivities. Although lactose intolerance is the most common food sensitivity, people can be sensitive to nearly any other food. The most likely culprits are sugars and grains. Careful charting of your foods and flatulence levels can help you detect which foods are giving you the most trouble.

Food sensitivities don't usually exist by themselves. If you have a number of food sensitivities, check for candida infection and dysbiosis.

Check for fermentation dysbiosis. An imbalance of intestinal flora often causes excessive gas. Candida fungi cause fermentation of sugars, fruits, and starches that we feel as gas and bloating. A comprehensive digestive and stool analysis, or small bowel bacterial overgrowth test, can determine whether or not you have a candida infection or other dysbiotic imbalance.

Avoid sorbitol and xylitol. Sorbitol and xylitol are indigestible sugars found in most sugarless candy and gum. They are used by diabetics and dieters because these sugars are sweet but don't affect blood sugar levels. Large amounts of sorbitol and xylitol cause gas, but even small amounts can cause a problem for those who are sensitive.

Check for parasites. Parasites often cause gas and bloating. If you have explored more obvious causes, you may want to have a stool test for parasites.

Take chlorophyll. Chlorophyll liquid or tablets can help prevent gas. Take 1 tablet two to three times daily with meals.

Use ginger, fennel, and anise. Most of us have at least one of these spices in our kitchen, and they are valuable tools for reducing gas. Put a few slices of fresh ginger or ½ teaspoon of dried ginger in a cup of boiling water and steep until cool enough to drink. It will soon begin to dispel your gas from both ends, and you'll be much more comfortable. Fennel and anise can be used in tea or you can simply chew on the seeds to relieve gas. In Indian restaurants, you find small bowls of these seeds. They also cleanse the palate with their sweet pungency.

Use herbs and drink herbal teas. Traditionally herbs and spices were added to foods to aid digestion. Nearly all our common kitchen herbs and spices have a beneficial effect, including basil, oregano, marjoram, parsley, thyme, celery seed, peppermint, spearmint, fennel, bayberries, caraway seed, cardamom seed, catnip, cloves, coriander, lemon balm, and sarsaparilla. You can find many digestive herbal tea blends in health-food stores.

Try activated charcoal tablets. Charcoal absorbs toxins and gases and can be found in nearly any pharmacy or health-food store. Your stools will turn black—that's the charcoal leaving your body. It has been rated "safe and effective" by the FDA for acute poisoning. It's inexpensive and very helpful. Take 1 to 4 tablets as needed, with a meal or immediately if you are having gas problems.

Parasites

Some symptoms of parasites appear to be like any other digestive problem. Chronic diarrhea is often a sign of a parasitic infection. Other symptoms include pain, constipation, bloating, gas, unexplained weight loss, fatigue, unexplained fever, coughing, itching, rashes, bloody stools, abdominal cramping, joint and muscle aches, irritable bowel syndrome, anemia, allergy, granulomas, nervousness, teeth grinding, chronic fatigue, poor immune response, and sleep disturbances. These symptoms can come and go due to the life cycles of the specific parasite involved. (See "Parasite Questionnaire" in Chapter 6.)

If your anus itches at night, you may have pinworms. They are most commonly found in children and parents of small children. It's fairly simple to determine whether or not you have them. When you feel the itching, put a piece of cellophane tape on your anus, and examine the tape for small white wiggly worms that look like white pieces of thread that move. Or, you can simply put your finger into your anus and see if you pull out any worms. With children, use tape or just look.

Recently, references in the scientific literature suggest that parasites may be the primary cause of allergies. Parasites cause damage to the lining of the digestive tract, which allows large molecules to enter the bloodstream. This provokes an antigenic response. This theory is revolutionary and additional research needs to be done to determine just how large a role parasites play in allergies of all types.

Parasite Testing

Many physicians request parasitology testing on random stool samples, but this type of testing is not very accurate. Even with repeated samples, accurate results are found only 85 to 90 percent of the time. Many parasites, like giardia, live farther up the digestive tract so that many labs now give an oral laxative to induce diarrhea when testing for parasites. This type of sample is called a stool purge. Stool purge tests and rectal swabs used with random stool samples give a much more accurate picture of colon health than single or multiple random stool samples. Many labs collect a random stool sample and a purge stool sample or two. The most accurate stool testing is usually done by labs that specialize in parasitology testing. Because of the high volume of samples, high-tech microscopes, and slow pace, their staffs have become experts in detection and recognition of parasites.

Healing Options

Prescription medication may be the most efficient treatment for most parasite infections. Within a week or two you are parasite-free. However, these medications can be hard on the liver and disruptive to the intestinal flora. After using them, it's wise to take probiotics to replace and rebalance the intestinal flora.

Natural options work more slowly—about a month—but are highly effective. They generally contain garlic, wormwood (artemisia), goldenseal, black walnut, and/or grapefruit seed extract. You can find many of these in combination products. Probiotic supplements should be used after therapy is finished.

Take garlic. Historically, garlic has been used for pinworms; it has antiviral, antibacterial, and antifungal properties. Allicin, the active component in garlic, has been shown to be effective against *Entamoeba histolytica* and *Giardia lamblia*. *Entamoeba histolytica* is an amoeba that has been used to evaluate the value of entamoeba drugs.

Try goldenseal. Historically, goldenseal has been used to balance infections of mucous membranes throughout the body. It is also effective with candida infections. Berberine sulfate, an active ingredient in goldenseal, has been shown to be effective against amoebas and giardia parasites.

Try artemisia (wormwood). Wormwood has been used for centuries in China and Europe for worms and parasites. It contains sesquiterpene lactone, which works like peroxide. It is believed to affect the parasite membranes, weakening them so our natural defense system kicks in. Artemisia also contains an ingredient that is effective against malaria even when it is resistant to quinine drugs. Tea of wormwood has been successfully used for pinworms and roundworms by Dr. Christopher, one of America's foremost herbalists. It's important to note that artemisia is safe when used in a tea or capsule, but pure wormwood oil is *poisonous*. Take ¼ to 1½ teaspoons powdered wormwood once or twice daily or make a tea using 2 teaspoons of fresh leaves or tops in 1 cup water. Drink ½ cup a day, 1 teaspoon at a time.

Try black walnut. The juice of unripe, green hulls of black walnuts has been traditionally used for treatment of parasites and fungal infections. Black walnut is a folk remedy for ringworm, athlete's foot, and healing cracks in the palms and feet.

*Try **Dichroa febrifuga** (saxifragaceae).* Dichroa is a Chinese herb called *changshan*, which is effective against malaria, amoebas, and giardia.

Use Jerusalem oak. A folk medicine used throughout the Americas, the Jerusalem oak (also called American wormseed or chenopod) expels roundworms, hookworms, and tapeworms, and is especially useful for children. More scientific studies need to be done to confirm the historical usage of this herb.

Eat pumpkin seeds. Pumpkin seeds have also been used historically as a folk medicine for tapeworms and roundworms. To be really effective, enormous amounts must be eaten: seven to fourteen ounces for children and up to twenty-five ounces for adults. Mash them and mix with juice. Two or three hours afterward, take castor oil to clear your bowels.

Celiac Disease, Sprue, or Gluten Intolerance

Celiac disease, also called celiac sprue, nontropical sprue, or gluten sensitive enteropathy, is caused by an inability to properly digest foods containing the gliadin fraction of gluten, which causes damage to the lining of the small intestine. People with celiac disease do not absorb nutrients well, and they are likely to become malnourished. Gluten is found in many grains including wheat, rye, barley, millet, and probably spelt. Most people with celiac disease can eat oats if they are in remission. Some people experience some gas when they first introduce oats, but their stool formation is better and they feel better. In a recent study of nineteen people with celiac disease, all but one improved when about two ounces (one-half cup dry) of oats were added to their daily diet. In a further study, several others with celiac were found to worsen with the addition of oats to their diet. So, once again, biochemical individuality plays an important role. With the addition of oats, most celiac sufferers feel better, have better nutritional status, are more satisfied with their diet, and have higher overall fiber and higher nutrient intake. Children with celiac disease often do poorly with oats, but then are able to eat them normally as adults.

Celiac disease is chronic and is genetic. In 90 to 95 percent of cases, it is associated with the HLA-DQ2 gene, and in 5 to 10 percent of cases with the HLA-DQ8 gene. It may affect several family members and occurs about twice as often in women as in men and mainly affects people of northwestern European ancestry. It rarely occurs among people of African, Jewish, Mediterranean, or Asian descent. A person who was breast-fed will find a delay in development of the disease, and research shows that the longer the baby was breast-fed, the greater the benefit.

While celiac disease was previously thought to be rare, new studies indicate that many people without obvious symptoms have subclinical celiac disease. According to analysis of IgG and IgA blood testing, an estimated 1 person in 250 to 300 may have celiac disease. Celiac disease often goes undiagnosed and can be mistaken for irritable bowel syndrome or other problems because many physicians are unfamiliar with the disease.

About 20 to 30 percent of those with celiac have classic symptoms of the disease. The rest may have other symptoms or be asymptomatic. Elimination of wheat, rye, barley, spelt, and possibly oats from the diet can eliminate many diverse symptoms. Symptoms are characterized by recurring attacks of diarrhea or constipation, abdominal cramping, bloating, gas, weakness, anemia, and steatorrhea (gray or tan fatty stools). Less typical symptoms are weight loss, arthritis, irritability, depression, fatigue, brain fog, bone pain, schizophrenia, fibromyalgia, bone pain, muscle cramps, tingling numbness in the legs, mouth sores, a skin rash (dermatitis herpetiformis), tooth discoloration, missed menstrual periods and miscarriage, neurological symptoms, and epilepsy. In children, the most common symptom is irritability. Infants may have failure to thrive.

Celiac disease is usually recognized early in childhood but may disappear in adolescence and reappear later in adulthood. Anemia is common in those with celiac disease. A recent pediatric study showed that half of the children tested were anemic, and a small percentage of children with anemia really had undiagnosed celiac disease.

Untreated celiac disease can lead to long-term complications that include lymphoma and adenocarcinoma, osteoporosis, miscarriage, and congenital birth defects such as neural tube defect, being shorter than you would have been otherwise, and seizure disorders. Other long-term consequences of celiac disease can be diminished calcium reserves and poor fat-soluble vitamin status, including vitamins A, D, E, and K.

About half of all people with celiac disease are also lactose intolerant at the time of their diagnosis. Lactase, the enzyme required to split lactose, is manufactured at the tips of the villi. Because these villi are damaged in people with untreated celiac disease, their bodies can't manufacture the lactase. Once people have gone onto a gluten-free diet and the intestinal lining is repaired, some will be able to tolerate dairy products. Remember that about 20 percent of Americans are lactose intolerant, so many people with controlled celiac disease will still be affected by dairy products.

Traditionally, diagnosis of celiac disease was made by excluding other possibilities and then performing an intestinal biopsy. New tests, such as the anti-endomysial antibodies, anti-gliadin antibodies, and the tissue transglutaminase antibodies tests more easily diagnose celiac disease. The anti-endomysial antibodies test appears to be the most accurate. It would be best to do at least two of these tests to have confirmation, because none of them is 100 percent conclusive.

A rectal gluten challenge test is available that determines gluten sensitivity. It appears that there are several types of gluten sensitivity: celiac disease, tropical sprue (caused by an infection or toxin and treated with antibiotics), and gluten sensitivity (caused by leaky gut syndrome). While symptoms may be similar for these problems, the treatments vary considerably. People with celiac disease must avoid gluten-containing foods for life. People with tropical sprue are generally treated with antibiotics and over time are able to use gluten-containing grains without further problems. People with wheat and/or gluten sensitivity often find that after avoidance of those foods for four to six months and a nutritional program that supports healing and friendly flora, they can then begin eating grain products without further problems.

People with celiac disease tend to have other autoimmune diseases as well, including:

- Dermatitis herpetiformis
- Thyroid disease
- Systemic lupus erythematosus
- Type 1 diabetes
- Liver disease
- Collagen vascular disease
- Rheumatoid arthritis
- Sjögren's syndrome

Fortunately, there is a cure: avoid grains that contain gluten. This stops the irritation to the gut and allows it to heal. Many people find quick relief in three to four days, although complete healing of the intestines will take longer. Nutritional therapies may help you heal faster. If you don't feel better in four to six weeks, you need to investigate other possibilities. Because of the malnourishment that celiac can cause, supplementation of nutrients is often necessary.

It's not easy to completely change your diet to avoid all gluten-containing foods. Americans depend on a wheat-based diet and many other foods that have gluten-containing grains. In addition to obvious sources of gluten, many products have hidden sources. Salad dressings, some hot dogs, ice cream, bouillon cubes, chocolate, and foods containing hydrolyzed vegetable protein may contain gluten. Fortunately, because of the many people who are intolerant of gluten, more gluten-free products are being introduced into the marketplace. Excellent breads, pastas, crackers, pancake mixes, cereals, and cookies are now available. A new home test kit may soon be on the market that can help you determine which foods contain gluten.

Functional Laboratory Testing
Anti-endomysial, anti-gliadin, and tissue transglutaminase antibodies testing. This is a specific way to screen for celiac disease. Anti-

endomysial antibodies are the most specific. If one of these tests is negative, do one of the others to make sure.

Food allergy/sensitivity screening. Test for wheat, oats, rye, barley, gluten, and gliadin; IgE and IgG antibody testing are all required. Gluten antibodies are positive in people with celiac disease and gluten intolerance. IgA levels are also higher in people with celiac disease, but a negative test does not always rule it out. Additional food sensitivities are likely.

Intestinal permeability screening. Test for leaky gut syndrome or intestinal hyperpermeability.

Iron status or nutrient status. Celiac disease causes malabsorption of nutrients. Many people with celiac disease have iron deficiency anemia; low vitamin A, D, E, and K; poor fat absorption; and other mineral deficiencies. Several labs have tests that help determine which nutrients need supplementation.

Comprehensive digestive stool analysis with parasitology. This test can be used to determine if there is an unidentified underlying cause of the celiac disease.

Rule out lactose intolerance. The lactose breath test determines lactose intolerance. Elimination of dairy products from your diet also helps determine if dairy products are contributing to your problem.

Healing Options

Make dietary changes. Avoid all gluten-containing grains and products that contain them, even in small amounts. Gluten-containing grains include wheat, rye, barley, millet, and spelt. It is essential to read all labels carefully and become an expert at reading between the lines. Switch to rice, quinoa, wild rice, and oats.

Try digestive enzymes. Either pancreatic or vegetable enzymes can be used to enhance digestive function. Take 1 to 2 with each meal. Specific amylase enzymes can be of particular benefit.

Foods That May Contain Hidden Gliadin

Texturized vegetable protein: It may contain wheat along with soy or corn.

Barley malt

Starch (when listed in the ingredient list): If it doesn't say "cornstarch," it may contain gluten.

Desserts: Ice cream cones, ice cream that contains gluten stabilizers, most cakes, cookies, and muffins.

Meats: Luncheon meats, hot dogs, and sausages may contain grains. Self-basting turkeys contain hydrolyzed vegetable protein that may contain gluten.

Cheese and dairy: Some processed cheeses contain wheat flour and/or oat gum.

Pasta: Most pasta is wheat. Semolina is a type of wheat that contains a high level of gluten. You can find gluten-free pasta at gourmet and health-food stores.

Miscellaneous (some brands contain gliadin): Curry powder, most white pepper, dry seasoning mixes, gravy mixes and extracts, meat condiments, catsup, chewing gum, pie fillings, baked beans, baking powders, salad dressings, sandwich spreads, muesli, cereals, instant coffee, breadcrumbs, vanilla and flavorings made with alcohol, and most dips.

Supplement with acidophilus and bifidobacteria. Probiotic flora enhance digestive function.

Try gut-healing nutrients. Glutamine, gamma oryzanol, and
N-acetyl-D-glucosamine are all healing to the intestinal lining.
While no specific testing has been done on therapeutic use of
these nutrients in people with celiac disease, clinical experience
with celiac and other diarrheal illnesses indicates their usefulness.
Take a multivitamin with minerals. Zinc; selenium; folic acid; iron;
and vitamins A, B₆, D, E, and K have all been shown to be deficient in people with celiac disease. Get a good quality multivitamin with minerals. Look for a supplement that is hypoallergenic
and contains no grains or dairy.

Colon or Large Intestine

Common problems in the large intestine, also called the colon,
include constipation, diarrhea, diverticular disease, irritable bowel
syndrome, inflammatory bowel disease, ulcerative colitis, Crohn's
disease, hemorrhoids, polyps, and colon cancer. Proper functioning of the colon requires a high-fiber diet. The colon is home to
trillions of beneficial bifidobacteria and other flora that ferment
dietary fiber that, in turn, produce short-chained fatty acids,
butyric acid, valerate acid, propionic acid, and acetic acid. These
short-chained fatty acids are the primary fuel of the colonic cells.
Without adequate fiber, we starve the colonic cells and weaken the
integrity of the colon. Butyric acid has been shown to stop the
growth of colon cancer cells in vitro and is used clinically to heal
inflamed bowel tissue.

The colon's main function is the reabsorption of nutrients and
water into our bodies and the elimination of toxic wastes. Adequate intake of liquids is essential for good colon health. Water,
juices, herbal teas, and fresh fruits contain liquids that are hydrat-
ing to the stool. Alcohol and soft drinks are more diuretic, which
increases our need for healthful fluids.

Constipation

Constipation affects four million Americans each year. Physicians write more than a million prescriptions for constipation annually, and we spend $725 million a year on laxatives. Constipation is a big problem. People are constipated when they strain to have a bowel movement, have hard stools, infrequent or incomplete bowel movements, discomfort, or a perception that bowel habits are different from usual. Some people feel fatigue, aches, and mental sluggishness from constipation; others get headachy. Constipation affects women twice as often as men and is more common in people over age sixty-five. Although aging is commonly listed as a cause of constipation, it is due more to the results of lifestyle. Elderly people often eat low-fiber foods, rely on packaged and prepared foods, take medications that interfere with normal bowel function, and have decreased mobility. Each of these factors by itself increases the risk of chronic constipation and is not necessarily a progression of aging.

Many other factors can be the underlying cause of constipation. Hormones play a role. Women often notice that their bowel habits change at various times in their menstrual cycles. Pregnancy is a common, but temporary, cause of constipation. Constipation can also be caused by an underactive thyroid. Some diseases can affect the body's ability to have bowel movements. Parkinson's disease, scleroderma, lupus, strokes, diabetes, kidney disease, low or high thyroid function, and certain neurological or muscular diseases, such as multiple sclerosis or spinal cord injuries, can cause constipation. Colon cancer can also cause it. Neurological problems, such as injuries to the spinal column, tumors that sit on nerves, nerve disorders of the bowel, and certain brain disorders are other causes.

Bowel movements should be painless. If you experience pain, see your physician. You may have a structural abnormality, fissure, hemorrhoid, or more serious problem. Pain during bowel movements can cause a muscle spasm in the sphincter, which can delay a stool. Magnesium helps relieve and prevent muscle spasms.

Bowel transit time is a newer parameter of constipation that is widely used in preventive health care. Bowel transit time is the amount of time it takes for food to go from the mouth, through the digestive system, and out in stool. Reports from the National Institutes of Health suggest that a "normal" range of bowel movements is from three to twenty-one each week. While this may show what is "average," it is not a good indicator of what is "normal."

It is normal to have one to three soft bowel movements each day. Optimal bowel transit time is twelve to twenty-four hours, so if you are only having three bowel movements each week, you have a transit time of fifty-six hours, which is way too long. Slow bowel transit times raise the risk of colon diseases and contribute to other health problems due to the reabsorption of toxins back into the body. A recent study showed an increased risk of colon cancer in people who are chronically constipated. This makes sense in light of current theories about fecal transit time. If you haven't done the transit time self-test, now would be a good time. (See section on bowel transit time in Chapter 2.)

Dennis Burkitt, M.D., studied bowel habits of Africans living in small towns and large cities. He found that people who ate indigenous, local foods had an average of a pound of feces each day, with twelve-hour transit times. Burkitt found that those who lived in cities on Western diets only excreted five-and-a-half ounces of stool each day, with average transit times of forty-eight to seventy-two hours. People on native diets had extremely low incidences of diseases common to Western civilization, such as appendicitis, diabetes, diverticulitis, gallstones, coronary heart disease, hiatal hernia, varicose veins, hemorrhoids, colon cancer, and obesity. When these people moved into cities and ate a Westernized diet, they too developed these diseases. Dr. Burkitt attributed much of this disease to poor dietary fiber intake in a modernized diet.

For most people, a diet high in fiber and fluids solves the problem. Be sure to drink six to eight glasses of water, juices, or herbal teas and eat at least five servings of fruits and vegetables each day. Brussels sprouts, asparagus, cabbage, cauliflower, corn, peas, kale, parsnips, and potatoes contain high amounts of fiber. Make whole grains the rule and processed grains the exception. The addition of high-fiber cereals at breakfast can make a big difference. Legumes, like kidney, navy, pinto, and lima beans, have a large amount of dietary fiber.

Make these dietary changes slowly. A quick change to a high-fiber diet can cause gas and bloating. As your body gets used to this new way of eating, it will adapt. Remember that the requirements for most of us are to double our daily fiber intake. Cut back on low-fiber foods, including meats, dairy products, pastries, candy, soft drinks, and white bread.

Exercise helps relieve constipation by massaging the intestines. Many of my clients have found that regular exercise keeps their bowels regular.

Overuse of laxatives is common and compounds the problem. Chronic use of laxatives, even herbal laxatives, causes the bowels to become lazy, and the muscles become dependent on laxatives to constrict. People often find they need more and more laxatives to have the same effect. Some laxatives can cause damage to the nerve cells in the wall of the colon. If you have used laxatives, you need to retrain your body to have bowel movements on its own. Try sitting on the toilet each morning for twenty minutes and relax. Over time your body will remember how to relax and function normally.

A recent study compared the use of psyllium seeds, a fiber supplement, with the use of docusate sodium, a common stool softener. The psyllium was more effective at relieving constipation than the stool softener. So use psyllium and eat more fiber.

Pay attention to your body's needs. When your body gives you the signals that it's time to defecate, stop what you are doing and go to the bathroom. When you ignore your body's urges, the rectum gets used to being stretched and fails to respond normally. Feces back up into the colon, causing discomfort. If you dislike having a bowel movement at work, school, or in a public restroom, readjust your attitude and get used to the idea. Everybody's doing it.

Healing Options

Double your fiber intake. Fresh produce, organically grown if possible, gives life to our cells. Eat a minimum of five fruits and vegetables every day. More is better. They are rich in fiber, vitamins, minerals, trace nutrients, fluids, and vitality. Eat whole grains such as whole wheat berries, oatmeal, millet, amaranth, quinoa, rye berries, and brown rice. Eat bran or whole grain cereals at breakfast; they can significantly boost your fiber intake in just one meal. Beans and peas are also loaded with healthful fibers. They are a low-fat protein source, and their soluble fiber and sitosterols help normalize cholesterol levels.

Try psyllium seed husks. Stop using laxatives and enemas and start using psyllium seeds. They add bulk and water to stool, which allows for easy passage. Though not a laxative, psyllium seeds do regulate bowel function, are beneficial for both diarrhea and constipation, and do not cause harmful dependencies. Build up gradually to 1 teaspoon of psyllium with each meal to avoid gas and cramping from sudden introduction of fiber. As your dietary fiber increases, you will probably find that you no longer need psyllium seeds.

Try wheat bran or corn bran. Wheat and corn bran can be used in the same way as psyllium seeds. They add bulk and moisture to stool, which allow it to pass more easily. Use 1 teaspoon with meals.

Increase fluids and start exercising. Drink at least six to eight glasses of water, fruit juice, or herbal teas each day. Alcoholic beverages and soft drinks have a dehydrating effect on the body. Improve bowel habits: Ignoring your body's natural urge to defecate can cause constipation. Take time each morning to have a bowel movement. If you go when nature calls, it takes just a minute or two. Additionally, begin an exercise or movement program.

Improve bowel flora. Poor bowel flora causes the digestive system to move sluggishly. Use of antibiotics, hormones, and steroid drugs; high stress levels; and poor diet can also cause an imbalance of intestinal flora. Bifidobacteria help regulate peristalsis. Take a probiotic supplement two to three times daily. If you are able to digest yogurt, it has a normalizing effect on the bowels and can be helpful for either constipation or diarrhea.

Add magnesium. Magnesium helps keep peristalsis—rhythmic muscle relaxation and contraction—working by proper relaxation of muscles. Americans have widespread magnesium deficiency that contributes to constipation. According to recent studies, 75 percent of magnesium is lost during food processing, and 40 percent of Americans fail to meet the RDA levels for daily magnesium intake. When magnesium deficiency or a calcium-magnesium imbalance is present, poor bowel tone can occur. On the other hand, too much magnesium can cause diarrhea. Take at least 400 milligrams daily. I've had clients who initially needed 2,000 milligrams of magnesium. Eventually, their deficiency lessens and they need less. If you need large amounts of magnesium, you may want to use 1 teaspoon daily of choline citrate to increase absorption.

Address lactose intolerance. People with lactose intolerance sometimes become constipated from dairy products. Avoid milk and dairy foods for two to three weeks and see if there is a change. Read the section on lactose intolerance in Chapter 6 to find hidden sources of lactose. Take the lactose breath test to determine if you are intolerant. Use Lactaid or Digestive Advantage LI to increase your tolerance to dairy.

Evaluate medications. Many medications can cause constipation: pain relievers, antacids that contain aluminum, antispasmodic drugs, antidepressants, tranquilizers, iron supplements, anticonvulsants, diuretics, anesthetics, anticholinergics, blood pressure medication, bismuth salts, and laxatives. If you noticed that constipation occurred suddenly after you began to take a new medication, discuss it with your doctor.

Investigate food sensitivities, dysbiosis, leaky gut syndrome. People with chronic constipation who do not respond to diet, fiber, liquids, and exercise should have digestive testing to see if dysbiosis, food allergies, or parasites are the underlying problem.

Take vitamin C. Vitamin C can help soften stool. The amount varies depending on individual needs. Use a vitamin C flush to determine your daily needs.

Try biofeedback. Biofeedback has been used successfully to treat constipation in people who have problems relaxing the pelvic floor muscles.

Diarrhea

Diarrhea is a symptom, not a disease. If you have chronic diarrhea, it's important to find the underlying cause. Chronic diarrhea can be the result of drugs, diverticular disease, foods or beverages that disagree with your system, infections (bacterial, fungal, viral, or parasitic), inflammatory bowel disease, irritable bowel syndrome, malabsorption, lactose intolerance, laxative use and abuse, contaminated water supply, or cancer. People with gallbladder problems often experience diarrhea after a fatty meal. With careful questioning and laboratory testing, your physician will be able to find the cause. Once you have a diagnosis, you can decide how to approach the problem.

Diarrhea occurs when you have a bowel transit time that is too fast. Feces don't sit in the colon long enough for water to be absorbed back into your body so the stool comes out runny. (It's truly amazing how much water is usually absorbed through the colon—two gallons every day.) If you have chronic diarrhea, you aren't getting the maximum benefit from foods because you aren't absorbing all the nutrients. Loss of fluids and electrolyte minerals can make us disoriented and weak. In infants, small children, and the elderly, dehydration can be dangerous and can happen suddenly. It's important to replace lost fluids to prevent dehydration. Drink eight to ten glasses of water, fruit and vegetable juices, or broths each day. Infants can be given a fleet enema, which is easily purchased at drugstores. Follow the directions in the package.

Most diarrhea is self-limiting. It is the body's way of getting rid of something disagreeable—food, microbes, or toxins. So for acute diarrhea, just let it flow and keep drinking plenty of water and fluids. If you have severe abdominal or rectal pain, fever of at least 102° Fahrenheit, blood in your stool, signs of dehydration— dry mouth, anxiety, restlessness, excessive thirst, little or no urination, severe weakness, dizziness or light-headedness—or your diarrhea lasts more than three days, call your doctor. Be more cautious with small children, people who are already ill, and the elderly.

You usually aren't very hungry when you have acute diarrhea. Many foods "feed" the bugs and you instinctively stop eating. The diet recommended for people with diarrhea is called the BRAT diet, which stands for bananas, rice, apples, and toast. These foods are bland and binding. You can make a pretty tasty rice pudding with apples, rice, eggs, and cinnamon. Soda crackers, chicken, and eggs can also be eaten.

Many other substances can cause diarrhea, including an excess of vitamin C and magnesium. For instance, antacids that contain magnesium salts can cause diarrhea. Sorbitol, mannitol, and xylitol are sugars found in dietetic candies and sweets that cause diarrhea. Even in small amounts, they can cause diarrhea in people sensitive to them. Some people have the same reaction to fructose or lactose.

Functional Laboratory Testing

Prolonged diarrhea is a symptom that warrants thorough investigation. These are a few of the tests that may give you information about what's causing your problem.

Comprehensive digestive stool analysis with parasitology
Hydrogen breath test for small bowel overgrowth
Lactose breath test
Food allergy and sensitivity testing IgG and IgE

Healing Options

Healing options depend on the cause of the diarrhea. See the appropriate sections for complete healing options.

Eliminate dairy products. Lactose intolerance is a common source of diarrhea. Avoid milk and dairy foods for two or three weeks to see if the diarrhea stops.

Supplement with acidophilus and bifidobacteria. These beneficial bacteria help normalize bowel function. They ferment fiber, which produces short-chained fatty acids to fuel the colonic tissue. You can also take probiotic supplements to help prevent traveler's diarrhea. Take 2 to 6 capsules daily.

Wash your hands frequently. The simple act of washing your hands with soap can help reduce the incidence of ongoing diarrhea. In a study done with mothers of children with prolonged diarrhea, the mothers were simply asked to wash their own hands with soap and water before preparing food and eating and to wash their children's hands before eating and as soon as possible after a bowel movement. There was an 89 percent reduction in diarrhea in the hand-washing mom's group in comparison with the control group.

Investigate food allergies and sensitivities. Diarrhea is a common symptom of food sensitivities and allergies. Blood testing can help you determine which foods you are reacting to. Or, you can go on an elimination diet for one week and slowly reintroduce foods. Although a painstaking process, you can find most food sensitivities and allergies this way. For more complete instructions, see food sensitivities and the elimination-provocation diet in Chapters 5 and 6.

Take goldenseal. This herb is highly effective for treatment of acute diarrhea caused by microbial infection. Be sure to use goldenseal in recommended dosages as it may also cause diarrhea if used in excessive amounts.

Use **Saccharomyces boulardii.** This friendly yeast has been used successfully to prevent and treat diarrhea caused by antibiotics, traveler's diarrhea, and diarrhea associated with AIDS. It boosts levels of secretory IgA, which is a protective part of the immune system. It is safe for all ages. Take 2 to 6 capsules daily.

Eat yogurt. This can help stop diarrhea. Yogurt contains active bacteria, *L. thermophilus* and *L. bulgaricus*, which help prevent and stop diarrhea. There have been several studies showing yogurt's effectiveness.

Use olive oil. One study showed that oleic acid, the main fatty acid in olive oil, slowed down transit time in people with chronic diarrhea. Because it's so nontoxic, it's worth a try. Oleic acid is also found in olives, almonds, and avocados.

Use psyllium. Adding psyllium fiber as a daily supplement can help solidify stools. Begin with 1 to 2 teaspoons in at least 8 ounces of water.

Avoid sorbitol. Sorbitol, mannitol, and xylitol are indigestible sugars found in sugar-free candy. They can easily cause diarrhea, gas, and bloating.

Take zinc. Much research has been done on zinc and diarrhea in children. It shortens the duration of acute diarrhea by boosting the body's immune system. Children can take 20 milligrams daily and adults can take 50 milligrams daily for up to two weeks.

Diverticular Disease

Diverticula are pea-sized pouches that have blown out of the intestinal wall, primarily in the colon. The underlying cause of diverticula formation is constipation. Soft, bulky stools easily pass through the colon and respond to peristaltic waves; hard, dehydrated stools are harder to push along, and the bowel wall has to work harder. As a result, the muscles in the colon thicken to help this abnormal situation, which results in greatly increased pressures within the bowel. Over time, this prolonged pressure can blow out portions of the bowel wall, causing diverticular pouches.

About half of all people over the age of sixty have diverticular disease, and about 10 percent will have it by the age of forty. It occurs more commonly in women than in men and with increasing frequency with age. Eighty-five percent of the people who have diverticula are symptom-free, and it's not a problem unless the pouches become inflamed or infected; this is called diverticulitis. The pouches usually heal on their own, but sometimes require surgery.

When the pouches become infected, causing diverticulitis, there is pain, most commonly around the left side of the lower abdomen, and often a fever with or without nausea, vomiting, chills, cramping, and constipation. It is usually at this point that a physician will order tests to discover diverticulitis and diverticulosis. These infections are treated with antibiotics and a soft-fiber diet or liquid. The possible complications of diverticulitis are bleeding, bowel obstruction, fistulas, abscesses, perforation, and peritonitis. So, if you think you are having a diverticular problem, call your doctor.

Once the inflammation resolves, a high-fiber diet is recommended. Diverticular pouches don't go away, but a high-fiber diet will prevent most future attacks. Repeated episodes of diverticulitis may require surgery. A disease of Western civilization, diverticular disease occurs rarely in people who consume a high-fiber diet.

Healing Options

Consume a high-fiber diet. A high-fiber diet is of first and foremost importance for preventing the development and recurrence of diverticular disease. If you are recovering from a flare-up of diverticulitis, begin with a soft-fiber diet. Cook vegetables until fairly soft, eat cooked fruits, use easy-to-digest grains like oatmeal, and make vegetable soups with tofu. Foods with seeds (such as strawberries, poppy seeds, sesame seeds, pumpkin seeds) can catch in your diverticula and cause irritation. Until healed, avoid seed foods.

Once you are feeling well, establish a high-fiber diet as a normal part of your life. Focus on fruits, vegetables, whole grains, and legumes. Meat, poultry, fish, and dairy products contain zero fiber and need to be eaten in moderation. Psyllium seeds are a good fiber supplement choice because they are nonirritating. Studies have shown that people eating a high-fiber, low-fat diet lower their risks of diverticular disease significantly. (Men who eat a high-red-meat, low-fiber diet have even higher incidences.) It may take you some time to get accustomed to a high-fiber, low-fat diet, but it will be worth the effort. The benefits reach further than your digestive tract, lowering your risk factors for cancer, heart disease, and diabetes. Be certain to drink plenty of water and other healthy beverages.

Supplement with acidophilus and bifidobacteria. Friendly flora can help fight the infection while it's active and protect you from future infection. Take 1 capsule two to three times daily for prevention; 2 capsules three times daily during flare-up.

Take gamma oryzanol. While studies of gamma oryzanol, a compound in rice bran oil, were not directly involved with diverticulitis, gamma oryzanol is known to have a healing effect on the colon. (See previous discussion of gastric ulcers and gastritis.) Take 100 milligrams three times daily for three to six weeks.

Take glutamine. The digestive tract uses glutamine, the most abundant amino acid in the body, as a fuel source and for healing. Studies have not been done with diverticulitis, but glutamine is regenerative for the colon in general. Begin with 8 grams daily for four to eight weeks. Then adjust dosage up or down depending on the response.

Take evening primrose oil. Evening primrose oil increases the levels of prostaglandin E2 series, which promote healing and repair. Take 1,000 to 2,000 milligrams three times a day.

Take aloe vera. Aloe vera, which contains vitamins, minerals, and amino acids, has been used by many cultures to heal the digestive tract. Its anti-inflammatory properties are soothing to mucous membranes, and it has been shown to reduce pain. It also stimulates the immune system, increasing white blood cell activity and formation of T-cells, and contains enzymes that help break down dead cells and toxins. It also reduces bleeding time, which is important with ruptured diverticula. Dosages vary from product to product, so read the label.

Take slippery elm bark. Slippery elm bark has demulcent properties and is gentle, soothing, and nourishing to mucous membranes. Drink as a tea, chew on the bark, or take in capsules. To make a tea, simmer 1 teaspoon of slippery elm bark in 2 cups of water for twenty minutes and strain. Sweeten if you want and drink freely; it can be used in large amounts without harm. Or, take 2 to 4 capsules three times daily.

Take a multivitamin with minerals.

Irritable Bowel Syndrome

Irritable bowel syndrome (IBS) affects 10 to 20 percent of all American adults and is the most common gastrointestinal complaint, although 75 percent of people who have it never seek a physician's help—they just learn to live with it. Over the years, IBS has had a variety of names: spastic colon, spastic bowel, mucous colitis, colitis, and functional bowel disease. It accounts for 10 percent of all doctor's visits and 50 percent of referrals to gastroenterologists. Associated symptoms are abdominal pain and spasms, bloating, gas, and abnormal bowel movements. Diarrhea alternating with constipation is the most common pattern. Bowel movements usually relieve the discomfort.

It's called functional bowel disease because people who have irritable bowel syndrome do not have any obvious changes in bowel structure or other serious complications and rarely require hospitalization. Nonetheless, IBS can significantly restrict one's lifestyle. Most of my IBS clients know where every public restroom is in town. They can't make morning appointments because of the unpredictability of the bowels and eating away from home can be tricky. Twice as many women as men seek medical help for IBS, and it often appears in the teen years or early adulthood.

Anemia, weight loss, rectal bleeding, and fever are *not* symptoms of irritable bowel syndrome. Bowel changes accompanied by these symptoms need to be checked out by a physician to discover the cause.

Irritable bowel syndrome has many causes. IBS can be caused by food sensitivities, stress, lactose intolerance, infection, mind-body interaction, malabsorption of nutrients, hormonal imbalances, endometriosis, AIDS, environmental sensitivities, and more. Many studies are flawed because they only test one factor at a time and generalize about results. There is no single cause for IBS, but hopefully we can find the causes for each person and work with him or her individually in response to the biochemical uniqueness. For instance, some people with IBS improve when they eliminate wheat from their diets, while the majority won't notice any benefit. Other people have an insulin rise after meals, causing an increase in serotonin, which can cause diarrhea. New medications for women with diarrhea-type IBS are based on lowering serotonin, also called 5-hydroxytryptamine (5-HT), levels.

IBS is originally triggered in about 25 percent of people by infection. The infection causes inflammation in the mucosal tissues, which stimulates T-cell mediated and smooth muscle changes. When this inflammatory response continues over time the bowels learn to be over- or underreactive to stimuli. People with postinfection IBS are more likely to have the diarrhea-type, have less psychiatric illness, and have an increase in enterochromaffin (EC) cells that secrete serotonin. There is usually a good response in postinfectious IBS with use of probiotic supplements. COX2 inhibitors decrease smooth muscle hypersensitivity and decrease bowel motility. Natural COX2 inhibitors include turmeric, boswellia, and Kaprex (a product by Metagenics).

Women may experience a flare-up in their symptoms around their menstrual period. The most common symptom associated with menstruation is pain. Because chronic pelvic pain can lead to hysterectomy, physicians need to be clear that IBS is not causing the pain. When IBS is the culprit, a hysterectomy won't eliminate it.

Low-fat, high-fiber diets are best. Eat small meals, and chew your food well. Dietary recommendations need to be tailored to your personal reactions. It is commonly advised to avoid alcohol and monitor sugar intake, coffee, beans, and cabbage family foods (broccoli, brussels sprouts, cauliflower) because they can be difficult to digest. You need only avoid those foods if they bother you.

Food sensitivities are found in half to two-thirds of people with IBS and are more prevalent in those who have allergies or come from allergic families. The most common foods that trigger IBS are wheat, corn, dairy products, coffee, tea, citrus fruits, and chocolate. In a study in which people were put on a food elimination diet for a year, bloating and distension was relieved by 88 percent, colic pain was reduced by 90 percent, diarrhea was reduced 85 percent, and constipation improved in 54 percent. Also, 79 percent of people who had other symptoms, such as hay fever, asthma, eczema, and hives, saw these symptoms improve.

Undiagnosed lactose insufficiency is often the cause of IBS. In a recent study of 242 people, it was found that 43 percent had total remission of IBS when they excluded dairy products from their diet, and another 41 percent had partial improvement. Taking the lactose hydrogen breath test is a valuable way to discover who would benefit from a lactose-free diet. You can also discover this by avoiding all dairy foods and products that contain dairy foods for at least two weeks to see how you feel. If you have only moderate improvement, other foods may also be playing a role in your symptoms.

Lactose is not the only sugar to cause problems. Our cells use single sugar molecules (monosaccharides), but many foods contain two-molecule sugars (disaccharides) that must be split. New research suggests that many people are unable to split mannitol, sucrose, sorbitol, fructose, and other disaccharides, and a high percentage of IBS sufferers are intolerant of one or more of these sugars. The result is diarrhea, gas, and bloating. These people find that fruit, especially citrus fruit, aggravates their symptoms.

Hydrogen breath tests are being experimentally used to diagnose fructose and sugar intolerance but are not on the market at present. You can do a self-test by avoiding all fruit and sugar for at least ten days. Be sure to read labels carefully and avoid any product that contains glucose, sucrose, malt, maltose, corn syrup, fructose, brown sugar, honey, maple syrup, molasses, and lactose. You'll find that sugar is everywhere, but if disaccharides are the cause of your IBS, it is worth the time and trouble. If sugars and fruits make you feel worse, do the self-test and a blood or stool test for candida infection. People with candida often feel worse after eating sugars and fruits.

Recent technology has provided new insight into the causes of IBS. High levels of methane shown in hydrogen breath tests are associated with IBS and indicate an infection in the small intestine, most commonly *Clostridium difficile*. (See more on lab testing in Chapter 6.) *C. difficile* often responds to *Saccharomyces boulardii* supplementation.

Parasites and candida overgrowth are overlooked causes of irritable bowel syndrome. One study showed that 18 percent of the study participants had treatable parasitic infections, while another found giardia in 9 percent and parasites in 15 percent of the study population. Leo Galland, M.D., has found that giardia was responsible for problems in nearly half of his patients with IBS. Even benign pinworms can cause severe colonic cramping at a certain stage of their life cycle. Ask your doctor to order a comprehensive digestive and stool analysis with parasitology to determine if parasites or candida are making you sick.

Antibiotics are well-known causes of temporary diarrhea and GI problems. Steroid medications can also affect the balance of flora. The good flora are eliminated, especially in people who are on repeated doses of antibiotics, which allows other microbes to dominate the intestinal tract. Acidophilus, bifidobacteria, and *Saccharomyces boulardii* supplements can help restore intestinal balance.

Irritable bowel syndrome has also been treated as a psychosomatic illness—"it's all in your head"—because there appears to be no other obvious reason for it. IBS sufferers often have reason to feel stressed, nervous, and depressed about their condition. Stressful situations can trigger IBS symptoms. People with IBS have no greater incidence of depression than others with chronic health problems. IBS can cause social embarrassment and is the second most common cause for missing work, after the common cold.

Functional Laboratory Testing
Comprehensive digestive stool analysis with parasitology
Lactose breath test
Hydrogen breath test for methane levels

Food allergy and sensitivity testing: IgE and IgG or IgG4,
    IgM
Intestinal permeability screening

Healing Options

Increase fiber intake. Fiber and high-fiber diets are recommended
for people with IBS. Focus on eating a minimum of five servings
of fresh fruits and vegetables daily, plus whole grains, beans, and
peas. You can use high-fiber cereals to boost fiber content, but
recent research indicates that wheat bran made the problem worse
in 55 percent of cases, whereas it only improved symptoms in 10
percent of patients. This is not surprising because a significant
number of people with IBS have a hypersensitivity to wheat
products.

If you want to add a fiber supplement, use psyllium seeds. Psyllium seeds were found to be more effective than wheat bran overall. They caused a decrease in abdominal bloating, whereas wheat
bran increased bloating. In a study in which psyllium was given
to people with IBS, it improved several parameters by increasing
the number of bowel movements per week, enlarging stool
weight, and speeding up transit times. No negative side effects
were reported.

Evaluate possible lactose intolerance. Lactose intolerance is often the
underlying cause of IBS. Take the hydrogen breath test or eliminate all dairy products and products containing dairy from your
diet for at least two weeks to help you determine whether lactose
intolerance is contributing to your problem.

Consider grain intolerance or other food allergies. While you are eliminating dairy, also eliminate wheat, rye, barley, and oats. (See the
section on celiac disease for more information.) You may experience a miraculous improvement in your symptoms. Then test to
see how much you can "get away with."

After you've tried the dietary approaches, consider these additional options.

Explore behavioral therapies. Biofeedback, self-hypnosis, and other relaxation techniques are widely used to help people with IBS. Stress often triggers bowel symptoms, and learning stress-modification techniques can alter our reactions. If we don't react with alarm to a situation, our body doesn't sense it as stressful.

Add probiotics. In numerous studies, probiotic supplements have been shown to help regulate IBS. Products with multiple strains of microbes would be best. Make sure they at least include lactobacilli and bifidobacteria. Studies on *E. coli Nissle* strain have also shown much promise.

Try gamma oryzanol. Gamma oryzanol, a compound found in rice bran oil, is a useful therapeutic tool for IBS. It acts on the autonomic nervous system to normalize production of gastric juice. (See previous discussion on gastric ulcers and gastritis.) Take 100 milligrams three times daily for a trial period of three to six weeks.

Add glutamine. Glutamine, the most abundant amino acid in the body, is used by the digestive tract as a fuel source and for healing IBS. Take 8 grams daily for a trial period of four weeks.

Take EPA/DHA fish oil. Fish oils inhibit the formation of inflammatory prostaglandins and leukotrienes. They may be effective in reducing the pain and inflammation associated with IBS. Take 1,000 to 2,000 milligrams daily in fish oil capsules, or 300 milligrams daily of Neuromins.

Take peppermint oil. Peppermint oil is a muscle relaxant that is widely used in England for IBS. To get the oil into the intestines intact, use enteric coated peppermint oil. (The coating prevents it from dissolving in the stomach.) Take 1 to 2 capsules daily between meals. During a spasm, you can rub a drop or two of the oil inside your anus with a finger. Caution: it stings!

Try herbs. Chamomile, melissa (balm), rosemary, and valerian all have antispasmodic properties. They help relieve and expel gas, strengthen and tone the stomach, and soothe pain. Valerian, hops, skullcap, and passionflower are all calming herbs, which can be found in a combination product. Antidepressant medication is often used by physicians for IBS; these gentle, effective calmatives may give you similar results. Use these herbs in capsules, tinctures, and teas.

Take ginger. Ginger, either fresh or powdered, helps relieve gas pains. It can be added to foods or used in tea. Within twenty to thirty minutes you'll be belching and/or passing gas, which will relieve the discomfort. To make a tea, take 2 or 3 slices of fresh ginger or ½ teaspoon dried ginger in one cup of boiled water. Combine it with other herbs, like peppermint or chamomile, to enhance the effect.

Take a multivitamin with minerals.

Take calcium-magnesium citrate. Anecdotally, many people have found that calcium-magnesium supplements prevent or alleviate the muscle spasms associated with IBS. Take 500 to 1,000 milligrams calcium, 300 to 750 milligrams magnesium. Be aware that too much magnesium will cause diarrhea.

Inflammatory Bowel Disease: Crohn's Disease and Ulcerative Colitis

Inflammatory bowel diseases (IBD) include two distinct illnesses: ulcerative colitis and Crohn's disease. IBD affects one to two million Americans and the incidence of both illnesses is rising. It is estimated that it costs us about $3 billion each year in direct and indirect costs.

IBD shares many of the symptoms of IBS, but they are very different problems. IBD involves inflammation of the digestive tract, which can occur anywhere from the mouth to the rectum. Symptoms include abdominal pain, bloody diarrhea, and cramping. If you are having these symptoms, go see your physician.

These symptoms may also be accompanied by fever, rectal bleeding, abdominal tenderness, abscesses, constipation, weight loss, awakening during the night with diarrhea, and a failure to thrive in children. Symptoms come and go and can go into remission for months or years, and about half of the people with IBD have only mild symptoms.

The two most common types of IBD are ulcerative colitis and Crohn's disease. Most cases are diagnosed before age forty. IBD tends to run in families and is more prevalent among people of Jewish descent. IBD affects half a million Americans. Ulcerative colitis and Crohn's disease are similar but have different characteristics.

Ulcerative colitis is a continuous inflammation of the mucosal lining of the colon and/or rectum. In the descending colon it is sometimes called left-sided disease, and in the rectum, it is called distal disease, ulcerative proctitis, or proctosigmoiditis. If sores are present, they are shallow, and it is generally milder and easier to treat in the rectum.

Crohn's disease can occur anywhere along the digestive tract, from mouth to rectum, but is most common in the colon and ileum near the ileocecal valve. It is sometimes called right-sided disease. Frequent symptoms are fevers that last twenty-four to forty-eight hours, canker sores in the mouth, clubbed fingernails, and a thickening of the GI lining, which may cause constrictions and blockage. Inflammation develops in a skip pattern, a little here and a little there, and goes more deeply into the tissues than with ulcerative colitis. In later stages, it can form abscesses and fistulas, little canals that lead to other organs or form tiny caves. If they become serious, surgery may be recommended. If you require surgery for Crohn's disease, it is important to know which part of the intestines were removed and which nutrients may have inadequate uptake. (See the absorption chart in Chapter 2.)

Leaky gut syndrome (increased intestinal permeability) is prevalent in IBD. Often an infectious or parasitic condition underlies it. A flare-up of symptoms commonly occurs with infections. The most common microbes involved are E. coli, staphylococcus, streptococcus, proteus, Mycoplasma pneumoniae, *Chlamydia psittaci*, *Clostridium difficile* toxin, and *Coxiella burnetii*. Bacterial infections occurred in one-quarter of all reoccurrence of IBD.

Research implicates measles as a possible cause of Crohn's disease. British scientists found measles virus in diseased parts of the colon. Swedish researchers found a high incidence of IBD in people who were exposed to measles in utero. Another British study showed that people who had received live measles vaccines had a threefold increase of Crohn's disease, while ulcerative colitis rose by two-and-a-half times. This study did not prove that the bowel disease was actually caused by measles, only that there was a correlation. Some people with Crohn's disease have flare-ups in a seasonal cycle, which suggests an allergy component to the illness. While studies have shown that allergy is a factor in a small number of people, a survey of members of the National Foundation of Ileitis and Colitis showed that 70 percent of people with IBD listed other symptoms which were probably allergic. This led one researcher to say "inflammatory bowel disease is just another possible facet of allergy." Mold sensitivity and allergies to candida and other types of fungus have also been proven to provoke IBD symptoms.

IBD is not caused by emotional illness or psychiatric disorder, though the condition may cause emotional problems because of its chronic nature, painful episodes, and lifestyle limitations. Prolonged treatment with steroid medications can cause side effects of depression, mania or euphoria, and bone loss.

There is a higher incidence of IBD in women who take oral contraceptives. Women with a history of IBD or with a family history of IBD may want to choose a different form of birth control.

People with IBD often develop complications, which include inflammation of the eyes or skin, arthritis, liver disease, kidney stones, and colon cancer. Of people with ulcerative colitis, 20 to 25 percent eventually require surgery because of massive bleeding, chronic illness, perforation of the colon, or risk of colon cancer. Five percent of people with ulcerative colitis ultimately develop colon cancer, and the degree of illness correlates with its incidence. For example, cancer levels aren't higher for people who are only affected in the rectum and distal end of the colon.

IBD is considered an autoimmune disease (your body begins attacking itself). The causes are many and have produced much debate. Current theories suggest that Crohn's and ulcerative colitis have a genetic component, which is triggered to a greater or lesser extent by either infection, a hypersensitivity to antigens in the gut wall, an inflammation of the blood vessels that causes ischemia (a lack of blood supply to the tissues), and food sensitivities. The first gene to be associated with Crohn's disease has been found, called NOD2. This gene apparently gives the person a rapid response to gut bacteria and/or their toxic by-products, which causes an overstimulation, and production of NF-kappa B and cytokine, which stimulate inflammation. The NOD gene is only found in 10 to 15 percent of people with Crohn's. Obviously, much work still needs to be done to explore the genetics of IBD.

Where this takes us on a practical level is to look at what we can do to have a healthy gut bacterial environment. Numerous studies have shown that use of probiotic supplements is beneficial for people with IBD. They have been shown to help maintain remission of flare-ups in Crohn's disease, ulcerative colitis, and pouchitis (infection of the diverticuli). Probiotic bacteria, like *L. acidophilus*, bifidobacteria, and the Nissle strain of E. coli, provide competition for other microbes and push them out. Commensal bacteria stimulate our immune response, increase beneficial antibodies such as sIgA, IgM, and IgG, balance pH, and enhance tight junction integrity. Probiotic therapy with *E. coli Nissle* strain has been shown to be effective in treatment for ulcerative colitis and was found to be equivalent to the drug mesalamine for short-term maintenance of the disease and after use of steroid treatment for remission. VSL#3 is a formula with eight different probiotic species and has been used for pouchitis.

Much more research needs to be done on IBD and probiotics. Different combinations will work for different people and to greater or lesser effect. You'll have to experiment with different brands and see which are most helpful. Remember to begin with a small dosage and increase slowly. You are changing your gut ecology and you want to do it gradually. You can think of them as a medicine that you'll probably need to take daily for life.

A 2004 study tested probiotic bacteria in mice. The exciting part of this study showed that sterilized probiotics worked as well as live probiotics in chemically induced ulcerative colitis. If the DNA in the dead probiotic bacteria work as well as live ones, there may be less possibility of adverse effects, but further studies need to be done.

Medical treatment for IBD consists of anti-inflammatory drugs, steroids, immune modulators, and sometimes antibiotics. While these medications can often relieve symptoms of IBD, they carry their own risks. Some specific drug side effects include bone loss due to use of steroid medications, and folic acid deficiency from use of sulfasalazine (Asulfadine). Infliximab is a new drug now in use for Crohn's disease and the fistulas caused by it. A monoclonal antibody, infliximab has a high specificity for tumor necrosis factor (TNF-alpha). This is an entirely new approach that focuses on stimulating the immune system to stop inflammation in people with severe disease. Many people are able to stop taking steroid medications and quality of life is increased. Research on infliximab in ulcerative colitis is in its infancy, but keep your heads up, it looks promising.

A very new approach to IBD is with the use of a protease inhibitor, called BBI; testing is in initial stages. BBI is derived from soybeans and is naturally found in all legumes. You'd need to eat huge amounts to get the same effects, but you might find them to be helpful. Remember that legumes are loaded with fiber, help lower serum cholesterol levels, and offer a vegetable protein of high quality.

Medications are often necessary, but use of complementary therapies can reduce the need, so that when you really need medication during a flare-up it works effectively. For example, repeated use of prednisone can lead to its failure as an available therapy. The good news is that effective natural therapies address the underlying factors of the disease, reduce the need for prescription medications, and heal the bowel. Among the hundreds of patients with IBD that Drs. Jonathan Wright and Alan Gaby, two nutritionally oriented M.D.s, have seen, most have improved, many dramatically. The key to success appears to be getting people into remission. To do this effectively, a combination of medication and supplements may be necessary. Once a flare-up has died down, natural therapies are highly successful in preventing a recurrence. It's also really important to take care of yourself when you are well and to practice stress-management techniques to help reduce the number and severity of flare-ups.

Diet plays an important role in IBD. The incidence of IBD is growing rapidly in Western countries, but is rare in cultures where people eat a native diet. People who eat a high amount of sugars and low-fiber diets have a higher incidence of IBD, and there are correlations of IBD with cigarette smoking and eating fast foods.

Food sensitivities play a significant role in IBD. Many IBD patients report significant improvement with use of an elimination diet over a three-week period. After this, they gradually add foods back into their diet to see which ones provoke bloating, pain, diarrhea, bleeding, or other symptoms. One study found that 13 percent of children with IBD were allergic to cow's milk during infancy. It is essential to check for food allergies and food sensitivities. Studies have shown reduction in symptoms and inflammation in people who adhere to a hypoallergenic diet. People with bowel disease are especially sensitive to most grains. Chemicals from some foods are irritating to the bowels. Truly, nearly any food can cause irritation and inflammation. In various studies, citrus, pineapple, dairy, coffee, tomatoes, cheese, bananas, sugar, additives, preservatives, spices, beverages other than water, bread, and so forth have been implicated. You'll need to be tested for both IgE and IgG antibodies. Testing of IgA and IgM antibodies is also useful.

No one diet will help all people with IBD, although the Elemental Diet and Haas Specific Carbohydrate Diet (details of the Haas program are discussed in "Healing Options") work especially well for people with Crohn's disease. The Elemental Diet, which has resulted in a reduction of intestinal permeability as well as its symptoms, includes synthetic foods you drink or are given through a tube. It has been found to be as good as steroids in reducing inflammation in a flare-up of Crohn's disease. But there are problems with use of the Elemental Diet. It is unpalatable to many people and they won't drink it. Newer products that are tastier are coming on the market.

The Haas Specific Carbohydrate Diet eliminates all simple sugars. As discussed under IBS, many people are unable to split disaccharide sugars (lactose, sucrose, maltose, and isomaltose) into single molecule sugars. This may explain, in part, why the diet is so successful. The Haas Specific Carbohydrate Diet also eliminates grains, which generally cause inflammation of the intestines in people with IBD, and it works especially well for people with Crohn's disease.

A low-sulfur diet may be of benefit in Crohn's disease. Studies have shown an increase in sulfur-eating bacteria in people with bowel disease in comparison with other people. In one study, people were advised to avoid high-sulfur foods including eggs, cheese, whole milk, ice cream, mayonnaise, soy milk, mineral water, sulfited drinks (including wine), nuts, and cruciferous vegetables (e.g., broccoli, cabbage, cauliflower, brussels sprouts, and so forth), and to reintroduce red meats. They were advised to get protein from fish and chicken. The researchers found significant changes—people had no relapses or attacks while on the diet, and there were no adverse effects from the diet itself. The expected relapse rate had been 22.6 percent. Of the four people in the study, one was able to stop taking steroid medication and had been attack-free for eighteen months, compared to the four attacks experienced in the eighteen months before the dietary changes. The other three showed microscopic improvement of inflammation. The number of daily bowel movements in all four was reduced from six to one and one-half.

Although there is not much research on the yeast connection and IBD, clinicians have often found antifungal therapies to be useful. Friendly flora have been found to be dramatically out of balance in people with IBD, so use of probiotic supplements is highly recommended. Use of the comprehensive digestive and stool analysis with parasitology screening and intestinal permeability tests will uncover many of these problems.

Because of bleeding and continued irritation, malabsorption of nutrients is often found in people with IBD. These same nutrients are often vital for repair, so the cycle worsens. Low serum levels of zinc, an important nutrient for wound repair, are often found in people with IBD. Folic acid helps repair tissue and prevents diarrhea. Prolonged bleeding can cause deficiencies of copper, zinc, iron, folic acid, and vitamin B_{12}.

Studies have shown an increased need for antioxidant nutrients such as vitamins A, E, K, and C, selenium, calcium, iron, zinc, glutathione, and superoxide dismutase (SOD). People with IBD have an increased level of leukotrienes, produced by neutrophils, which increase pain and inflammation. Many natural substances can modulate these effects. For instance, omega-3 fatty acids, found in cold-water fish, can reduce inflammation caused by leukotrienes and the arachidonic acid cascade. When supplementing with antioxidants, use more than you'd expect.

One unusual twist in the story is that nicotine appears to be protective for ulcerative colitis. While normally I wouldn't recommend nicotine patches, the severity of the disease could warrant a try. It's certainly less toxic than the usual drugs that are used. The studies show positive results, using 15- to 25-milligram patches over periods of four to six weeks along with mesalamine. Many people stayed in remission for up to three months after stopping the patch. One study gave people who were in relapse either nicotine or prednisone with mesalamine for five weeks. The relapse rate was much better in the nicotine group—only 20 percent in comparison to a 60 percent relapse rate for those on prednisone. In the long term, nicotine patches appear to help with flare-ups and maintenance when used with mesalamine.

There are many additional approaches for IBD. One promising approach involves photopheresis, a process that exposes blood to light and many herbal therapies. Natural COX2 inhibitors, like curcumin and boswellia, also show promise. You won't believe this, but researchers took three men and three women with ulcerative colitis and gave them colonic enemas with the bowel movements of healthy people for five consecutive days. Four of the six had total remission of their symptoms within four months. One to thirteen years later, they were still completely well and without use of any medications. They call this method fecal bacteriotherapy. We'll keep our ears open for more research on this!

Several studies have shown bone loss in people with Crohn's disease and ulcerative colitis. While incidence of loss in some studies is correlated with use of steroid medications, in others it appears to be independent. It is advisable to do at least a baseline bone density study to see if you are at risk. If so, increasing all bone nutrients would be advised. A study on low-impact exercise in people with Crohn's disease found that bone density was significantly increased. So get out there and exercise regularly. Exercise is not optional for any of us!

A new lab test can help monitor people with ulcerative colitis and Crohn's, and can also distinguish them from people with irritable bowel syndrome. Calprotectin is an indicator of inflammation and increased levels are seen in people with inflammatory bowel disease, GI infections, and inflammatory arthritis, like rheumatoid arthritis. Calprotectin can be used to monitor the effectiveness of treatment and to screen people to see if a flare-up of the disease is likely.

Functional Laboratory Testing
Comprehensive digestive stool analysis with parasitology
Lactose breath test
Food and environmental sensitivity testing
Calprotectin
Intestinal permeability screening
Antioxidant analysis
Bone density testing
Immunogenetics testing
Nutritional analysis of blood

Healing Options
Make dietary changes. Eliminate simple sugars, alcohol, and fast foods (one study showed that flare-ups occurred almost four times as frequently when fast foods were eaten twice a week in people with ulcerative colitis). Grains and dairy products often aggravate the condition.

Try the Specific Carbohydrate Diet. Many people have found relief from using the Specific Carbohydrate Diet outlined in Elaine Gottschall's book *Breaking the Vicious Cycle*. Foods that are allowed are beef, lamb, pork, poultry, fish, eggs, fruits, nuts, pure fruit juices, weak coffee or tea, and peppermint and spearmint teas. Also allowed are corn, soy, safflower, sunflower, and olive oils. No grains, dairy products, legumes, potatoes, yams, or parsnips are allowed on the diet. No sugars or alcoholic beverages are consumed. For delicious recipes and more detail, read the book.

This diet is beneficial because it eliminates most foods that cause sensitivities—grains and dairy products. Similar to the candida diet, it helps restore intestinal balance. While going on the diet alone may be effective, it is most effective after laboratory testing has determined your unique biochemistry.

Explore possible lactose intolerance. Hydrogen breath testing or elimination of all dairy products and foods containing dairy from your diet for at least two weeks can help determine whether lactose intolerance is contributing to your problem. Definitely eliminate dairy during a flare-up of your illness.

Consider food sensitivities. Food sensitivities play a significant role in ulcerative colitis and Crohn's disease, occurring approximately half the time. The most common offenders are dairy products, grains, and yeast, followed in frequency by egg, potato, rye, coffee, apples, mushrooms, oats, and chocolate. Some people are sensitive to more than one food or type of food. Going on an elimination-provocation diet is a simple way to eat foods that are less likely to trigger symptoms. The slow addition of new foods in the challenge stage will give you an idea of which foods make you feel worse. You can also do a blood test for food sensitivities. For example, if you find that you are not sensitive to grains or dairy products, you'll be able to include them in your food plan. Most foods can be added back into your diet within six months, while fixed sensitivities must be avoided long-term.

Take glutamine. Glutamine is the first nutrient I recommend for bowel and intestinal health. It is the most abundant amino acid in our bodies. The digestive tract uses glutamine as the primary nutrient for the intestinal cells, and it is effective for healing stomach ulcers, irritable bowel syndrome, and ulcerative bowel diseases.

Douglas Wilmore, M.D., has been using high doses of glutamine to heal digestive tracts in people with IBD who have had surgery in which part of the colon was removed. When only a short portion of the colon remains, people develop chronic diarrhea, a condition called short bowel syndrome. With a high-fiber, high-glutamine diet, and short-term use of growth hormones, Dr. Wilmore is able to help normalize bowel function. Studies have shown reduced glutathione levels specifically in colon cells. Glutathione is also synthesized from glutamine. Glutathione levels are low in both inflamed and normal bowel tissue. Glutamine is also great for building muscle mass. Begin with 8 to 20 grams daily for a trial period of four weeks. In clinical settings, up to 40 grams daily have been used.

Take folic acid. One of folic acid's main functions is to help with the repair and maintenance of epithelial cells, such as those in the bowel. The drug Asulfadine causes a 30 percent loss of folic acid. Even those who don't take Asulfadine may benefit greatly from folic acid supplementation. In a study, twenty-four people with bowel disease were given either a placebo or 15 milligrams of folic acid daily. Beneficial changes to the cells were observed in those receiving the folic acid. In my own clinical experience, I have found that a combination of glutamine and folic acid can often rapidly reduce inflammation and irritation in bowel disease. Take 5 to 15 milligrams when the disease is active, less for maintenance.

Increase consumption of omega-3 fatty acids. Omega-3 fatty acids are found in cold-water fish and have been used to reduce inflammation in rheumatoid arthritis, psoriasis, and ulcerative colitis by reducing the production of leukotrienes. Salmon, mackerel, herring, tuna, sardines, and halibut are all excellent sources of EPA/DHA oils. Eating these fish several times a week can supply your body with these essential fats. Seaweeds also provide generous amounts of omega-3 oils, but carrageenan, an extract from seaweed, may increase the inflammation in the colon. While carrageenan is used in animals to produce IBD, in humans the research is not yet clear. To be on the safe side, avoid red and brown seaweeds.

You can also take capsules of EPA/DHA oils daily. In a recent study, it was found that use of Max/EPA decreased disease activity by 58 percent over a period of eight months. No patient worsened, and eight out of eleven were able to reduce or discontinue use of medication. The dosage was 15 capsules of Max/EPA, which contained 2.7 grams of EPA and 1.8 grams of DHA, per day. Many other studies also show the benefit of fish oils with dosages between 3.5 and 5.5 grams daily.

Take quercetin. Quercetin, the most effective anti-inflammatory bioflavonoid, can be used to reduce pain and inflammatory responses and control allergies. Take 500 to 1,000 milligrams three to four times daily.

Take acidophilus, bifidobacteria, E. coli Nissle *strain, or* Saccharomyces boulardii. Imbalance of friendly flora allows for proliferation of pathogenic microbes, such as candida, bacteroides, citrobacter, and more. It is believed that dysbiosis is a primary cause of IBD in many cases. Use of probiotic supplements can help restore balance of intestinal flora. Take 1 to 2 capsules three times daily.

Take gamma oryzanol. Gamma oryzanol, a compound found in rice bran oil, is a useful therapeutic tool for gastritis, ulcers, and irritable bowel syndrome. (See previous discussion of gastric ulcers and gastritis.) Try taking 100 milligrams three times daily for a period of three to six weeks.

Take boswellia. Boswellia has been used in Ayurvedic medicine as an anti-inflammatory for ulcerative colitis. Only one study has been done so far, but in comparison with sulfasalazine it was equivalent. Take 350 milligrams three times daily.

Try butyrate enemas. Butyrate is the preferred fuel of the colonic cells. It is produced when fiber in the colon is fermented by intestinal flora, predominantly bifidobacteria. A few studies have shown that butyrate enemas, taken twice daily, helped heal active distal ulcerative colitis.

Explore herbal remedies. Demulcent herbs—marshmallow, slippery elm, acacia, chickweed, comfrey, mullein, and plantain—are beneficial and soothing to the intestinal membranes and help stimulate mucus production. All are gentle enough to be used at will; try them in capsule or tea form. Other herbs used by people with bowel disease include wild indigo, purple cornflower, echinacea, American cranesbill, goldenseal, cabbage powder, wild yam, bayberry, agrimony, neem, aloe vera, chamomile, feverfew, ginger, ginkgo biloba, St.-John's-wort, milk thistle, valerian, peppermint, hawthorn, and La Pacho.

Take a multivitamin with minerals and antioxidant nutrients. Because of general malabsorption and poor dietary habits in people with Crohn's disease and ulcerative colitis, it is wise to add a good-quality multivitamin with minerals to your daily routine. Deficiencies of many nutrients have been found in people with IBD: calcium/magnesium; folic acid; iron; selenium; vitamins A, B_1, B_2, B_6, C, D, E; and zinc. Because oxidative damage plays a significant role in IBD, the supplement should contain adequate amounts of antioxidant nutrients: at least 10,000 IU of beta-carotene or other carotenoids, 400 IU of vitamin E, 250 milligrams of vitamin C, 200 micrograms of selenium, 5 milligrams of zinc, plus other nutrients. It may also contain CoQ10, glutathione, NAC, pycnogenol, superoxide dismutase (SOD), and other antioxidants. It is best to buy a supplement that is free of foods, herbs, colorings, and common allergens.

Try wheat grass juice. People with ulcerative colitis have had great results reducing flare-ups of the disease by drinking wheat grass juice. In 2002 Israeli researchers finally put it to the test. Twenty-three people with active distal ulcerative colitis were given either

3½ ounces of wheat grass juice daily or a green placebo daily for one month. People who received the wheat grass juice had less severe flare-ups of the disease and less blood loss. This is certainly a nontoxic and easy remedy to try.

Drink aloe vera juice. Aloe vera juice has been used as a traditional remedy for digestive disorders of all types. A randomized, double-blind, placebo-controlled trial was done using oral aloe vera gel in people with active colitis. Forty-four people were given 3½ ounces daily of either aloe vera gel or a placebo for four weeks. People who received the aloe vera had a significant reduction of all disease symptoms in comparison with people who received the placebo.

Try bovine cartilage. Bovine cartilage is shown to have anti-inflammatory and wound-healing properties. Its benefit has been documented in many illnesses, including ulcerative colitis, hemorrhoids and fissures, rheumatoid arthritis, and osteoarthritis.

Hemorrhoids

About half of Americans over the age of fifty have hemorrhoids. They are not life-threatening or dangerous, but can be painful or might bleed. They occur when blood vessels in and around the anus get swollen and stretch under pressure, similar to varicose veins in the legs. They are found either inside the anus (internal hemorrhoids) or under the skin around the anus (external hemorrhoids). Internal hemorrhoids may become so swollen that they push through the anus. When they become irritated, inflamed, and painful, they are called protruding hemorrhoids.

Straining during bowel movements is a common cause of hemorrhoids. The most common symptom is bright red blood with a bowel movement. Hemorrhoids are also common but temporary during pregnancy. Hormonal changes cause the blood vessels to expand. During childbirth, extreme pressure is put on the anus. Hemorrhoids also occur in people with chronic constipation or diarrhea. Sitting for long periods, heavy lifting, and genetics are other influential factors. In most cases, hemorrhoids go away in a few days. If you have bleeding that lasts longer, have your doctor examine you to rule out a more serious problem.

A high-fiber diet with plenty of fluids—water, fruit juices, and herbal teas—helps prevent hemorrhoids because fiber and fluids soften stool so they pass through easily. No straining with bowel movements means less pressure on the blood vessels near your anus. So, increase your intake of fruits, whole grains, legumes, and vegetables, especially those containing the most fiber: asparagus, brussels sprouts, cabbage, carrots, cauliflower, corn, peas, kale, and parsnips. Eating a high-fiber breakfast cereal significantly increases your fiber intake.

Hemorrhoids generally don't itch. If your anus itches mainly at night, you might have pinworms. The best time to check for them is at night while you itch. Place a piece of tape around your finger, sticky side out. Put the tape on your anus, pull it off and check for worms, which look like moving white threads. If you are checking one of your children, you can use the tape method or just look. Another cause of rectal itching is called pruritus ani, which can be caused by food sensitivities, contact with irritating substances (laundry detergent or toilet paper), fungi, bacterial infection, parasites, antibiotics, poor hygiene, or tight clothing. If you have hemorrhoids, you might find relief from the following suggestions.

Prevention

Improve your diet. A high-fiber diet usually prevents hemorrhoids and allows them to heal. Increase your intake of fruits, vegetables, whole grains and legumes, and drink plenty of fluids, including water, fruit juices, and herbal teas.

Use psyllium seed husks. Psyllium seeds add bulk and water to stool, which allows for easy passage. They regulate bowel function and can be beneficial for both diarrhea and constipation. Because they are not a laxative, they do not cause harmful dependency. Gradually build up to 1 teaspoon of psyllium with each meal to avoid gas and cramping from the sudden introduction of fiber. As your dietary fiber increases, you will probably find you no longer need to take psyllium seeds.

Try wheat or corn bran. Wheat and corn bran can be used in the same way as psyllium seeds to add bulk and moisture to stool, allowing them to pass more easily. Take 1 teaspoon with meals or eat a high-fiber breakfast cereal. Be sure to add fiber to your diet slowly to prevent any gas or discomfort.

Take probiotics. Poor bowel flora causes the digestive system to move sluggishly. Use of antibiotics, hormones, or steroid drugs; high-stress levels; and poor diet can cause an imbalance of intestinal flora. Take acidophilus and bifidobacteria two to three times daily to help regulate peristalsis. If you are able to digest yogurt, it also has a normalizing effect on the bowel and can be helpful for either constipation or diarrhea.

Address magnesium deficiency. Americans have widespread magnesium deficiency that contributes to constipation. According to recent studies, we lose 75 percent of magnesium during food processing, and 40 percent of Americans fail to meet the RDA levels for daily magnesium intake. One of the many functions of magnesium is the proper relaxation of muscles, and peristalsis is a rhythmic muscle relaxation and contraction. When magnesium deficiency or a calcium-magnesium imbalance is present, poor bowel tone can occur. On the other hand, too much magnesium can cause diarrhea. Take 400 to 500 milligrams daily.

Explore possible lactose intolerance. People with lactose intolerance can become constipated from dairy products. (See discussion in Chapter 6.)

Examine hormone changes. Women often notice that their bowel habits change at various times in their menstrual cycle. Pregnancy is a common but temporary cause of constipation and hemorrhoids. An underactive thyroid can also cause constipation.

Take vitamin C. Vitamin C can be used to help soften stool. The amount needed depends on your individual needs. Use a vitamin C flush to determine your daily need for vitamin C. (See Chapter 8.)

Healing Options

Change your bathroom habits. In many countries, people squat to relieve themselves. A squatting position on the toilet takes pressure off the rectum and can help during a flare-up of hemorrhoids. (You may feel a little silly, but who's watching!) Also, wipe gently with soft toilet paper. It may help to wash your anal area with warm water after each bowel movement, or if you have a bidet, now is the time to use it.

Use salves. Salves can soothe inflamed tissues. Spread vitamin E oil, comfrey, calendula ointment, or goldenseal salve gently on the anus with your fingers. Witch hazel is also soothing to hemorrhoidal tissue. Put some on a cotton ball and press gently. Repeat treatments several times daily.

Take sitz baths. Sitz baths are an old-fashioned remedy for hemorrhoids that are still in favor with the medical profession.

Place three to four inches of warm water in the bathtub, and sit in it for ten minutes several times daily. You can improve the results by adding ¼ cup Epsom salts or healing herbs. Chamomile, chickweed, comfrey, mullein, plantain, witch hazel, and yarrow are all healing and soothing to mucous membranes. Most of these are weeds and may even be growing in your yard. (Comfrey is a very easy herb to grow; just put it in a place where it can spread. It helps with wound healing of any sort and is also soothing for colds and lung problems.) Bring a large pot of water to a boil. Steep 1 to 2 cups of fresh herbs or 1½ cups of dried herbs until cool; strain and add to bathwater.

Use horse chestnuts. Horse chestnuts, also called buckeye, help tone blood vessels, improve their elasticity, and reduce inflammation.

They can also be used in a sitz bath. Chop up two cups of horse chestnuts, add to boiled water, strain, and add infusion to bathwater. Sit in bath twice daily for ten to fifteen minutes. You can also take 500 milligrams of the bark orally three times daily. Horse chestnut salves are also available.

Use butcher's broom. Butcher's broom helps strengthen blood vessels and improves circulation. Take 100 milligrams extract three times daily.

Take vitamin E. Vitamin E helps bring oxygen to the tissues and promotes healing. You can use it topically or take it internally. Take 400 to 800 IU of d-alpha tocopherol and mixed tocopherols daily.

Take vitamin C and bioflavonoids. Vitamin C and bioflavonoids increase capillary and blood vessel strength so that they don't rupture easily. Bioflavonoids are also essential to collagen formation and elasticity of blood vessels. Berries of all types and cherries have high amounts of protective bioflavonoids. Take 500 to 2,000 milligrams vitamin C daily plus 100 to 1,000 milligrams bioflavonoids, which can usually be purchased in a single supplement.

Use dimethylsulfoxide (DMSO). In the literature, there is one anecdotal study in which a physician used DMSO topically for hemorrhoids. By his report, a 70 percent solution of DMSO will dissolve blood-engorged hemorrhoids almost overnight. It may be worth trying.

Natural Therapies for the Diverse Consequences of Faulty Digestion

"When one comes into a city to which he is a stranger, he ought to consider its situation, how it lies as to the winds and the rising of the sun; for its influence is not the same whether it lies to the north or to the south, to the rising or to the setting sun. . . . From these things he must proceed to investigate everything else. For if one knows all these things well, or at least the greater part of them, he cannot miss knowing, when he comes into a strange city, either the diseases peculiar to the place, or the particular nature of the common diseases. . . ."
—HIPPOCRATES, *ON AIRS, WATERS, AND PLACE*, c. 400 B.C.

This chapter discusses functional approaches to arthritis, eczema, psoriasis, migraine headaches, fibromyalgia, schizophrenia, scleroderma, chronic fatigue syndrome, asthma, Behcet's disease, and food and environmental sensitivities. All these seemingly diverse medical problems have digestive connections, including leaky gut syndrome, parasites, and dysbiosis. When the intestinal lining heals and intestinal flora regain balance, these conditions often improve dramatically. When pH is balanced, symptoms usually improve.

For each health condition, I have provided general information about the disease, recommendations for functional laboratory testing, and healing options, with the most important ones discussed first. With careful investigation and patience, you may find the underlying conditions that influence how you feel. You won't need to follow every remedy, but many of them can be found in combination products. You will note that although these health conditions are different, many of the healing options are the same.

Of course, you'll need to clean up your diet, correct any nutrient imbalances, get regular exercise, and find time to nurture yourself. If at first you don't find major improvement, keep working at it. You may not have found the best remedy or combination of therapies on the first try. Patience and perseverance bring the best results. It takes time to resolve chronic illnesses.

Arthritis

Arthritis refers to more than a hundred diseases that cause inflammation of the joints. The old-fashioned term for arthritis is *rheumatism*, and today physicians who specialize in arthritis are called rheumatologists. Arthritis affects forty million Americans and accounts for forty-six million medical visits per year. It affects about 15 percent of our population and 3 percent of those severely, but it is severe in 11 percent of people age sixty-five and older.

The two most common types of arthritis are osteoarthritis and rheumatoid arthritis. Other common types include psoriatic arthritis, ankylosing spondylitis, gout, Lyme disease, and Sjögren's syndrome. Each of these diseases has its own characteristics, but they all share the symptoms of pain and inflammation in joints.

There are many causes for arthritis: genetics, infections, physical injury, nutritional deficiencies, allergies, metabolic and immune disorders, stress, and environmental pollutants and toxins. Several types of arthritis have well-documented associations with faulty digestive function, and osteoarthritis responds well to dietary changes. Rheumatoid arthritis, ankylosing spondylitis, lupus, Sjögren's syndrome, and Reiter's syndrome may be caused by a combination of genetics, dysbiosis, food or environmental sensitivities, and leaky gut syndrome.

The current drugs of choice for arthritis pain are nonsteroidal anti-inflammatories (NSAIDs). However, NSAIDs block the production of prostaglandins, which stimulate repair of the digestive lining. This causes increased leaky gut syndrome. Use of NSAIDs in children with rheumatoid arthritis showed that 75 percent had gastrointestinal problems caused by the drugs. And the more NSAIDs people take, the leakier the gut wall becomes, the more pain and inflammation follows, which sets up a continuously escalating problem. To make matters worse, many NSAIDs also have a negative effect on the ability of cartilage to repair itself. They block our body's ability to regenerate cartilage tissue by lowering the amounts of healing prostaglandins, glycosaminoglycans, and hyaluronan, and by raising leukotriene levels.

Other drugs commonly used to ameliorate the symptoms of arthritis also have well-known adverse effects. Natural therapies for arthritis reduce the need for such medications and their accompanying side effects. These natural therapies can be astonishingly effective.

The dietary connection between rheumatoid arthritis and food sensitivities was first noted by Michael Zeller in 1949 in *Annals of Allergy*. He found a direct cause and effect by adding and eliminating foods from the diet. He joined forces with Drs. Herbert Rinkel and Theron Randolph to publish a book called *Food Allergy* in 1951.

Theron Randolph, M.D., is the father of a field of medicine called clinical ecology, which studies how our environment affects health. He found that people with rheumatoid arthritis who were not reacting to foods had at least one sensitivity to an environmental chemical. Randolph sent questionnaires to more than two hundred of his patients with osteoarthritis and rheumatoid arthritis to assess how well treatments were working. Their responses showed that when they avoided food and environmental allergens, there was a significant reduction in arthritic symptoms. Randolph also felt that other types of arthritis, including Reiter's syndrome, ankylosing spondylitis, and psoriatic arthritis, have an ecological basis.

Since then, other studies have been done on the relationship between food sensitivities and arthritis. In a study of forty-three people with arthritis of the hands, a water fast of three days brought improvement in tenderness, swelling, strength of grip, pain, joint circumference, function, and SED rate (a simple blood test that determines a breakdown of tissue somewhere in the body). When some of these people were tested with single foods, symptoms reoccurred in twenty-two out of twenty-seven people. In other studies, the foods most likely to provoke symptoms after an elimination diet were, in order of most to least: corn, wheat, bacon or pork, oranges, milk, oats, rye, eggs, beef, coffee, malt, cheese, grapefruit, tomato, peanuts, sugar, butter, lamb, lemon, and soy. Cereals were the most common food, with wheat and corn causing problems in more than 50 percent of the people.

In another study, it was found that forty-four out of ninety-three people with rheumatoid arthritis had elevated levels of IgG to gliadin. Among these forty-four people, 86 percent had positive RA factors. In yet another study, fifteen out of twenty-four people had raised levels of IgA, rheumatoid factor, and wheat protein IgG with a biopsy of the jejunum. Six of the wheat-positive people and one of the wheat-negative people had damage to the brush borders of their intestines. The researchers felt that the intestines play an important role in the progression of rheumatoid arthritis. Increased intestinal permeability allows more food particles to cross the intestinal mucosa, which triggers a greater sensitivity response.

The concept of food sensitivity and increased intestinal permeability is gaining acceptance as more physicians see the clinical changes in their patients when they use this approach. Testing for food and environmental sensitivities, parasites, toxic metals, candidiasis, and intestinal permeability and a comprehensive digestive stool analysis often provide an understanding of an underlying cause of the disease.

Candidiasis frequently plays a role in arthritis and is a possible aggravator in rheumatoid arthritis. Yeast in the gastrointestinal system may be the result of antibiotics, oral contraceptives, steroid medications, increased use of alcohol or sugar, or a stressed immune system. Treatment of candida infections in the digestive system has improved rheumatoid symptoms in many cases. To find out if it complicates your symptoms, do the self-test in this book as well as a blood or stool test.

Infection can trigger arthritis and joint inflammation. Why they move to the joints or cause joint pain is unknown at this time. But the phenomenon is well documented. If candida, Lyme disease, chlamydia, klebsiella, salmonella, or another infection is present, your physician can recommend a variety of therapeutics, including both natural and pharmaceutical remedies.

If you have increased intestinal permeability, nutrients such as glutamine, quercetin, gamma oryzanol, and beneficial flora can help heal the leaky cells. An elimination diet or fasting can significantly reduce joint inflammation, pain, and stiffness and increase mobility. By careful addition of foods over the course of three months, you can see which foods cause symptoms to recur. Blood testing can significantly aid in this process because you have a much clearer idea of which foods you are sensitive to. No blood test is 100 percent accurate, so you still need to go through the dietary regimen. After a period of four to six months of avoiding a particular food, you will be able to tolerate most of the troublesome foods. Repeat blood testing at that time is advised.

After that, many people will be pain-free, while others may still have some arthritic symptoms. There is documentation in the literature about arthritis and deficiencies of nearly every known nutrient. When the needed nutrients are supplied, the body can begin to balance itself. Though many additional nutritional and herbal products help arthritis sufferers, no one thing works for everyone, so persist until you find the therapies that work best for you. Give each one at least a three-month trial before giving up on it. I remember Abraham Hoffer, M.D., telling about a patient at a conference many years ago. He had recommended the man take 1,000 milligrams of vitamin C daily for his arthritis. The man took the vitamin C faithfully each day without any improvement. After a whole year, he suddenly became pain-free.

People with arthritis are often too acidic. To buffer this acidity, the body pulls alkaline minerals out of the bones. These minerals are sometimes deposited in joints throughout the body. Use of litmus paper to test the first morning urine can determine whether an acid-alkaline imbalance is contributing to arthritis. (See Chapter 6.)

Exercise and stretching are useful for all types of arthritic conditions. Yoga has been found to help with range of motion, pain, stiffness, and joint tenderness. Walking, swimming, physical therapy, and massage therapy may all play a role in reduction of symptoms. Movement is *not* optional. Even small amounts can give great relief.

Osteoarthritis

Osteoarthritis is the most common type of arthritis and the one we associate with aging, although nutritionally oriented physicians believe it has more to do with poor dietary habits and biochemical imbalances. Pain is usually the first symptom. The main characteristics are stiffness, aches, and painful joints that creak and crack. Stiffness may be worse in the morning and after exercise. Osteoarthritis begins gradually and usually affects one or a few joints, most commonly in the knee, hip, fingers, ankles, and feet. As joints enlarge, cartilage degenerates. Eventually, hardening leads to bone spurs. You lose flexibility, strength, and the ability to grasp, accompanied with pain. Risk of osteoarthritis, especially arthritis in the knee, increases if you are overweight; losing weight helps. Acid-alkaline balance is also important in treating this illness.

Rheumatoid Arthritis (RA)

Rheumatoid arthritis is characterized by inflammation of joints most often in the hands, feet, wrists, elbows, and ankles with symmetrical involvement. It can start in virtually any joint. The onset may be sudden, with pain in multiple joints; or it may come on gradually, with more and more joints becoming involved. Joints become swollen and feel tender and can degenerate and become misshapen. Joints are often stiffest in the mornings and also feel worse after movement. The rheumatoid factor (RF) is a blood test that will become elevated in most cases of rheumatoid arthritis. While it may get better or worse, once established it is nearly always present to some extent. Treatment is aimed at lowering inflammation and TNF-alpha.

Many drugs are being used to treat rheumatoid arthritis, and all have complicating side effects. Natural therapies are an adjunct or replacement for medical intervention. For example, fish oils and curcumin lower TNF-alpha.

Rheumatoid arthritis has a genetic component, often running in families. When genes meet the environment, the illness is triggered. It's not a one-to-one correlation; many genes may be involved and many environmental triggers. The gene marker HLA-DR4 is present in 50 to 75 percent of people with rheumatoid arthritis. *Proteus mirabilis*, a bacteria commonly found in the digestive tract, typically doesn't cause illness, but when present in a person who is HLA-DR4 positive, it may trigger an auto-immune response that leads to rheumatoid arthritis. *Proteus mirabilis* antibodies are often found in people with RA. Vegetarian diets have long been shown to be of benefit. In a unique study, a decrease in antibodies to *Proteus mirabilis* was observed in subjects on a vegetarian diet. Proteus infections can be treated with either natural or pharmaceutical therapy.

Vegetarian, vegan, and raw-food diets have been shown in numerous studies to be successful at reducing the symptoms of rheumatoid arthritis. Vegetable-based diets help balance pH levels. They also provide an abundance of antioxidants, natural anti-inflammatory factors, vitamins, minerals, and phytonutrients. This diet also tends to be more hypoallergenic. Food sensitivities play a role in RA. Add fish oil to increase the benefits. Short-term fasting prior to beginning the vegetarian diet has also been shown to provide long-term benefits. These approaches are definitely worth trying. You'll want to work with a nutritionist on this.

Food and environmental sensitivities, malabsorption, parasites, candida, and leaky gut syndrome also play a role in rheumatoid arthritis. Any food may trigger a reaction, but the most common aggravators, in descending order, are corn, wheat, bacon or pork, oranges, milk, oats, rye, eggs, beef, coffee, malt, cheese, grapefruit, tomato, peanuts, sugar cane, butter, lamb, lemons, and soy. Some people with it are gliadin sensitive (sensitive to grain; see information on celiac disease in Chapter 10). It's hard to generalize or predict which of these factors will be found in each person, but usually one or more is present. Each of them needs to be investigated. Leaky gut is probably not a primary cause of rheumatoid arthritis, but long-term use of NSAID medication often makes it a factor.

Psoriatic Arthritis

Psoriatic arthritis affects 3 to 7 percent of people with psoriasis, about 1.4 million Americans. In addition to the usual symptoms of psoriasis, they also have joint pain, tenderness, or swelling in the fingers, toes, or spine. Other symptoms include reduced range of motion, morning stiffness, redness and pain of the eye that is similar to conjunctivitis, and nail changes with pitting or lifting of the nail. Psoriatic arthritis is rarely found in people who do not also have psoriasis. Skin and joint symptoms may flare up or improve simultaneously. Psoriatic arthritis closely resembles rheumatoid arthritis, although people with psoriatic arthritis usually have a negative rheumatoid factor. This disease can be mild, but it can also be severely deforming and disabling.

Like other types of autoimmune disease, psoriatic arthritis has genetic, environmental, and immunologic origins. The gene marker HLA-B27 is present in most people with this disease.

Inflammation of psoriatic arthritis is involved with arachidonic acid pathways and TNF-alpha. New drug therapies, like injectable infliximab and etanercept, aim at lower TNF-alpha levels. A healthful diet plus essential fatty acids help reduce and prevent further inflammation. Evening primrose, borage, and fish oils; turmeric; curcumin; bromelain; and quercetin all work on these pathways.

Ankylosing Spondylitis (AS)

Ankylosing spondylitis is characterized by a progressive fusion of joints in and around the spine. Caucasian men constitute 90 percent of those with the illness, and it typically becomes evident between the ages of ten and thirty. It starts off as a low backache, which is often worse in the mornings. Symptoms get progressively worse and spread from the lower back to the midback and up to the neck. The spine gradually becomes fused. Later, shoulders, hips, and knees may be affected. Symptoms flare and subside. Secretory IgA levels are usually elevated in people with ankylosing spondylitis.

The role of dysbiosis in ankylosing spondylitis is the most researched and best understood of all the arthritic diseases. Most researchers believe that AS is triggered by an inherited gene and interactions with the environment. Much research has been done on the role of infection as a primary trigger of AS. The gene implicated is HLA-B27, although others may still be found. HLA-B27 is present in 96 percent of people with ankylosing spondylitis. This marker is also present in 8 percent of the general population. Research shows 70 to 80 percent of people with ankylosing spondylitis have the klebsiella bacteria in their stools. Yersinia, shigella, and salmonella bacteria are also associated with this process and may contribute to the disease in people who are not infected with klebsiella. These bacteria may not normally cause disease, but in people with the HLA-B27 gene marker, antibodies produced to kill the bacteria cross-react, causing pain and inflammation. This concept of autoimmune disease may explain why some people get certain illnesses and others don't. It's the presence not only of a specific gene, but also of a microbe or other environmental trigger that activates the disease process.

What begins as a local infection triggers an autoimmune disease. Finnish rheumatology researcher Marjatta Leirisalo-Repo states, "An association between inflammatory bowel disease and enteroarthritis and the spondyloarthropathies has been known for awhile . . . and it now seems evident that chronic gut inflammation is either associated with or is even the cause of chronicity of peripheral arthritis and the development of ankylosing spondylitis."

It is important to make an early diagnosis of ankylosing spondylitis so that progression of the disease can be slowed or halted. Because it usually appears as a low backache, many people will tend to seek chiropractic help or massage therapy or take anti-inflammatory medications. But such remedies can't correct dysbiosis in the intestinal tract. Because many men commonly have low-back pain, they often have irreversible damage before a correct diagnosis is made.

About half the people with ankylosing spondylitis experience dramatic improvement when they eliminate dairy products. Thirteen out of twenty-five people who were studied had good results, and another four had moderate improvements. Of the respondents whose results were good, eight were able to discontinue NSAID medication. Six patients remained dairy-free for more than two years because they were so satisfied with the results. The elimination of dairy products is a simple and effective treatment to try. Although the mechanism for this improvement is unclear, it is suggested that a dairy-free diet modifies the bacterial ecosystem of the gut, which may have benefits. Another hypothesis is that milk allergy causes chronic irritation to the gut as well as gut permeability.

Klebsiella and other disease-producing microbes that can contribute to ankylosing spondylitis use sugars as their main food source. Some physicians are experimenting with a low-starch diet and getting good results. Eliminate all breads, grains, pasta, cookies, candy, root vegetables, and legumes. Be patient: you may get amazing results, but you will need to stay on the diet for at least six months before you really reap the benefits.

Leaky gut syndrome is present in people with ankylosing spondylitis. Unfortunately, NSAIDs are commonly used to treat ankylosing spondylitis, causing even greater intestinal permeability. This, in turn, causes more sensitivity to foods and environmental substances.

Functional Laboratory Testing

The letters following each list item indicate the illness that that test can be used to detect. Note that O = osteoarthritis, RA = rheumatoid arthritis, PA = psoriatic arthritis, and AS = ankylosing spondylitis.

Elisa/Act allergy testing for foods. (O, RA, PA, AS)

Comprehensive digestive stool analysis. (O, RA, PA, AS)

Intestinal permeability screening. Stop use of NSAIDs for three weeks prior to test. (O, RA, PA, AS)

Candida testing, either separately or in CDSA. (O, RA, PA, AS)

Heidelberg capsule testing for HCl status. (RA)

Small bowel bacterial overgrowth breath test. (RA)

Liver function testing. People with rheumatoid arthritis are also shown to have reduced function in the detoxification pathways. (RA)

Healing Options

Some of these suggestions will significantly help your arthritis; others may not help at all. You can look for products that combine these nutrients and herbs. Be patient and give whatever you try time to work. Try one or two at a time until you find a program that suits your body's unique needs and your lifestyle. Recommendations work for all types of arthritis, unless I've specifically noted a type after the suggestion.

Try an alkalizing diet. Bring your body into acid–alkaline balance. Read instructions in Chapter 6.

Exercise. It's important to use your body as much as you can without aggravating the condition. Yoga, walking, swimming, stretching, water exercises, physical therapy, massage, and acupressure massage may all be of help. Do something nearly every day.

Do the elimination-provocation diet. Follow the directions outlined in Chapter 6. For best results, work with a nutritionist or physician who is familiar with food sensitivity protocols.

Try the Nightshade Diet. In the 1970s, Norman Childers, a horticulturist, popularized the Nightshade Diet. Elimination of nightshade foods helps only about 15 percent of people with arthritis, but the people who respond are usually helped a great deal. The nightshade foods are potatoes, tomatoes, eggplant, and peppers (red, green, yellow, and chili). An elimination diet of one week followed by a reintroduction of these foods provides a good test. Blood testing also picks up these sensitivities.

Take a multivitamin with minerals. People with arthritis are often deficient in many nutrients. Aging, poor diet, medications, malabsorption, and illness all contribute to poor nutritional status. At least seventeen nutrients are essential for formation of bone and cartilage, so it's important to find a supplement that supports these needs. Look for a supplement that contains 800 to 1,000 milligrams calcium, 400 to 500 milligrams magnesium, 15 to 45 milligrams zinc, 1 to 2 milligrams copper, 10,000 IU vitamin A, 200 micrograms selenium, 50 milligrams vitamin B_6, and 5 to 10 milligrams manganese in addition to other nutrients. Follow dosage on bottle to get nutrients in the appropriate amounts.

Address hypochlorhydria or low HCl levels (RA). Low levels of hydrochloric acid (HCl) were found in 32 percent of people tested with rheumatoid arthritis. Half of these people had small bowel bacterial overgrowth. Thirty-five percent of patients with normal levels of HCl had small bowel bacterial overgrowth compared with none of the normal controls. Small bowel overgrowth was found most in people with active arthritic symptoms.

The dosage will vary from person to person. To find the optimal amount for you, begin by taking one HCl tablet with each meal for one day. The next day, take two tablets with each meal, gradually increasing the dosage. At some point you will feel a warm, burning sensation in your stomach; your optimal dose is one tablet less than this. If the burning sensation is uncomfortable, quickly drink a glass of milk or water with a teaspoon of baking soda.

Take vitamin E. Twenty-nine people with osteoarthritis were given 600 IU of vitamin E or a placebo daily. Out of fifteen who received vitamin E, 52 percent reported improvement. Another study showed no improvement in those with osteoarthritis who were given vitamin E supplementation of 1,200 IU daily. Try 800 IU for two to three months. It is very safe and may help some people. Best is the "d" form of mixed tocopherols.

Take vitamin C. Vitamin C is an essential nutrient for every antiarthritis program. It is vital for formation of cartilage and collagen, a fibrous protein that forms strong connective tissue necessary for bone strength. Vitamin C also plays a role in immune response, helping protect us from disease-producing microbes. Many types of arthritis are caused by microbes, which vitamin C helps combat. It also inhibits formation of inflammatory prostaglandins, helping to reduce pain, inflammation, and swelling. Vitamin C is also an antioxidant and free radical scavenger; free radical formation has been noted in arthritic conditions. Take 1 to 3 grams daily in an ascorbate or ester form.

For best results, try a vitamin C flush weekly for four weeks.

Take glucosamine and chondroitin. Glucosamine sulfate and chondroitin sulfate are nutrients used therapeutically to help repair cartilage, reduce inflammation, and increase mobility. Studies have consistently shown benefits of both glucosamine and chondroitin supplementation. Green-lipped mussels are a rich source of glycosaminoglycans. Use of glucosamine sulfate has no associated side effects, although anecdotally it may raise serum cholesterol levels.

It either works or it doesn't. Give it a three-month trial. It's important to buy a product that has been broken down into a molecular size that your body can use. It's worth it to spend more on this product.

Take alfalfa. Alfalfa is a tried and true folk remedy for arthritis. Many people attest to its benefits, but more research is needed on it. Alfalfa is an abundantly nutritious food, high in minerals, vitamins, antioxidants, and protein. Alfalfa may help because of its saponin content or its high nutrient and trace mineral content. It is widely used as a nutritional supplement in animal feed.

Take 14 to 24 tablets in two or three dosages daily, or grind up alfalfa seeds and take 3 tablespoons of ground seeds each day. You can mix them with applesauce, cottage cheese, or oatmeal or sprinkle them on salads. Another method is to cook 1 ounce of alfalfa seeds in 3 cups of water. Do not boil them, but cook gently in a glass or enamel pan for thirty minutes and strain. Toss away the seeds and keep the tea. Dilute the tea with an equal amount of water. Add honey if you like. Use it all within twenty-four hours. Yet another method is to soak 1 ounce of alfalfa seeds in 3 cups of water for twelve to twenty-four hours. Strain and drink the liquid throughout the day.

Try yucca. Yucca has been used by Native Americans of the Southwest to alleviate symptoms of arthritis and improve digestion. It's a rich source of saponins with anti–inflammatory effects. Studies have been done with both rheumatoid and osteoarthritis with significant improvement in 56 to 66 percent of the people who tried it. People taking yucca for more than one-and-a-half years also had the additional advantage of improved triglyceride and cholesterol levels and reduction in high blood pressure, with no negative side effects. Take 2 to 8 tablets daily.

Increase omega-3 fatty acids and fish oils. Fish oils come from cold-water fish and contain eicosapentaenoic acid (EPA) and docosahexaenoic acid (DHA). The fish with the highest levels are salmon, mackerel, halibut, sardines, tuna, and herring. These omega-3 fatty acids are essential because we cannot synthesize them and must obtain them from our foods. Fish oils inhibit production of inflammatory prostaglandin E2 series, inhibit cyclooxygenase and thromboxane A2, all of which come from arachidonic acid. Fish oils shift the production to thromboxane A3, which causes less constriction of blood vessels and platelet stickiness than thromboxane A2.

Research has shown fish oils are really helpful for some people with arthritis. Fish-oil capsules reduce morning stiffness and joint tenderness. They produce moderate, but definite improvement in arthritic diseases at dosages from 8 to 20 capsules daily. Similar results can be obtained by eating fish with high EPA/ DHA two to four times a week. Because fish oils increase blood clotting time, they should not be used by people who have hemophilia or who take anticoagulant medicines or aspirin regularly.

It's easier for most people to eat fish two to four times each week. High dosages in capsule form should be monitored by a physician.

Take gamma-linolenic acid (GLA) (RA). Patients with rheumatoid arthritis were given 1.4 grams of GLA from borage oil daily. It significantly reduced their symptoms: swollen joints by 36 percent, tenderness by 45 percent, swollen joint count by 28 percent, and swollen joint score by 41 percent. (Some people responded in more than one area.) Use of evening primrose oil in the study group and olive oil for the control group showed that both oils helped reduce pain and morning stiffness. Several people were able to reduce use of NSAIDs, but none were able to stop the medication. The modest results in this study were probably due to the use of NSAIDs with the evening primrose oil. The same results could be obtained by use of evening primrose or borage oil alone. Take 1,400 milligrams.

Take ginger. Ginger is an old Ayurvedic remedy that was given to people with rheumatoid and osteoarthritis. It reduced pain and swelling in various amounts in 75 percent of the people tested, with no reported side effects over three months to two-and-a-half years. Ginger can be used as an ingredient in food and tea or taken as a supplement. Take 2 ounces fresh ginger daily or 3,000 to 7,000 milligrams powdered ginger.

Take niacinamide. Most of the B-complex vitamins have been shown to reduce inflammation and swelling associated with arthritis. Dr. Kaufman, M.D., Ph.D., an expert on arthritis, recommends using niacinamide at a rather high dosage with excellent results. It doesn't cure the arthritis, but it really helps while you take it. If you are going to try this, do so with your physician's supervision. High levels of niacinamide can be liver toxic. Take 250 to 500 milligrams daily. Soft gel capsules are recommended. Make sure to get a brand without colors, preservatives, or solvents.

Take cetyl myristoleate (CM). Harry Diehl, a researcher at the National Institutes of Health, found that mice did not develop arthritis when CM was given. When he himself developed arthritis, Diehl took CM and his arthritis resolved. Jonathan Wright, M.D., has found CM to be clinically valuable in about half of his patients. CM appears to actually "cure" arthritis in many instances. I was able to find two studies on CM that had astounding results. CM was found to be best used in combination with glucosamine sulfate, sea cucumber, and methylsulfonylmethane (MSM). Recommended duration of use is two to four weeks. Carbonated beverages, caffeine, chocolate, and cigarettes are not allowed while taking CM and its associated supplements.

Take superoxide dismutase (SOD). SOD plays an important role in reducing inflammation and has been used alone, with copper, manganese or copper, and zinc for various arthritic conditions. Oral

SOD doesn't seem to work as well, except when used in a copper-zinc preparation. Some physicians are using SOD in injections. Wheat grass extracts of SOD can be purchased at health-food stores. Most people who try them experience benefits, but there is little scientific research to date. Some veterinarians are using wheat grass SOD with arthritic animals with excellent results.

Take methylsulfonylmethane (MSM) or dimethylsulfoxide (DMSO). DMSO is highly effective for reducing arthritis pain when used on skin. It has a distinct odor that prevents many people from using it, but MSM is odorless. MSM, a naturally occurring derivative of dimethylsulfoxide, is now being used as a supplement. MSM has been found to be an antioxidant and anti-inflammatory in animal studies probably because of its high sulfur content. It helps reduce pain and inflammation and gives the body the sulfur compounds necessary to build cartilage and collagen. It is also useful in allergies, blood sugar control, and asthma. Take 1,000 to 5,000 milligrams daily. It is best when taken with 1,000 to 5,000 milligrams of vitamin C for absorption. Or use DMSO topically on skin.

Take S-adenosylmethionine (SAMe). A recent player on the scene is SAMe, a chemical that is found naturally in every living cell. Research in ten studies on SAMe that included more than 22,000 people has shown it to have powerful antidepressant effects without the side effects of pharmaceutical antidepressant medications. SAMe has also been shown to be as potent an anti-inflammatory drug as indomethacin and other NSAIDs with fewer negative effects. This product is expensive because it is difficult to stabilize. Use it with a good multivitamin that contains B-complex vitamins. Take 400 milligrams twice daily. Adjust up or down as needed.

Take bromelain. Bromelain is an enzyme derived from pineapple that acts as an anti-inflammatory in much the same way that evening primrose, fish, and borage oils do. It interferes with production of arachidonic acid, shifting to prostaglandin production of the less inflammatory type. It also prevents platelet aggregation and interferes with the growth of malignant cells. It appears to be as effective as NSAID medications. Bromelain can be taken with meals as a digestive aid, but as an anti-inflammatory, it must be taken between meals. Take 500 to 1,000 milligrams two to three times daily between meals.

Take quercetin. Quercetin is the most effective bioflavonoid in its anti-inflammatory effects; others include bromelain, curcumin, and rutin. Bioflavonoids help maintain collagen tissue by decreasing membrane permeability and cross-linking collagen fibers, making them stronger. Quercetin can be used to reduce pain and inflammatory responses and for control of allergies. Take 500 to 2,000 milligrams daily. It appears to reduce inflammatory cytokines.

Take boswellia. Boswellia is taken over the long term as a treatment for rheumatoid arthritis, not specifically for immediate pain. *Boswellia serrata*, an Ayurvedic remedy that has been traditionally used for arthritis, pain, and inflammation, has been shown to moderate inflammatory markers such as nitric oxide and 5-lipoxygenase. A specific preparation of boswellia called H–15 was given to 260 people and found to be effective in treating rheumatoid arthritis. Fifty to 60 percent of the subjects had good results. Take 1,200 milligrams two or three times daily.

Take turmeric or curcumin. Turmeric has been shown to have powerful anti-inflammatory properties. Some of the mechanisms involved include its ability to block leukotrienes and arachidonic acid, both of which cause inflammation and pain. An effective dosage of turmeric is 10 to 60 grams daily. Curcumin, the active pain-relieving ingredient, can be taken in much smaller doses of 500 milligrams three times daily. For those lucky enough to live in warm areas where turmeric can be grown and used fresh, it can be juiced, grated, used in stir-fry, and eaten freely. Turmeric is also a lovely flowering garden plant.

Take folic acid plus vitamin B_{12}. In a recent study, those with osteoarthritis in their hands were given 20 micrograms vitamin B_{12} plus 6,400 micrograms folic acid daily. They reported a significant reduction in symptoms. This is a tiny amount of vitamin B_{12} and a large amount of folic acid, which is nontoxic even at these high levels.

Take devil's claw. Devil's claw (*Harpagophytum procumbens*) is a South African root that is commonly used as an arthritis remedy. It reduces pain and inflammation. Several studies have shown it to work as well as phenylbutazone, a common NSAID medication. It is commonly used in low-potency homeopathic dilutions of 2X in Germany.

Use black cohosh. Black cohosh (*Cimicifuga racemosa*) has long been used by European and American herbalists to reduce muscle spasm, pain, and inflammation. It can be used as either a tincture or in capsules.

Use capsicum (cayenne pepper). Cayenne has been well studied for its temporary relief of arthritis pain. Creams with capsicum are used topically to relieve pain. (These creams may burn when first applied.) They work by blocking leukotrienes and arachidonic acid, thereby reducing pain and inflammation. Eighty percent of the topical-cream users experience pain relief.

Try DL-phenylalanine (DLPA) (for RA). DLPA is an amino acid that is used therapeutically for pain and depression. It is effective for treating rheumatoid arthritis, osteoarthritis, low-back pain, and migraines. "D" is the naturally found form, and "L" is its synthetic mirror. The combination of DL slows down the release of the phenylalanine. It appears to inhibit the breakdown of endorphins, our body's natural pain relievers. Take 400 to 500 milligrams three times daily.

Use copper to treat RA symptoms. Copper is involved in collagen formation, tissue repair, and anti-inflammatory processes. Rheumatoid arthritis sufferers often have marginal copper levels. Traditionally, copper bracelets have been worn to help reduce arthritic symptoms. W. Ray Walker, Ph.D., tested those who had benefited from copper bracelets by having them wear copper-colored aluminum bracelets for two months. Fourteen out of forty participants deteriorated so much they couldn't finish the two months. More than half reported that their arthritis had worsened. Dr. Walker found that 13 milligrams of copper per month was dissolved by sweat, and presumably much of that was absorbed through the skin. Supplementation with copper increases levels of superoxide dismutase (SOD). Wear a copper bracelet or supplement with 1 to 2 milligrams daily in a multivitamin preparation. If you are working with a physician, you may temporarily add a supplement of copper salicylate or copper sebacate until copper levels return to normal.

Examine side effects of breast implants. Silicone breast implants may cause rheumatoid-like symptoms in some women, although research is divided. If you have rheumatoid arthritis and silicone or saline breast implants, it would be smart to be tested for silicone antibodies or allergies on an annual basis. Many women feel remarkably better once breast implants have been removed.

Diagnose and treat dysbiosis. In ankylosing spondylitis, an infection is often present. Your physician can prescribe an appropriate antibiotic, or you can use colloidal silver, goldenseal, and/or grapefruit seed extract. This treatment may be useful for other types of arthritis as well.

Supplement with acidophilus and bifidobacteria. Because treatment for dysbiosis will alter your intestinal flora, take probiotic supplements of supportive healthy bacteria to reestablish them. Take 1 to 2 capsules two to three times daily or, between meals, ¼ to ½ teaspoon powder mixed with a cool or room-temperature beverage.

Asthma

Asthma affects about 5 to 8 percent of the U.S. population, more than 14.9 million. It is more common in children and people of African descent. Asthma is more common in boys than in girls during childhood, but the incidence evens out between genders in adulthood. The incidence of asthma has been rising at an alarming rate. Between 1980 and 1993–94, there was a 75 percent increase overall, 74 percent in children aged five to fourteen, and 160 percent increase in children up to age four. These rates continue to rise.

Symptoms of asthma include shortness of breath, wheezing, chest tightness, and coughing. Its more technical name is reversible obstructive pulmonary disease (ROPD). Asthma can be a chronic or an occasional problem. Most people with asthma also have allergies. The causes of asthma are multifactorial and not well understood. Exposure to stress, poor air quality, grasses, molds, smoke, chemicals, bacterial infections, colds, viruses, pollens, dust, and sensitivity to cockroaches and pets can trigger asthma attacks. Increasing ozone levels are directly correlated with an increase in hospital admissions for asthma. Anyone can be sensitive to these events, but people with asthma are much more sensitive. During an attack, changes take place in the lungs that make breathing difficult. The lungs begin to produce more mucus than normal. It's very thick and sticky, and tends to clog up the tubes. The air tubes become inflamed and swell, which causes them to narrow, and breathing becomes labored. Oxygen supply to the rest of the body is limited, carbon dioxide builds up, and the body becomes more acidic.

On a biochemical level, exposure to allergens stimulates mast cell activity and production of cytokines as interleukins, which play a central role in initiating and sustaining the inflammation associated with asthma.

Asthma attacks can come on suddenly or build over several hours or days. Medical treatment consists of medications, inhalers, allergy shots, and peak flow meter machines, which help breathing. Reducing allergen exposure also helps. Excellent air-filtration systems, efficient vacuum cleaners, laundering bedding in hot water, and keeping bedrooms scrupulously clean and uncluttered can be effective in preventing asthma attacks.

When exposed to allergens, asthma sufferers have inflammation in their digestive tract that causes a leaky gut syndrome. Although the symptoms are felt in the lungs, it is believed that people with asthma have mucous membrane problems in general. Candida and other fungal infections have been linked to asthma. This may initially be due to steroid medications, such as inhalers and prednisone, which are well-known triggers of candida. One study found fungal infections in fifty-two out of sixty-four subjects. After two years of treatment for candida, a significant decrease in asthmatic symptoms was reported in 60 percent of the subjects. Other studies have found a high incidence of candida in asthmatics who don't use steroids. I've had several clients whose asthma significantly cleared by treating the candida infection. There is also a deficiency of secretory IgA found in mucous membranes throughout the body as a consequence of asthma.

Asthma seems to respond best to lifestyle changes and stress-management techniques. Learning to develop emotional hardiness and a relaxed manner in stressful situations can greatly reduce the incidence and severity of asthma attacks. Exercise is usually beneficial for people with asthma, although there is one type of asthma that only occurs post exercise. Cleaning up your diet is essential. Get rid of sugars, alcohol, processed foods, and food additives.

Test for specific food sensitivities and allergies and then avoid those that you react to. Reactions will be individual and cannot be generalized. In children, the most common food allergens are fruits, eggs, dairy products, and nuts. Dairy products have been shown to be protective in other studies, which is why it's important to test. Allergies and asthma are a problem with total load of stress on the body. If you can keep the total below the threshold, you stay symptom-free.

When children are born to a parent who has asthma, it's advised to breast-feed for at least four months. This significantly reduces the likelihood that the children will develop asthma.

Functional Laboratory Testing

IgE and IgG food allergy testing
Intestinal permeability testing
Candida antibodies and sensitivity testing

Healing Options

Make dietary changes. Eliminate sugar, alcohol, processed foods, and food additives from your diet. Focus on fresh fruits and vegetables and natural foods. Discover food allergens by testing. Avoid all reactive foods for four to six months. Slowly reintroduce those foods. The most likely foods to cause reactions are dairy, nuts, fruits, and eggs, but virtually any food can be a problem. Remember, we breathe in about five grams of pollen and dust each year, but we eat about a thousand pounds of food during that same time. Sensitivity to foods is often a major problem in asthma.

Exercise. Research shows that twenty to thirty minutes of aerobic exercise four or five times each week will reduce use of medications and symptoms of asthma. It is important to go at your own pace and to not overdo—you don't want to cause exercise-induced asthma. If you are not already exercising, build up slowly and ask your doctor or a fitness instructor for a personalized program.

Focus on healing mucous membranes. People with asthma benefit from nutrients that promote healthful mucous membranes in the lungs and gut. Helpful nutrients include vitamin A, glutamine, N-acetyl glucosamine, N-acetyl cysteine (NAC), and folic acid.

Take vitamin C. Vitamin C is well documented in the literature to be of use in asthma protection. It protects lung responsiveness and function and reduces asthma symptoms. Vitamin C has antioxidant, antiallergy, antiviral, and antimicrobial properties. Take at least 1,000 milligrams. For best results, start with a vitamin C flush (see Chapter 8) once a week for four weeks.

Take magnesium. Magnesium deficiency is common in people with asthma. Magnesium is a powerful muscle relaxant and can help prevent and reduce the severity of asthma attacks. Take 400 to 800 milligrams daily. I also recommend increasing the dosage until you get diarrhea, then back off. If the dose you need is more than 1,000 milligrams, you may benefit from a teaspoon of choline citrate daily to help increase magnesium uptake into the cells.

Increase fish oil consumption. The research on fish oils and asthmatics has been extensive and mixed. Some people benefit tremendously, while others don't. You have nothing to lose from a month-long trial. It is well known that fish oils decrease inflammatory leukotrienes, cytokines, and arachidonic acid. Cod liver oil may be a good supplement because it also contains vitamin A, which is protective of the lung mucosa. Eat fish high in EPA/ DHA at least twice each week, take 2,000 to 2,500 milligrams EPA/DHA fish oil daily, or take 2,000 to 2,500 milligrams cod liver oil.

Try quercetin. Quercetin is a powerful and gentle mast cell inhibitor and antihistamine. Take at first sign of lung tightness and through the duration of the asthma attack, 1,000 to 3,000 milligrams daily as needed. As far as I know, there is no toxic dose.

Try arginine. Nitric oxide (NO) acts as a bronchodilator. The amino acid arginine is a precursor to NO release. Take 250 to 1,500 milligrams daily.

Use ginkgo biloba. One study on ginkgo showed improvement in symptoms, lung function, and reduced airway hyper-reactivity. Ginkgo is a known free radical scavenger, enhances circulation, protects nerves, and has an anti-inflammatory effect. Take ginkgo biloba standardized extract, 180 to 240 milligrams daily.

Take a multivitamin with antioxidants. Research documents the increased need for glutathione peroxidase, vitamin C, and vitamin E in asthma sufferers. The enzyme glutathione peroxidase depends on both selenium and glutathione. Vitamin B_6 and B_{12} levels have also been found to be lower in asthmatics. Look for a multivitamin that contains at least 400 IU vitamin E, 1,000 milligrams vitamin C, 200 micrograms selenium, reduced glutathione or NAC, and 5 or more milligrams of manganese. If you look for a multivitamin that has a dosage of three or more tablets, you may also find 400 to 600 milligrams magnesium as well.

Try bee propolis. Propolis is a resin that bees collect from trees and buds and is used to repair their hives. It has antibiotic and anti-fungal properties. One study looked at the benefits from use of bee propolis in adults with asthma. After two months, the number and severity of nighttime attacks had decreased, pulmonary function tests had improved, and inflammatory cytokines had decreased. *Caution*: some people are really allergic to all bee products. If you are one, don't use this. Otherwise, take 1,000 milligrams daily.

Try Traumeel S. Traumeel S is a homeopathic product that was used in a double-blind, placebo-controlled study. Subjects continued to use their corticosteroid medications along with Traumeel S during the study. Over twenty weeks, the use of medications was reduced from 4.6 milligrams daily to 2.6 milligrams daily. Their general symptoms improved significantly, and people had an increased sense of well-being. Take 1 ampoule subcutaneously every five to seven days.

Take coleus forskohli or forskolin. Coleus forskohli is an Ayurvedic herb in wide usage. Forskolin is one of the active ingredients and is now marketed as a separate product. This herb has been shown to have bronchodilating effects on the lungs and to be beneficial for asthma. It stimulates the production of cyclic AMP. Impaired cyclic AMP production is believed to be an underlying cause of asthma. Take 50 to 100 milligrams coleus forskohli daily or 9 to 18 milligrams forskolin daily.

Provide adrenal support. Asthma, like all allergies, responds to adrenal support. Corticosteroid drugs mimic the body's natural adrenal hormones. Anything you can do to enhance your body's own production of steroid hormones will be of benefit. Although literature is scant, animal studies with licorice hold promise. Use DGL licorice unless blood pressure is extremely low. Most licorice candy does not contain any licorice, but some gourmet licorice does. Be careful, as too much may raise your blood pressure. Adrenal glandulars, pantothenic acid, vitamin B_2, and Siberian ginseng (Eleutherococcus) may also be of use.

Try Meyer's cocktail. IV nutrients, given by a physician, can quickly help revitalize your nutrient status. Nutrients can be absorbed and used at higher concentrations. Meyer's cocktail is a combination of magnesium, calcium, vitamins B_{12} and B_6, pantothenic acid, and vitamin C. It has been used successfully in people with a variety of ailments.

Behcet's Disease (BD)

Behcet's disease (BD) is an inflammatory autoimmune disease that affects blood vessels throughout the body, causing vasculitis, an inflammation of the blood or lymph vessel. It was first recognized in 1937 by a Turkish doctor, Hulusi Behcet. It is also known as Silk

Road Disease because the incidence is greatest in the Mediterranean, the Middle East, and the Far East, although there have been cases in people of all nationalities and descent. In the United States, it is more common in women than in men. In the Middle Eastern countries, it is more common in men than women. Symptoms most commonly appear in one's twenties or thirties but can begin anytime. Fifteen thousand to 20,000 Americans have been diagnosed, and many more are undiagnosed.

Symptoms vary depending on where the inflammation is in your body and are due to an *overactive* immune system. It is chronic and the course is unpredictable. Some people are debilitated by the disease, while a lucky few may go into complete remission. The most common symptoms are recurrent sores in the mouth and genitals and eye inflammation. The sores often have a white or yellow center with redness at the edges and are very painful. There may also be additional symptoms, including skin lesions, painful joints, bowel inflammation, and meningitis. Symptoms may involve the nervous system, causing Parkinson-like symptoms; memory loss; impaired speech; hearing loss; loss of balance; blindness; headaches; stroke; and digestive complications, such as bloating, gas, bloody stools, and diarrhea. About 15 percent of people with BD also have heart disease complications. Sufferers sometimes experience a profound sense of fatigue. BD usually presents itself in a rhythm of remissions and flare-ups of disease activity. It may be worsened by extremes of hot and cold climates or menstrual cycles.

There is no known cause for Behcet's disease. It is suspected that an environmental exposure, such as a viral or bacterial infection, can trigger the illness in people who are already genetically susceptible.

A large body of research focuses on the insufficiency of antioxidant nutrients and enzymes in people with BD. Glutathione peroxidase levels are lower in people with BD. Glutathione is an enzyme that depends upon vitamin E and selenium for optimal function. Superoxide dismutase (SOD) activity is also diminished. It appears that production of nitric oxide (NO) is excessive in people with BD. Use of antioxidant nutrients can bring NO into control.

One recent study examined levels of vitamin C and malondi-aldehyde in people with BD. Malondialdehyde is a metabolite that is produced when there is lipid-peroxidation, which is a chain reaction requiring antioxidant nutrients. Vitamin C levels were lower in people with BD than in controls and malondialdehyde levels were higher than in controls. Vitamin C levels were low in people with BD even when the illness was in remission. Different researchers looked at vascular health and found that one hour after IV vitamin C was given there was improved function in the blood vessels.

Another study looked at vitamin E supplementation in BD. It was found that vitamins A and E, beta-carotene, and glutathione levels were lower in people with BD than in controls. When given vitamin E supplementation for six weeks, levels of blood antioxidants rose in the treatment group and were higher than in the untreated control groups.

BD sufferers have significantly increased intestinal permeability. Leaky gut syndrome can be aggravated by use of certain foods. Use of dairy products, gluten-containing foods (see section on celiac disease in Chapter 10), and other foods may trigger an immune response and symptoms. Testing for food and environmental sensitivities and allergies makes sense. Use of nutrients such as glutamine, quercetin, probiotics, and antioxidants can be helpful. See Chapter 5 or my booklet called *Leaky Gut Syndrome*.

No specific diagnostic test exists for Behcet's disease. Diagnosis is made by elimination of other possibilities and through symptom analysis and is best done by a physician experienced in the treatment of Behcet's patients. A list of patient-recommended physicians is available at the American Behcet's Disease Association website at behcets.com. BD may begin gradually at first, with sores that come and go and may be undiagnosed for a long time; it may also be misdiagnosed as herpes. Like patients with chronic fatigue syndrome, people with BD are often told it's "all in your head" because they look so healthy. Most of the inflammations are internal and not readily apparent to family and friends. To be diagnosed with BD, a person must have had recurrent oral ulcers, at least three times in a year. They must also meet two of four additional criteria: recurrent genital ulcers, eye lesions, skin lesions, or a positive "pathergy test." The pathergy test is simple. The forearm is pricked with a sterile needle, and if a small red bump or pustule occurs, the result is positive. This is very useful in Middle-Eastern populations, where 70 percent of people with BD test positive, but less so in Europe and America where the majority test negative.

Conventional treatments are similar to those for other autoimmune conditions and involve the use of immunosuppressive medications such as steroids, interferon alpha 2A and B, Levamisole, cyclosporine, Cytoxan, colchicine, Trental, and thalidomide. Not a group to be dealt with lightly.

Functional Laboratory Testing
Intestinal permeability testing
Lactose tolerance test
Testing for gluten and anti–gliadin antibodies
IgE, IgG, IgM food and environmental sensitivity testing

Healing Options
After testing, you'll have a better idea of any underlying problems. Look up related sections in this book to help you with the specifics. Then detoxify if necessary, clean up your diet, take pro-

biotics, and increase intake of vitamins, minerals, and other antioxidants.

Try metabolic cleansing. Metabolic cleansing involves going on a hypoallergenic food plan for one to three weeks and taking a nutrient-rich protein powder designed to help restore your liver's detoxification capacities. For a thorough discussion of metabolic cleansing, see Chapter 8.

Take antioxidants. You'll find fruits and vegetables to be great natural sources of antioxidants. Make sure you eat at least five to twelve servings daily. They probably won't give enough protection by themselves so add nutritional supplements. Vitamin C, vitamin E, glutathione, trace minerals, and other antioxidants may be helpful in decreasing the incidence and severity of flare-ups. Research shows that BD patients have an increased need for antioxidants. Therefore, supplementation with trace elements involved in the antioxidative processes may increase scavenger enzyme activities, and consequently, an improvement in clinical symptoms may be expected. While much more research is needed in this area, there is no reason not to add them to your daily routine. Take an antioxidant combination with carotenoids, selenium, glutathione, or N-acetyl cysteine, and that may contain lipoic acid, grape seed extract, pycnogenol, or other antioxidant nutrients.

Take vitamin E. Take 800 to 1,000 IU d-alpha tocopherol with mixed tocopherols daily.

Take vitamin C. Take a minimum of 2,000 milligrams of vitamin C daily. To maximize effects see section on vitamin C flush in Chapter 8.

Try BG-104. This is a Chinese herbal supplement. One study looked at the effectiveness of BG-104 in people with BD and Sjögren's diseases. Both BG-104 and vitamin E were found to have an anti-inflammatory effect. They enhanced antioxidant activity to reduced sedimentation rates (a measure of tissue breakdown) and number of neutrophils (white blood cells), and lowered C-reactive protein levels, which is a measure of inflammation.

Balance your pH. Cells work best in a neutral pH. When we have long-standing illness we tend to have acidic urine. See the section on pH testing and the food charts in Chapter 6. Also make use of baking soda and Epsom salt baths. Use ½ cup of each and soak on a regular basis.

Try acupuncture. There is limited research in this area, but the one study showed a positive effect on improving immune function and trace mineral status; however, a 2002 letter in the *British Journal of Ophthalmology* (Murray and Aboteen, 86, 2002: 476–77) discussed a BD patient who developed pathergy-like pustules at the sites of acupuncture needle placement, indicating caution in the use of this treatment.

Investigate allergies and sensitivities. Although more research needs to be done in this area, one study indicated an immune response when patients were given cow's milk. Eliminate dairy products for two weeks. See if you have improvement in symptoms. Then add back cultured dairy, such as yogurt, kefir, and cottage cheese. See how you feel. It may be necessary to avoid dairy products. Rule out other food sensitivities with the elimination-provocation diet and/or food-allergy or -sensitivity blood testing.

Cigarettes, toothpaste, mouthwash, and flavored dental floss can cause irritation. According to Joanne Zeis, the author of several books on Behcet's disease, "ironically, according to some research studies people who quit smoking cigarettes sometimes develop excessive oral ulcers, which can be a real problem for BD patients who quit—some go right back to smoking again. Toothpastes containing sodium lauryl sulfate may create aphthous ulcers in some BD patients, and should be avoided."

Use probiotics. Lactobacillus acidophilus is often beneficial in prevention and treatment of canker sores and may be useful in BD. No clinical research has been done in this area, but it makes sense.

Take 1 to 2 capsules or ¼ to ½ teaspoon of the powder three times daily; take between meals.

Practice stress-management skills. Stress can contribute to a flare-up of the disease. Development of strong support systems is vital. This is a lifelong illness and you can greatly benefit from support groups, many of which are available on the Internet. Exchange of information and dialogue with others who understand what you are going through can expedite recovery. Take time for yourself, rest, and relax.

Chronic Fatigue Syndrome

Fatigue is one of the most common complaints that bring people into a physician's office. Fatigue can be caused by nearly every illness and is part of the natural healing process. Excessive fatigue that lasts and lasts may be a sign of illness or of chronic fatigue syndrome. Also called CFIDS (chronic fatigue and immune dysfunction syndrome), CFS, myalgic encephalomyelitis, chronic Epstein-Barr virus (CEBV), and yuppie flu, chronic fatigue syndrome is a long-lasting, debilitating fatigue that is not associated with any particular illness. Although people have been fatigued for millennia, the term *chronic fatigue syndrome* was only coined in 1988. CFIDS affects more than half a million people. According to the Centers for Disease Control (CDC), 200 people per 100,000 experience CFIDS. About 50 percent eventually return to normal health within five years. The rest may be affected for decades.

By definition, individuals with chronic fatigue syndrome have been extremely tired for at least six months for no obvious reason. The CDC has provided the following criteria for diagnosis of CFIDS. First, the fatigue is not eliminated by rest, and the fatigue substantially reduces the person's ability to function normally. Second, the diagnosis includes at least four of the following symptoms for a period of at least six months: loss in ability to concentrate or short-term memory function; sore throat; swollen and tender lymph nodes; muscle pain; multiple-joint pain without swelling or redness; headaches of a new type, pattern, or severity; sleep disturbances; and exercise-caused fatigue that lasts more than twenty-four hours.

People with CFIDS share many common symptoms, but not everyone has all the same ones. CFIDS often begins with an infectious flu-like disease accompanied by fevers that come and go. There is often accompanying joint stiffness and pain, sore throat, cough, sleep disturbances, light sensitivity, night sweats, and extreme exhaustion after the slightest exertion. Commonly, a short walk or bit of exercise will wipe out your energy for days afterward. Some people have the Epstein-Barr virus, or cytomegalovirus, but others don't. Sometimes healthy people have high blood antibodies for these viruses and have no symptoms of CFIDS. It's possible that these viruses trigger CFIDS, but it's also possible that the low immune function in people with CFIDS increases their chances of catching a wide variety of infectious illnesses.

Many with CFIDS cannot hold down a job and become depressed because the fatigue is so extreme. Those who do work come home exhausted and go immediately to bed so they can generate enough energy for work the next day. Because there isn't any apparent cause and no observable symptoms (like boils or measles), people with CFIDS are often confronted by people and doctors who just don't believe it's real.

In 1990, the CDC in Atlanta began to keep records and study people with CFIDS to understand more about possible causes and therapies. We now know that CFIDS is multifactorial and affects many biochemical systems. Cytokine production of interleukin-2 (IL-2) is low and causes poor immune function. Other immune

Common Symptoms of Chronic Fatigue Syndrome

Symptom	Percentage Affected
Fatigue	100
Mental sluggishness, foggy thinking, inability to concentrate	50–85
Depression	50–85
Pharyngitis	50–75
Exhaustion after minimal exertion that can last for days	50–60
Stiffness and muscle pain	50–60
Muscle weakness	40–70
Joint pain, arthritis-like symptoms	40–50
Headache	35–85

Komaroff, A.L. *"Clinical Presentation of Chronic Fatigue Syndrome."* Chronic Fatigue Syndrome. *New York: Wiley and Sons, 1993.*

parameters appear to be overstimulated. Although this seems paradoxical, it's probably not. According to Hans Selye, an expert on stress, our systems initially react to stress by overproducing. If working harder doesn't eventually solve the problem, they underproduce. Many people with CFIDS have exhausted adrenal glands and produce low amounts of cortisone and other adrenal hormones. They almost always have dysbiosis, and most have candida infections. Leaky gut syndrome is usually present, accompanied by a host of food and environmental sensitivities. The liver is overburdened and overworked, so the toxic by-products of life accumulate in tissues, and the cycle deepens.

Eventually, the mitochondria are affected. Mitochondria are the energy factories inside our cells, creating ATP from glucose in a complicated process called the citric acid cycle, or Krebs cycle.

Mitochondrial function can be tested with an organic acid test, which has provided evidence that mitochondrial DNA is damaged much more easily and is more susceptible to environmental toxins and other stressors. As chronic fatigue symptoms progress, the mitochondria often need nutritional support of their own. Products to facilitate this include Mitochondrial Resuscitate, Krebs Cycle Nutrients, and others.

With the blood pressure test used with a tilt table, researchers have found that many people with CFIDS have low postural blood pressure. Complementary medicine physicians have long used reclining and standing blood pressures to detect poor adrenal function. Individuals with healthy adrenal function experience only a five- to ten-point rise in blood pressure when they move from a reclining to a standing position. In people with poor adrenal function, blood pressure remains the same or drops. So, is the tilt-table hypotension the primary culprit or an indicator of poor adrenal function? In any case, some people with low blood pressure respond to an increase in salt intake to at least 1,000 milligrams daily or by taking medication to increase blood pressure.

There aren't any panaceas for CFIDS, but there are therapies that can gradually help restore people to health. It's important to address detoxification, viral load, digestive function, dysbiosis (including candida and parasites), mitochondrial function, intestinal flora, environmental contaminants, heavy metals, underlying allergies, and hormone imbalances (especially thyroid and adrenal), as well as to restore the immune system. If this seems daunting, it can be. The causes and specifics are different for each person. Careful partnership between practitioner and patient will give the very best results. CFIDS is one area in which conventional, mainstream medicine has little to offer. If you've tried everything that your doctor has recommended and still aren't any better, you need to broaden your approach.

Restoration of digestive competency and nutrition go a long way toward normalizing CFIDS. Work with a nutritionally oriented health professional to design a program that meets your specific needs. The first steps are discovering any underlying problems that aggravate and drive the condition using the tests listed. It's important to check carefully for parasites; one study found giardia in 28 percent of subjects with CFIDS. Giardia hangs out in the mucous membranes and is difficult to detect with random stool samples. Develop and follow a diet based upon foods that are healthful for you and a nutrient-rich program designed to boost immune, brain, and cellular function. When you are ready, add exercise, a little bit at a time. People with CFIDS often feel worse after exercise, so go slowly.

The biological, rather than medical, approach to chronic fatigue saves money and works better. In one study of cost-effectiveness it was determined that a nutritional approach costs $2,000 compared to $10,000 for a medical approach. The patients on nutritional programs reported greater improvements in function and subjective well-being. They were able to significantly reduce the amount of medications they used.

The CFIDS Association in Charlotte, North Carolina, offers a wealth of information for people with CFIDS. You can obtain information about medications, herbs, nutritional supplements, diet, exercise, and additional therapies.

Functional Laboratory Testing

Comprehensive digestive stool analysis with parasitology
Elisa/Act testing for food, airborne, and chemical
    sensitivities
Liver function profile
Intestinal permeability screening
Organic acids
Hair analysis or urine test for heavy metals

Healing Options

After testing, you'll have a better idea of any underlying problems. Look up related sections in this book to help you with the specifics.

Try metabolic cleansing. Metabolic cleansing involves going on a hypoallergenic food plan for one to three weeks and taking a nutrient-rich protein powder designed to help restore your liver's detoxification capacities. For a thorough discussion of metabolic cleansing, see Chapter 8.

Investigate food and environmental sensitivities. Eliminate all foods and chemicals that you are sensitive to from your diet for four to six months. Use shampoos, soaps, and toiletries that are hypoallergenic for your specific needs and natural household cleaning products that are healthier for you, your family, and the environment. Some people are sensitive to their mattresses, gas stoves, carpeting, and upholstery. You may need to wear 100 percent cotton or other natural fiber clothes and use 100 percent cotton sheets and blankets. Work with a health professional who can help you thread your way through the details.

Try an alkalizing diet. Read the section on acid-alkaline diets in Chapter 6. Use pH paper to determine your levels. Use alkalizing foods, alkalizing salts, baking soda, Epsom salt baths, and vegetable juicing to bring your body into balance.

Supplement with acidophilus and bifidobacteria. Supplemental use of beneficial bacteria can make a tremendous difference in your ability to digest foods. Beneficial flora can help reestablish the normal microbial balance in your intestinal tract. The supplements you purchase may have additional microbes. Take 1 to 2 capsules two to three times daily or, between meals, ¼ to ½ teaspoon powder mixed with a cool or room-temperature beverage.

Try digestive enzymes. Pancreatic or vegetable enzymes supply the enzymes that your body needs to digest fats, proteins, and carbohydrates. Products differ. Some contain lactase, the milk-digesting enzyme; others have additional hydrochloric acid to assist the stomach; and some contain ox bile to help with emulsification and digestion of fats. Take 1 to 2 capsules with meals.

Take a multivitamin with minerals. Because people with CFIDS have difficulty with absorption and utilization of nutrients, a highly absorbable, hypoallergenic nutritional supplement is necessary. Although products that contain herbs, bee pollen, spirulina, and other additional food factors are good for many people, people with CFIDS often feel worse after taking food-based supplements. Make sure you buy the supplements that are herb and food free. Choose a supplement that contains the following nutrients: 25 to 50 milligrams zinc, 5,000 to 10,000 IU vitamin A, 10,000 to 25,000 IU carotenes, 200 or more IU vitamin E, at least 200 micrograms selenium, 200 micrograms chromium, at least 25 milligrams of most B-complex vitamins, 400 to 800 micrograms folic acid, and 5 to 10 milligrams manganese.

Take vitamin C. Vitamin C boosts immune function and helps detoxification pathways and has been shown to have antiviral effects. Clinicians have found it useful in people with CFIDS. Take 3,000 to 5,000 milligrams daily. Do a vitamin C flush (detailed instructions in Chapter 8).

Increase magnesium. Found in green leafy vegetables and whole grains, magnesium is involved in over three hundred enzymatic reactions in the body. It is essential for energy production, nerve conduction, muscle function, and bone health. People with CFIDS are often deficient in magnesium. Supplemental magnesium can improve energy levels and emotional states, while decreasing pain. Most people improve with use of oral magnesium supplements, but some need intravenous injections. Physicians can give 1,000 milligrams magnesium sulfate by injection. In one study, magnesium injections improved function in twelve out of fifteen people, compared to only three receiving the placebo. Magnesium can be hard for many people to use. Adding 1 teaspoon of choline citrate daily can significantly improve magnesium uptake. Take 500 to 2,000 milligrams magnesium citrate or magnesium-potassium aspartate (aspartic acid helps mobilize magnesium into the cells).

Try coenzyme Q10 (CoQ10). CoQ10 is necessary for energy production, immune function, and repair and maintenance of tissues. It also enhances cell function. CoQ10 is widely used in Japan for heart disease and has been researched as an antitumor substance. Take 60 to 300 milligrams daily.

Take essential fatty acids. Several studies have shown people with CFIDS to have fatty acid imbalances. In a recent study, a combination of evening primrose oil and fish oil or a placebo of olive oil was given to seventy people with CFIDS. Of the people taking fish and evening primrose oils, 74 percent showed improvement at five weeks, and 85 percent showed improvement at fifteen weeks. In comparison, the placebo group showed 23 percent improvement at five weeks and 17 percent at fifteen weeks. Another study of the use of supplemental fatty acids showed improvement in twenty-seven out of twenty-nine people with CFIDS over twelve to eighteen weeks. Twenty people who had previously been unable to work full-time for an average of more than three years were able to go back to work full-time after an average of sixteen weeks. Sixteen months later twenty-seven out of twenty-eight remained improved, and twenty were still progressing.

Take 2 to 3 grams flaxseed oil capsules daily or EPA/DHA fish oil once or twice daily plus 1 to 2 grams evening primrose or borage oil daily. Because magnesium and vitamin B_6, as well as the proper genetics, are necessary to convert flaxseed oil into EPA and DHA, it is advisable to take at least some preformed DHA.

Add methionine. Methionine, an essential sulfur-containing amino acid, is commonly deficient in people with CFIDS. It acts as a methyl donor for transmethylation reactions throughout the body, especially in the brain. It also helps sulfoxidation for liver detoxification pathways and is a precursor for other sulfur-containing amino acids such as cysteine and taurine. People with CFIDS probably have an increased need for methionine. Some people find improvement with a general amino acid supplement that supplies methionine, lysine, and carnitine simultaneously. Take 500 to 1,000 milligrams daily.

Try SAMe. S-adenosylmethionine (SAMe), a compound that is naturally found in every cell in our body, is made from methionine. Research on SAMe shows it to have powerful antidepressant effects without the side effects of pharmaceutical antidepressant medications. SAMe has also been shown to be as potent an anti-inflammatory drug as indomethacin without the negative side effects in people with arthritis.

Try acetylcarnitine. The vast majority of people with CFIDS have low levels of acetylcarnitine, although their levels of free carnitine are normal. Carnitine, vital for the conversion of fats into energy, also plays some role in detoxification and is believed to be essential for heart function. Finally, carnitine helps transport long-chain fatty acids into the mitochondria. Carnitine deficiencies result in muscle weakness, aches, and poor tone. When people were supplemented with 4 grams daily of acetylcarnitine, half showed improvement in their symptoms. Take 4 grams acetylcarnitine daily. For those on a budget, L-carnitine will also work.

Try lysine. Often people with CFIDS also have herpes infections. Some people find good results with a general amino acid supplement, which supplies carnitine, lysine, and methionine as well as other amino acids. Take 1 to 2 grams lysine daily at the first sign of an outbreak; 500 milligrams daily for prevention.

Try malic acid. Malic acid comes from apples and is important in energy production at a cellular level. Several physicians have found malic acid supplementation reduces fatigue and pain of fibromyalgia. Take 6 to 12 tablets daily, decreasing dosage over time. Each tablet contains 300 milligrams malic acid–magnesium hydroxide.

Use immune-modulating herbs. Echinacea, goldenseal, astragalus, phytolacca (pokeweed), licorice, and lomatium all have immune-stimulating properties. They can also help prevent secondary infections while you are in a susceptible state. Take them preventively or therapeutically as directed.

Provide adrenal support. People with CFIDS often need adrenal support, such as adrenal glandular supplements or herbal supplements, such as licorice and Siberian ginseng. Vitamin C and pantothenic acid (vitamin B_5) are also needed for proper adrenal function. If your blood pressure is low, you can use whole licorice; if not, use DGL, which will not affect blood pressure. It's best to take adrenal support in the morning and at lunch. If taken too late in the day, adrenal support can stimulate energy when you want to be winding down.

Consider nicotinamide adenine dinucleotide (NAD). In a study monitoring the effect NAD has on people with CFIDS, twenty-six subjects were given the reduced form of it for four weeks and a placebo for an additional four weeks. Thirty-one percent showed improvement when on NAD, while only 8 percent improved when taking the placebo. Subjects were less fatigued and had improvement in quality of life. NAD is integral to the citric acid cycle of energy production. Once again, we are reminded that each person has unique needs. While most people did not benefit, NAD may be a useful treatment for some people. More research needs to be done to see if 10 milligrams daily, the amount given in the study, is the proper dosage; if a longer treatment program would be of additional benefit; and what, if any, are the long-term benefits.

Try Meyer's cocktail. IV nutrients, given by a physician, can quickly help revitalize your nutrient status. Nutrients can be absorbed and used at higher concentrations. Meyer's cocktail is a combination of magnesium, calcium, vitamins B_{12} and B_6, pantothenic acid, and vitamin C. It has been used successfully in people with a variety of ailments.

Exercise. People with CFIDS find exercise to be totally exhausting and draining. It is common for one period of exercise to be followed within six to twenty-four hours by two to fourteen days of exhaustion and muscle aches. Paradoxically, exercise is helpful for restoring function in people with CFIDS, and so it's advisable to begin with simple walking, swimming, or biking for five minutes daily. If you can, increase by one or two minutes a day each week. If you feel that you are at your maximum, maintain your present length of exercise time until your fatigue decreases. Don't push yourself hard. Slow and steady wins the race. Studies have shown that two-thirds of people with CFIDS benefit through exercise, although it is critical to not overdo.

A new hypothesis suggests that those with CFIDS are functioning in an anaerobic state, so light anaerobic exercise may be most beneficial. Working with light weights, leg lifts, and use of weight machines to your capacity without causing fatigue may be more beneficial than aerobic exercise. As you begin to feel better, incorporate aerobic exercise—walking, biking, swimming, and dancing. Prioritize, so you have energy for what's most important. Be patient, kind, and loving to yourself.

Practice stress-management skills. Development of strong support systems is vital. People with CFIDS often have the illness for a long time and can greatly benefit from support groups. Exchange of information and dialogue with others who understand what you are going through can expedite recovery. Take time for yourself, rest, and relax.

Eczema or Atopic Dermatitis

Eczema, or atopic dermatitis, is a chronic skin condition characterized by redness, itching, and sometimes oozing, crusting, and scaling. The itch makes us scratch, which causes redness and inflammation. It affects fifteen million Americans. Approximately 0.5 to 1 percent of us have eczema and it affects 10 to 20 percent of all infants. Fifty percent of children outgrow it by age fifteen; the rest may have mild to severe eczema throughout their lives. It can first appear at any age, but most often during the first year of life. Babies can have eczema on their faces, scalp, bottom, hands, and feet. In children and adults, it may be more localized. Eczema is on the rise in industrialized countries. The causes are multifactorial and include imbalanced intestinal flora; leaky gut syndrome; food allergies; environmental contaminants, such as air pollution and tobacco smoke; and genetic predisposition.

The red patches are itchy, scaly, and dry, which encourages people to use lotions and creams to which they are often allergic. This complicates the problem further. Eczema varies over time, flaring up and calming down, at times better and worse. Emotional stress, heat, increase in humidity, bacterial skin infections, sweat, pets, hormone fluctuations, dust, molds, pollens, toiletries, cosmetics, and wool clothing commonly aggravate eczema. As children age, they may continue to have eczema; it may disappear; or they may develop other allergies, including asthma. People with eczema have high levels of IgE, secretory IgA, and eosinophils, all allergy signs.

Strong connections exist between eczema and food, microbial, and inhalant allergies. The word *atopy*, which is often used by physicians synonymously for *allergy*, refers to inflammations of the skin, nasal passages, and lungs. People with eczema often have allergies to dust, mold, dander, pollens, and foods.

Food allergies diagnosed through IgE and skin testing is apparent in most children with eczema. In a study of 165 children between the ages of four months and twenty-two years, researchers found that 60 percent had at least one positive skin-prick test for food allergies. When they challenged these results with a double-blind, placebo-controlled study, thirty-nine of sixty-four subjects had a positive test, with milk, egg, peanut, soy, wheat, codfish, catfish, and cashews accounting for 89 percent of the positive food-allergy challenges. Undoubtedly, many more would be borne out by IgG, IgA, and IgM testing. Studies of children with eczema have shown that eczema improved in forty-nine out of sixty-six children after elimination of the particular foods. Foods that aggravate eczema, in descending order, were eggs, cow's milk, food coloring, tomatoes, fish, goat's milk, cheese, chocolate, and wheat.

A study was made of 122 children, aged four months to six years, with food intolerance. Of them, 52 children had eczema; the rest had chronic diarrhea. The allergies caused damage to the intestinal lining, and there was a decrease in the body's ability to defend itself because of lactose intolerance and dysbiosis, which caused leaky gut syndrome, leading to more food antigens and sensitivity. Children with eczema had more intestinal damage than those with chronic diarrhea.

Breast-feeding dramatically reduces a baby's risk of developing eczema and allergies. Babies with eczema, and probably most babies, should not be given cow's milk, milk products, eggs, or wheat before one year of age. As their digestive system matures, they can better handle these complex foods. Babies with eczema who drink formula should be tested by skin prick to determine which formulas are most suitable for them. Because babies are born without intestinal flora in their digestive tracts, giving supplemental flora to the baby (and the mother, if she's nursing) can quickly alleviate baby eczema. The best flora for infants is *Bifidobacteria infantis.*

Elimination of foods, stress, and allergens can significantly alter the course of the disease. Even though you cannot control all factors, controlling enough of them will allow you to stay under the symptom threshold. Jonathan Wright, M.D., had success in thirty-nine out of forty patients with eczema who followed this program: 50 milligrams zinc three times daily for six weeks, plus 2 milligrams copper daily, 5 grams omega-3 fatty acids (evening primrose or borage oil) twice a day for three months, and 1 to 2 grams omega-6 fatty acids (EPA/DHA fish oils) three times daily for four weeks.

The most common treatment for eczema is cortisone cream, which suppresses your body's normal immune function. However, there is often a rebound effect after you stop using the cream, and your symptoms return worse than before. A new class of medications, called topical immunomodulators, is available by prescription. In test studies, they relieve symptoms in most people without an equal number of the adverse effects of steroid creams. Natural creams with chamomile, licorice, and comfrey root are also very effective at soothing and healing eczema without negative side effects. It's important to remember that even though eczema shows up on the skin, it is a systemic problem. Use creams to decrease irritation, but look for the underlying irritants.

Exercise may be especially beneficial for people with eczema. A recent study indicated that exercise reduced the inflammation associated with eczema by increasing the body's adaptability to stress.

Vacuum fastidiously and use air purifiers in bedrooms and other rooms you are in frequently to reduce eczema. One recent study attributed a reduction in eczema severity to a reduction in mattress dust and carpet mites by using a high-filtration vacuum cleaner and bedcovers. Keep your bedroom clean and clutter-free.

Functional Laboratory Testing
Allergy testing for IgE, food, mold, dust, and inhalants

Sensitivity testing for IgG, IgA, and IgM

Comprehensive digestive stool analysis (CDSA). Check to see if there is dysbiosis and how well the body is digesting.

Some studies indicate a low level of hydrochloric acid in

people with eczema, and the CDSA can give a general indication of HCl production.

Intestinal permeability screening

Heidelberg capsule test for adequacy of hydrochloric acid production

Healing Options

Investigate food and environmental sensitivities. Follow the directions in Chapter 6. An elimination-provocation diet can significantly reduce eczema. Foods that you are sensitive to will generally make you itch. Often the itching starts soon after the meal, but it can be delayed up to forty-eight hours, which makes tracking down the foods a bit tricky. Food allergy and sensitivity testing can help you determine which foods to eliminate from your diet.

Eliminate all foods and chemicals that you are sensitive to for four to six months. Use natural household cleaning products and shampoos, and soaps and toiletries that are hypoallergenic. If you are sensitive to mattresses, gas stoves, carpeting, and upholstery, you may need to use cotton and other natural fiber clothing and sheets that allow the skin to breathe naturally. Work with a health professional who knows how to help you meet your needs.

Supplement with lactobacillus and bifidobacteria. Restoring the normal balance of flora in your intestinal tract can help reduce eczema. Use of supplemental beneficial bacteria can make a tremendous difference in your ability to thoroughly digest foods. The supplement you purchase may have additional microbes, such as saccharomyces. Take 1 to 2 capsules two to three times daily, or ¼ to 1½ teaspoons powder two to three times daily. Mix powdered supplement with a cool beverage. It works best on an empty stomach.

Babies are born with sterile digestive tracts, and as soon as they are born they are exposed to microbes of all sorts. Dairy and soy products are difficult to digest until the baby's digestive system has mature flora. Supplementing with beneficial flora, such as *Bifidobacteria infantis* and others, will help your baby digest food more easily and heal the eczema. Use probiotic formulas specifically designed for infants, toddlers, or small children. Give ⅛ to ¼ teaspoon to baby three times daily. If the mother is breast-feeding, she should also take ¼ teaspoon three times daily.

Check for candida infection. Fungal infections are a common cause of eczema. In a study of 115 men and women with eczema, 85 were sensitive to fungus and after they were treated with fungal creams, oral ketoconazole, or a yeast-free diet, there was much improvement. Take the yeast self-test and do blood testing or CDSA to determine if yeast is contributing to your eczema.

Try black cumin seed oil. In four human studies, black cumin seed oil (*Nigella sativa*) has been shown to alleviate the symptoms of eczema and other allergies. It also moderately helps to normalize serum triglycerides and cholesterol. Black cumin seeds are a food, so there is low toxicity. Take 20 to 40 milligrams daily per pound of body weight. For example, a 20-pound baby could take 40 to 80 milligrams. A 150-pound adult could take 300 to 600 milligrams. Take internally, but could also be mixed with lotion and put on the skin.

Use natural eczema creams. Herbal creams can be as effective as cortisone creams in reducing eczema, and they don't have the negative side effects. Licorice root stimulates production of healing and anti-inflammatory prostaglandins. Use of a 2 percent licorice cream is recommended. Chamomile creams are widely used in Europe. A recent study compared a chamomile product, Kamillosan, against 0.5 percent hydrocortisone cream. After two weeks, the Kamillosan was reported to give slightly better results than the hydrocortisone cream. Look in health-food stores or ask your health professional to find a product that works for you.

Take a multivitamin with minerals. It is wise to add a good-quality multivitamin with minerals to your daily routine. However, you probably cannot get all the nutrients you require from a single tablet or capsule. Look for a supplement that has at least 100 micrograms chromium, 100 micrograms selenium, 5 to 10 milligrams manganese, 500 milligrams calcium, 250 milligrams magnesium, 25 to 50 milligrams zinc, 1 to 2 milligrams copper, 10,000 to 25,000 IU vitamin A (*not* beta-carotene; pregnant women should not exceed 10,000 IU daily), and 400 IU vitamin E. Zinc and vitamin A are essential for healthy skin and mucous membranes, and zinc is also necessary for production of anti-inflammatory prostaglandins and formation of hydrochloric acid. There are many anecdotal reports of the effectiveness of vitamin E and eczema, but no controlled studies have been done.

It is best not to buy a supplement that contains many different foods and herbs because you may be unknowingly sensitive to one or more of the ingredients. Be sure to buy a supplement that is free of common allergens.

Take vitamin C. A study of ten young people with severe eczema showed that supplementation with vitamin C significantly improved eczema and immune function. They needed only half as many antibiotics for treating skin infections as the control group. Take 1,000 to 3,000 milligrams mineral ascorbates or Ester-C daily. Do a vitamin C flush once a week.

Try evening primrose, flaxseed, and borage oils. Studies show that people with eczema generally have low levels of both omega-3 and omega-6 fatty acids. The first step in metabolism of linoleic acid, which allows for the conversion into gamma-linolenic acid (GLA), is often impaired in people with eczema. Taking GLA directly in evening primrose, flax, or borage oil circumvents blockage. GLA has an anti-inflammatory effect and benefits immune function. Take 1 to 2 grams three times daily of any of these oils or a combination.

Increase fish oil consumption. One recent study on people with eczema showed a 30 percent improvement in a four-month trial of 8 capsules of fish oil per day. Though the placebo group was given corn oil, which gave an improvement of 24 percent, results suggest that people with eczema have a generalized need for essential fatty acids.

Eating cold-water fish—salmon, halibut, sardines, herring, tuna—two to four times each week can provide you with the omega-3 oils you need. If you use fish oil capsules, do so under the supervision of a physician. They cause a significant increase in clotting time and should not be used by people with hemophilia or those on aspirin or anticoagulant drugs.

Try quercetin. Quercetin, the most effective bioflavonoid for anti-inflammation, can be used to reduce pain and inflammatory responses and control allergies. Take 500 to 1,000 milligrams three to four times daily.

Use turmeric. For eczema, turmeric can be used in combination with neem, an Ayurvedic remedy for parasites and infections.

Try a nickel-restricted diet. The relationship between nickel sensitivity and eczema has appeared recently in scientific literature. Nickel is an essential nutrient that is found in many enzymes. However, excess nickel is an irritant to the GI lining. You can be tested for nickel sensitivity through skin testing or an oral challenge. Nickel is used as an alloy in jewelry, so if jewelry irritates your skin or turns it gray, you may be sensitive to nickel. If you are, a low-nickel diet should be followed for a limited period of time. High-nickel foods are chocolate, nuts, dried beans and peas, and grains.

Neutralize reactions. There are many ways to minimize the effects of food sensitivities. Clinical ecologists can provide neutralization drops to counteract your reaction to particular foods. These drops work like allergy shots—a small amount of what you are sensitive to helps stimulate your body's natural immune response. Malic acid can also curtail sensitivity reactions.

Fibromyalgia

Fibromyalgia is characterized by long-term muscle pain and stiffness. According to the American College of Rheumatology, fibromyalgia affects 3 to 6 million Americans, 85 to 90 percent of whom are women. It affects about 2 percent of the general population and 20 percent of people with arthritic disease. It used to be called fibrositis, which implies an inflammation of fibrous and connective tissues such as muscles, tendons, fascia, and ligaments. Myofascial pain syndrome is similar, but is characterized by just a few painful and achy places, most often in the jaw, that are tender when trigger points are touched.

Fibromyalgia is characterized by generalized aching, pain, and tenderness throughout the body. People complain of neck, shoulder, lower back, and hip pain that seems to move around from place to place. People often report fatigue and changes in sleep patterns. They often wake up during the night with a feeling of achiness or stiffness. About 40 to 70 percent of people with fibromyalgia also report irritable bowel symptoms: abdominal pain, constipation, diarrhea, gas, or bloating. Other symptoms that occur with frequency include headaches, jaw pain or temporomandibular joint (TMJ) problems, and depression. Symptoms that occur less often are heightened sensitivity to chemicals; intolerance to cold, heat, or bright lights; bladder problems; Raynaud's phenomenon; difficulty concentrating; mood changes; dry eyes, skin, and mouth; painful menstruation; chest or pelvic pain; dizziness; nasal congestion; teeth grinding; or numbness or swelling in hands and/or feet.

People with fibromyalgia often report a traumatic event that triggered initial symptoms: emotional or physical stress, an accident, or a severe infectious illness. Though common, this doesn't occur in everyone.

Fibromyalgia shares many symptoms with chronic fatigue syndrome, though it is classified as its own disease. People with fibromyalgia, unlike those with chronic fatigue syndrome, usually do not have low acetylcarnitine levels or have a viral infection as a trigger. Recent studies indicate that myofascial pain, fibromyalgia, and CFIDS are on a continuum of the same disease path, with myofascial pain being the mildest, fibromyalgia moderate, and CFIDS the most severe.

It's important to be checked for vitamin D status. About half of all people with fibromyalgia are deficient in this nutrient. We make vitamin D from sunlight, but in northern climates or if people aren't outdoors, they don't make nearly enough. Best food source is cold-water fish such as salmon, sardines, mackerel, and herring. Vitamin D also helps facilitate magnesium absorption. An increased need for magnesium is found in most people with fibromyalgia.

People with fibromyalgia are generally put on anti-inflammatory drugs and antidepressants. One study showed that 90 percent of people treated with anti-inflammatory drugs were still symptomatic after three years. Conventional medical therapies for fibromyalgia usually are unsuccessful. They fail to address possible underlying causes of the illness. Food and environmental sensitivities, candida, or parasites can be causal factors in fibromyalgia. A stool test may be useful in diagnosing the cause of fibromyalgia. When the underlying problem has been identified and treated, fibromyalgia resolves.

A very small but promising study was done with thirty-two people who had fibromyalgia for five to ten years. There were twenty-five active participants and seven controls. The participants were tested for food and environmental sensitivities with the Elisa/Act test and given dietary restrictions. They were put on a detoxification program and personalized nutritional therapies to meet their needs and stimulate repair of cells and tissues. The final component was stress management, with recommendations for relaxation training, exercise, and biofeedback. In six to twelve weeks, these people showed a reduction of 80 to 90 percent in their symptoms. They also showed a significant reduction in the number of foods and environmental sensitivities in repeated testing. More research needs to be done in this area.

Nutritional therapies have been successful in the reduction of symptoms. Fifty people with either CFIDS or fibromyalgia were given products made by Mannatech, a multilevel supplement company, including freeze-dried aloe, plant-derived saccharides with freeze-dried fruits and vegetables, and a wild yam product with multivitamins and minerals. Although all subjects in the study had previous unsuccessful medical treatment, a remarkable reduction in symptoms was noted, with continued improvement over the nine-month test period. Although this was a small, preliminary study, it shows promise for the nutritional approach to fibromyalgia and CFIDS.

One approach to fibromyalgia is the use of guaifenesin, a gout medication. Endocrinologist R. Paul St. Amand, M.D., believes that people with fibromyalgia have calcium phosphate deposits on muscles, tendons, and ligaments. St. Amand developed his theory after observing a high level of dental calculus (calcium phosphate deposits) among his fibromyalgia patients. His therapy (which includes a healing crisis, or a period of worsening of symptoms before improvement) begins with a dose of 300 milligrams of guaifenesin per day. He reports this working in 20 percent of his patients, but if no healing crisis occurs after two weeks, St. Amand increases the dose to 600 milligrams daily. At this level, another 50 percent of his patients improve, while the remaining 30 percent seem to require higher doses. In two months of treatment, one year of fibromyalgia can be reversed; however, the longer you've had the disease, the longer you need to stay on the medication. While doing this therapy, avoid all salicylates, because they negate the treatment. This would include aspirin; herbs such as willow bark and aloe; and some common products that may contain salicylates, such as topical pain-relieving cream, some mouthwashes, eyeliner, and some herbal hair sprays. As guaifenesin is a weak anti-gout medication with few side effects, the therapy certainly seems worth trying.

Use of a single supplement may bring some relief, but a total program is necessary to bring dramatic relief and true healing. Taking coenzyme Q10; vitamins B_1, B_6, and arginine; 5-HTP; SAMe; essential fatty acids; antioxidants; niacin; and magnesium malate (magnesium plus malic acid), in addition to a hypoallergenic diet has been shown to have positive effects. Acupuncture has been proven useful in treating fibromyalgia. Chiropractic or osteopathic adjustments and massage treatments may also be of help.

Functional Laboratory Testing

Comprehensive digestive stool analysis (CDSA)
Liver function profile
Elisa/Act food and environmental sensitivity testing
Intestinal permeability screening
Oxidative stress evaluation

Healing Options

Take vitamin D. Vitamin D deficiency is often diagnosed as fibromyalgia. About half of people with fibromyalgia have low serum vitamin D levels. We make vitamin D in our skin from exposure to sunlight. So, get outdoors more. Fatty, cold-water fish is your best dietary source of vitamin D, and includes salmon, tuna, herring, sardines, and mackerel. Milk, some orange juices, and some cereals are fortified with synthetic vitamin D. A trial of 1,000 IU daily for three to four weeks may be a great starting point. Check vitamin D levels with your physician to prevent vitamin D toxicity over time.

Try an alkalizing diet. Balancing cellular metabolism by eating an alkalizing diet may be of great help in fibromyalgia. Use pH testing to determine the best diet for you. Include fresh fruits and vegetables, vegetable juices, and sea vegetables. Use baking soda and Epsom salt baths. (See Chapter 6.)

Try metabolic cleansing. Metabolic cleansing involves going on a hypoallergenic food plan and taking a nutrient-rich protein powder designed to help restore your liver's detoxification capacities. Use this protocol for one to three weeks. See Chapter 8 on detoxification and metabolic cleansing.

Investigate food and environmental sensitivities. Eliminate all foods and chemicals that you are sensitive to for four to six months (see Chapter 6). Get tested to find the specifics. Work with a health professional who can help you find your way through the details.

Try ascorbigen and broccoli powder. A study on twelve patients with fibromyalgia was done with ascorbigen and broccoli powder. Ascorbigen is the most common indole found in cooked cabbage, broccoli, brussels sprouts, and other cabbage family foods. In one month, symptoms improved by nearly 20 percent. After the supplements were discontinued, symptoms returned to usual levels within two weeks. Take 100 milligrams ascorbigen plus 400 milligrams broccoli powder daily.

Take a multivitamin with minerals. A high-quality, hypoallergic nutritional supplement is necessary. Although products that contain herbs, bee pollen, spirulina, and other additional food factors are good for many people, it's best to buy supplements that are herb- and food-free. Look for the following levels of specific nutrients: 50 to 100 milligrams vitamin B_1, 50 to 100 milligrams vitamin B_6, 200 to 400 IU vitamin E, 10,000 IU vitamin A, 10,000 to 25,000 IU carotenes, 200 micrograms selenium, 200 micrograms chromium, 5 to 10 milligrams manganese, glutathione, cysteine, or N-acetyl cysteine (NAC), plus additional nutrients. Antioxidant nutrients—carotenes, vitamins C and E, selenium, glutathione, CoQ10, cysteine, and NAC—have been shown to be needed in larger quantities in people with fibromyalgia.

Take vitamin B₁ (thiamin). People with fibromyalgia have lower levels of red blood cell transketolase, which is a functional test for vitamin B (thiamin) status. Researchers found that supplemental thiamin pyrophosphate worked better than other forms. This suggests a metabolic defect rather than a true deficiency. This may also reflect a magnesium deficiency because thiamin-dependent enzymes require magnesium. Take 25 to 100 milligrams daily.

Take vitamin C. Vitamin C boosts immune function, helps detoxification pathways, and has antiviral effects. Take 3,000 milligrams daily. Once a week, do a vitamin C flush (see Chapter 8).

Take magnesium. It is very common for people with fibromyalgia to be deficient in magnesium. Serum magnesium levels are often normal, but if more sophisticated tests like red blood cell magnesium are done, magnesium levels are often low. Supplemental magnesium can improve energy levels and emotional states while decreasing pain. Most people improve by using oral magnesium supplements, but some need an intravenous injection of 1,000 milligrams magnesium sulfate by a physician (for more on magnesium, see discussion on chronic fatigue syndrome). Choline citrate can greatly enhance oral magnesium utilization (available from Perque, listed in Resources). Take 500 to 1,000 milligrams magnesium citrate or magnesium/glycinate.

Try arginine. People with fibromyalgia have been shown to have lower levels of arginine than other people. Take 500 to 1,000 milligrams or a mixed free amino acid supplement.

Try 5-hydroxytryptophan (5-HTP). People with fibromyalgia have lower tryptophan levels than controls. Studies have shown 5-HTP to be of benefit in fibromyalgia. Tryptophan is a precursor to serotonin, a neurotransmitter that helps us sleep and prevents depression. Tryptophan itself is only available by prescription at a few pharmacies nationwide because of a contaminated batch a decade ago. Fortunately, 5-HTP, the intermediary metabolite between tryptophan and serotonin, is available as a supplement. Passion-flower, an herb with high levels of tryptophan, has been used historically for depression, anxiety, and insomnia, all of which are symptoms of fibromyalgia. Tryptophan is also found in cashews, cheddar cheese, eggs, halibut, peanuts, salmon, sardines, shrimp, turkey, and tuna. Our body produces it when we eat starchy foods. Take 200 to 600 milligrams daily of 5-HTP, or 500 to 2,000 milligrams daily of tryptophan. Doses can be divided between morning and bedtime.

Try capsaicin (cayenne pepper cream). The prescription drug capsaicin was used in a study of forty-five people with fibromyalgia. It was found to improve grip strength and reduce pain over a two-week period. Capsaicin cream burns temporarily, but this diminishes over time.

Try S-adenosylmethionine (SAMe). A recent study of forty-seven people with fibromyalgia showed that injections and oral supplementation of SAMe significantly reduced muscle tenderness and the number of tender points, lowered pain severity, and benefited depression and anxiety. SAMe is produced in our bodies from methionine. It is the active methylating agent for many enzyme reactions throughout the body, especially in the brain. It is probably the sulfur that is needed. People with fibromyalgia can probably make this conversion, so oral methionine may be useful clinically (1,000 to 2,000 milligrams). Other sulfur-containing supplements are dimethylsulfoxide (DMSO), taurine, glucosamine or chondroitin sulfate, and reduced glutathione. In the study, dosages of SAMe were 200 milligrams given daily as intramuscular injection, plus 400 milligrams taken orally twice daily.

Try Meyer's cocktail. IV nutrients, given by a physician, can quickly help revitalize your nutrient status. Nutrients can be absorbed and used at higher concentrations. Meyer's cocktail is a combination of magnesium, calcium, vitamins B_{12} and B_6, pantothenic acid, and vitamin C. It has been used successfully in people with a variety of ailments.

Try electroacupuncture. In a study of electroacupuncture with people with fibromyalgia, half the people received acupuncture on four points; the other half received acupuncture 20 millimeters away from the actual point. Seven out of eight symptom parameters improved in the four-point electroacupuncture treated group. None changed in the placebo group. In the electroacupuncture group, a quarter had no improvement, half improved satisfactorily, and a quarter had their symptoms disappear completely. Although this study was done with electroacupuncture, similar results would occur with classical acupuncture.

Try malic acid. Malic acid found in apples is important in energy production at a cellular level. Several physicians have found malic acid supplementation reduces fatigue and the pain of fibromyalgia. It also helps alkalize. Take 6 to 12 tablets of 300 milligrams malic acid/magnesium hydroxide daily, decreasing dosage over time.

Take quercetin. Quercetin is the most effective bioflavonoid in its anti-inflammatory effects and can be used to reduce pain and inflammatory responses and control allergies. Take 500 to 1,000 milligrams three to four times daily.

Take glucosamine sulfate. Glucosamine sulfate is used therapeutically to help repair cartilage, reduce swelling and inflammation, and restore joint function, with no reported side effects. Take 500 milligrams two to four times daily.

Try digestive enzymes. Pancreatic or vegetable enzymes supply the enzymes your body needs to digest fats, proteins, and carbohydrates. Some products contain lactase, the milk-digesting enzyme, others have additional hydrochloric acid to assist the stomach, and some contain ox bile to help with emulsification and digestion of fats. Take 1 to 2 tablets or capsules with meals.

Supplement with acidophilus and bifidobacteria. Use of supplemental beneficial bacteria can help reestablish the normal microbial bal-

ance in your intestinal tract. The supplement you purchase may
have additional microbes as well. Take 1 to 2 capsules two to three
times daily or ¼ to 1½ teaspoons powder two to three times daily.
Mix powdered supplement with a cool beverage.

Try coenzyme Q10 (CoQ10). CoQ10 is necessary for energy production, immune function, repair and maintenance of tissues, and
enhanced cell function. Take 60 to 100 milligrams daily.

Try glutamine. Glutamine, the most abundant amino acid in our
bodies, is used in the digestive tract as a fuel source and for healing stomach ulcers, irritable bowel syndrome, ulcerative bowel
diseases, and leaky gut syndrome. Begin with 8 grams daily for
four weeks.

Food and Environmental Sensitivities

Two types of allergies cause reactions: acute or immediate hypersensitivity reactions (Type I) and delayed hypersensitivity reactions
(Type II–IV).

True food *allergies* (Type I) are rare. They affect from 0.3 to 7.5
percent of children and 1 to 2 percent of adults. Type IgE antibodies bind to the offending food antigens and cause the release
of cytokines and histamines, which results in hives, skin rashes,
closing of the throat, respiratory distress, runny nose, itching, and
sometimes severe reactions of asthma and anaphylactic shock.
These symptoms can occur within minutes to hours after the food
is eaten. Foods that most often trigger these reactions are eggs,
cow's milk, nuts, wheat, soy, white fish, and shellfish. Physicians
diagnose food allergies through the use of patch skin tests and
RAST blood testing, but these tests do not accurately determine
food or environmental *sensitivities*.

Type II–IV reactions are the result of food or environmental
factors and cause symptoms that are delayed, taking several hours

to several days to appear. This makes tracking them down very difficult. They are more common than true food allergies, affecting 24 percent of American adults. Food sensitivities cause a wide number of symptoms resulting from a typical leaky gut reaction. Food molecules enter the bloodstream through damaged mucosal membranes, the body recognizes them as foreign substances (antigens), and triggers an immune reaction to get rid of them. Prolonged antibody response overwhelms the liver's ability to eliminate the antigens, so the toxins enter the bloodstream and trigger delayed hypersensitivity response, inflammation, cell damage, and disease. Almost any food can cause a reaction, although the foods that provoke 80 percent of food sensitivity reactions are wheat, beef, dairy products, egg, pork, and citrus. It's important to discover the underlying cause of this gut leakiness, which may be parasites, candida infection, bacterial or viral infection, pancreatic insufficiency, medications, or poor lifestyle habits. See Chapter 6 for more information on food allergies and sensitivities.

Doctors of preventive medicine and clinical ecology recognize two types of food sensitivities: cyclic and fixed. Cyclic account for 80 to 90 percent of food sensitivities. These reactions occur after a specific food has been eaten over and over, causing a reaction. If you avoid eating the food for four to six months, your body will most likely tolerate it again. However, you must correct the underlying leaky gut syndrome, or the problem will reoccur with that or other foods. With the fixed type, sensitivities don't go away, even if you have avoided eating the foods for periods of time. Occasionally, you can eat it after years of avoidance without provoking symptoms.

These reactions happen when antibodies are triggered in response to foods, chemicals, and bacterial toxins. They damage cells and inflammation occurs because of the damage. Many people are aware of which foods and chemicals bother them, but just as often the cause is hidden. With repeated exposure to these foods, our bodies slowly adapt to the irritants and the symptoms that are provoked.

Usually, we learn to live with the symptoms. Remember your first cigarette or glass of beer? It was probably distasteful to you. You probably didn't like the feeling of the smoke in your throat and lungs and didn't like the taste of beer. With continual use of beer or cigarettes, those initial reactions disappear, and eventually we like and even crave them. They still have a negative effect on our system, but our body has adapted to it. This model works for our relation to foods and chemicals as well. Habitual use dulls our ability to recognize their negative health effects. Because of this phenomenon, we can make use of the elimination-provocation challenge.

The idea behind the elimination-provocation challenge is simple—only eat foods that you are unlikely to be sensitive to for a week or two, and then add back the foods you normally eat to "challenge" your system. Removal of offending foods calms down symptoms. Challenging yourself with these foods allows you to determine which foods trigger symptoms. Careful addition of only one food every two days makes it easier to determine which foods caused the reaction.

While the elimination-provocation challenge sounds simple, the administration of it can be tricky. In general, people have no problem with the elimination part—a restricted food plan for a week can be accomplished with a bit of planning and discipline. Adding foods back into your diet slowly is more difficult. Symptoms are delayed and recipes contain a combination of foods, so that you can't easily tell which ones cause the reaction. Eating simple or single foods is helpful for determining which foods you may be sensitive to. You may feel bad after eating something, but you might not be certain which ingredient caused the distress. It then becomes necessary to remove all suspected foods for four days, and try them again one at a time. If you have the same reaction each time you add the food, you've found the culprit. If you have a food sensitivity to one food, you are often sensitive to all foods in the same food family. For example, some people who are sensitive to wheat are sensitive to all grains in the grass family. People who are sensitive to milk are often sensitive to cheese and yogurt. It is common to be sensitive to more than one food or food family.

Environmental illness, also called multiple chemical sensitivities, is becoming more and more common. In fact, two subspecialties of medicine are now devoted to it: environmental medicine and clinical ecology. Chronic exposure to food additives, household chemicals, building materials, recirculating air, and impure water can so depress and weaken our immune systems that even a small amount of toxic exposure makes us ill.

To test for food *allergies*, run a RAST or modified RAST test, which checks for elevation of IgE antibodies. To test for food and environmental *sensitivities*, check levels of IgG and, if possible, IgM and IgA antibodies. You can also do an elimination-provocation test at home. Though highly accurate, it can be frustrating. I prefer to use it along with a blood test, which helps reinforce and simplify the program.

If you have cyclic food or environmental sensitivities, you'll do best with a holistic approach. By avoiding substances you're sensitive to for a period of six months, your body will gradually stop reacting to most of them. It really helps the process if you also detoxify the body and the liver. (See Chapter 8.) Natural foods, organically grown and nutrient rich, also help repair the body.

For people who are highly sensitive to foods, a four-day food rotation may be helpful in addition to complete avoidance of foods you are highly sensitive to. The theory behind the rotation diet is that when you eat a food, your body begins to produce antibodies against it. If you don't eat it again for several days, the antibodies are no longer present. When you eat the food on day five, the process begins again, but you never develop symptoms because the antibodies are never prepared at the correct moment. There are many good books on the four-day food rotation diet. My favorite is *Dr. Sally's Allergy Recipes* by Sally Rockwell, Ph.D.

To set up the rotation, make four lists, dividing all foods into four groups, with a quarter of your fruits, vegetables, grains, proteins, oils, nuts, seeds, and beverages in each group. Keep all foods from the same family in the same group. For example, all grains are in one family because of the similarity of their makeup. Follow these food lists in order and then begin again with the first list on the fifth day.

A comprehensive program of nutritional supplements will also help the cells regenerate and generally aid the healing process. People with food sensitivities have a heightened need for supplementation because their metabolism isn't functioning optimally. Exercise programs and stress-management tools also play a part in recovery. If you follow a holistic program, you'll find that over time, you will become less and less sensitive to foods and the environment.

Functional Laboratory Testing

Elisa/Act testing—IgG4 and possibly IgM and IgA
RAST or modified RAST for IgE
Comprehensive digestive stool analysis (CDSA) with
   parasite screening
Intestinal permeability test
Candida testing, either serum or through CDSA

Healing Options

Avoid the culprits. Eliminate all foods and chemicals that you are sensitive to for four to six months. Health-food stores specialize in wheat-free breads, rice noodles, and a plethora of foods for people with food allergies. If you are sensitive to chemicals, use natural household cleaning products. Some people are sensitive to mattresses, gas stoves, carpeting, and upholstery, which can make elimination tricky. Work with a health professional who can help you with the details.

Neutralize reactions. You can find many ways to help minimize the effects of food sensitivities. Clinical ecologists can provide neutralization drops to desensitize you to reactive foods. These drops work like allergy shots—a small amount of what you are sensitive to stimulates your body's natural immune response. Malic acid is also useful to neutralize sensitivity reactions.

Use glutamine. The most abundant amino acid in our bodies, glutamine is effective for healing the intestinal tract. Take 8 grams daily for a trial period of four weeks.

Try quercetin. Quercetin, the most effective bioflavonoid thanks to its anti-inflammatory effects, can help heal a leaky gut. Take 500 to 1,000 milligrams three to four times daily.

Try N-acetylglucosamine (NAG). NAG helps promote good flora and protects against some microbes. It is high in mucopolysaccharides, which are critical to intestinal health.

Take vitamin C. Vitamin C helps flush toxins from our bodies and helps minimize allergic responses, so be sure to get plenty of vitamin C. Take 1,000 to 3,000 milligrams mineral ascorbates or Ester-C daily. Do a vitamin C flush once every week or two.

Try probiotics. Probiotic supplements, such as lactobacilli and bifidobacteria, protect the mucous lining of the digestive tract. Take 2 to 6 capsules daily or ¼ to ½ teaspoon twice daily.

Take tri-salts or malic acid. Alkalizing mineral salts that generally contain calcium, magnesium, and/or potassium bicarbonates help minimize reactions to foods. Alka-Seltzer Gold can be used in this capacity because it contains sodium and potassium salts. Malic acid is also useful for stopping or slowing reactions to foods.

Try gamma oryzanol. Gamma oryzanol is found in rice bran oil and products that help heal leaky gut syndrome. Take 100 milligrams three times daily for a trial period of three to six weeks.

Try digestive enzymes. If the pancreas cannot make or recirculate enough digestive enzymes, we don't digest foods sufficiently. Use of either vegetable or pancreatic enzymes helps you break down foods more completely. Take 1 to 2 capsules or tablets with meals. *Take a multivitamin with minerals.* To cure problems with leaky gut syndrome, it is wise to add a good quality, allergen-free multivitamin with minerals to a daily routine. Look for a supplement that has at least 100 micrograms chromium, 100 micrograms selenium, 5 to 10 milligrams manganese, 500 milligrams calcium, 250 milligrams magnesium, and 15 milligrams zinc. It is best to buy a supplement that does not contain a lot of foods and herbs because you may be sensitive to one or more of the ingredients in the supplement itself.

Migraine Headaches

Migraine headaches cause periodic disruption in the lives of twenty-eight million Americans, affecting 6 percent of men and more than 18 percent of women every year. It averages just over 10 percent of our population, making it the most prevalent neurological illness. Costs to the society are $13 billion annually, which includes 157 million work days that are lost each year. Migraines have genetic, hormonal, immune, and environmental components.

Migraines usually begin with a throbbing pain on one side of the head, which can spread to both sides. About 60 percent of people experience symptoms twenty-four hours prior to the actual migraine, which include mood changes, food cravings, repetitive yawning, thirst, fluid retention, stiff neck, irritability, fatigue, numbness or tingling on one side of the body, lack of appetite, diarrhea, constipation, a feeling of coldness, lethargy, changes in vision, or seeing bright spots. Medications and other techniques work best if used at this point. These symptoms may disappear when the headache appears or remain. Although symptoms vary from person to person, they have a consistent pattern in each individual. Migraine attacks may last from hours to days and may be accompanied by nausea, vomiting, and extreme sensitivity to light.

Migraines usually come on in response to a "trigger." Common triggers are foods and beverages, alcohol, stress, emotions, hormone changes, medications such as estrogen therapy, visual stimuli, or changes in routine. A recent study of 494 people with migraines cited the following triggers: stress in 62 percent, weather changes in 43 percent, missing a meal in 40 percent, and bright sunlight in 38 percent. Cigarettes, perfumes, and sexual activity also provoked migraines in some people. Other triggers are red wines, exhaustion, and monosodium glutamate (MSG).

Jean Munro, M.D., an English doctor who specializes in working with people with multiple-chemical sensitivities, breaks migraines into four types. The first type is a classic migraine, which begins with a visual disturbance of some sort—flashing lights, blackening, or blurred vision. It usually involves one side of the head, and people often vomit. The migraine usually lasts one to three days and can be quite severe. The second type is called a common migraine and is almost identical to the first except that there is no visual warning. It begins on one side, sometimes progressing to both, and there may be vomiting. The third type is called a basilar migraine, when the blood vessels at the base of the head dilate. It can be quite frightening and often causes a panicky feeling, accompanied by a sense of doom. A generalized headache is accompanied by a pins-and-needles sensation around the mouth, nausea, and tingling hands. The fourth type, called a motor migraine, is a variation on the basilar and may be quite severe. Half the body feels weak, head pain centers around the eye, and vision is distorted.

Of 282 patients with migraines whom Dr. Munro studied, 100 percent had food allergies or sensitivities; more than 200 of them were sensitive to wheat and/or dairy products. Other common trigger foods were tea, oranges, apples, onions, pork, and beef. She found that foods eaten daily provoked more reactions than chocolate, alcohol, and cheese, which are thought to be the most common triggers. Dr. Munro also found that people who eliminated these foods from their diet and cleared their homes of environmental contaminants had the best results in prevention of migraines. Using mild household cleaners, getting rid of gas appliances, removing house plants with molds and fungus, frequent cleaning, and making a bedroom an oasis by removing carpets and curtains resulted in fewer migraines. Although these people were still exposed to smoke, perfume, and other environmental triggers outside, changing the home environment and diets lowered their threshold enough so that they became more tolerant. More recent studies show that IgG4 and anti-IgG antibodies increased after food challenges in people with migraines, which supports the food-sensitivity or -allergy hypothesis. Other researchers have confirmed that many of the foods identified by Dr. Munro provoked symptoms. However, virtually any food can be a trigger.

John Diamond, M.D., of the Diamond Headache Clinic in Chicago believes that foods high in amines also provoke migraines in some people. Dietary amines, which promote constriction of blood vessels, are normally broken down by enzymes, but some people with migraines have lower than normal amounts of the appropriate enzymes. The amines that provoke vasoconstriction are serotonin, tyramine, tryptamine, and dopamine. They are found in the greatest quantities in avocados, bananas, cabbage, eggplant, pineapple, plums, potatoes, tomatoes, cheese, canned fish, wine (especially red), beer, aged meats, and yeast extracts.

Some physicians give intravenous M nutrients to people with migraines. An IV with 23 grams of magnesium sulfate, 200 to 300 milligrams of vitamin B_6, and 1,000 milligrams of arginine will often give migraine relief in just minutes. This injection must be given slowly to prevent a sudden drop in blood pressure.

Hormone fluctuations in women can worsen, improve, or trigger migraines. Many women only experience migraines at specific times in their menstrual cycle from ovulation through menstruation. Birth control pills and other estrogen-containing medications are widely recognized to trigger migraines in susceptible women. When women stop taking the medications, their migraines typically disappear.

The truth is that migraines have many triggers that vary from person to person. Finding your triggers and the treatments that work best for you is the key. You certainly won't need all the therapies listed below, but hopefully you'll find relief from some of them.

Functional Laboratory Testing

Intracellular magnesium, either RBC or lymphocytes

IgG, IgE, and if possible IgA and IgM Elisa/Act testing for food and environmental allergies or sensitivities

Intestinal permeability screening

Comprehensive digestive stool analysis with parasitology

Candida antibodies or CDSA

Healing Options

Make dietary changes. Remove all sugars, alcohol, refined carbohydrates, and caffeine. One study found that a low-fat diet of less than 20 grams daily lowered the incidence of headache from nine each month to three each month. Headache intensity and the need for medications also dropped substantially. This information shows the importance of the diet and the quality of fats. In combination with good-quality omega-3 fatty acids, this could give great results for many people.

Be sure to eat often. Low blood sugar levels often trigger migraines so don't skip meals. You may find that eating five to six small meals each day works better for you than three main meals.

Investigate food sensitivities and allergies. Avoid foods you are sensitive to. Make your home environmentally safe by using only natural cleaning supplies, removing gas appliances, cleaning out mold and mildew, using a dehumidifier, and making your bedroom into a safe harbor by removing unnecessary items, such as carpeting and drapery.

Use riboflavin (vitamin B₂). Forty-nine people with recurrent migraines were given 400 milligrams of vitamin B_2 daily with breakfast for three months. The number of migraines declined by 67 percent and the severity diminished by 68 percent. Its maximum effect is reached after two or three months, so be patient and give it a good try. In another study, fifty-five people were given either a placebo or 400 milligrams of riboflavin daily. Over three months, 59 percent of the people on riboflavin improved by at least 50 percent. There were minor side effects in two people—one had diarrhea and the other had frequent urination. If you experience either of these side effects, decrease the dosage.

Take vitamin B₁₂. Twenty people with a history of migraines for more than one year and with a frequency of two to eight per month were given 1 milligram vitamin B_{12} daily for three months in a nasal spray. Half of the people had a 53 percent reduction in migraines. In these people there was a reduction from 5.2 to 1.9 attacks per month. In the other half, there was virtually no improvement. Vitamin B_{12} is nontoxic, inexpensive, and widely available in sublingual and nasal sprays. Oral forms are not well-absorbed. Take 1 milligram daily for three months. If you get good results, continue. Over time, dosage needs may decrease.

Explore possible candida infection. A recent study of the relationship between candida and migraines found that thirteen out of seventeen migraine sufferers responded to a three-month program of diet and medication with fewer and less severe headaches. Blood testing showed a lowering of candida antibodies as well. The four people who did not respond well didn't stick to the program. If you have migraines, take the home test for candida infections and have your physician order additional testing.

Take magnesium. Numerous studies have documented the relationship between low magnesium levels and migraine headaches. It is estimated that magnesium plays a role in at least half of all people with migraines. When magnesium is supplemented at levels of 600 milligrams daily, the number of migraines significantly decreases. Alan Gaby, M.D., offers his patients magnesium injections (of B complex, vitamin C, and calcium), which alleviate their migraine headaches within minutes. A recent study used injectable magnesium sulfate with good results. Try 600 to 2,000 milligrams magnesium citrate or magnesium glycinate daily for at least three to four months. When you've reached saturation, you'll get diarrhea. I use this with my clients to figure out the correct dose. If you need more than 1,000 milligrams daily before your stools loosen, add 1 teaspoon choline citrate to facilitate the magnesium absorption.

Increase consumption of omega-3 fatty acids, olive oil, and polyunsaturated fats. Fish oil supplements contain high levels of DHA and EPA oils. They have been shown in many studies to reduce the severity, duration, and frequency of migraine headaches. Most of us can produce EPA and DHA by using flaxseed oil, borage oil, or evening primrose oil, or by taking alpha-linolenic acid (ALA) and gamma-linolenic acid (GLA) supplements. However, this conversion requires that we have not only the genetic ability to complete the conversion, but also adequate vitamin B_6 and magnesium. One study gave subjects 1,800 milligrams of GLA and ALA in 6 capsules daily, plus 3 milligrams of niacin, 20 milligrams of vitamin C, 25 IU of vitamin E, 20 milligrams of soy phosphatides, 50 milligrams of magnesium, 1.3 milligrams of beta-carotene, and 0.3 milligrams of vitamin B_6. Of the 128 people who participated in the study, 86 percent had a reduction in the severity, frequency, and duration of their migraine headaches, 22 percent became migraine-free, and 90 percent had reduced nausea and vomiting.

Fourteen percent of the subjects were able to reduce their medication to simple pain relievers. Stress reduction and relaxation are also recommended. Take 1,800 milligrams GLA/ALA and 2,000 to 3,000 milligrams of fish oil daily.

Try feverfew. Numerous studies have shown the herb feverfew (*Tanacetum parthenium*) to be effective in preventing and minimizing the severity of migraines. Others show no effectiveness. You can try it for yourself and see if it works for you.

Feverfew needs to be taken on a daily basis as a preventive measure rather than as a medication. There is a difference between fresh and dried feverfew and between various samples. If you don't get relief from one type, try another. Fresh feverfew seems to work best. It is easy to grow, so you could just eat a few leaves each day. Tinctures are available and would best approximate fresh leaves. It also comes in a freeze-dried form that seems to be effective. Twice daily, take 15 to 20 drops tincture, or take 1 to 3 capsules or 1 to 3 fresh leaves daily.

Try butterbur (Petadolex). Butterbur (*Petasites hybridus*) is a European herb that has been used for centuries for such diverse problems as plaque, cough, asthma, and skin wounds. It works by lowering inflammatory markers that cause pain. Most recently it has been shown to be effective for hay fever. In its natural state it contains liver toxins, but a patented product, Petadolex, has removed these substances. In a 2004 study of sixty people with migraines, thirty-three were given 25 milligrams Petadolex twice daily and 27 were given a placebo twice daily. After three months, incidence of migraines decreased from 3.4 per month to 1.8 per month. Forty-five percent of the people responded really well and accounted for most of the results. If you are one of the lucky, this could be a great remedy for you. Take 25 milligrams twice daily.

Try acupuncture. Acupuncture has been shown to reduce the incidence and severity of migraine headaches in some people. Study results vary. You may find great or no benefit.

Explore behavioral techniques. Many studies have been done and biofeedback, hypnotherapy, and stress-reduction techniques have all proven useful to some migraine sufferers. They may be 35 to 50 percent effective. Plus, you'll have better stress-management skills to use in all areas of life. Behavioral techniques help us better understand stressors and how to cope more effectively.

Avoid monosodium glutamate (MSG). MSG can provoke migraine headaches, asthma, diarrhea, vomiting, and gastric symptoms. These problems can occur immediately after eating or may be delayed up to seventy-two hours, which makes their relationship to MSG more difficult to discover. Food product labels may be misleading, with MSG labeled as "natural coloring"; some hydrolyzed vegetable protein contains MSG. You can challenge yourself with MSG to see if it brings on a migraine. The Elisa/Act blood test includes tests for MSG and glutamate sensitivity.

Try quercetin. Quercetin, the most effective bioflavonoid because of its anti-inflammatory effects, can be used to reduce pain and inflammatory responses and control allergies. Take 500 to 1,000 milligrams three to four times daily at onset of migraine; take 500 milligrams daily as a preventive measure.

Try chiropractic manipulation and massage. Chiropractic manipulation and massage can help blood and lymphatic supply and relax muscle tension.

Examine effects of caffeine. Caffeine plays a mixed role in migraines. For some people, it significantly reduces the number and severity of headaches; for others it triggers them.

Try niacin. Some physicians use niacin intravenously during a migraine to decrease the severity and duration of headaches. The dose contains at least 100 milligrams niacin, which is infused slowly.

Take antioxidants. Migraines are often triggered by substances that promote free radicals, such as cigarette smoke, perfume, hair spray, pollution, and household chemicals. One researcher found lower levels of superoxide dismutase (SOD) in platelets of people with migraines than in people with tension headaches. More research needs to be done in this area, but taking adequate antioxidants in a multivitamin with minerals may help prevent migraines.

Psoriasis

Psoriasis is a chronic skin rash characterized by scaling, patchy, or silvery-looking skin. It can affect just knees, elbows, or scalp or can spread over most of the body. It often occurs at the site of a previous injury. Psoriasis often runs in families and usually develops gradually. It has genetic, immune, and environmental aspects. It affects 4.5 million Americans.

Psoriasis occurs when skin cells mature too quickly. Skin cells build up on the surface causing red, scaly patches that often itch or are uncomfortable. Psoriasis flares up because of stress, severe sunburn, irritation, skin creams, antimalarial therapy, or from withdrawal from cortisone, or it can be brought on by other triggers. It tends to flare up and then go into remission. Arachidonic acid and leukotrienes are elevated in the urine of people with active psoriasis, which indicates that omega-3 fatty acids may be of benefit. Psoriasis affects about 1 percent of the American population as a whole, but 2 to 4 percent of Caucasians.

Psoriasis can also occur with joint inflammation as psoriatic arthritis (see discussion on arthritis) and is found in 3 to 7 percent of people with psoriasis. It isn't clear whether psoriasis and psoriatic arthritis are the same disease or two almost identical diseases.

Michael Murray, N.D., and Joe Pizzorno, N.D., have documented a number of factors that influence the progression of psoriasis, including incomplete digestion of protein, bowel toxemia, food sensitivities, poor liver function, reaction to alcoholic beverages, and eating high amounts of animal fats. Let's look at each of these factors.

When protein digestion is incomplete or proteins are poorly absorbed, bacteria can break them down and produce toxic substances. One group of these toxins is called polyamines, which have been found to be higher in people with psoriasis than in the average population. Polyamines contribute to psoriasis by blocking production of cyclic AMP. Vitamin A and goldenseal inhibit the formation of polyamines. Because protein digestion begins in the stomach, low levels of hydrochloric acid there can also cause incomplete protein digestion. Digestive enzymes and/or hydrochloric acid supplementation aid protein digestion.

Bowel toxemia plays an important role in psoriasis. A poor balance of intestinal flora because of stress, diet, medications, or other factors often leads to bacterial and fungal infection. In fact, many people with psoriasis have colonization of fungus in their digestive system and on their skin. In a recent study, twenty-one out of thirty-four people with psoriasis were found to have *Candida albicans* in the spaces between their fingers or toes, and the majority were also affected by fungi from the tinea family. Other research found a 56 percent increase in nail fungus in people with psoriasis. Another study looked at stool samples of people with psoriasis and other skin disorders. Researchers found a high number of disease-producing microbes, predominantly yeasts, in the colon. This may not be the cause of psoriasis, but rather an indication of poor gut ecology. Treatment for yeast infection corresponded with a decrease in skin inflammation.

Elimination diets and hypersensitivity testing have also produced profound results. People with psoriasis have high levels of IgE antibodies, which indicate an allergic component. Sixteen percent of people with psoriasis have antibodies to gliadin, the protein found in wheat, rye, and barley. Even though when tested for gliadin intolerance their endomysium antibodies were normal, a gluten-free diet for three months greatly improved the psoriasis. Intestinal dysbiosis predisposes people to food and environmental sensitivities, so people with hypersensitivities need to heal the intestinal lining by taking appropriate bacterial supplements.

Poor liver function may contribute to psoriasis as well. Liver function profile tests and the metabolic screening questionnaire can help you determine liver function, and the metabolic screening questionnaire can also be used to follow your progress. Incorporate a detoxification program with an elimination-provocation diet to determine which foods may trigger your psoriasis. (See Chapters 5, 6, and 8.)

Alcohol consumption contributes to psoriasis because it contains many toxic substances, which stress an overburdened liver. *Candida albicans* (yeast) thrive when beer and wine are consumed. Even one glass can provoke symptoms. Alcohol also increases intestinal permeability.

The causes and treatment of psoriasis are complex. Successful treatment must encompass several approaches reflecting its complexity. Look for underlying causes and develop a personal program based on your needs.

Functional Laboratory Testing
Food and environmental sensitivity testing, IgE and IgG4 testing
Candida testing (either blood or stool)
Liver function profile
Intestinal permeability testing
Blood testing for vitamin and mineral status

Healing Options
Try the elimination-provocation diet. Explore the relationship between your psoriasis and food and environmental sensitivities through laboratory testing and the elimination-provocation diet.

(See Chapters 5 and 6.) For best results work with a nutritionist or physician who is familiar with food sensitivity protocols.

Take a multivitamin with minerals. Take a good-quality multivitamin with minerals every day. Look for a supplement that contains at least 25,000 IU vitamin A, 400 IU vitamin D, 400 IU vitamin E, 800 micrograms folic acid, 200 micrograms selenium, 200 micrograms chromium, and 25 to 50 milligrams zinc. Each of these nutrients has been shown to be deficient in people with psoriasis. There are several vitamin A topical creams used by dermatologists for psoriasis. Vitamin A is a critical nutrient for healthy skin.

Practice stress-management skills. Flare-ups of psoriasis often occur after a stressful event. Because stress has to do with our own internalization of an event, even a mildly stressful situation can trigger psoriasis. Learning stress-modification techniques can change your attitudes about stressful situations, allowing you to let them roll by more easily. In a recent study, four out of eleven people showed significant improvement in psoriatic symptoms with meditation and guided imagery. Hypnotherapy, biofeedback, and walks in nature are other effective tools. Regular aerobic exercise is a powerful stress reducer.

Increase consumption of fish oils and EPA/DHA. The research on fish oils is mixed. Eating fish or taking fish oils has been shown to have an anti-inflammatory effect on psoriasis for some people. Fatty acids contribute to healthy skin, hair, and nails, and fish oils promote production of anti-inflammatory prostaglandins. It is also possible that fish oils increase the activity of vitamin D and sunlight. Eat cold-water fish—salmon, halibut, mackerel, sardines, tuna, and herring—two to four times per week or take EPA/DHA capsules.

Enjoy some sunlight and get your vitamin D. Sunlight stimulates our bodies to manufacture vitamin D, which has been shown to be an effective treatment for psoriasis. Ask your doctor to test your vitamin D levels. If low, supplement. Cod liver oil is a good source of vitamin D because it also contains fish oil and vitamin A, both of benefit in psoriasis. A good multivitamin usually has 400 IU vitamin D. An additional 400 IU of vitamin D could be beneficial. In general, slow tanning improves psoriasis, with sunshine and sunlamps prescribed as part of standard therapy.

A recent study done in Israel at the Dead Sea, long renowned for its treatment of psoriasis, showed that natural sunlight stimulated significant improvement in disease activity. One group was just given sunlight therapy, and the other received additional therapy in mud packs and sulfur baths. Both groups showed significant improvement in skin symptoms and with psoriatic arthritis, where present. Sunlight and ultraviolet light therapy are regular therapies for psoriasis.

Use aloe vera cream. A placebo-controlled study of sixty people with psoriasis found that a 0.5 percent aloe vera cream cured 86 percent of the subjects. Each person used the aloe vera cream three times each day for a period of one year, and the researchers concluded that aloe vera cream is a safe and effective cure for psoriasis.

Try glucosamine. A new hypothesis is that glucosamine, a component of connective tissue widely used for arthritic conditions, may benefit people with psoriasis. There is no human research as yet, but glucosamine has little risk.

Try milk thistle (silymarin). Extracts of the herb milk thistle have been used since the fifteenth century for ailments of the liver and gallbladder. Milk thistle, also known as silymarin, contains anti-inflammatory flavonoid complexes that promote the flow of bile and help tone the spleen, gallbladder, and liver. An excellent liver detoxifier, milk thistle has also been shown to have a positive effect on psoriasis. Take 3 to 6 capsules of 175 milligrams standardized 80 percent milk thistle extract daily with water before meals.

Take zinc. Zinc is necessary for maintenance and repair of skin, immune function, and healing. Copper and zinc compete for the same receptor sites during absorption. When zinc is deficient, copper is usually elevated. This is true for people with psoriasis.

Many studies have determined that people with psoriasis have lower levels of zinc than people in control groups. However, studies using oral zinc supplementation haven't always shown a clear improvement in psoriasis, though such studies have been of short duration—only six to ten weeks. Even though they didn't show improvement in the skin, they did show improvement in immune function and dramatic improvement in joint symptoms. It's possible that either zinc needs to be used along with other nutrients, or the time frame of these studies was too brief to see improvement. Take 50 milligrams zinc picolinate (an easily absorbed form) daily.

Take selenium. Many studies have shown that people with psoriasis are deficient in selenium. Selenium is part of a molecule called glutathione peroxidase that protects against oxidative damage (free radicals). Giving supplemental selenium to people with psoriasis showed an increase in glutathione peroxidase levels and improvement in immune function, though not an improvement in skin condition. However, they were studies of short duration with selenium the only supplement. This underscores the concepts of patience when using natural therapies and of using more than one nutrient or approach at a time. Take 200 micrograms daily, which you can get in a good multivitamin. Selenium can be toxic, so more is not necessarily better.

Try **Saccharomyces boulardii.** *Saccharomyces boulardii* is a cousin to baker's yeast. It has been shown to raise levels of secretory IgA, which are low in psoriatic arthritis and psoriasis. Take 6 capsules daily.

Try topical creams. Many topical creams, oils, and ointments help psoriasis. Capsaicin, a cayenne pepper cream, helped 66 to 70 percent of the people who used it in a recent trial. The main side effect was that of a burning feeling associated with chili peppers, which quickly subsided. Vitamins A and E have also been used topically with success; one physician alternates them, one each day. Creams containing zinc are also effective, as are salves containing sarsaparilla. Goldenseal ointment or oral supplements can also be helpful.

Try Honduran sarsaparilla. Sarsaparilla, a flavoring in root beers and confections, has proven to be effective in psoriasis, especially the more chronic, large-plaque forming type. Sarsaparilla binds bacterial endotoxins. Take 2 to 4 teaspoons liquid extract daily; 250 to 500 milligrams solid extract daily.

Try lecithin and phosphatidylcholine. Lecithin was used in a ten-year study from 1940 to 1950. People consumed 4 to 8 tablespoons of lecithin daily, along with small amounts of vitamins A, B_1, B_2, B_5, B_6, D, thyroid and liver preparations, and creams. Out of 155 patients, 118 people responded positively. Lecithin-rich foods include soybeans, wheat germ, nuts, seeds, whole grains, eggs, and oils from soy, nuts, and seeds. Lecithin granules can be purchased in health-food stores and added to foods as a cooking ingredient. Lecithin can also be purchased in capsule form, as can the active ingredient in lecithin, phosphatidylcholine. Take 4 to 8 tablespoons daily or 1 to 4 capsules of phosphatidylcholine.

Take folic acid. There is much research on folate deficiency caused by the drug methotrexate, which is a folate antagonist medication often used for psoriasis. This seems ironic, because folic acid is one of the primary nutrients needed for proper skin formation. Jonathan Wright, M.D., recommends extremely high-dose folic acid therapy for psoriasis—50 to 100 milligrams daily. Although I have never used dosages in such high ranges, a dose of 10 to 15 milligrams daily is considered safe. Be aware that if folic acid is taken by someone with a vitamin B_{12} deficiency, nerve damage can go undetected. If you are going to use high levels of folic acid, have your doctor test your vitamin B_{12} status with homocysteine or methylmalonic acid testing.

Schizophrenia

Schizophrenia is a chronic, disabling brain disease. People with schizophrenia experience altered realities, including hallucinations, hearing voices, delusions, and confused or paranoid thoughts. Their speech and behavior can be very disorganized, which can be disturbing or confusing to those around them. This is very disorienting. During acute periods, people with schizophrenia experience a loss of energy, sense of humor, and interest in living. It affects one million Americans each year and 1 percent of us will have it during our lifetime. It can be progressive or episodic. Medication is useful for many people with schizophrenia, but some are not greatly helped by it. Fortunately there are other therapies.

This is definitely an illness where a complete approach must be taken to get the best results. An entire field of nutritional medicine, called orthomolecular medicine (named by Linus Pauling), is based upon treatment of schizophrenia and other mental illnesses, although its original definition was broader. Specific testing of amino acids, food sensitivities, fatty acids, heavy metals, and gut health will reveal information relevant to each person. Often, studies of schizophrenia using nutritional models have been disappointing because all patients are lumped into one group. When groups are broken into subtypes or patients are seen individually, improvements are seen.

Abraham Hoffer, M.D., and Humphry Osmond, M.D., are pioneers in the field. Their protocols are based around use of niacin at 3,000 milligrams daily (vitamin B_3), vitamin C at 3,000 milligrams daily, and loving care. Niacin therapy works best when used early after the diagnosis. Be patient: it can take months before it begins to work. Niacin causes a skin-flush caused by the release of prostaglandins in the skin; in people who don't flush, it probably indicates a problem with fatty acid deficiency. A niacin challenge offers a simple way to test for this group of people. Loving care expedites the healing process.

Carl Pfeiffer, M.D., Ph.D., found that some people with schizophrenia had faulty metabolism of specific B-complex vitamins. He once stated, "for every drug that yields a beneficial result, there is a nutrient, which can produce the same effect."

Fatty acid metabolism is faulty in people with schizophrenia. Schizophrenics have shown altered fatty acid panels. Arachidonic acid, the omega-3 fatty acids, EPA, and DHA levels are often low. Schizophrenics are found to have high levels of interleukin-2, an inflammatory substance known to have the potential to cause symptoms similar to schizophrenia. Fish oils can help reduce levels of interleukin-2 and cytokines. Doing a fatty acid test would make sense.

One subtype of schizophrenics responds well to gut-healing protocols and elimination of wheat products. Wheat sensitivity can stimulate the production of chemicals in the brain that resemble opiates and cause hallucinations and behavior disturbances. Other classic food offenders in schizophrenia include dairy products, food additives, and chocolate, although nearly any food can cause problems.

People with schizophrenia have an increased need for antioxidant nutrients. Other antioxidants have also been found to be deficient. Poor free radical protection can damage fat-dependent membranes, the nervous system, and the brain. Testing for specific antioxidants would be advised.

Schizophrenia appears to have an autoimmune component, which may be a result of the disease itself. Many studies have shown a correlation between a mother getting the flu while pregnant and an increase in schizophrenia in the children.

Functional Laboratory Testing

Essential fatty acids

SpectraCell functional nutrient, oxidative, and cardiovascular profiles

IgE and IgG food allergy testing, and IgM and IgA testing if possible

Hair mineral analysis, for detection of heavy metals

Urinary amino acids

Healing Options

Rule out food sensitivities. Do blood testing for food allergies and sensitivities. Eliminate foods that test positive and see how you respond.

Take niacin. Abraham Hoffer, M.D., has long used niacin therapy for schizophrenia. It is believed that there is faulty niacin metabolism in this condition, because people with schizophrenia often do not experience the intense flushing that usually occurs with niacin ingestion. Take up to 3,000 milligrams daily.

Increase intake of tryptophan or 5-hydroxytryptophan (5-HTP). In fourteen patients tested, dietary restriction of tryptophan worsened their symptoms. Tryptophan can easily be converted to niacin, which may be one reason why it is of benefit. Tryptophan is also a precursor to serotonin, which affects mood, behavior, sleep, and carbohydrate cravings. Take 1,000 to 2,500 milligrams tryptophan daily (only available by prescription) or 300 to 600 milligrams 5-HTP (available over the counter).

Increase consumption of good fats. Schizophrenics have been well documented to have low omega-3 fatty acid levels, low arachidonic acid levels, and low levels of polyunsaturated fatty acids. Benefit would be found by increasing good fats in the diet from sources such as nuts, seeds, whole grains, unprocessed vegetable oils, and cold-water fish, including salmon, halibut, tuna, mackerel, sardines, or herring. Twenty hospitalized patients were given

10 grams of MaxEPA daily. There were significant improvements in psychological symptoms, behavior, and tardive dyskinesia (uncontrollable movements) after six weeks. Another study used a smaller dose: 180 milligrams EPA, 120 milligrams DHA, plus 400 IU vitamin E and 500 milligrams vitamin C twice daily. There was improvement in lab testing and also in schizophrenic symptoms.

Try serine. Much research has been done showing that high-dose glycine is beneficial for schizophrenia. Concern has been posted as to the possible long-term neurological effects of high-glycine supplementation. The mechanism of the response was believed to be the effect on NMDA, a neurotransmitter, receptor sites. NMDA function is low in people with schizophrenia. Newer research on serine shows that the positive effects of enhancing NMDA function can be achieved by taking serine, without the risks of high-dose glycine. Dosage in one study was glycine 0.8 grams per kilogram of body weight daily. It would be advisable to do a urine amino acid test before using this type of therapy. Work with a physician.

Take folic acid. Folic acid levels are often lower in those with schizophrenia, while homocysteine levels are often higher. Thirty-three percent of patients with acute psychiatric disorders were given 15 milligrams of folic acid daily for six months in addition to standard treatment. The benefits in the folic acid–treated group increased over time. Folic acid deficiency does not cause the disease but correlates with its severity, flare-ups, and use of medications. Folic acid is also required by our bodies for the synthesis of serine, which has also been shown to have a positive effect in schizophrenia. High levels of homocysteine due to a folate metabolism error have also been found consistently in people with schizophrenia. The amount of folic acid you can take is limited because it can mask a vitamin B_{12} deficiency. If you do not have a vitamin B_{12} anemia, you can take up to 15 milligrams daily.

Take magnesium. Magnesium deficiency can produce depression, agitation, confusion, and disorientation. Twenty schizophrenic patients were evaluated for serum magnesium levels. Twenty-five percent were found to be magnesium deficient. Serum magnesium is not a sensitive test of magnesium deficiency, so if red blood cell magnesium had been analyzed, the results would probably have been much higher. Half of the magnesium-deficient patients were exhibiting psychotic behavior, including hallucinations. In drug-treated schizophrenics, magnesium levels have been found to be consistently low. Supplementing with magnesium does not always show improvement in symptoms. Magnesium injections or use of choline citrate may be necessary at first to "prime the pump." Because so many enzymes are dependent on magnesium, a deficiency could affect other nutrients including vitamins B_1, B_6, E, and C and minerals such as zinc, copper, and selenium.

Scleroderma

Scleroderma is a connective-tissue disease characterized by a thickening and loss of elasticity in the skin, joints, digestive tract (especially in the esophagus), lungs, thyroid, heart, and kidneys. Mild or severe, it can flare up and subside in intensity. There are two forms of the disease: *localized* to one or two locations or *generalized* throughout the body. The most common initial complaint is loss of circulation in toes or fingers (Raynaud's syndrome), characterized by swelling and a thickening of skin. About 300,000 Americans have scleroderma.

Joint pain is an early symptom. As the disease progresses, the skin becomes taut and shiny, with the face becoming masklike. There may be red blotches on the skin where capillaries have broken. Small calcifications occur under the skin on the fingers. People become malnourished and may need supplemental foods or total parenteral feeding (tube feeding).

Scleroderma has definite digestive components in 80 to 100 percent of people and can affect any part of the digestive tract. In scleroderma, people begin to lose peristalsis. Early in the disease, the esophageal sphincter becomes stiff and loses elasticity, which causes gastric juices to go up into the esophagus and burn the lining, which causes heartburn. Sometimes there is regurgitation back into the mouth. Eventually, the acids damage the esophagus and may lead to Barrett's disease, bleeding, or ulceration. It is common to have fungal or candida infections in the esophagus, often called thrush. Because there is loss of peristalsis, the small intestines are prone to bacterial overgrowth. The bacteria break down bile acids and gut mucosa causing malabsorption of nutrients, which leads to weight loss and diarrhea. The large intestine may develop diverticular pouches. Constipation is common. Late in the disease, the stomach may become involved.

Malabsorption leads to poor movement, dysbiosis, and semiobstructions in the small intestines. Small bowel bacterial overgrowth is common because of a loss of peristaltic function in the intestines. Use of steroid medications increases the likelihood of yeast infections in the digestive tract. Treatment with antimicrobial medications will cure the infection temporarily but doesn't change the fact that there is a loss of movement in the area. Small bowel overgrowth must be routinely monitored and treated if an infection is present.

There is no single known cause of scleroderma. It is caused by a combination of genetics and environmental factors. Evidence suggests that prolonged exposure to silica, silicone, and chemical solvents significantly increases the risk of developing scleroderma. (Another possible association is in workers with repetitive hand and arm vibration.) In some individuals, solvents trigger the illness. An evaluation was made of 178 people with scleroderma, in comparison to 200 controls. People with scleroderma were more likely to have higher concentrations of and levels of exposure to solvents, especially trichloroethylene.

Scleroderma may also be linked to autoimmune disease. In a small study, forty-four women and six men went through extensive testing and examination to see if there was a relationship between their work and autoimmune disease. They had been working for an average of six years in a factory that produced scouring powder with a high silica content. Thirty-two, or 64 percent, showed symptoms of a systemic illness, six with Sjögren's syndrome, five with scleroderma, three with systemic lupus, five with a combination syndrome, and thirteen who didn't fit into any definite pattern of disease. Seventy-two percent had elevated ANA (antinuclear antibodies), an indicator of autoimmune connective tissue diseases. The conclusion was that workers who are continually exposed to silica have a high probability of developing an autoimmune problem.

The research on breast implants is mixed. Silicone breast implants may also play a role in some women with scleroderma. Twenty-six women with either lupus or scleroderma had breast implants removed. Three had complete remission of at least two years. If you have breast implants, testing for silicone and chemical antibodies would help you determine if you might benefit from their removal.

Some evidence suggests that people with scleroderma have a genetic block of the delta-6-desaturase enzyme. This enzyme system converts fatty acids from linolenic acid to EPA and DHA. Supplementation with fish oils would circumvent this. There haven't been a lot of studies using fish oils, but the small amount of literature shows them to be of benefit. Fatty acid testing would be advisable.

Antioxidants are beneficial in people with scleroderma. Raynaud's causes a surge of free radicals that need to be quenched. Studies have shown that blood levels of vitamin C, vitamin E, selenium, and carotenoids are all lower in people with sclero-derma, despite normal levels in their diets. Supplementation with antioxidant nutrients and testing for antioxidant status to see if levels are adequate is advisable. Specific use of N-acetyl cysteine increases glutathione levels and is also advised. Use of several antioxidant supplements may be necessary for optimal results. Resveratrol, from red grapes, may also be of use.

Homocysteine may be elevated in people with scleroderma. Use of vitamin B_6, B_{12}, folic acid, and betaine (TMG) may be use-ful in normalizing levels.

Natural therapies can work along with medical therapies for scleroderma. Infections must be treated, and beneficial flora given. Nutrients that help with collagen maintenance and repair are essential to help prevent loss of elasticity in skin and organs. Think of vitamin C, quercetin, zinc, glucosamine, and chondroitin. Foods and supplements that help reduce production of arachidonic acid will reduce inflammation and pain. Good-quality oils, fish, nuts, and seeds work in this way. It's also important to increase cir-culation and oxygen supply to the tissues. Finally, a nutrient-dense food plan must be developed that works to offset the problems of malnutrition, which are common.

Functional Laboratory Testing

Methane breath test for small bowel bacterial overgrowth

Elisa/Act IgE and IgG testing for food and environmental sensitivities

Free DHEA/cortisol saliva test

Candida testing

Comprehensive digestive stool analysis

Liver function profile

Testing for silicone antibodies should be done for women with breast implants. Saline implants have a silicone casing that may also cause problems.

Healing Options

Treat infections. Small bowel infections, esophageal candida, and other infections are likely to recur. You may be able to keep the infections at bay with use of colloidal silver, grapefruit seed extract, or garlic capsules. Each of these substances has wide antimicrobial properties, low toxicity, and a low incidence of negative side effects. Your doctor may prescribe antibiotics or antifungal medications.

Try probiotics. Flora supplements containing acidophilus, bifidobacteria, *Saccharomyces boulardii*, and other beneficial bacteria may help control infections of the intestines. No research has been done on this specifically for scleroderma, but they have been helpful in other cases of small bowel bacterial overgrowth. Take 4 to 6 capsules daily.

Detoxify. A liver function panel can determine whether your phase I and phase II liver detoxification pathways are working normally. Because the risk of scleroderma increases with solvent exposure, a liver detoxification program may be of significant benefit. In the few people I've worked with who have scleroderma, this has proven to be an effective starting point.

Try DHEA. DHEA is an adrenal hormone that has been found to be beneficial for people with scleroderma, especially in perimenopausal women. Because DHEA is a hormone, I recommend that you have a free DHEA/cortisol saliva test to determine if you actually need supplementation and to monitor your dosage levels. Dosages will vary, depending on your personal needs.

Try the elimination-provocation diet. Explore the relationship between your scleroderma and food and environmental sensitivities through laboratory testing and the elimination-provocation diet. Follow directions in Chapters 5 and 6. For best results, work with a nutritionist or physician who is familiar with food sensitivity protocols.

Make dietary changes. People with scleroderma are often malnourished. So eat at least five servings of fruits and vegetables daily and as many organic and natural foods as possible. You may want to supplement your diet with nutrient-rich protein powder drinks and spirulina or blue-green algae, available at health-food stores. Eliminate nearly all foods that don't contribute to your nutritional well-being (see Chapter 9). Make changes gradually.

Take a multivitamin with minerals. Poor diet, loss of movement in the digestive tract, loss of elasticity of the organs, infections, and medications all contribute to the malabsorption of nutrients. Selenium and vitamin C deficiencies are common in people with scleroderma. At least seventeen nutrients are essential for formation of bone and cartilage, so it's important to find a supplement that supports these needs. Look for a supplement that contains 10,000 IU vitamin A, 800 to 1,000 milligrams calcium, 400 to 500 milligrams magnesium, 400 IU vitamin E, at least 250 milligrams vitamin C, 50 milligrams vitamin B_6, 15 to 50 milligrams zinc, 5 to 10 milligrams manganese, 12 milligrams copper, and 200 micrograms selenium in addition to other nutrients. Follow the dosage on the bottle to get nutrients in appropriate amounts.

Take vitamin C. Vitamin C is vital for formation of cartilage and collagen, which is a fibrous protein that forms strong connective tissue necessary for bone strength. Vitamin C also plays an important role in immune response, helping protect us from disease-producing microbes. Vitamin C also inhibits formation of inflammatory prostaglandins, helping to reduce pain, inflammation, and swelling. If you have candida or bacterial overgrowth, vitamin C can boost your body's ability to defend itself. Vitamin C is also an antioxidant, needed to counter free radical formation noted in sclerotic conditions. Take 1 to 3 grams daily in an ascorbate or ester form. For best results, do the vitamin C flush. (See Chapter 8.)

Try gamma-linolenic acid (GLA). One gram of evening primrose oil was given to four women with scleroderma three times daily for one year. They experienced a reduction in pain, improved skin texture, and healing of sores; red patches on skin due to broken capillaries were much improved. The researchers suggest that 6 grams daily may be of greater benefit. Take 3 to 6 grams of evening primrose oil, borage oil, or flaxseed oil daily.

Increase consumption of omega-3 fatty acids and fish oils. Fish oil capsules reduce morning stiffness and joint tenderness. Similar results can be obtained by eating fish high in EPA and DHA—salmon, mackerel, halibut, tuna, sardines, and herring—two to four times a week. Fish oils increase blood-clotting time and should not be used by people with hemophilia or those who take anticoagulant medicines or aspirin regularly. It's easier for most people to eat fish two to four times each week. You can also take fish oil capsules, 4 to 10 daily.

Try licorice. Deglycyrrhized (DGL) licorice helps heal mucous membranes by increasing healing prostaglandins that promote mucus secretion and cell proliferation. Licorice also enhances the blood flow and health of intestinal tract cells. Be sure to use DGL licorice to avoid side effects caused by whole licorice. Chew or swallow 2 tablets three to four times daily.

Try slippery elm bark. Slippery elm bark has demulcent properties, so it's gentle and soothing to mucous membranes. It has been a folk remedy for both heartburn and ulcers in European and Native American cultures and was used as a food by Native Americans. Slippery elm bark can be used in large amounts without harm. Drink as a tea or chew on the bark. To make a tea, simmer 1 teaspoon of slippery elm bark in 2 cups of water for twenty minutes and strain. Sweeten if you wish, and drink freely. You can also purchase slippery elm lozenges at health-food stores and some drugstores.

Take glutamine. Although I was unable to find any references for use of glutamine to heal the esophagus, it makes theoretical sense. The digestive tract uses glutamine as a fuel source and for healing. It is effective for healing stomach ulcers, irritable bowel syndrome, and ulcerative bowel diseases, and it is likely to be useful in the upper GI tract as well. Begin a one-month trial with 8 grams daily in divided doses. If it's helpful, continue.

Try glucosamine. Glucosamine sulfate is used therapeutically to help repair cartilage, reduce swelling and inflammation, and restore joint function. Green-lipped mussels are a rich source of glycosaminoglycans. Use of glucosamine sulfate has no associated side effects. Take 500 milligrams two to four times daily.

Take ginger. Ginger can provide temporary relief, it has some anti-inflammatory properties, and it can help expel gas. Ginger can be used as an ingredient in food or taken as a supplement. To make a tea, take ½ teaspoon of powdered ginger or a few slices of fresh ginger per cup of boiled water. Steep for ten minutes and drink. If you'd like, sweeten it with honey. Cook with ginger and use it freely.

Try meadowsweet herb. A demulcent, meadowsweet soothes inflamed mucous membranes. To make a tea, take 1 to 2 teaspoons of the dried herb in 1 cup of boiled water. Steep for ten minutes, and sweeten with honey if you like. Drink 3 cups daily.

Try bromelain. Bromelain is an enzyme from pineapple that acts as an anti-inflammatory in much the same way that evening primrose oil, fish oils, and borage oils do. It interferes with production of arachidonic acid, which reduces inflammation. It also prevents platelet aggregation and interferes with growth of malignant cells. Bromelain can be taken with meals as a digestive aid, but as an anti-inflammatory it must be taken between meals. Take 500 to 1,000 milligrams two to three times daily between meals.

Try quercetin. Quercetin is the most effective bioflavonoid in its anti-inflammatory effects. It can be used to reduce pain and inflammatory responses and for control of allergies. Take 500 to 1,000 milligrams two to four times daily.

Appendix

Resources

This is a limited resource list. You'll find many more resources on my website at www.elizabethlipski.com.

Professional Organizations

Clinical Nutrition Certification Board: (972) 250-2829, www.cncb.org

Functional Medicine Institute: (800) 228-0622, www.functionalmedicine.org

International and American Association of Clinical Nutritionists: (972) 407-9089, www.iaacn.org

Laboratories

The tests listed in *Digestive Wellness* are not the ordinary tests you will find in your local medical lab or hospital, although many tests that were originally performed only by these laboratories have found their way into local and national labs. Your physician may be unfamiliar with these tests. Don't let that deter you from asking him or her to order any you feel may be appropriate for you and your condition. Your physician can call these labs for complete information packages and test kits. These labs also provide competent staff to assist your doctor with interpretation of the results.

Diagnos-Techs, Inc.: (800) 878-3787, www.diagnostechs.com. Provides many laboratory tests including adrenal stress profile, DHEA, male and female salivary hormones, parasitology testing, candida, helicobacter, digestion efficiency, secretory IgA, gastric pH, and liver function testing.

Doctor's Data Inc. and Reference Laboratory: (800) 323-2784, www.doctorsdata.com. Hair mineral testing, blood mineral analysis, urine and blood complete amino acid testing, mercapturic acid testing, D-glucaric acid, functional folic acid result, methylmalonic acid (B_{12} status), and diet analysis.

Elisa/Act Biotechnologies: (800) 553-5472, www.elisaact .com. Comprehensive food and environmental blood testing that measures more than 350 foods, environmental chemicals, preservatives, mercury sensitivity, and three major classes of yeasts.

Great Smokies Diagnostic Laboratory: (800) 522-4762, www.gsdl.com. CDSA 2.0, lactose, and small bowel breath tests; liver detoxification profiles; intestinal permeability; *Helicobacter pylori*; vitamin analysis; hair analysis; male and female hormone testing; DHEA/cortisol; secretory IgA; essential fatty acids; bone resorption; and homocysteine.

Immuno Laboratories, Inc.: (800) 231-9197, www.immunolabs.com. Food sensitivity testing.

Immunosciences Lab., Inc.: (800) 950-4686, www.immuno-sci-lab.com. Immune function testing, immunotoxicology, silicone-related immune panels, chronic fatigue panels, gastrointestinal evaluation, viral antibodies, parasite antibodies, candida antibodies, bacterial antibodies, and secretory IgA.

Meridian Valley Clinical Laboratory: (425) 271-8689, www.meridianvalleylab.com. DHEA screening, cortisol, IgE and IgG food allergies, essential amino acids, adrenal steroids, parasitology, CDSA, essential fatty acids, and fractionated estrogens.

Meta Metrix Medical Laboratory: (800) 221-4640,
www.metametrix.com. Amino acid analysis; fatty acid
analysis; lipid peroxides; antioxidant vitamin status;
minerals in blood, urine, and hair; whole blood reduced
carnitine; organic acids; glutathione; ATP, IgG, and IgE
food allergies; inhalant allergy testing; functional liver
detoxification; intestinal permeability; plasma homocysteine; cysteine; total glutathione; and bone
resorption.

Pacific Toxicology Laboratories: (800) 328-6942, www
.pactox.com. Environmental pollutants and contaminants,
including panels for solvents and metabolites, pesticides,
herbicides, polychlorinated and polybrominated
biiphenyls, PCBs, and heavy metals, as well as OSHA
compliance panels.

SpectraCell Laboratories, Inc.: (800) 227-5227, www
.spectracell.com. Provides functional vitamin, mineral,
and antioxidant panels; comprehensive functional
cardiovascular profiles.

US BioTek Laboratories, Inc.: (206) 365-1256 or (877) 318-
8728, www.usbiotek.com. Organic acid testing, food
allergy testing, salivary hormone testing.

Nutritional and Herbal Products

You will find a more comprehensive list of supplement companies
on my website (www.elizabethlipski.com). Companies listed with
an asterisk (★) will accept orders directly from readers of *Digestive
Wellness*. They carry health-professional-line products.

★Perque/Thinking of You: (800) 806-8671 to order,
www.perque.com for product information. Nutritional
and hypoallergenic products. My favorite for people with

autoimmune or complicated illnesses, but great for everyone. Mention *Digestive Wellness* for a discount.

★Emerson Ecologics: (800) 654-4432, www.emersonecologics.com. Emerson is a distributor for eighty high-quality professional supplement manufacturers and health books. Mention *Digestive Wellness* and receive a 15 percent discount. Companies include: Perque, Allergy Research, Douglas Labs, Vital Nutrients, Pure Encapsulations, Designs for Health, AMNI, NF, MMS-Pro, Metabolic Maintenance, Karuna, Seacure, Gaia Herbs, and dozens more.

★Ann Louise Gittleman and Uni Key Health Systems: (800) 888-4353, www.annlouise.com or www.unikeyhealth.com. Parasite products: Para Kek, Para Plus, Verma Key, Verma Plus.

★Metagenics: (800) 692-9400, www.metagenics.com. Nutritional and herbal products; UltraClear products.

★Integrative Therapeutics: (800) 931-1709 with PIN 90088, www.integrativeinc.com. Tyler Encapsulations, NF Formulas, Phytopharmica, and Vitaline.

★Biotics Research Southeast: (800) 874-7318, www.bioticsse.com. Nutritional and herbal products.

Associations for Specific Illnesses

A list of associations for specific illnesses can be found at www.elizabethlipski.com.

References

Chapter 1 The American Way of Life Is Hazardous to Our Health

Boris, J., and F.S. Mandel. "Foods and Additives Are Common Causes of the Attention Deficit Hyperactive Disorder in Children." *Ann Allergy* 72, no. 5 (May 1994): 462–68.

Carter, C.M., et al. "Effects of a New Food Diet in Attention Deficit Disorder." *Arch Dis Child* 69, no. 5 (November 1993): 564–68.

CFSAN Office of Nutritional Products, *Labeling and Dietary Supplements*, July 9, 2003, U.S. Food and Drug Administration, "Questions and Answers About Trans Fat Nutrition Labeling," www.cfsan.fda.gov/~dms/qatrans2.html#s2q1.

Chakurski, I., et al. "Treatment of Duodenal Ulcers and Gastroduodenitis with an Herbal Combination of *Symphitum officinalis* and *Calendula officinalis* with and Without Antacids." *Vutr Boles* 20 (6) (1981): 44–47.

Di Mario, F., et al. "Use of Bovine Lactoferrin for *Helicobacter pylori* Eradication." *Dig Liver Dis* 35 (10) (October 2003): 706–10.

———. "Use of Lactoferrin for *Helicobacter pylori* Eradication—Preliminary Results." *J Clin Gastroenterol* 36 (5) (May–June 2003): 396–98.

Economic Research Service, U.S. Department of Agriculture, "Adoption of Genetically Engineered Crops in the U.S." www.ers.usda.gov/Data/BiotechCrops.

"Exclusive Interview with Gary Gibbs, D.O., Authority on Food Radiation." *Health & Healing* 2, no. 5 (May 1995): 5–6.

Gallo, A.E. "Food Advertising in the United States," www.ers.usda.gov/publications/aib750/aib750i.pdf.

Guttner, Y., et al. "Human Recombinant Lactoferrin Is Ineffective in the Treatment of Human *Helicobacter pylori* Infection." *Aliment Pharmacol Ther* 17 (1) (January 2003): 125–29.

Hemilia, H. "Vitamin C and Plasma Cholesterol." *Crit Rev Food Sci Nutr* 32, no. 1 (1992): 35–37.

Jacques, P. "Effect of Vitamin C on High-Density Lipoprotein Cholesterol and Blood Pressure." *J Am Coll Nutr* 11, no. 2 (1992): 139–44.

Jaffe, R., and P. Donovan. *Guided Health: A Constant Professional Reference*. Reston, Va.: Health Studies Collegium Publishing, 1989.

Kennedy, S.H. "Vitamin Supplements Win Newfound Respect: Skeptics Are Changing Their Minds Over the Value of These Compounds." *Mod Med* 60 (July 1992): 15–18.

Losey, J.E., L.S. Rayor, and M.E. Carter. "Transgenic Pollen Harms Monarch Larvae." *Nature* 399 (6733) (May 1999): 214.

Quan, R., et al. "Effects of Microwave Radiation on Anti-Infective Factors in Human Milk." *Pediatrics* 89 (1992): 667–69.

Mokdad, A.H., et al. "Prevalence of Obesity, Diabetes, and Obesity-Related Health Risk Factors, 2001." *JAMA* 289 (1) (January 1, 2003): 76–79.

National Institutes of Health. *Clinical Guidelines on the Identification, Evaluation, and Treatment of Overweight and Obesity in Adults.* Bethesda, Md.: Department of Health and Human Services, National Institutes of Health, National Heart, Lung, and Blood Institute, 1998.

Neher, J.O., and J.M. Borkan. "A Clinical Approach to Alternative Medicine." *Arch Fam Med* 3 (October 1994): 859–61.

Pauling, L. "Prevention and Treatment of Heart Disease: New Research Focus at the Linus Pauling Institute." *Linus Pauling Institute of Science & Medicine Newsletter* (March 1992): 1.

Sigman, M., et al. "Effects of Microwaving Human Milk: Changes in IgA Content and Bacterial Count." *J Am Diet Assoc* 89 (1989): 690–92.

U.S. Department of Agriculture Economic Research Service. *Food Consumption: Prices and Expenditures, 1980–1982.* Washington, D.C.: 1995.

U.S. EPA. "America's Children and the Environment (ACE), Measure E8: Pesticide Residues on Foods Frequently Consumed by Children," October 2003. www.epa.gov/envirohealth/children/contaminants/e8.htm.

Wolfe, S.M. *Health Letter of the Public Citizen Health Research Group* 5, no. 7 (1989): 1–5.

Chapter 2 A Voyage Through the Digestive System

Bland, J. *20-Day Rejuvenation Diet*. Los Angeles: Keats Publishing, 1997.

Gershon, M.D. *The Second Brain*. New York: HarperCollins Publishers, 1998.

Robbins, J. *May All Be Fed*. New York: William Morrow & Co., 1992.

Thompson, T. "Approach to Gastrointestinal Immune Dysfunction and Related Health Problems." Lecture given at the Fourth International Functional Medicine Meeting, Aspen, Colo., 1997.

Tips, J. *The Liver Triad*. Austin, Tex.: Apple A Day Publishing, 1989.

Chapter 3 The Bugs in Your Body: Intestinal Flora

Biffi, A., et al. "Antiproliferative Effect of Fermented Milk on the Growth of a Human Breast Cancer Cell Line." *Nutr Cancer* 28 (1) (1997): 93–99.

Bland, J., et al. *Clinical Nutrition: A Functional Approach*. Gig Harbor, Wash.: Functional Medicine Institute, 1999.

Campieri, C., et al. "Reduction of Oxaluria After an Oral Course of Lactic Acid Bacteria at High Concentration." *Kidney Int* 60 (3) (September 2001): 1097–1105.

Carper, Jean. *Food Pharmacy*. New York: Bantam Books, 1988.

Casas, I.A., F.W. Edens, and W.J. Dobrogosz. "*Lactobacillus reuteri*: An Effective Probiotic for Poultry and Other Animals." In *Lactic Acid Bacteria: Microbiology and Functional Aspects*, 2nd ed., edited by S. Salminen and A. von Wright. New York: Marcel Dekker, Inc., 1998.

Chaitow, L., and N. Trenev. *Probiotics*. London: Thorsons, 1990.

Czerucka, D., I. Roux, and P. Rampal. "*Saccharomyces Boulardii* Inhibits Secretagogue-Mediated Adenosine 3',5'-Cyclic Monophosphate Induction in Intestinal Cells." *Gastroenterology* 106, no. 1 (January 1994): 65–72.

Florastor website: www.florastor.com/ProductInformation.asp.

Galland, Leo. *Dysbiosis & Disease*. Audiotape from Great Smokies Diagnostic Lab and HealthComm International, 1993.

Great Smokies Diagnostic Lab and HealthComm International, "Solving the Digestive Puzzle." Conference manual. San Francisco: May 1995.

Gibson, G.R., and M.B. Roberfroid. "Dietary Modulation of the Human Colonic Microbiota: Introducing the Concept of Probiotics." *J Nutr* 125, no. 6 (June 1995): 1401–12.

Gibson, G.R., and X. Wang. "Regulatory Effects of Bifidobacteria on the Growth of Other Colonic Bacteria." *J Appl
Bacteriol* 77 (1994): 412–20.

Guandalini, S., et al. "Lactobacillus GG Administered in Oral
Rehydration Solution to Children with Acute Diarrhea: A
Multicenter European Trial." *J Pediatr Gastroenterol Nutr* 30 (1)
(January 2000): 54–60.

Kajiwara, S., H. Gandhi, Z. Ustunol. "Effect of Honey on the
Growth of and Acid Production by Human Intestinal Bifidobacterium spp.: An In Vitro Comparison with Commercial
Oligosaccharides and Inulin." *J Food Prot* 65 (1) (January
2002): 214–18.

Kalliomaki, M., and E. Isolauri. "Role of Intestinal Flora in the
Development of Allergy." *Curr Opin Allergy Clin Immunol* 3
(1) (2003): 15–20.

Kimmey, M.B., et al. "Prevention of Further Recurrences of
Clostridium difficile Colitis with *Saccharomyces boulardii*." *Dig
Dis Sci* 35, no. 7 (July 1990): 897–901.

Macfarlane, G., and J.H. Cummings. "Probiotics and Prebiotics:
Can Regulating the Activities of Intestinal Bacteria Benefit
Health?" *BMJ* 318 (April 10, 1999): 999–1003.

Mitsuuoka, T. "Intestinal Flora & Aging." *Nutr Rev* 50, no. 12
(December 1992): 438–46.

Plein, K., and J. Hotz. "Therapeutic Effects of *Saccharomyces
boulardii* on Mild Residual Symptoms in a Stable Phase of
Crohn's Disease with Special Respect to Chronic Diarrhea—

A Pilot Study." *Gastroenterology* 31, no. 2 (February 1993): 129–34.

Plummer, N., P. Quilt, and C. Crockett. "Fructooligosaccharides (FOS) and Other Prebiotics," Townsend Letter for Doctors and Patients. June 2003, www.findarticles.com/cf_0/moISW/2003_June/102372155.

Reid, G. "Probiotic Agents to Protect the Urogenital Tract Against Infection." *Am J Clin Nutr* 73 (Suppl) (2001): S437–43.

Reid, G., and A.W. Bruce. "Selection of Lactobacillus Strains for Urogenital Probiotic Applications." *J Infect Dis* 183 (Suppl 1) (2001): S77–80.

Resnick, Corey, N.D. Telephone conversation. Winter 1994.

Roberfroid, M.B. "Prebiotics and Synbiotics: Concepts and Nutritional Properties." *Br J Nutr* 80, no. 4 (October 1998): S197–S202.

Sehnert, K. "The Garden Within." *Health World Magazine* (1989): 9.

Sekine, K., et al. "Analysis of Antitumor Properties of Effector Cells Stimulated with a Cell Wall Preparation (WPG) of *Bifidobacterium Infantis*." *Biol Pharm Bull* 18 (1) (January 1995): 148–53.

Sellars, R.L. "Acidophilus Product." *Therapeutic Properties of Fermented Milks*, New York: Elsevier Applied Science, 1991.

Seppo, L., et al. "A Fermented Milk High in Bioactive Peptides Has a Blood Pressure–Lowering Effect in Hypertensive Subjects." *Am J Clin Nutr* 77 (2) (February 2003): 326–30.

Sghir, A., J.M. Chow, and R.I. Mackie. "Continuous Culture Selection of Bifidobacteria and Lactobacilli from Human Fecal Samples Using Fructooligosaccharide as a Selective Substrate." *J Appl Microbiol* 84, no. 4 (October 1994): 769–77.

Trenev, Natasha. Telephone conversation. Winter 1994.

Van Niel, C.W., et al. "Lactobacillus Therapy for Acute Infectious Diarrhea in Children: A Meta-Analysis." *Pediatrics* (4) (April 2002): 678–84.

Chapter 4 Dysbiosis: A Good Neighborhood Gone Bad

Begley, S. "The End of Antibiotics." *Newsweek* (March 28, 1994): 46–51.

Bjarnason, I., et al. "Side Effects of Non-Steroidal Anti-Inflammatory Drugs on the Small and Large Intestine in Humans." *Gastroenterology* 104, no. 6 (June 1993): 1832–47.

Bland, J. "Preventive Medicine Update." May 1994. Audiotape.

Crook, W. *The Yeast Connection and the Woman*. Jackson, Tenn.: Professional Books, 1995.

Garrett, L. *The Coming Plague*. New York: Farrar, Straus, Giroux, 1994.

Hoffer, A. Preface to *The Yeast Syndrome*, by John Trowbridge and Morton Walker. New York: Bantam Books, 1986.

Koelz, H.R. "Ulcer Prevention During Anti-Rheumatism Therapy and in Intensive Medicine." *Schweiz Rundsch Med Prax* 3, nos. 25–26 (June 21, 1994): 768–71.

Lee, M., of the Great Smokies Diagnostic Laboratory. Personal correspondence. Spring 1995.

Loosli, A.R. "Reversing Sports-Related Iron & Zinc Deficiencies." *Phys Sportsmed* 21, no. 6 (June 1993): 70–78.

McBride, J. "Nutrient Deficiency Unleashes Jekyll-Hyde Virus." *Agric Res* 42, no. 8 (August 1994): 14–16.

Mfitsuoka, T. "Intestinal Flora & Aging." *Nutr Rev* 50, no. 12 (December 1992): 438–46.

The Nutrition Screening Initiative, American Dietetic Association, the National Council on Aging, and the American Academy of Family Physicians. "Providers Estimate One in Four Seniors Malnourished." *Nutr Week* (April 30, 1993): 3.

Tippett, K., and J.D. Goldman. "Diets More Healthful, but Still Fall Short of Dietary Guidelines." *Food Review, U.S.D.A.* 17, no. 1 (January–April 1994): 8–14.

Chapter 5 Leaky Gut Syndrome: The Systemic Consequences of Faulty Digestion

Bahna, S.L. "Unusual Presentations of Food Allergy." *Ann Allergy Asthma Immunol* 86 (2001): 414–20.

D'Adamo, P. *Eat Right 4 Your Type.* New York: Putnam Publishing Group, 1997.

Dagci, H., et al. "Protozoon Infections and Intestinal Permeability." *Acta Tropica* 81 (2002): 1–5.

Diebel, L.N., et al. "Enterocyte Apoptosis and Barrier Function Are Modulated by SIgA After Exposure to Bacteria and Hypoxia/Reoxygenation." *Surgery* 134 (4) (October 2003): 574–80.

Elisa/Act Patient Handbook. Reston, Va.: Serammune Laboratories, 1994.

Galland, L. "Solving the Digestive Puzzle." Conference manual, Great Smokies Diagnostic Lab and HealthComm International, San Francisco, May 1995.

Guide to Health. Fort Lauderdale, Fla.: Immuno Laboratories, Inc., 1994.

Jaffe, R. "Gut Hyperpermeability." Serammune Physicians Lab Newletter 2, no. 1 (January 1992).

Hang, C.H., et al. "Alterations of Intestinal Mucosa Structure and Barrier Function Following Traumatic Brain Injury in Rats." *World J Gastroenterol* 9 (12) (December 2003): 2776–81.

Holden, W., T. Orchard, and P. Wordsworth. "Enteropathic Arthritis." *Rheum Dis Clin North Am* 29 (3) (August 2003): 513–30, viii.

Hollander, D. "Intestinal Permeability, Leaky Gut, and Intestinal Disorders." *Curr Gastroenterol Rep* 1 (5) (October 1999): 410–16.

Kashavarzian, A., et al. "Preventing Gut Leakiness by Oats Supplementation Ameliorates Alcohol-Induced Liver Damage in Rats." *J Pharm Exp Therap* 229 (2) (2001): 442–48.

"The Leaky Gut." *Great Smokies Digest* (Summer 1990): 4.

Lipski, Elizabeth. *Leaky Gut Syndrome*. Los Angeles: Keats Publishing, 1998.

Marks, D., and L. Marks. "Food Allergy: Manifestations, Evaluation, and Management." *Food Allergy, Postgraduate Medicine* 93, no. 2 (February 1, 1993): 191–201.

Ren, H., et al. "Short-Chain Fatty Acids Induce Intestinal Epithelial Heat Shock Protein 25 Expression in Rats and IEC 18 Cells." *Gastroenterology* 121 (2001): 631–39.

Ryan, C.M., et al. "Increased Gut Permeability Early After Burns Correlates with the Extent of Burn Injury." *Crit Care Med* 20 (11) (November 1992): 1508–12.

Schmitz, H., et al. "Altered Tight Junction Structure Contributes to the Impaired Epithelial Barrier Function in Ulcerative Colitis." *Gastroenterology* 116 (2) (February 1999): 301–9.

Sturniolo, G.C., et al. "Effect of Zinc Supplementation on Intestinal Permeability in Experimental Colitis." *J Lab Clin Med* 138 (5) (May 2002): 311–15.

Suenaert, P., et al. "Anti-Tumor Necrosis Factor Treatment Restores the Gut Barrier in Crohn's Disease." *Am J Gastroenterol* 97 (8) (August 2002): 2000–2004.

Swanson, M. "Comprehensive Digestive Stool Analysis and Intestinal Permeability." Great Smokies Diagnostic Lab, 1993. Audiotape.

Trenev, N. Lecture to California State Meeting IAACN. April 1994.

Weber, P., et al. "Gastrointestinal Symptoms and Permeability in Patients with Juvenile Idiopathic Arthritis." *Clin Exp Rheumatol* 21 (5) (September–October 2003): 657–62.

Zhou, Y.P., et al. "The Effect of Supplemental Enteral Glutamine on Plasma Levels, Gut Function, and Outcome in Severe Burns: A Randomized, Double-Blind, Controlled Clinical Trial." *JPEN J Parenter Enteral Nutr* 27 (4) (July–August 2003): 241–45.

Chapter 6 Functional Medicine and Functional Testing

Application Guide, *Bacterial Overgrowth of the Small Intestine*. Asheville, N.C.: Great Smokies Diagnostic Laboratory, 1994.

Application Guide, *Functional Liver Testing*. Asheville, N.C.: Great Smokies Diagnostic Laboratory, 1994.

Bland, J. "New Clinical Breakthroughs in the Management of Chronic Fatigue Syndrome, Intestinal Dysbiosis, Immune

Dysregulation, and Cellular Toxicity." Gig Harbor, Wash.: Health Comm International, 1992.

Brown, S., and R. Jaffe. "Acid–Alkaline Balance and Its Effect on Bone Health." *International Journal of Integrative Medicine* 2 (6) (November–December 2000). Reprint available from Serammune Laboratory.

Cusak, M.A., M.S. O'Mahony, and K. Woodhouse. "Giardia in Older People." *Age and Aging* 30 (2001): 419–21.

Gittleman, A.L. *Guess What Came to Dinner?* Garden City Park, N.Y.: Avery Publishing, 1993.

Kirsch, M. "Bacterial Overgrowth." *Am J Gastroenterol* 85, no. 3 (1990): 231–37.

Jaffe, R., and P. Donovan. "Your Health: A Professional User's Guide." Sterling, Vir.: Health Studies Collegium, 1993.

Lab manual. Asheville, N.C.: Great Smokies Diagnostic Laboratory, 1995.

Rider, M.S., et al. "Effect of Immune System Imagery on Secretory IgA." *Biofeedback Self-Regulation* 15, no. 4 (December 1990): 317–33.

Chapter 7 Moving Toward a Wellness Lifestyle

Eisenberg, D.M., et al. "Trends in Alternative Medicine Use in the United States, 1990–1997: Results of a Follow-Up

National Survey." *JAMA* 280, no. 18 (November 11, 1998): 1569–75.

Sokol Green, N. *Poisoning Our Children: Surviving in a Toxic World*. Chicago: Noble Press Inc., 1991.

Tubesing, N.L., and D. Tubesing. *Structured Exercises in Wellness*, vol. 3. Duluth, Minn.: Whole Person Press, 1986.

Wetzel, M.S., D.M. Eisenberg, and T.J. Kaptchuk. "Courses Involving Complementary and Alternative Medicine at U.S. Medical Schools." *JAMA* 280, no. 9 (September 2, 1998): 784–87.

Chapter 8 First Things First: Detoxification

Jaffe, R. Women and Children's Health Update, syllabus, 1994–1995.

National Research Council. *Environmental Neurotoxicity*. Washington, D.C.: National Academy Press, 1992.

Sokol Green, N. *Poisoning Our Children: Surviving in a Toxic World*. Chicago: Noble Press Inc., 1991.

Stone, I. *The Healing Factor*. New York: Grosset & Dunlap, 1982.

Ultrabalance Workbook. Gig Harbor, Wash.: HealthComm International, 1988.

Chapter 9 Diet Means "A Way of Living"

Carper, J. *The Food Pharmacy*. New York: Bantam Books, 1989.

Erasmus, Udo. *Fats That Heal, Fats That Kill*. Burnaby, B.C.: Alive Books, 1993.

Jaffe, R., and P. Donovan. *Guided Health: A Constant Professional Reference*. Reston, Va.: Health Studies Collegium Publishing, 1989.

Moore Lappe, F. *Diet for a Small Planet*. New York: Ballantine, 1991.

―――. *Food First*. New York: Ballantine, 1988.

Robbins, J. *Diet for a New America*. Walpole, N.H.: Stillpoint, 1998.

―――. *May All Be Fed*. New York: William Morrow, 1992.

Schauss, A. "Dietary Fish Oil Consumption and Fish Oil Supplementation." In *A Textbook for Natural Medicine*, edited by Joseph E. Pizzorno and Michael T. Murray. St. Louis, Mo.: Churchill Livingstone, 1991.

Schnohr, P., et al. "Egg Consumption and High-Density Lipoprotein Cholesterol." *J Intern Med* 235 (1994): 249–51.

Shinitsky, M. "Egg Consumption, Serum Cholesterol, and Membrane Fluidity." *Biomembranes and Nutrition* 195 (1989): 391–400.

Smith, B. "Organic Foods vs. Supermarket Foods, Element Levels." *Doctor's Data Labs*, 1993.

Weir, D., and M. Schapiro. *Circle of Poison*. San Francisco: Institute for Food & Development Policy, 1981.

Chapter 10 Natural Therapies for Common Digestive Problems

Aldoori, W.H., et al. "A Prospective Study of Diet and the Risk of Symptomatic Diverticular Disease in Men." *Am J Clin Nutr* 60 (1994): 757–64.

Andreone, P., et al. "Vitamin E as Treatment for Chronic Hepatitis B: Results of a Randomized Controlled Pilot Trial." *Antiviral Res* 49 (2) (February 2001): 75–81.

Aslan, A., and G. Triadafilopoulos. "Fish Oil Fatty Acid Supplementation and Active Ulcerative Colitis: A Double-Blind, Placebo-Controlled Crossover Study." *Am J Gastroenterol* 87, no. 4 (April 1992): 432–33.

Babbs, C.F. "Oxygen Radicals in Ulcerative Colitis." *Free Radic Biol Med* 13, no. 2 (1992): 169–81.

Bacon, B.R., et al. "Nonalcoholic Steatohepatitis: An Expanded Clinical Entity." *Gastroenterology* 107 (4) (October 1994): 1103–9.

Baran, E., and C. Dupont. "Modification of Intestinal Permeability During Food Provocation Procedures in Pediatric Irritable Bowel Syndrome." *J Pediatr Gastroenterol Nutr* 11 (1990): 72–77.

Barnard, N. "Fiber, Health, and Research; The Work of Dennis Burkitt, M.D." *PCRM Update* (May–June 1990): 1–9.

Batmanghelidj, F. *Your Body's Many Cries for Water.* Falls Church, Va.: Global Health Solutions, 1995.

Bazzocchi, G., et al. "Intestinal Microflora and Oral Bacteriotherapy in Irritable Bowel Syndrome." *Dig Liver Dis* 34 (Suppl
2) (September 2002): S48–S53.

Bean, P. "The Use of Alternative Medicine in the Treatment of
Hepatitis C." *Am Clin Lab* 21 (4) (May 2002): 19–21.

Bell, I.R., et al. "Symptom and Personality Profiles of Young
Adults from a College Student Population with Self-
Reported Illness from Foods and Chemicals." *J Am Coll Nutr*
12, no. 6 (1993): 693–702.

Ben-Ayre, E., et al. "Wheat Grass Juice in the Treatment of
Active Distal Ulcerative Colitis: A Randomized Double-
Blind Placebo-Controlled Trial." *Scand J Gastroenterol* 37 (4)
(April 2002): 444–49.

Berkson, B.M. "A Conservative Triple Antioxidant Approach to
the Treatment of Hepatitis C. Combination of Alpha lipoic
Acid (Thioctic Acid), Silymarin, and Selenium: Three Case
Histories." *Med Klin* (Munich) 94 (Suppl 3) (October 15,
1999): 84–89.

Biasco, G., et al. "Folic Acid Supplementation and Cell Kinetics
of Rectal Mucosa in Patients with Ulcerative Colitis." *Cancer
Epidemiol Biomarkers Prev* 6 (June 1997): 469–71.

Bjarnason, I. "Intestinal Permeability." *Gut* (Suppl 1) (1994):
S18–S22.

Bland, J. *Glandular-Based Food Supplements: Helping to Separate
Fact from Fiction.* Bellevue, Wash.: Bellevue-Redmond Medical Lab, Inc., 1984.

Bleijenberg, G., and H.C. Kuijpers. "Biofeedback Treatment of Constipation: A Comparison of Two Methods." *Am J Gastroenterol* 89, no. 7 (July 1994): 1021–26.

Bolin, T.D., A.E. Davis, and V.M. Duncombe. "A Prospective Study of Peristent Diarrhea." *Australia/New Zealand Journal of Medicine* 12, no. 1 (February 1982): 22–26.

Bonkovsky, H.L., R.W. Lambrecht, and Y. Shan. "Iron as a Co-Morbid Factor in Nonhemochromatotic Liver Disease." *Alcohol* 30 (2) (June 2003):137–44.

Born, P., et al. "Fructose Malabsorption and Irritable Bowel Syndrome." *Gastroenterology* 101, no. 5 (1991): 1454.

Borody, T.J., et al. "Treatment of Ulcerative Colitis Using Fecal Bacteriotherapy." *J Clin Gastroenterol* 37 (1) (July 2003): 42–47.

Borok, G. "Irritable Bowel Syndrome and Diet." *Gastroenterology Forum* (April 1994): 29.

Boyko, E.J., et al. "Increased Risk of Inflammatory Bowel Disease Associated with Oral Contraceptive Use." *Am J Epidemiol* 140, no. 3 (1994): 268–78.

Breneman, J. "Allergy Elimination Diet as the Most Effective Gallbladder Diet." *Ann Allergy* 26, no. 2 (February 1968): 83–87.

Campan, P. "Pilot Study on n-3 Polyunsaturated Fatty Acids in the Treatment of Human Experimental Gingivitis." *J Clin Periodontol* 24 (1997): 907–13.

Capper, W., et al. "Gallstones, Gastric Secretion, and Flatulent Dyspepsia." *Lancet* 1 (February 25, 1967): 413–15.

Capron, J.P., et al. "Meal Frequency and Duration of Overnight Fast: A Role in Gallstone Formation?" *BMJ* 283 (1981): 1435.

Catassi, C., et al. "Celiac Diseases in the Year 2000: Exploring the Iceberg." *Lancet* 343 (1994): 200–203.

Centers for Disease Control website: www.cdc.gov/ncidod/diseases

Challacombe, S.J. "Hematological Abnormalities in Oral Lichen Planus, Candidiasis, Leukoplakia, and Non-Specific Stomatitis." *Int J Oral Maxillofacial Surg* 15, no. 1 (February 1986): 72–80.

Chang, W.S., et al. "Inhibitory Effects of Flavonoids on Xanthine Oxidase." *Anticancer Res* 13 (6A) (November–December 1993): 2165–70.

Chambers, J.C., D.O. Haskard, and J.S. Kooner. "Vascular Endothelial Function and Oxidative Stress Mechanisms in Patients with Behcet's Syndrome." *J Am Coll Cardiol* 37 (2) (February 2001): 517–20.

Charnow, J. A. "Vitamin A, Fiber May Cut Risk of Duodenal Ulcer." *Med Trib Med News* (February 6, 1997): 15.

Chaturvedi, G.N., and R.H. Singh. "Jaundice of Infectious Hepatitis and Its Treatment with an Indigenous Drug, Picrorhiza Kurrooa [sic]." *J Res Ind Med* 1 (1966): 1–13.

Chen, L. "Bile Acid Pool in the Formation of Pigment Stones: An Experimental Study." *Chung Hua Wai Ko Tsa Chih* 30, no. 8 (August 1992): 496–98.

Constipation Fact Sheet. Publication no. 92-2754. Washington, D.C.: National Institutes of Health, National Institute of Diabetes and Digestive & Kidney Diseases, 1992.

Correa, P., et al. "Chemoprevention of Gastric Dysplasia: Randomized Trial of Antioxidant Supplements and Anti-*Helicobacter pylori* Therapy." *J Nat Can Inst* 200 (92): 1881–88.

"Crohn's Disease Linked to Measles." *Med Trib Med News* (May 13, 1993): 10.

Dahl, H., and M. Degre. "The Effect of Ascorbic Acid on Production of Human Interferon and the Antiviral Activity In Vitro." *Acta Pathol Microbiol Scand* 84:5 (October 1976): 280–84.

Delilbasi E., et al. "Selenium and Behcet's Disease." *Biol Trace Elem Res* 28 (1) (January 1991): 21–25.

Dieleman, L.A., and W.D. Heizer. "Nutritional Issues in Inflammatory Bowel Disease." *Gastroenterol Clin North Am* 27, no. 2 (June 1998): 435–51.

Di Prisco, M.C. "Possible Relationship Between Allergic Disease and Infection by Giardia Lamblia." *Ann Allergy* 70 (March 1993): 210–12.

Drinka, P., et al. "Nutritional Correlates of Atrophic Glossitis: Possible Role of Vitamin E and Papillary Atrophy." *J Am Coll Nutr* 12, no. 1 (1993): 14–20.

Drinka, P., et al. "Laboratory Measurements of Nutritional Status as Correlates of Atrophic Glossitis." *J Gen Intern Med* 6, no. 2 (March–April 1991): 137–40.

Dubey, S.S., G.R. Palodhi, and A.K. Jain. "Ascorbic Acid, Dehydroascorbic Acid, and Glutathione in Liver Disease." *Indian J Physiol Pharmacol* 31 (4) (October–December 1987): 279–83.

Dunlop, S.P., D. Jenkins, and R.C. Spiller. "Distinctive Clinical, Psychological, and Histological Features of Postinfective Irritable Bowel Syndrome." *Am J Gastroenterol* 98 (7) (July 2003): 1578–83.

Dunlop, S.P., et al. "Relative Importance of Enterochromaffin Cell Hyperplasia, Anxiety, and Depression in Postinfectious IBS." *Gastroenterology* 125 (6) (December 2003):1651–59.

Drossman, D.A., et al. "Irritable Bowel Syndrome and Sexual/Physical Abuse History." *J Gastroenterol Hepatol* 9 (4) (April 1997): 327–30.

Emerson Ecologics, Clinical Essentials, hepatitis, www.emersonecologics.com/ClinicalEssentials

Evaluating Silymarin for Chronic Hepatitis C, www.nccam.nih.gov

Fasano, A. "Celiac Disease: How to Handle a Clinical Chameleon." *N Engl J Med* 34 (25) (June 19, 2003): 2568–70.

"Fasting May Cause Stones." *Med Trib Med News* (July 25, 1991): 13.

Fernandez-Banares, F., et al. "Enteral Nutrition as a Primary Therapy in Crohn's Disease." *Gut* (1994): S55–S59.

Fernandez-Banares, F., et al. "Role of Fructose-Sorbitol Malabsorption and Irritable Bowel Syndrome." *Gastroenterology* 101, no. 5 (November 1991): 1453–54.

Floch, M.H. "Probiotics, Irritable Bowel Syndrome, and Inflammatory Bowel Disease." *Curr Treat Options Gastroenterol* 6 (4) (August 2003): 283–88.

Francis, C.W., et al. "Bran and Irritable Bowel Syndrome: Time for Reappraisal." *Lancet* 334 (July 2, 1994): 339–40.

Fresko, I., et al. "Intestinal Permeability in Behcet's Syndrome." *Ann Rheum Dis* 60 (1) (January 2001): 65–66.

Frezza, M., et al. "Oral S-Adenosylmethionine in the Symptomatic Treatment of Intrahepatic Cholestasis: A Double-Blind Placebo Controlled Study." *Gastroenterology* 99 (1990): 211–15.

Gaby, A., and J. Wright. "Ulcerative Colitis." *Nutrition & Healing* 2, no. 1 (January 1995).

Galland, L., M.D. Telephone conversation. June 1995.

———. Telephone conversation. Winter 1995.

Gershon, M.D. "Serotonin and Its Implication for the Management of Irritable Bowel Syndrome." *Rev Gastroenterol Disord* 3 (Suppl 2) (2003): S25–S34.

———. *The Second Brain.* New York: HarperCollins Publishers, 1998.

Gottschall, E. *Food and the Gut Reaction*. Kirkton, Ontario: Kirkton Press, 1986.

Gross, V., et al. "Free Radicals and Inflammatory Bowel Diseases, Pathophysiology and Therapeutic Implications." *Hepatogastroenterology* 41 (1994): 320–27.

Gryboski, J.D. "Ulcerative Colitis in Children 10 Years Old or Younger." *J Pediatr Gastroenterol Nutr* 17, no. 1 (July 1993): 24–31.

Gulati, R.K., S. Agarwal, and S.S. Agarwal. "Hepatoprotective Studies on Phyllanthus Emblica Linn. and Quercetin." *Indian J Exp Biol* 33 (4) (April 1995): 261–68.

Gupta, I., et al. "Effects of Boswellia Serrata Gum Resin in Patients with Ulcerative Colitis." *Eur J Med Res* 2 (1) (January 1997): 37–43.

Hamilton, C. Clinical Pearls Database version 5.02, IT Services, Sacramento, Calif. www.clinicalpearls.com.

Hanauer, S.B. "Inflammatory Bowel Disease: Novel Aspects of Clinical Genetics and Potential for Probiotic Therapy." *Medscape* June 7, 2002. www.medscape.com/viewarticle/434522.

Hanaway, P. "Achieving Clinical Excellence, Optimizing Gut Function: Improving Diagnostic and Therapeutic Decisions in Common GI Complaints," Great Smokies Diagnostic Lab. Conference, Spring 2004.

Harnyk, T.P. "The Effect of Plant Preparations on the Malondialdehyde Indices of Patients with Chronic Hepatitis." *Lik Sprava* (6) (September 1999): 129–31.

Head, K.A., and J.S. Jurenka. "Inflammatory Bowel Disease, Part 1: Ulcerative Colitis—Pathophysiology and Conventional and Alternative Treatment Options." *Altern Med Rev* 8 (3) (August 2003): 247–83.

"*Helicobacter pylori* in Peptic Ulcer Disease." National Institutes of Health Consensus Statement 12, no. 1 (February 1994).

Hepatitis B Foundation, www.hepb.org

"Hepatitis Viral Load Correlates to Glutathione Levels." *Posit Health News* no. 17 (Fall 1998): 14–15.

Hoffman, R. *7 Weeks to a Settled Stomach*. New York: Pocket Books, 1990.

Hollen, E., et al. "Antibodies to Oat Prolamines (Avenins) in Children with Coeliac Disease." *Scand J Gastroenterol* 38 (7) (July 2003): 742–46.

Hotz, J., and K. Plein. "Effectiveness of Plantago Seed Husks in Comparison with Wheat Bran on Stool Frequency and Manifestations of Irritable Colon Syndrome with Constipation." *Med Klin* 89, no. 12 (December 15, 1994): 645–51.

Husebye, E., et al. "Fasting Hypochlorhydria with Gram Positive Gastric Flora Is Highly Prevalent in Healthy Old People." *Gut* 33 (October 1992): 133–37.

Iijima, K., et al. "Novel Mechanism of Nitrosative Stress from Dietary Nitrate with Relevance to Gastro-Esophageal Junction Cancers." *Carcinogenesis* 24 (12) (December 2003): 1951–60. Published online September 11, 2003. http://carcin.oopjournals.org/cgi/content/fall/24/12/1951.

Jacobs, E.J., and E. White. "Constipation, Laxative Use, and Colon Cancer Among Middle-Aged Adults." *Epidemiology* 9, no. 4 (1998): 385–91.

Jain, S.K., et al. "Oxidative Stress in Chronic Hepatitis C: Not Just a Feature of Late Stage Disease." *J Hepatol* 36 (6) (June 2002): 805–11.

Jancin, B. "Gastroesophageal Disease Linked to Long Antacid Use." *Fam Pract News* 26, no. 13 (July 1, 1996): 12.

Johnston, S.D., et al. "A Comparison of Antibodies to Tissue Transglutaminase with Conventional Serological Tests in the Diagnosis of Coeliac Disease." *Eur J Gastroenterol Hepatol* 15 (9) (September 2003):1001–4.

Jones, E.L. "Does DMSO Dissolve Hemorrhoids?" *Cortlandt Forum* 103 (May 1994).

Kapur, G., et al. "Iron Supplementation in Children with Celiac Disease." *Indian J Pediatr* 70 (12) (December 2003): 955–58.

Karamanlioglu, B., et al. "Hepatobiliary Scintigraphy for Evaluating the Hepatotoxic Effect of Halothane and the Protective Effect of Catechin in Comparison with Histo-Chemical Analysis of Liver Tissue." *Nucl Med Commun* 23 (1) (January 2002): 53–59.

Karnam, U.S., L.R. Felder, and J.B. Raskin. "Prevalence of Occult Celiac Disease in Patients with Iron-Deficiency Anemia: A Prospective Study." *South Med J* 97 (1) (January 2004): 30–34.

Katz, J.P., and G.R. Lichtenstein. "Rheumatologic Manifestations of Gastrointestinal Diseases." *Gastroenterol Clin North Am* 27 (3) (September 1998): 533–62, v.

Kim, H.J., et al. "A Randomized Controlled Trial of a Probiotic, VSL#3, on Gut Transit and Symptoms in Diarrhea-Predominant Irritable Bowel Syndrome." *Aliment Pharmacol Ther* 17 (7) (April 2003): 895–904.

Kimikazu, I., J. Kiyonana, and M. Ishikawa. "Studies on Gamma-Oryzanol II—The Anti-Ulcerogenic Action." Tokushima: Research Institute, Otsuka Pharmaceutical Co., Ltd., 1976.

Kokcam, I., and M. Naziroglu. "Effects of Vitamin E Supplementation on Blood Antioxidants Levels in Patients with Behcet's Disease." *Clin Biochem* 35 (8) (November 2002): 633–39.

Komar, V.I., and V.S. Vasil'ev. "The Use of Water-Soluble Vitamins in Viral Hepatitis A." *Klin Med* (Mosk) 70 (1) (January 1992): 73–75.

Kratzer, W., et al. "Gallstone Prevalence in Relation to Smoking, Alcohol, Coffee Consumption, and Nutrition." *Scand J Gastroenterol* 32 (1997): 953–58.

Kumar, K.S., and P.F. Malet. "Nonalcoholic Steatohepatitis." *Mayo Clin Proc* 75 (7) (July 2000): 733–39.

Langmead, L., et al. "Randomized, Double-Blind, Placebo-Controlled Trial of Oral Aloe Vera Gel for Active Ulcerative Colitis." *Aliment Pharmacol Ther* 19 (7) (April 1, 2004): 739–47.

Lazzari, R., et al. "Sideropenic Anemia and Celiac Disease." *Pediatr Med Chir* 16, no. 6 (November–December 1994): 549–50.

Lichtenstein, G.R., and R.P. MacDermott. "Recent Advances in the Treatment of Inflammatory Bowel Disease: The Role of biologics and Immunomodulators." Medscape 2002. www.medscape.com/viewarticle/434521

Leitzmann, M.F., et al. "The Relation of Physical Activity to Risk for Symptomatic Gallstone Disease in Men." *Ann Intern Med* 128, no. 6 (March 15, 1998): 417–25.

Lewin, S. *Vitamin C: Its Molecular Biology and Medical Potential.* Academic Press, 1976.

Li, J., L. Zhou, and Y. Zhang. "Studies on the Effects of Tea Catechins Against Hepatitis B Virus Infection." *Zhonghua Yu Fang Yi Xue Za Zhi* 35 (6) (November 2001): 404–7.

Lin, H.C., et al. "Slowing of Gastrointestinal Transit by Oleic Acid: A Preliminary Report of a Novel, Nutrient-Based Treatment in Humans." *Dig Dis Sci* 46 (2) (2001): 223–29.

Loguercio, C., and A. Federico. "Oxidative Stress in Viral and Alcoholic Hepatitis." *Free Radic Biol Med* 34 (1) (January 2003): 1–10.

Lucena, M.I., et al. "Effects of Silymarin MZ-80 on Oxidative Stress in Patients with Alcoholic Cirrhosis. Results of a Randomized, Double-Blind, Placebo-Controlled Clinical Study." *Int J Clin Pharmacol Ther* 40 (1) (January 2002): 2–8.

Lundin, K.E., et al. "Oats Induced Villous Atrophy in Coeliac Disease" *Gut* 52 (11) (November 2003): 1649–52.

Luper, S. "A Review of Plants Used in the Treatment of Liver Disease: Part 1." *Altern Med Rev* 3 (6) (December 1998): 410–21.

Malstrom, M., O.P. Salo, and F. Fyhrquist. "Immunogenetic Markers and Immune Response in Patients with Recurrent Oral Ulceration." *Int J Oral Surg* 12, no. 1 (February 1983): 23–30.

Mahmood, S., et al. "Effect of Vitamin E on Serum Amino-transferase and Thioredoxin Levels in Patients with Viral Hepatitis C." *Free Radic Res* 37 (7) (July 2003): 781–85.

Manton, D., N.D., et al. "Non-Alcoholic Steatohepatitis in Children and Adolescents." *MJA* 173 (2000): 476–79.

Markell, E.K., and M.P. Udkow. "Blastocystis Hominis: Pathogen or Fellow Traveler?" *Am J Trop Med Hyg* 35, no. 5 (September 1986): 1023–26.

Marleau, D. Hepnet: www.hepnet.com/hepc/uldh98/marleau.html, Saint-Luc Campus, University of Montreal.

Maruyama, K., and K. Kashiwzaki. "Clinical Trial of Gamma-Oryzanol on Gastrointestinal Symptoms at 375 Hospitals." Japan: Department of Internal Medicine, Keio University, 1977.

McRorie, J.W., et al. "Psyllium Is Superior to Docusate Sodium for Treatment of Chronic Constipation." *Aliment Pharmacol Ther* 12 (1998): 491–97.

Mendeloff, A.I., and J.E. Everhart. "Diverticular Disease of the Colon." In *Digestive Diseases in the United States: Epidemiology and Impact*. Washington, D.C.: U.S. Department of Health and Human Services, National Institutes of Health, 1994.

Merck Manual, 16th ed. Rahway, N.J.: Merck Research Laboratories, 1992.

Minakuchi, C., et al. "Effectiveness of Gamma-Oryzanol on Various Gastrointestinal Complaints." *Shinyaku to Rinsho* 25, no. 10 (1976): 29.

Moerman, C. "Dietary Risk Factors for Clinical Diagnosed Gallstones in Middle-Aged Men: A 25-Year Follow-Up Study." *Ann Epidemiol* (1994): 248–54.

Moller, E., and R. Schmitt. "A Contribution to the Treatment of Chronic Liver Diseases." *Med Klin* 71 (43) (October 22, 1976): 1831–53.

Moscarella, S., et al. "Lipid Peroxidation, Trace Elements and Vitamin E in Patients with Liver Cirrhosis." *Eur J Gastroenterol Hepatol* 6 (1994): 633–36.

Murray, M., and J. Pizzorno. *Encyclopedia of Natural Medicine*. Rocklin, Calif.: Prima Publishing, 1991.

Murray, M. "Indigestion, Antacids, Achlorhydria, and *H. Pylori.*" *American Journal of Natural Medicine* (January–February 1997): 11–16.

Nellist, C.C. "Elemental Diet Therapy a Good Option for Crohn's." *Fam Pract News* (March 1, 1994): 7.

Nolan, A., et al. "Recurrent Apthous Ulceration: Vitamin B_1, B_2, and B_6 Status and Response to Replacement Therapy." *J Oral Path Med* 20, no. 8 (September 1991): 389–91.

Noyan, T., et al. "Serum Vitamin C Levels in Behcet's Disease." *Yonsei Med J* 44 (5) (October 30, 2003): 771–78.

Ofarrelly, C., et al. "Gliadin Antibodies Identify Gluten-Sensitive Oral Ulceration in the Absence of Villous Atrophy." *J Oral Path Med* 20, no. 10 (November 1991): 476–78.

Orem, A., et al. "The Evaluation of Autoantibodies Against Oxidatively Modified Low-Density Lipoprotein (LDL), Susceptibility of LDL to Oxidation, Serum Lipids and Lipid Hydroperoxide Levels, Total Antioxidant Status, Antioxidant Enzyme Activities, and Endothelial Dysfunction in Patients with Behcet's Disease." *Clin Biochem* 35 (3) (May 2002): 217–24.

Ozick, L.A., C. Salazar, and S.S. Donelson. "Pathogenesis, Diagnosis and Treatment of Diverticular Disease of the Colon." *Gastroenterologist* 2, no. 4 (December 1994): 299–310.

Palopoli, J., and J. Waxman. "Recurrent Apthous Stomatitis and Vitamin B_{12} Deficiency." *South Med J* 83, no. 4 (April 1990): 475–77.

Patrick, L. "Hepatitis C: Epidemiology and Review of Complementary/Alternative Medicine Treatments." *Altern Med Rev* 4 (4) (August 1999): 220–38.

Pauling, L., and E. Cameron. *Cancer and Vitamin C*, Linus Pauling Institute of Science and Medicine, 1979, p. 114.

Pessayre, D., A. Mansouri, and B. Fromenty. "Nonalcoholic Steatosis and Steatohepatitis. V. Mitochondrial Dysfunction in Steatohepatitis." *Am J Physiol Gastrointest Liver Physiol* 282 (2) (February 2002): G193–99.

Phillipson, J.D., and C.W. Wright. "Medicinal Plants in Tropical Medicine: Medicinal Plants Against Protozoal Diseases." *Transactions of the Royal Society of Tropical Medicine and Hygiene* 85 (1991): 18–21.

Porter, S.R., C. Scully, and S. Flint. "Hematologic Status in Recurrent Apthous Stomatitis Compared with Other Oral Disease." *Med Oral Path* 66, no. 1 (July 1988): 41–44.

Prokopova, L. "Celiac Disease—A Severe Disease." *Vnitr Lek* 49 (6) (June 2003): 474–81.

Pronai, L., and S. Arimori. "BG-104 Enhances the Decreased Plasma Superoxide Scavenging Activity in Patients with Behcet's Disease, Sjögren's Syndrome or Hematological Malignancy." *Biotherapy* 3 (4) (1991): 365–71.

Prudden, J.F., and L.L. Balassa. "The Biological Activity of Bovine Cartilage Preparations." *Semin Arthritis Rheum* 3, no. 4 (Summer 1974): 287–320.

Rachmilewitz, D., et al. "Toll-Like Receptor 9 Signaling Mediates the Anti-Inflammatory Effects of Probiotics in Murine Experimental Colitis." *Gastroenterology* 126 (2) (February 2004): 520–28.

Radebold, K., Achlorhydria, E-medicine July 2002. http://www.emedicine.com/med/topic18.htm

Reinisch, W., et al. "Extracorporeal Photochemotherapy in Patients with Steroid-Dependent Crohn's Disease: A Prospective Pilot Study." *Aliment Pharmacol Ther* 15 (2001): 1313–22.

Resnick, C. "The Effects of Gamma-Oryzanol on Ulcers, Gastritis, Hyperlipidemias, and Menopausal Disorders." Research review. Tyler Encapsulations, 1993.

Robinson, R.J., et al. "Effect of a Low-Impact Exercise Program on Bone Mineral Density in Crohn's Disease: A Randomized Controlled Trial." *Gastroenterology* 115 (1998): 36–41.

Rode, D. "Comfrey Toxicity Revisited." *Trends Pharmacol Sci* 23 (11) (November 2002): 497–99.

Roediger, W.E.W. "Decreased Sulfur Amino Acid Intake in Ulcerative Colitis." *Lancet* 351 (May 23, 1998): 1555.

Rogers, S. "Chemical Sensitivity: Breaking the Paralyzing Paradigm: How Knowledge of Chemical Sensitivity Enhances the Treatment of Chronic Disease." *Internal Medicine World Report* 7, no. 8 (1992): 13–41.

Rumessen, J.J. "Functional Bowel Disease: The Role of Fructose and Sorbitol." *Gastroenterology* 101 (1991): 1452–60.

Russell, R. Quoted in *Clinical Pearls*, 1991, by Kirkham R. Hamilton. Sacramento, Calif.: IT Services, 1992.

Saglam, K., et al. "Trace Elements and Antioxidant Enzymes in Behcet's Disease." *Rheumatol Int* 22 (3) (July 2002): 93–96.

Sancak, B., et al. "Nitric Oxide Levels in Behcet's Disease." *J Eur Acad Dermatol Venereol* 17 (1) (January 2003): 7–9.

Scheppach, W. "Effects of Short-Chain Fatty Acids on Gut Morphology and Function." *Gut* (Suppl 1) (1994): S335–38.

Scheppach, W., et al. "Effect of Butyrate Enemas on the Colonic Mucosa in Distal Ulcerative Colitis." *Gastroenterology* 103 (1992): 51–56.

Siegel, B.V., and J.I. Morton. "Vitamin C and Immunity: Natural Killer (NK) Cell Factor." *Int J Vitam Nutr Res* 53 (2) (1983): 179–83.

Seigel, J. "Inflammatory Bowel Disease: Another Possible Effect of the Allergic Diathesis." *Ann Allergy* 47, no. 2 (August 1981): 92–94.

Seigel, M.A., and B.A. Balciunas. "Medication Can Induce Severe Ulcers." *J Am Dent Assoc* 122, no. 10 (September 1991): 75–77.

Shabert, J. *The Ultimate Nutrient Glutamine*. Garden City Park, N.Y.: Avery, 1994.

Shanahan, F., "Host-Flora Interactions in Inflammatory Bowel Disease." *Inflamm Bowel Dis* vol. 10, Suppl 1, (February 2004): S16–S24.

Shibasaki, T. "The Relationship of Nutrition and Dietary Habits to Gingivitis, Dental Calculus Deposit, and Dental Plaque Adhesion in High School Students." *Shoni Shikagaku Zasshi* 27, no. 2 (1989): 415–26.

Shimizu, I. "Sho-saiko-to: Japanese Herbal Medicine for Protection Against Hepatic Fibrosis and Carcinoma." *J Gastroenterol Hepatol* 15 (Suppl) (March 2000): S84–S90.

Siblerud, R.L. "Relationship Between Mercury from Dental Amalgam and Oral Cavity Health." *Ann Dent* (Winter 1990): 6–10.

Simon, J.A. "Ascorbic Acid and Cholesterol Gallstones." *Med Hypotheses* 40, no. 2 (February 1993): 81–84.

Simon, J.A., and E.S. Hudes. "Serum Ascorbic Acid and Other Correlates of Gallbladder Disease Among U.S. Adults." *Am J Public Health* 88, no. 8 (August 1998): 1208–12.

Singh, G. "Recent Considerations in Nonsteroidal Anti-Inflammatory Drug Gastropathy." *Am J Med* 105, no. 1B (July 27, 1998): 31S–38S.

Sipos, P., et al. "Effects of Black Radish Root (*Raphanus Sativus L. Var Niger*) on the Colon Mucosa in Rats Fed a Fat-Rich Diet." *Phytother Res* 16 (7) (November 2002): 677–79.

Stone, I. *The Healing Factor.* New York: Putnam Publishing Group, 1974.

Storsrud, S., L.R. Hulthen, and R.A. Lenner. "Beneficial Effects of Oats in the Gluten-Free Diet of Adults with Special Reference to Nutrient Status, Symptoms and Subjective Experiences." *Br J Nutr* 90 (1) (July 2003): 101–7.

Sky, P.R. "Of Parasites and Pollens." *Discover* (September 1993): 56–62.

Tamboli, C.P., et al. "Dysbiosis in Inflammatory Bowel Disease." *Gut* 53 (1) (January 2004): 1–4.

Teselkin, Y.O., et al. "Dihydroquercetin as a Means of Antioxidative Defence in Rats with Tetrachloromethane Hepatitis." *Phytother Res* 14 (3) (May 2000): 160–62.

Thompson, N.P., et al. "Is Measles Vaccination a Risk Factor for Inflammatory Bowel Disease?" *Lancet* 345 (1995): 1071–74.

Thompson, T. "Oats and the Gluten-Free Diet." *J Am Diet Assoc* 103 (3) (March 2003): 376–79.

Thyagarajan, S., et al. "Herbal Medicines for Liver Diseases in India." *J Gastroenterol Hepatol* 17 (Suppl 3) (December 2002): S370–76.

Tomas-Ridocci, M., et al. "The Efficacy of Plantago, Ovata as a Regulator of Intestinal Transit." *Rev Esp Enferm Dig* 82, no. 1 (July 1992): 17–22.

Triolo, G., et al. "Humoral and Cell Mediated Immune Response to Cow's Milk Proteins in Behcet's Disease." *Ann Rheum Dis* 61 (5) (May 2002): 459–62.

Tuzhilin, S.A., et al. "The Treatment of Patients with Gallstones by Lecithin." *Am J Gastroenterol* 65 (1976): 231.

Van den Worm, E., et al. "Effects of Methoxylation of Apocynin and Analogs on the Inhibition of Reactive Oxygen Species Production by Stimulated Human Neutrophils." *Eur J Pharmacol* 433 (2–3) (December 21, 2001): 225–30.

Vernia, P., et al. "Lactose Intolerance and Irritable Bowel Syndrome: Relative Weight in Inducing Abdominal Symptoms in High Prevalence Area." *Gastroenterology* 102, no. 4, Part II (April 1992): A5–30.

Von Herbay, A., et al. "Vitamin E Improves the Aminotransferase Status of Patients Suffering from Viral Hepatitis C: A Randomized, Double-Blind, Placebo-Controlled Study." *Free Radic Res* 27 (6) (December 1997): 599–605.

Walker, D.M., et al. "Effect of Gluten-Free Diet on Recurrent Apthous Ulceration." *Br J Derm* 103, no. 1 (July 1980): 111.

Watanabe, A., et al. "Nutritional Therapy of Chronic Hepatitis by Whey Protein (Non-Heated)." *J Med* 31 (5–6) (2000): 283–302.

Wang, S.W., et al. "The Trace Element Zinc and Apthosis: The Determination of Plasma Zinc and the Treatment of Apthosis with Zinc." *Rev Stomatol Chir Maxillofac* 87, no. 5 (1986): 339–43.

Whitehead, W.E. "Biofeedback Treatment of Gastrointestinal Disorders." *Biofeedback Self-Regul* 17, no. 1 (1992): 59–76.

Wilhelm, K.P., et al. "Halothane Hepatotoxicity in Glutathione Depleted Rats." *J Appl Toxicol* 7 (2) (April 1987): 105–10.

Wilhelmsen, I., and A. Berstad. "Quality of Life and Relapse of Duodenal Ulcer Before and After Eradication of *Helicobacter pylori*." *Scand J Gastroenterol* 29, no. 10 (October 1994): 874–79.

Wilmore, D. Personal conversation. Spring 1995.

Wilson, J.M. "Hand Washing Reduces Diarrhea Episodes: A Study in Lombok Indonesia." *Transactions of the Royal Society of Tropical Medicine and Hygiene* 85 (1991): 819–21.

Wray, D. "Gluten-Sensitive Recurrent Arthritis Stomatitis." *Dig Dis Sci* 26, no. 8 (August 1981): 737–40.

Wright, J. *Dr. Wright's Guide to Healing with Nutrition.* Emaus, Penn.: Rodale Books, 1984.

Yesilada, E., I. Gurbuz, and H. Shibata. "Screening of Turkish Anti-Ulcerogenic Folk Remedies for Anti-*Helicobacter pylori* Activity." *J Ethnopharmacol* 66 (3) (September 1999): 289–93.

Yoshinari, T. "Usefulness of Hi-Z Fine Granule (Gamma-Oryzanol) for the Treatment of Autonomic Instability in Gastrointestinal System." *Shinyaku to Rinsho* 225, no. 3 (1976): 56.

Yadav, D., et al. "Serum and Liver Micronutrient Antioxidants and Serum Oxidative Stress in Patients with Chronic Hepatitis C." *Am J Gastroenterol* 97 (10) (October 2002): 2634–39.

Yu, P., et al. "Effects of Acupuncture on Humoral Immunologic Function and Trace Elements in 20 Cases of Behcet's Disease." *J Tradit Chin Med* 21 (2) (June 2001): 100–102.

Zeis, J. "Behcet's Disease." website:
www.behcetsdisease.com/basics.htm#WhatisBD

Chapter 11 Natural Therapies for the Diverse
Consequences of Faulty Digestion

21st Century Prevention and Management of Migraine
Headaches, Clinical Courier, 9; September 8, 2001. *NINDS
and Amer Acad Neurol.* www.ninds.nih.gov/doctors/OP129D_
Clinical_Courier_fa.pdf

Abyad, A., and J.T. Boyer. "Arthritis and Aging." *Curr Opin
Rheumatol* 4, no. 2 (April 1992): 153–59.

Aggarwal, B.B., A. Kumar, and A.C. Bharti. "Anticancer Potential of Curcumin: Preclinical and Clinical Studies." *Anticancer
Res* 23 (1A) (January–February 2003): 363–98.

Al-Allaf, A.W., et al. "Bone Health in Patients with Fibromyalgia." *Rheumatology* (Oxford) 42 (10) (October 2003): 1202–6.

Ali, B.H., and G. Blunden. "Pharmacological and Toxicological
Properties of Nigella Sativa." *Phytother Res* 17 (4) (April
2003): 299–305.

Alteras, I. "The Incidence of Skin Manifestations by Dermato-
phytes in Patients with Psoriasis." *Mycopathologia* 95, no. 1
(July 1986): 37–39.

Ammon, H.P. "Boswellic Acids (Components of Frankincense)
as the Active Principle in Treatment of Chronic Inflammatory Diseases." *Wien Med Wochenschr* 152 (15–16) (2002):
373–78.

Appleboom, T., and P. Durez. "Effect of Milk Product Deprivation on Spondyloarthropathy." *Ann Rheum Dis* 53, no. 11 (1994): 481–82.

Arvindakshan, M., et al. "Supplementation with a Combination of Omega-3 Fatty Acids and Antioxidants (Vitamins E and C) Improves the Outcome of Schizophrenia." *Schizophr Res* 62 (3) (August 1, 2003): 195–204.

Barrie, S. "Dysbiosis & Immune Disease, a Retrospective Study." Audiotape from lecture given at the Great Smokies Diagnostic Laboratory, Asheville, N.C., 1993.

Bates, B. "Low-Fat, High-Carbohydrate Diet Averts Migraines." *Fam Pract News* (August 1, 1996): 16.

Berbis, P., et al. "Essential Fatty Acids and the Skin." *Allergy Immunol* 22, no. 6 (June 1990): 225–31.

Bigal, M.E., et al. "Intravenous Magnesium Sulphate in the Acute Treatment of Migraine Without Aura and Migraine with Aura: A Randomized, Double-Blind, Placebo-Controlled Study." *Cephalalgia* 22 (5) (June 2002): 345–53.

Black, M. "Nicotinic Acid and Headache." *Cortlandt Forum* (August 1990): 26–30.

Bland, J. "Advancement in Clinical Nutrition HealthComm." Taken from Komaroff, A.L. "Clinical Presentations of Chronic Fatigue Syndrome." In *Chronic Fatigue Syndrome*, edited by Bock and Whelan. New York: Wiley and Sons Ltd., 1993.

———. *Applying New Essentials in Nutritional Medicine.* Gig Harbor, Wash.: HealthComm International, 1995.

Boris, M., and F.S. Mandel. "Foods and Additives Are Common Causes of the Attention Deficit Hyperactive Disorder in Children." *Ann Allergy* 72, no. 5 (May 1994): 462–68.

Bornstein, R.A., et al. "Plasma Amino Acids in Attention Deficit Disorder." *Psychiatry Research* 33, no. 3 (September 1990): 301–6.

Bottiglieri, T. "S-Adenosyl-L-Methionine (SAMe): From the Bench to the Bedside—Molecular Basis of a Pleiotrophic Molecule." *Am J Clin Nutr* 76 (5) (November 2002): 1151S-57S.

Bou-Holaigah, I., et al. "The Relationship Between Neurally Mediated Hypotension and the Chronic Fatigue Syndrome." *JAMA* 74, no. 12 (September 27, 1995): 961–67.

Bramwell, B., et al. "The Use of Ascorbigen in the Treatment of Fibromyalgia Patients: a Preliminary Trial." *Altern Med Rev* 5 (5) (October 2000): 455–62.

Briggs, N.C., and P.H. Levine. "A Comparative Review of Systemic and Neurological Symptomatology of 12 Outbreaks Collectively Described as Chronic Fatigue Syndrome, Epidemic Neuromyasthenia, and Myalgic Encephalomyelitis." *Clin Infect Dis* 18 (Suppl) (January 1994): S32–S42.

Brzeski, M., et al. "Evening Primrose Oil in Patients with Rheumatoid Arthritis and Side Effect of Non-Steroidal Anti-Inflammatory Drugs." *Br J Rheumatol* 30 (1991): 370–72.

Burks, W.A., et al. "Atopic Dermatitis and Food Hypersensitivity Reactions." *J Pediatr* 132 (1998): 132–36.

Caramaschi, P., et al. "Homocysteine Plasma Concentration Is Related to Severity of Lung Impairment in Scleroderma." *J Rheumatol* 30 (2) (February 2003): 298–304.

Chandra, R.K. "Food Hypersensitivity and Allergic Diseases." *Eur J Clin Nutr* 56 (Suppl 3) (August 2002): S54–S56.

Corbo, J., et al. "Randomized Clinical Trial of Intravenous Magnesium Sulfate as an Adjunctive Medication for Emergency Department Treatment of Migraine Headache." *Ann Emerg Med* 38 (6) (December 2001): 621–27.

Corrocher, R., et al. "Effect of Fish Oil Supplementation on Erythrocyte Lipid Pattern, Malondialdehyde Production and Glutathione-Peroxidase Activity in Psoriasis." *Clin Chim Acta* 179, no. 2 (February 15, 1989): 121–31.

Czirjak, L., et al. "Localized Scleroderma After Exposure to Organic Solvents." *Dermatology* 189, no. 4 (1994): 399–401.

Darlington, L.G. "Dietary Therapy for Arthritis." *Nutr Rheumatic Dis* 17, no. 2 (May 1991): 273–85.

Darlington, L.G., and N.W. Ramsey. "Clinical Review of Dietary Therapy for Rheumatoid Arthritis." *Br J Rheumatol* 32 (1993): 507–14.

Dawson-Hughes, B., et al. "Rates of Bone Loss in Postmenopausal Women Randomly Assigned to One of Two Dosages of the Vitamin D." *Am J Clin Nutr* 6 (1) (1995): 1140–45.

Deal, C.L., et al. "Treatment of Arthritis Pain with Topical Capsaicin: A Double-Blind Trial." *Clinical Therapy* 13, no. 3 (1991): 383–95.

Deluze, C., et al. "Electroacupuncture in Fibromyalgia: Results of a Controlled Trial." *BMJ* 305 (November 21, 1992): 1249–51.

Diener, H.C., V.W. Rahlfs, and U. Danesch. "The First Placebo-Controlled Trial of a Special Butterbur Root Extract for the Prevention of Migraine: Reanalysis of Efficacy Criteria." *Eur Neurol* 51 (2) (January 2004): 89–97.

Disilvestro, R.A. "Effects of Copper Supplementation on Ceruloplasmin and Copper-Zinc Superoxide Dismutase in Free-Living Rheumatoid Arthritis Patients." *J Am Coll Nutr* 11, no. 23 (1992): 177–80.

Dochao, A., et al. "Therapeutic Effects of Vitamin D and Vitamin A in Psoriasis: A 20-Year Experiment." *Actas Dermosfiliogr* 66, nos. 3, 4 (1975): 121–30.

Dominguez-Lopez, M.L., et al. "IgG Antibodies to Enterobacteria 60 kDa Heat Shock Proteins in the Sera of HLA-B27 Positive Ankylosing Spondylitis Patients." *Scand J Rheumatol* 31 (5) (2002): 260–65.

Dykman, K.D., et al. "The Effects of Nutritional Supplements on the Symptoms of Fibromyalgia and Chronic Fatigue Syndrome." *Integr Physiol Behav Sci* 33, no. 1 (January–March 1998): 61–71.

Ebringer, A., and C. Wilson. "HLA Molecules, Bacteria and Autoimmunity." *J Med Microbiol* 49 (4) (April 2000): 305–11.

Eisinger, J., et al. "Glycolysis Abnormalities in Fibromyalgia." *J Am Coll Nutr* 13, no. 2 (1994): 144–48.

Elisa/Act Patient Handbook. Reston, Va.: Serammune Laboratories, 2000.

Ellis, C. "Hot Pepper Cure: Capsaicin Relieves Psoriatic Itch." *Mod Med* 61 (1993): 31.

Emsley, R., P. Oosthuizen, and S.J. van Rensburg. "Clinical Potential of Omega-3 Fatty Acids in the Treatment of Schizophrenia." *CNS Drugs* 17 (15) (2003): 1081–91.

Etzel, R. "Special Extract of Boswellia Serrata (H-15) in the Treatment of Rheumatoid Arthritis." *Phytomedicine* 3, no. 1 (1996): 91–94.

Fahrer, H., et al. "Diet and Fatty Acids: Can Fish Substitute for Fish Oil?" *Clin Exp Rheumatol* 9, no. 4 (July–August 1991): 403–6.

Failli, P., et al. "Effect of N-Acetyl-L-Cysteine on Peroxynitrite and Superoxide Anion Production of Lung Alveolar Macrophages in Systemic Sclerosis." *Nitric Oxide* 7 (4) (December 2002): 277–82.

Fairris, G.M., et al. "The Effect of Supplementation with Selenium and Vitamin E in Psoriasis." *Ann Clin Biochem* 26, Part 1 (January 1989): 83–88.

Faivelson, S. "Electroacupuncture Tried for Pain of Fibromyalgia." *Med Trib Med News* (December 24, 1992): 24.

Fenton, W.S., J. Hibbeln, and M. Knable. "Essential Fatty Acids, Lipid Membrane Abnormalities, and the Diagnosis and Treatment of Schizophrenia." *Biol Psychiatry* 47 (1) (January 1, 2000): 8–21.

Flynn, M. "The Effect of Folate and Cobalamine on Osteoarthritis and Hands." *J Am Coll Nutr* 13, no. 4 (1994): 351–56.

———. "A Follow-Up on Malic Acid: CFIDS Buyer's Club." *Health Watch* 3, no. 1 (Spring 1993): 1–3.

Forsyth, L.M., et al. "Therapeutic Effects of Oral NADH on the Symptoms of Patients with Chronic Fatigue Syndrome." *Ann Allergy Asthma Immunol* 82, no. 2 (February 1999).

Gabay, C., and M.F. Kahn. "Male-Type Scleroderma: The Role of Occupational Exposure." *Schweiz Med Wocheschr* 122, no. 46 (November 14, 1992): 1746–52.

Gaby, A.R. "Natural Treatments for Osteoarthritis." *Altern Med Rev* 4 (5) (October 1999): 330–41.

———. "Intravenous Nutrient Therapy: The 'Meyers' cocktail.'" *Altern Med Rev* 7 (5) (2002): 389–403.

Galland, L., et al. "Giardia Lamblia Infection as a Cause of Chronic Fatigue." *J Nutr Med* (1990): 27–31.

Galland, L., M.D. Telephone conversation. June 1995.

Garfinkel, M.S., et al. "Evaluation of a Yoga-Based Regimen for Treatment of Osteoarthritis of the Hands." *J Rheumatol* 21 (12) (December 1994): 2341–43.

Gaston, L., et al. "Psychological Stress and Psoriasis: Experimental and Prospective Correlation Studies." *Acta Derm Venereol* (Suppl 156) (1994): 37–43.

Germain, B.F. "Silicone Breast Implants and Rheumatic Disease." *Bull Rheum Dis* 41, no. 6 (October 1992): 1–4.

Godfrey, P.S., et al. "Enhancement of Recovery from Psychiatric Illness by Methylfolate." *Lancet* 336, no. 8712 (August 1990): 392–95.

Goldenberg, D.L. "Fibromyalgia, Chronic Fatigue Syndrome, and Myofascial Pain Syndrome." *Curr Opin Rheumatol* 6, no. 2 (March 1994): 223–33.

Golos, N., and F. Golos-Golbritz. *If It's Tuesday, It Must Be Chicken.* Los Angeles: Keats Publishing, 1979.

Grassetto, M., and A. Varotto. "Primary Fibromyalgia Is Responsive to S-Adenosyl-L-Methionine." *Curr Ther Res Clin Exp* 55, no. 7 (July 1994): 797–806.

Gray, J.B., and A.M. Martinovic. "Ecoisanoids and Essential Fatty Acid Modulation in Chronic Disease and Chronic Fatigue Syndrome." *Med Hypotheses* 43 (July 1994): 31–42.

Grimminger, F., et al. "A Double-Blind Randomized, Placebo-Controlled Trial of N-3 Fatty Acid Based Lipid Infusion in Acute, Extended Guttate Psoriasis: Rapid Improvement of Clinical Manifestations and Changes in Neutrophil Leukotriene Profile." *Clin Investig* 71 (1993): 634–43.

Grossman, M., J. Kirsner, and I. Gillespie. "Basal and Histalog-Stimulated Gastric Secretion in Control Subjects and in Patients with Peptic Ulcer or Gastric Cancer." *Gastroenterology* 45 (1963): 15–26.

Gumowski, P., et al. "Chronic Asthma and Rhinitis Due to *Candida albicans*, Epidermophyton, and Trichophyton." *Ann Allergy* 59, no. 1 (July 1987): 48–51.

Hagerman, R.J., and A.R. Falkenstein. "An Association Between Recurrent Otitis Media in Infancy and Later Hyperactivity." *Clin Pediatr* 26, no. 5 (May 1987): 253–57.

Hamilton, C. Clinical Pearls Database, version 5.02, IT Services, Sacramento, CA. www.clinicalpearls.com

Harel, Z., et al. "Supplementation with Omega-3 Polyunsaturated Fatty Acids in the Management of Recurrent Migraines in Adolescents." *J Adolesc Health* 31 (2) (August 2002): 154–61.

Harvima, R.J., et al. "Screening of Effects of Selenomethionine-Enriched Yeast Supplementation on Various Immunological and Chemical Parameters of Skin and Blood in Psoriatic Patients." *Acta Derm Venereol* 73, no. 2 (April 1993): 88–91.

Hendel, L., et al. "Esophageal Candidosis in Progressive Systemic Sclerosis: Occurrence, Significance, and Treatment with Fluconazole." *Scand J Gastroenterol* 23, no. 10 (December 1988): 1182–86.

Henricksson, A.E.K. "Small Intestinal Bacterial Overgrowth in Patients with Rheumatoid Arthritis." *Ann Rheum Dis* 52 (1993): 503–10.

Herrick, A.L., et al. "Dietary Intake of Micronutrient Antioxidants in Relation to Blood Levels in Patients with Systemic Sclerosis." *J Rheumatol* 23 (4) (April 1996): 650–53.

Herrick, A.L., et al. "Micronutrient Antioxidant Status in Patients with Primary Raynaud's Phenomenon and Systemic Sclerosis." *J Rheumatol* 21 (8) (August 1994): 1477–83.

Hesse, J., et al. "Acupuncture Compared with Metoprolol for Migraine Gave Mixed Results." *Ann Intern Med* 235 (May 1994): 451–56.

Hesse, J., et al. "Acupuncture Versus Metoprolol in Migraine Prophylaxis: A Randomized Trial of Trigger Point Inactivation." *J Intern Med* 235 (1994): 451–56.

Hesslink, R., Jr., et al. "Cetylated Fatty Acids Improve Knee Function in Patients with Osteoarthritis." *J Rheumatol* 29 (8) (August 2002): 1708–12.

Heuser, G., et al. "*Candida albicans* and Migraine Headaches: A Possible Link." *J Adv Med* 5, no. 3 (Fall 1992): 177–87.

Hippocrates. "On Airs, Waters, and Places." In *The Genuine Works of Hippocrates*, translated by Francis Adams. London; Leslie P. Adams, Jr., 1849.

Holden, W., T. Orchard, and P. Wordsworth. "Enteropathic Arthritis." *Rheum Dis Clin North Am* 29 (3) (August 2003): 513–30, viii.

Holick, M.F. "Vitamin D: Importance in the Prevention of Cancers, Type 1 Diabetes, Heart Disease, and Osteoporosis." *Am J Clin Nutr* 79 (3) (March 2004): 362–71.

Horrobin, D.F. "Loss of Delta-6-Desaturase Activity as a Key Factor in Aging." *Med Hypotheses* 7 (9) (September 1981): 1211–20.

———. "Essential Fatty Acid and Prostaglandin Metabolism in Sjögren's Syndrome, Systemic Sclerosis and Rheumatoid Arthritis." *Scand J Rheumatol* 61 (Suppl) (1986): 242–45.

———. "Fatty Acid Metabolism in Health and Disease: The Role of Delta-6 Desaturase." *Am J Clin Nutr* 57 (Suppl) (1993): S732–37.

Houston, L. "Dietary Change in Arthritis." *Practitioner* 238 (June 1994): 443–48.

Huisman, A.M., et al. "Vitamin D Levels in Women with Systemic Lupus Erythematosus and Fibromyalgia." *J Rheumatol* 28 (11) (November 2001): 2535–39.

Ianniello, A., et al. "S-Adenosyl-L-Methionine in Sjögren's Syndrome and Fibromyalgia." *Curr Ther Res Clin Exp* 55, no. 6 (June 1994): 699–706.

Joe, B., and B.R. Lokesh. "Effect of Curcumin and Capsaicin on Arachidonic Acid Metabolism and Lysosomal Enzyme Secretion by Rat Peritoneal Macrophages." *Lipids* 32, no. 11 (1997): 1173–80.

Johnson, E.S., et al. "Efficacy of Feverfew as Prophylactic Treatment of Migraine." *BMJ* 2291, no. 6495 (August 31, 1985): 569–73.

Jones, M. "Migraine Headaches and Food." *NOHA News* 14, no. 2 (Spring 1989).

Kalimo, K. "Yeast Allergy in Adult Atopic Dermatitis." *Immunol Pharmacol Aspects* 4 (1991): 164–67.

Kalin, P. "The Common Butterbur (*Petasites hybridus*)—Portrait of a Medicinal Herb." *Forsch Komplementarmed Klass Naturheilkd* 10 (Suppl 1) (April 2003): 41–44.

Kalus, U., et al. "Effect of *Nigella Sativa* (Black Seed) on Subjective Feeling in Patients with Allergic Diseases." *Phytother Res* 17 (10) (December 2003): 1209–14.

Kanofsky, J.D. "Magnesium Deficiency in Chronic Schizophrenia." *Int J Neurosci* 61 (1991): 87–90.

Katz, J.P., and G.R. Lichtenstein. "Rheumatologic Manifestations of Gastrointestinal Diseases." *Gastroenterol Clin North Am* 27 (3) (September 1998): 533–62, v.

Keough, C. *Natural Relief for Arthritis.* New York: Pocket Books, 1983.

Khayyal, M.T., et al. "A Clinical Pharmacological Study of the Potential Beneficial Effects of a Propolis Food Product as an Adjuvant in Asthmatic Patients." *Fundam Clin Pharmacol* 17 (1) (February 2003): 93–102.

Khoo, J., et al. "Pattern of Sensitization to Common Environmental Allergens Amongst Atopic Singapore Children in the First 3 Years of Life." *Asian Pac J Allergy Immunol* 19 (4) (December 2001): 225–29.

Kielar, M.L., et al. "Docosahexaenoic Acid Decreases IRF-1 mRNA and Thus Inhibits Activation of Both the IRF-E and

NF kappa d Response Elements of the iNOS Promoter." *Transplantation* 69 (10) (May 27, 2000): 2131–37.

Kimikazu, I., J. Kiyonana, and M. Ishikawa. *Studies on Gamma-Oryzanol II—The Anti-Ulcerogenic Action, Research Institute.* Tokushima, Japan: Otsuka Pharmaceutical Co., Ltd.

Kimmatkar, N., et al. "Efficacy and Tolerability of *Boswellia Serrata* Extract in Treatment of Osteoarthritis of Knee—A Randomized Double-Blind, Placebo-Controlled Trial." *Phytomedicine* 10 (1) (January 2003): 3–7.

Kjeldsen-Kraugh, J. "Dietary Treatment of Rheumatoid Arthritis." *Scand J Rheumatol* (1996): 63.

Kopelson, J. "Clinician of the Month." *Functional Medicine Update* (January 1999). Audiotape.

Kozielec, T., and B. Starobrat-Hermerlin. "Assessment of Magnesium Levels in Children with Attention Deficit Hyperactivity Disorder (ADHD)." *Magnes Res* 10, no. 2 (1997): 143–48.

Kuratsune, H., et al. "Acylcarnitine and Chronic Fatigue Syndrome." *Carnitine Today* 10 (1997): 195–213.

Kurkcuoglu, N., and F. Alaybeyi. "Topical Capsaicin for Psoriasis." *Br J Dermatol* 123, no. 4 (October 1990): 549–50.

Javitz, H.S., et al. "The Direct Cost of Care for Psoriasis and Psoriatic Arthritis in the United States." *J Am Acad Dermatol* 46 (6) (June 2002): 850–60.

Johnson, S. "The Multifaceted and Widespread Pathology of Magnesium Deficiency." *Med Hypotheses* 56 (2) (February 2001): 163–70.

La Montagna, G., et al. "Dehydroepiandrosterone Sulphate Serum Levels in Systemic Sclerosis." *Clin Exp Rheumatol* 19 (1) (January–February 2001): 21–26.

Lahesmaa, R., et al. "Molecular Mimicry: Any Role in the Pathogenesis of Spondyloarthropathies?" *Immunol Res* 12, no. 2 (1993): 193–208.

Lamm, S.H. "Silicone Breast Implants and Long-Term Health Effects: When Are Data Adequate?" *J Clin Epidemiol* 48, no. 4 (April 1995): 507–11.

Lapp, C.W., and P. Cheney. "Chronic Fatigue Syndrome: Self-Care Manual, February 1991." *The CFDS Chronicle Physicians' Forum* 1, no. 1 (March 1991): 14–17.

Lawrence, R.C., et al. "Estimates of the Prevalence of Arthritis and Selected Musculoskeletal Disorders in the United States." *Arthritis Rheum* 41, no. 5 (May 1998): 778–99.

Leirisalo-Repo, M. "Enteropathic Arthritis, Whipple's Disease, Juvenile Spondyloarthropathy, and Uveitis." *Curr Opin Rheumatol* 6, no. 4 (July 1994): 385–90.

Leung, R.S., et al. "Neutrophil Zinc Levels in Psoriasis and Seborrheoic Dermatitis." *Br J Dermatol* 123, no. 3 (September 1990): 319–23.

Leventhal, L.J., et al. "Treatment of Rheumatoid Arthritis with Gamma-Linolenic Acid." *Ann Intern Med* 119, no. 9 (November 1, 1993): 867–73.

Li, M.H., H.L. Zhang, and B.Y. Yang. "Effects of Ginkgo Leave Concentrated Oral Liquor in Treating Asthma." *Chung Kuo Chung Hsi I Chieh Ho Tsa Chih* 17, no. 4 (April 1997): 216–18.

Looker, A.C., et al. "Prevalence of Low Femoral Bone Density in Older U.S. Adults from NHANES III." *J Bone Miner Res* 12 (11) (November 1997): 1761–68.

Lundberg, A.C., A. Akesson, and B. Akesson. "Dietary Intake and Nutritional Status in Patients with Systemic Sclerosis." *Ann Rheum Dis* 51 (10) (October 1992): 1143–48.

Lyon, M., and J. Cline. "The Effect of a Loligoantigenic Diet with or Without a Prescribed Medical Food Product on the Behavior and Physiological Parameters of Children with Attention Deficit Hyperactivity Disorder." Unpublished data, quoted in the proceedings of the Sixth International Symposium on Functional Medicine, page 346, Institute for Functional Medicine, Gig Harbor, Wash., 1999.

Machtey, I. "Vitamin E and Arthritis/Vitamin E and Rheumatoid Arthritis." *Arthritis Rheum* 34, no. 9 (September 1991): 1205.

Marasini, B., et al. "Homocysteine Concentration in Primary and Systemic Sclerosis Associated Raynaud's Phenomenon," *J Rheumatol* 27 (2000): 2621–23.

Marks, D., and L. Marks. "Food Allergy: Manifestations, Evaluation and Management." *Postgrad Med* 93, no. 2 (February 1, 1993): 191–201.

Martelletti, P. "T Cells Expressing IL-2 Receptor in Migraine." *Acta Neurol* 13, no. 5 (October 1991): 448–56.

Matusiewicz, R. "The Homeopathic Treatment of Corticosteroid-Dependent Asthma: A Double-Blind, Placebo-Controlled Study." *Biomedical Therapy* 15, no. 4 (1997): 117–22.

McCarthy, G., and D. Kenny. "Dietary Fish Oil and Rheumatic Diseases." *Semin Arthritis Rheum* 21, no. 6 (June 1992): 368–75.

McCarty, D.J., et al. "Treatment of Pain Due to Fibromyalgia with Topical Capsaicin: A Pilot Study." *Semin Arthritis Rheum* 23, no. 6 (Suppl) (June 1994): 41–47.

McCarty, M.F. "Glucosamine for Psoriasis?" *Med Hypotheses* 48 (1997): 437–41.

"Methylsulfonylmethane (MSM)." *Monograph Altern Med Rev* 8 (4) (November 2003): 438–41.

McMillan, E.M., et al. "Diurnal Stage of Circadian Rhythm of Plasma Zinc in Healthy and Psoriatic Volunteers." *Prog Clin Biolog Res* 227B (1987): 295–303.

McSherry, J. "Chronic Fatigue Syndrome: A Fresh Look at an Old Problem." *Can Fam Phys* 39 (February 1993): 336–40.

Melton, L.J., III. "The Prevalence of Osteoporosis: Gender and Racial Comparison." *Calcif Tissue Int* 69 (4) (October 2001): 179–81.

Menzel, I., and H. Holzmann. "Reflections on Seborrheic Scalp Eczema and Psoriasis Capillitii in Relation to Intestinal Mycoses." *Z Hautkr* 61, no. 7 (April 1986): 451–54.

Messamore, E. "Relationship Between the Niacin Skin Flush Response and Essential Fatty Acids in Schizophrenia." *Prostaglandins Leukot Essent Fatty Acids* 69 (6) (December 2003): 413–19.

Messamore, E., W.F. Hoffman, and A. Janowsky. "The Niacin Skin Flush Abnormality in Schizophrenia: A Quantitative Dose-Response Study." *Schizophr Res* 62 (3) (August 1, 2003): 251–58.

Michaelsson, G., and L.K. Ljunghall. "Patients with Dermatitis Herpetiformis, Acne, Psoriasis, and Darier's Disease Have Low Epidermal Zinc Concentrations." *Acta Derm Venereol* 70, no. 4 (1990): 304–8.

Michaelsson, G., et al. "Selenium in Whole Blood and Plasma Is Decreased in Patients with Moderate and Severe Psoriasis." *Acta Derm Venereol* 69, no. 1 (1989): 29–34.

Miller, F.W., and D.R. Germolec. "Occupational Exposures and Autoimmune Diseases." *Cooper Int Immunopharmacol* 2 (2002): 303–13.

Moldofsky, H. "Fibromyalgia, Sleep Disorder and Chronic Fatigue Syndrome." *Ciba Foundation Symposium* 173 (1993): 262–71, 272–79.

Moreshead, J., and R. Jaffe. "Fibromyalgia: Clinical Success Through Enhanced Host Defenses: A Case-Controlled Outcome Study." IAACN Syllabus, Dallas, Tex., September 1994.

Mulbert, A.E., et al. "Identification of Nonsteroidal Anti-Inflammatory Drug-Induced Gastroduodenal Injury in Children with Juvenile Rheumatoid Arthritis." *J Pediatr* (April 1993): 645–46.

Murray, M., and J. Pizzorno. *The Encyclopedia of Natural Medicine*. Rocklin, Calif.: Prima, 1991.

National Institute of Neurological Disorders and Stroke, www.ninds.nih.gov/health_and_medical/pubs/migraineupdate.htm

"The Neglect of Glucosamine as a Treatment for Osteoarthritis—A Personal Perspective." *Med Hypotheses* 42, no. 5 (May 1994): 323–27.

Nielsen, G.L., et al. "The Effects of Dietary Supplementation with N-3 Polyunsaturated Fatty Acids in Patients with Rheumatoid Arthritis." *Eur J Clin Investig* 22 (1992): 687–91.

Nietert, Paul J., et al. "Is Occupational Organic Solvent Exposure a Risk Factor for Scleroderma?" *Arthritis Rheum* 41, no. 6 (June 1998): 1111–18.

Noy, S., et al. "Schizophrenia and Autoimmunity—A Possible Etiological Mechanism?" *Neuropsychobiology* 30 (1994): 157–59.

Oliwiecki, S., et al. "Levels of Essential and Other Fatty Acids in Plasma and Red Cell Phospholipids from Normal Controls in Patients with Atopic Eczema." *Acta Derm Venereol* (Stockholm) 71 (1990): 224–28.

Palladino, M.A., et al. "Anti-TNF-Alpha Therapies: The Next Generation." *Nat Rev Drug Discov* 2 (9) (September 2003): 736–46.

Patzelt-Wenczler, R., and E. Ponce-Poschl. "Proof of Efficacy of Kamillosan® Cream in Atopic Eczema." *Eur J Med Res* 5 (4) (April 19, 2000): 171–5.

Peet, M., et al. "Essential Fatty Acid Deficiency in Erythrocyte Membranes from Chronic Schizophrenic Patients, and the Clinical Effects of Dietary Supplementation." *Prostaglandins Leukot Essent Fatty Acids* 55, nos. 1, 2 (1996): 71–75.

Pelmear, P.L., J.O. Roos, and W.M. Maehle. "Occupationally Induced Scleroderma." *J Occup Med* 34, no. 1 (January 1992): 20–25.

"*Petasites hybridus* Monograph." *Altern Med Rev* 6 (2) (April 2001): 207–9.

Pfaffenrath, V., et al. "The Efficacy and Safety of *Tanacetum Parthenium* (Feverfew) in Migraine Prophylaxis—A Double-Blind, Multicentre, Randomized, Placebo-Controlled Dose-Response Study." *Cephalalgia* 22 (7) (September 2002): 523–32.

Picco, P., et al. "Increased Gut Permeability in Juvenile Chronic Arthritides. A Multivariate Analysis of the Diagnostic Parameters." *Clin Exp Rheumatol* 18 (6) (November–December 2000): 773–78.

Pignet, M., and A. Lecomte. "The Effects of Harpogophytum Capsules in Degenerative Rheumatology." *Medicine Actuelle* 12, no. 4 (1985): 65–76.

Pittler, M., and E. Ernst. "Feverfew for Preventing Migraine." *Cochrane Database Syst* Rev. 1 (2004): CD002286.

Polli, E., et al. "Pharmacological and Clinical Aspects of Sadenosylmethionine (SAMe) in Primary Degenerative Arthropathy." *Minerva Medical* 66, no. 83 (December 5, 1975): 4443–59.

Procter, A. "Enhancement of Recovery from Psychiatric Illness by Methylfolate." *Br J Psychiatry* 159 (August 1991): 271–72.

Puri, B.K., et al. "A Volumetric Biochemical Niacin Flush-Based Index That Noninvasively Detects Fatty Acid Deficiency in Schizophrenia." *Prog Neuropsychopharmacol Biol Psychiatry* 26 (1) (January 2002): 49–52.

Rance, F., et al. "Food Allergy and Asthma in Children." *Rev Pneumol Clin* 59 (2 Part 1) (April 2003): 109–13.

Randolph, T., and R.W. Moss. *An Alternative Approach to Allergies*. New York: Harper Perennial, 1990.

Reddy, R., M. Keshavan, and J.K. Yao. "Reduced Plasma Antioxidants in First-Episode Patients with Schizophrenia." *Schizophr Res* 62 (3) (August 1, 2003): 205–12.

Resnick, C. "The Effects of Gamma-Oryzanol on Ulcers, Gastritis, Hyperlipidemias, and Menopausal Disorders." In *Res Rev.* Greshem, Oreg.: Tyler Encapsulations, 1993.

Rigden, S., and J. Bland. "UltraClear Program and Cost Effectiveness." In *Advancement in Clinical Nutrition.* Gig Harbor, Wash.: HealthComm International, 1994.

Robbins, L. "Precipitating Factors in Migraine: A Retrospective Review of 494 Patients." *Headache* 34, no. 4 (April 1994): 214–16.

Rockwell, Sally. *Dr. Sally's Allergy Recipes.* Seattle: Diet Designs, 1997.

Rupprecht, M., et al. "Physical Stress-Induced Secretion of Adrenal and Pituitary Hormones in Patients with Atopic Eczema Compared with Normal Controls." *Clin Endocrinol Diabetes* 105 (1997): 39–45.

Saeedi, M., K. Morteza-Semnani, and M.R. Ghoreishi. "The Treatment of Atopic Dermatitis with Licorice Gel." *J Dermatolog Treat* 14 (3) (September 2003): 153–57.

Sampson, H.A. "The Immunopathogenic Role of Food Hypersensitivity in Atopic Dermatitis." *Acta Derm Venereol Suppl* (Stockholm) 176 (1992): 34–37.

Sanchez-Roman, J., et al. "Multiple Clinical and Biological Autoimmune Manifestations in 50 Workers After Occupational Exposure to Silica." *Ann Rheum Dis* 52, no 7 (July 1993): 534–38.

Sazanova, N.E., et al. "Immunological Aspects of Food Intolerance in Children During First Years of Life." *Pediatriia* 3 (1992): 14–18.

Schafer, T., et al. "Epidemiology of Food Allergy/Food Intolerance in Adults: Associations with Other Manifestations of Atopy." *Allergy* 56 (12) (December 2001): 1172–79.

Schoenen, J., et al. "Effectiveness of High-Dose Riboflavin in Migraine Prophylaxis: A Randomized Controlled Trial." *Neurology* 50 (1998): 466–70.

Schoenen, J., et al. "High-Dose Riboflavin as a Prophylactic Treatment of Migraine: Results of an Open Pilot Study." *Cephalalgia* 14 (1994): 328–29.

Seignalet, J. "Diet, Fasting, and Rheumatoid Arthritis." *Lancet* 339 (January 4, 1993): 68–69.

Shafran, S.D., et al. "Chronic Fatigue Syndrome." *Am J Med* 90 (June 1991): 730–40.

Sharma, R.P., et al. "Acute Dietary Tryptophan Depletion: Effects on Schizophrenic Positive and Negative Symptoms." *Neuropsychobiology* 35 (1997): 5–10.

Shimomura, T., et al. "Platelet Superoxide Dismutase in Migraine and Tension Type Headaches." *Cephalalgia* 14 (1994): 215–18.

Silberstein, S.D., and R.B. Lipton. "Epidemiology of Migraine." *Neuroepidemiol* 12, no. 3 (1993): 179–84.

Simonini, G., et al. "Emerging Potentials for an Antioxidant Therapy as a New Approach to the Treatment of Systemic Sclerosis." *Toxicol* 155 (1–3) (November 30, 2000): 1–15.

Smith, R. "Chronic Headaches in Family Practice." *J Am Board Fam Pract* 5, no. 6 (November–December 1992): 589–99.

Soeken, K.L., et al. "Safety and Efficacy of S-Adenosylmethionine (SAMe) for Osteoarthritis." *J Fam Pract* 51 (5) (May 2002): 425–30.

Soriani, S., et al. "Serum and Red Blood Cell Magnesium Levels in Juvenile Migraine Patients." *Headache* 35, no. 1 (January 1995): 14–16.

Soyland, E., et al. "Dietary Supplementation with Very Long-Chain Omega-3 Fatty Acids in Patients with Atopic Dermatitis." *Br J Dermatol* 130 (1994): 757–64.

Srivastava, K.C., and T. Mustafa. "Ginger (*Zingiber officinale*) in Rheumatism and Musculoskeletal Disorders." *Med Hypotheses* 39 (1992): 342–48.

St. Amand, R.P., M.D. Communication with author.

Starobrat-Hemerlin, B. "The Effect of Deficiency of Selected Bioelements on Hyperactivity in Children with Certain Specified Mental Disorders." *Ann Acad Med Stetin* 44 (1998): 297–314.

Starobrat-Hemerlin, B., and R. Kozielec. "The Effects of Magnesium Physiological Supplementation on Hyperactivity in Children with Attention Deficit Hyperactivity Disorder (ADHD). Positive Response to Magnesium Oral Loading Test." *Magnes Res* 10, no. 2 (1997): 149–56.

Stewart, W.F., A. Schechter, and B.K. Rasmussen. "Migraine Prevalence. A Review of Population-Based Studies." *Neurology* 44, no. 6 (Suppl 4) (June 1994): S17–S23.

Straub, R.H., et al. "High Prolactin and Low Dehydroepiandrosterone Sulphate Serum Levels in Patients with Severe Systemic Sclerosis." *Br J Rheumatol* 36 (4) (April 1997): 426–32.

Stokes, D.G., and J.M. Kremer. "Potential of Tumor Necrosis Factor Neutralization Strategies in Rheumatologic Disorders Other than Rheumatoid Arthritis." *Semin Arthritis Rheum* 33 (1) (August 2003): 1–18.

Strong, A.M.M., et al. "The Effect of Oral Linoleic Acid and Gamma-Linolenic Acid (Efamol)." *Br J Clin Pract* 39, nos. 11–12 (November–December 1985): 444–45.

Sukenik, S., et al. "Treatment of Psoriatic Arthritis at the Dead Sea." *J Rheumatol* 21, no. 7 (July 1994): 130–59.

Syed, T.A., et al. "Management of Psoriasis with Aloe Vera Extract in a Hydrophilic Cream: A Placebo-Controlled, Double-Blind Study." *Trop Med Intern Health* 1, no. 4 (August 1996): 505–9.

Tan, B. B., et al. "Double-Blind Controlled Trial of Effect of Housedust-Mite Allergen Avoidance on Atopic Dermatitis." *Lancet* 347 (January 26, 1996): 15–18.

Taubert, K. "Magnesium in Migraine. Results of a Multicenter Pilot Study." *Portschreit Medizin* 112, no. 24 (August 30, 1994): 228–30.

Thomas, J., et al. "Migraine Treatment by Oral Magnesium Intake and Correction of the Irritation of Buccofacial and Cervical Muscles as a Side Effect of Mandibular Imbalance." *Magnes Res* 7, no. 2 (June 1994): 123–27.

Tiwana, H., et al. "Antibody Responses to Gut Bacteria in Ankylosing Spondylitis, Rheumatoid Arthritis, Crohn's Disease, and Ulcerative Colitis." *Rheumatol Int* 17, no. 1 (1997): 11–16.

Trock, D.H., et al. "A Double-Blind Trial of the Clinical Effects of Pulsed Electromagnetic Fields in Osteoarthritis." *J Rheumatol* 20, no. 3 (1993): 456–60.

Troughton, P.R., and A.W. Morgan. "Laboratory Findings and Pathology of Psoriatic Arthritis." *Baillieres Clinical Rheumatology* 8, no. 2 (May 1994): 439–63.

Tuthill, R.W. "Hair Lead Levels Related to Children's Classroom Attention-Deficit Disorder." *Arch Environ Health* 51, no. 3 (May–June 1996): 214–20.

Uhlig, T., et al. "Topographic Mapping of Brain Electrical Activity in Children with Food-Induced Attention Deficit

Hyperkinetic Disorder." *Eur J Pediatr* 156, no. 7 (July 1997): 557–61.

Van der Kuy, P.H., et al, "Hydroxocobalamin, a Nitric Oxide Scavenger, in the Prophylaxis of Migraine: An Open, Pilot Study," *Cephalalgia* 22 (2002): 513–19.

Van den Worm, E., et al. "Effects of Methoxylation of Apocynin and Analogs on the Inhibition of Reactive Oxygen Species Production by Stimulated Human Neutrophils." *Eur J Pharmacol* 433 (2–3) (December 21, 2001): 225–30.

Von Tirpitz, C., et al. "Osteoporosis in Inflammatory Bowel Disease—Results of a Survey Among Members of the German Crohn's and Ulcerative Colitis Association." *Z Gastroenterol* 41 (12) (December 2003): 1145–50.

Wager, W., and U. Nootbaar-Wagner. "Prophylactic Treatment of Migraine with Gamma-Linolenic and Alpha-Linolenic Acids." *Cephalalgia* 17 (1997): 127–30.

Wallace, D.J. "Silicone Breast Implants Do Not Cause Rheumatic Diseases, but Can They Influence Them?" *Arthritis Rheum* 46 (9) (September 2002): 25–45.

Weber, P., et al. "Gastrointestinal Symptoms and Permeability in Patients with Juvenile Idiopathic Arthritis." *Clin Exp Rheumatol* 21 (5) (September–October 2003): 657–62.

Wehren, L.E., et al. "Gender Differences in Mortality After Hip Fracture: The Role of Infection." *J Bone Miner Res* 18 (12) (December 2003): 2231–37.

Werbach, M. *Healing with Nutrition*. New York: HarperCollins Publishers, 1993.

Witte, S., R. Lasek, and N.Victor. "Meta-Analysis of the Efficacy of Adenosylmethionine and Oxaceprol in the Treatment of Osteoarthritis." *Orthopade* 31 (11) (November 2002): 1058–65.

Wood, N.C., et al. "Abnormal Intestinal Permeability. An Aetiological Factor in Chronic Psychiatric Disorders." *Br J Psychiatry* 150 (June 1987): 853–56.

Woods, R.K., et al. "Food and Nutrient Intakes and Asthma Risk in Young Adults." *Am J Clin Nutr* 78 (3) (September 2003): 414–21.

Yunus, M.B., et al. "Plasma Tryptophan and Other Amino Acids in Primary Fibromyalgia: A Controlled Study." *J Rheumatol* 19, no. 1 (1992): 90–94.

Index

About the Author

Elizabeth Lipski first became interested in holistic healing while in college. There she spent much of her time stalking the woods for edible plants and roots and studying and making herbal medicines. It became apparent to Lipski that herbs were another type of medicine, and that people's lifestyles and attitudes are the foundation for great health.

Lipski has been working in the field of wellness and holistic nutrition since receiving her master's degree in 1979. She became board certified as a clinical nutritionist in 1991 and received her doctorate in clinical nutrition in 2001. She has had a varied career. Along with a private practice, she has run weight-management programs; worked in holistic medical and allopathic medical clinics, a health-food store, several spas, and several health clubs; created and provided wellness programs for businesses and corporations; and taught and lectured extensively. *Digestive Wellness* was first published in 1995 and is accompanied by the *Leaky Gut Syndrome* booklet. Lipski's proudest achievement is being a mom of two amazing young men, Kyle and Arthur.

The website www.elizabethlipski.com has additional information about private telephone consultations, and on workshops for health professionals and community groups on nutritional medicine and digestive wellness. You'll also find information about Lipski's services, products, some articles, and a variety of resources.

Lipski has a great passion for this work, seeking balance in her own life in order to be a model for those she serves. If she can be of assistance to you, she welcomes the opportunity.